Global Search
for *Justice*

Third Edition

COLLEGE *of* ST. CATHERINE

Copley Custom Publishing Group
Acton, Massachusetts 01720

ISBN 1-58152-345-9

Cover: Photo of Bolivian women courtesy of Clara R. Burgert.

College of St. Catherine Website: www.stkate.edu

Printed on recycled paper with soy ink

Contents

Preface

On behalf of the Global Search for Justice subcommittee, I am pleased to write this introduction to the third edition of *The Global Search for Justice* reader. This edition includes revisions and questions for discussion and review as well as a new entry. *The GSJ* reader represents the culmination of years of conversation with our colleagues, years of searching for common readings that never quite fit the needs of GSJ instructors or students. As a result, we have created our own course-specific readings—readings that will hopefully serve to highlight the central themes of GSJ and strengthen the connections with The Reflective Woman.

Like The Reflective Woman, GSJ is an interdisciplinary course, the second of what many have called the "bookends" of the core liberal arts requirements at the College of St. Catherine. Unlike TRW, however, GSJ is guided by common themes that are explored in a variety of topic areas. (At this writing, the common elements of GSJ are addressed in several topic areas: Dismantling Racism, Environmental Justice, The Immigrant Experience, Latin America, Voices of Dissent: Movements for Social Change, Women and Work, and Women's Health Issues.)

Several GSJ documents (i.e., the principles document, the GSJ concept paper and the common course objectives paper) identify the following conceptual foundations:

- Focus on justice issues in at least one non-U.S., non-western European culture or in an historically oppressed non-western European culture within the U.S.

- Examination of a situation of injustice

- Reflection on what justice is—from several perspectives, including law, Catholicism, feminism, non-Western cultures

- Interdisciplinary focus on the examination of method in the search for justice

- Attention to artistic expression from a situation of injustice

- Identification of possible actions to address the justice issue

- Students' reflection on and articulation of personal responsibility in the search for justice, including identification of justice frameworks and action plans

The selections in *The GSJ* reader are designed to reinforce these common themes across all sections. The CSC faculty authors represent a variety of disciplines—biology, business administration, English, philosophy, sociology, Spanish and theology. All have infused their selections with interdisciplinary perspectives and attention to examples that are relevant to all GSJ topic areas.

I am the author of the first article, "Justice and Action: Frameworks and Foundations for Social Change." Here, I have attempted to provide a descriptive overview of justice frameworks (i.e., the sources, standards and scope of justice arguments) and action parameters (i.e., the goals, conditions and strategies that shape action). I hope that this overview might provide some analytical tools that might aid both faculty and students in identifying justice arguments and exploring the options for action. Although my expertise is in sociology, this meta-analysis is informed by a wide range of disciplines and includes an extensive bibliography that provides a starting point for further study. In fact, as I was writing this, I came to a greater appreciation of my own liberal arts education and the breadth of perspective it affords me now.

The next two selections focus more specifically on Catholic and feminist views of justice and action. Russell Connors, associate professor of theology, is the author of "Catholic Social Teaching—Convictions and Connections." Dr. Connors provides an excellent overview of the central convictions of Catholic social teaching—its history and contemporary centrality to social issues. Dr. Connors also explores the connections between Catholic social teaching and the specific current examples of capital punishment, immigration and the place of gays and lesbians within the Church. Throughout, Dr. Connors emphasizes Catholic social teaching as a work in progress that has implications for the Church as well as the community at large.

Feminist theory and practice is integrated throughout "Creativity in Chaos: Feminist Social Justice" by Sharon Doherty, assistant professor of women's studies; Amy Hilden, assistant professor of philosophy; and Cecilia Konchar Farr, associate professor of English. Using examples from first-, second- and third-wave feminism, they explore the shifting concerns of the women's movement, the connections between feminism and other social movements past and present, the role of women in the civil rights, labor and Catholic worker movements and current feminist concerns and issues. Again, this article offers examples that should be applicable to a variety of GSJ topic areas.

John Pellegrini, associate professor of biology, has compiled the sample poster assignment. The poster assignment and attendance at the poster session are also required elements of all GSJ sections and this sample assignment reflects the collective efforts of many GSJ faculty.

New to this edition is "A Call to Action: GSJ and Community Partnerships," by Karen Harris (CSC Office of Community Work and Learning) and Lynne Gildensoph. This should serve as an excellent guide to both faculty and students who are currently engaged in community work in their GSJ courses. It will hopefully be an inspiration to those who may be contemplating community projects for their GSJ sections.

The third edition of *The GSJ* reader also includes "Eastern Perspectives: A Contrasting View of Justice and Action (with a Buddhist Commentary on the Ones Who Walk Away from Omelas)" by Sherry Tousley, assistant professor, Department of Business Administration. Dr. Tousley brings her vast experience to this piece, which offers the readers a non-western view of justice and action as well as an application.

The GSJ reader again includes a glossary to help guide students through challenging terms and theories. Marilyn Bennett, assistant professor of philosophy, has created the glossary that defines and clarifies some key concepts that appear throughout the original selections. Included here are brief overviews of philosophical theories of justice.

And, finally, Marilyn Bennett, assistant professor of philosophy, has created the glossary that defines and clarifies some key concepts that appear throughout the original selections. Included here are brief overviews of philosophical theories of justice.

In addition to original works by the college's faculty, *The GSJ* reader includes the bridge readings from the "Engaging Communities" unit of *The Reflective Woman*. In the context of TRW, these readings encourage students to direct their thoughts globally to the questions of justice and action that frame GSJ. Here, the inclusion of these readings may encourage students to reconsider the connections between TRW and GSJ. In addition, many of these readings (e.g., Gandhi, King, and Lorde) are classics that must be addressed in any discussion of justice and action. Some are cited in the original selections in this text. Faculty and students who wish to explore these ideas further will have immediate access to them.

I hope that *The GSJ* reader will enhance the GSJ experience for both faculty and students. I personally have been enriched by my involvement with this course and express my gratitude to all those who have contributed to its conception and implementation. Special thanks are also in order for Suzanne Hendricks, Core Director 2003–2006; the 2003–2004 GSJ subcommittee (Susan Hames, CSJ, Karen Harris, Lynne Gildensoph, Sharon Stoffel, and Mary Wagner); Jackie Schroeder, and all GSJ faculty. My best wishes for an exciting and rewarding Global Search for Justice!

Nancy A. Heitzeg
Associate Professor, Sociology
Chair, GSJ Subcommittee

Course Readings

Nancy A. Heitzeg, Ph.D. is an associate professor of sociology and program director for critical studies of race/ethnicity. Nancy has taught several sections of GSJ, in the topic areas of environmental justice, voices of dissent, and dismantling racism. As a sociologist, Nancy has long been interested in issues of inequality and their intersection. The role of race, class, gender, sexual orientation, ability and age are central and consistent themes in every course she teaches, all her writings and professional presentations, and all her interdisciplinary work in Global Search for Justice, women's studies, critical studies of race/ethnicity, and the honors program. In addition, these issues, and, most importantly, their eventual resolution are her personal passion.

Justice and Action: Frameworks and Foundations for Social Change

Nancy A. Heitzeg, Ph.D.

"We are the ones we have been waiting for. . . ."

—June Jordan

Introductory Remarks

Consider the following points:

- The wealthiest 1% of Americans controls over 20% of all annual income and 60% of all wealth. The richest 10 Americans have a combined net worth of over $300 billion. They are overwhelmingly white, male, and over 50 years of age. Over 60% of the richest 1% has directly inherited their wealth.

- The richest 400 Americans have a net worth of nearly $1 trillion, which is 1,000 times greater than the net worth of the 40 million poorest Americans.

- Only 31 women are listed among the 400 richest Americans. Of those, 25 directly inherited their wealth. Oprah Winfrey is one of two African Americans on the list and the only "rags to riches" story of the Forbes 400.

- Over 32 million Americans live in official poverty (i.e., annual income of approximately $8,000 for a single person, $11,000 for a two-person household, and $17,000 for a family of four). A more accurate indication (i.e., relative poverty) would count 50 million Americans as poor.

- The poorest Americans control 3% of annual income and less than 1% of wealth in the U.S.

- 40% of the poor are children; another 10% are 18 to 24 years of age. 10% of the poor are elderly, most of them are women and/or racial/ethnic minorities. Among the adults (18 to 64 years of age) poor, 40% are working.

- People of color, women, and children are disproportionately in poverty. Female-headed single-parent households represent 60% of the poor and one-third of all female-headed households, one-fourth of racial/ethnic minorities, over 50% of minority children, and 20% of all children in the U.S. live in official poverty.

- The U.S. has the highest rate of child poverty and the greatest extremes of income/wealth inequality, of any First World country.

- The U.S. government annually disperses $200 billion in corporate welfare (i.e., subsidies, tax write-offs/breaks, overseas marketing grants, etc.) and a mere $60 billion in individual welfare, including $16 billion for TANF (Temporary Assistance to Needy Families).

- One to two million Americans are homeless at some point during the course of a year. Over 50% are families with children; 10% are over 65 years of age.

- Need-based welfare expenditures represent a fraction of the $2 trillion Federal budget ($60 billion). The top expenditures include age-graded entitlement programs (i.e., Social Security, $491 billion, and Medicare, $241 billion); Defense, $400 billion plus the nearly $2 trillion dollars spent on the War in Iraq; and interest on the $7 trillion debt, $318 billion.

- In average, the maximum state welfare payment represents only 15% of the annual estimated living wage.

- Federal minimum wage is still $5.25 an hour, although most independent estimates suggest that a living wage is $13 per hour.

- Women still earn only 76 cents for every dollar men make.

- Women and people of color remain under-represented in the professions and over-represented in blue- and "pink-"collar occupations.

- The typical woman with a Ph.D. degree earns less than the typical male with a B.A. degree.

- The U.S. has more than 2 million persons in prison; this is the highest incarceration rate in the world. The majority of inmates are serving time for non-violent property and drug offenses.

- Although there are no racial differences in participation in crime, African Americans and Latinos are approximately 10 times more likely to be arrested and 7 times more likely to be incarcerated than whites.

- "Corporate crime" results in 5 times more deaths and at least 10 times more economic loss every year than "street crime."

- There are nearly 4,000 prisoners on death rows in the 38 states that allow for capital punishment. African Americans and Latinos comprise 25% of the U.S. population, but account for nearly 70% of death row inmates.

- The best predictor of who will receive a death sentence requires consideration of the race of both the victim and offenders. African Americans who kill whites are most likely to receive the death penalty.

- Globally, women do over 65% of the world's unpaid labor.

- Two of every three illiterate people worldwide are women.

- Nearly one half of the world's 6 billion people live on the equivalent of $2 per day.

- In addition to the 20 million people who have already died of AIDS, 40 million people globally are living with HIV. The overwhelming majority of these are living in the Third World; over 50% are women and children.

- Every 3.6 seconds, someone dies of hunger.

- 80% of the grain produced in the U.S. each year is fed to livestock, and 70% of all antibiotics produced annually are used for the production of meat.

- Over 12 billion animals are killed in the U.S. each year for food, fur, laboratory research, or entertainment.

- The U.S. represents 5% of the world's population and consumes over 25% of all fossil fuels, 20% of metals, and 33% of paper. The U.S. is responsible for the creation of nearly 75% of the world's hazardous waste every year.

- Although scientists have identified only a fraction of the world's life forms, it is estimated that anywhere from 15 to 150 plant, animal, aquatic, or insect species become extinct every year.

- 60% of the earth's forests have already been destroyed and continue to disappear at the rate of 30 million acres per year.

(Ehrenreich; Gans; Kozol; McChesney; Saign; Seager; Simon; Walker, Spohn and DeLone; Wilson; www.peta.org; www.arc.org; www.census.gov; www.gpo.gov; www.factoryfarming.org; www.bjs.gov; www.prb.org)

Are these justice issues? It is likely that most of us would answer yes. When pressed, however, to elaborate as to why, and how, and for what reasons, we may have more difficulty responding. Justice, it seems, is easy to intuitively acknowledge, more difficult to articulate. And, if we agree that the aforementioned facts represent justice issues, we are then faced with the question of action.

One of the goals of both TRW and GSJ is to clarify our place in the community, be it local, national or global. This requires, in part, an interdisciplinary understanding of justice and action—what these words mean for us as well as others. Justice is difficult to define, perhaps uncomfortable to act upon. For our purposes, there are several dimensions of justice and action that we should consider.

First of all, justice is ultimately a collective, rather than individual concern. Justice issues have a broad impact, and even seemingly isolated incidents often have global connections. Many grassroots actions for justice emerge at the local level only to uncover links with global goals. Consider Lois Gibbs and Love Canal. In 1978, Lois Gibbs was a lower-middle-class housewife in Niagara Falls, who, with other women in her neighborhood, "became politicized by the life and death issues directly affecting their children and their homes" (Merchant, pp. 192–193). Gibbs and other members of the Love Canal Homeowners Association conducted studies documenting the health problems associated with the Hooker Chemical and Plastic waste site and succeeded in obtaining redress from the state of New York. As the involvement of these women deepened, they came to realize that the hazardous waste was not an isolated local problem. Similar action by women globally linked them together as cultural ecofeminists. As Carolyn Merchant writes, "From initial Not In My Back Yard (NIMBY) concerns, the movement has changed to Not In Anybody's Back Yard (NIABY) to Not On Planet Earth (NOPE)" (p. 193).

Second, justice issues are often systemic issues, i.e., they reflect larger structural patterns of inequality and disparity. All of the aforementioned statistics reveal structured inequality both globally and nationally. They all represent the consequences of systemic and institutionalized classism, racism, sexism, heterosexism, ageism, ableism, speciesism, and anthropocentrism. Consideration of justice issues as systemic requires distinguishing between what sociologist C. Wright Mills calls "personal troubles and social issues" (p. 45). If, for example, someone becomes poor due to laziness, bad habits, and inertia, that is a personal trouble. When, however, more than 30 million people (most of them women, children, and senior citizens) live in absolute poverty in the richest nation in the world, this can no longer be attributed to personal failing. That is an issue of structured inequality, an issue of justice.

Third, justice issues imply, indeed, impel action. Justice and action are inextricably linked. Justice claims are more often than not accompanied by calls to action. Conversely, spontaneous action is often later linked to broader justice issues. The Stonewall riots provide an example. On the fringes of the emerging gay liberation movement, the gay men, lesbians, and street queens who frequented the Stonewall Inn (a Greenwich Village bar) wanted to dance and socialize. But a night in late June 1969 changed all that. Fed up with perpetual police harassment and arrests, the patrons fought back as yet another police raid unfolded. The officers were out-numbered, and three days of street fights and skirmishes ensued. The event, now referred to as the Stonewall Riots, is widely regarded as the symbolic beginning of the gay liberation movement. Action led to activism (out of the closets and into the streets . . .) and many disenfran-chised Stonewall patrons became part of the general movement for GLBT rights (Duberman). What was initially a very specific response to per-ceived injustice became linked with general justice issues and broader goals and, in many respects, became a symbolic rallying point.

Finally, justice and action, despite their complexities and often emotional overtones, can be critically analyzed. That is our primary objective here, to ferret out the general themes and common threads that link the wide range of perspectives on justice and action. What follows is an overview of the existing literature on justice and action, an acknowledgment of its limitations for interdisciplinary analysis, and the suggestion of a schema for analyzing justice frameworks and action parameters.

Prevailing Approaches to Justice and Action

What is justice? What actions might we take to achieve it? These seemingly simple questions become increasingly complex, and we are immediately left with more questions. Justice for whom? By what standards? According to which perspectives—social, economic, political, legal, divine, ecological? To what end? What exactly do fairness, equality, and freedom mean? What rights do we have, should we have? And by which means is justice to be achieved? What actions are acceptable in the pursuit of justice? Is civil dis-obedience ever called for? Must resistance be nonviolent? May we arm our-selves in self-defense? In revolution? In short, what is to be done, and how shall we endeavor to do it?

Debates over justice and action are timeless and as varied as historical experience. Questions of justice and action have been raised and dis-puted, asked, answered, and re-asked by theologians, philosophers, political theorists, and grassroots activists as well. All of the disciplines of the Liberal Arts and Sciences offer us either explicit or implicit perspec-tives on justice and action and might offer us some guidance in dis-cussing justice and action. (See Appendix A.)

Often these discussions are explicit, expressly directed towards defining justice and delineating the conditions and contingencies of action. Such is the case with many religious tracts, political treatises, and philosophical essays. Similarly, analyses of justice and action are also found in the writ-ings of sociologists, social workers, historians, and political scientists, among others. Issues of justice and action also form the foundation for many areas of interdisciplinary studies, which emphasize the vantage point of disenfranchised groups. Women's Studies, GLBT Studies, Multi-cultural and Post-Colonial Studies are all cases in point. In all the afore-mentioned areas, issues of justice and action are at the fore; indeed, a primary goal of the discussion/discipline is to advance discourse on issues of justice and related options for action.

On other occasions, perspectives on justice and action are emergent, less overtly articulated, but present nonetheless. Some of these are implicit in the theoretical paradigms and applications of various disciplines includ-ing the natural and social sciences, the humanities, and certain areas of professional study. Here, notions of equity, of balance, of resource alloca-tion, provide a seminal justice/action framework. Other emergent views of justice and action emanate from the grassroots, from everyday under-standings of the cosmos, from patterns of interaction with others, nature, and the unseen. These are worldviews, ways of life which are based on a taken for granted notion of what constitutes justice and right action. Grassroots perspectives on justice and action also arise under duress, from spontaneous collective responses (e.g., demonstrations, riots, and revolt) to perceived injustice. Latent definitions of justice and action may become manifest in the face of oppression, and what was unclear becomes certain as the people respond. In other words, notions of justice and action may be embedded in ways of thinking and being; these are implied rather than explicitly stated, but become apparent under closer examination.

Both implicit and explicit approaches are essential to a comprehensive interdisciplinary understanding of justice and action. Indeed, they pro-vide the foundation for the ensuing discussion. For our purposes, how-ever, detailed analysis of the specific points of each approach is limiting. For example, the explicit theoretical discourse on justice is often disci-pline-specific, fettered by academic jargon and abstraction. And, with some noted exceptions, it has been dominated by Western, often Euro-centric, male points of view, particularly those of philosophers, political theorists, and theologians. Implicit claims, on the other hand, are just that. Awareness of the justice/action issues requires extrapolation, inter-pretation, case-by-case analysis, and post-hoc speculation. In many cases, we are unguided by firsthand accounts and documentation.

Further, even in combination, these perspectives per se constrain our dis-cussion by failing to consistently draw the connection between justice and action. In many cases, one is emphasized at the expense of the other, with very few acknowledgements of the conceptual and practical link-ages between the two.

And, finally, any systematic examination of the range of viewpoints represents an insurmountable task. It is impossible to quantify perspectives on justice/action—there may be 6 or 600 or 6 billion. Such an endeavor is fruitless and loses sight of the common threads that run through these discussions. Over-attention to the specifics here leads to the proverbial dilemma of losing sight of the forest for the trees. What is needed, and what is lacking is an overview of the common themes that provide a basis for comparing perspectives on justice and action.

A New View of Justice and Action

How, then, are we to proceed in untangling an endless web of justice and action? Perhaps a broader view, a meta-analysis of justice frameworks and action parameters will offer a starting point. Interdisciplinary analysis of justice and action may require a search for themes and patterns among the vast array of perspectives and experiences.

As noted earlier, there is a dearth of literature that provides an overarching look at the similarities, differences, common questions, points of contention, and convergence. All the explicit and implicit approaches to justice and action grapple with comparable concerns. They emerge from identifiable sources and also name certain contingencies of justice and action that translate into concrete goals and strategies. Those proverbial trees, in short, do constitute a forest, and it is that forest that will be explored here. The goal of the ensuing discussion is to provide an overview of the conceptual variations in justice frameworks and action parameters. There are certainly other ways of organizing these ideas, and while what is presented is representative, it may not exhaust all the complexities of justice and action. Consider this a beginning, rather than a definitive end point for this discussion.

Further, the goal is to provide a descriptive, general outline of justice frameworks and action parameters. Hopefully, this might illuminate more specific discussions of justice frameworks and action parameters. The aim here is not to advocate for any particular perspective on justice, nor to evaluate the relative efficacy of various actions. Those indeed are valid discussions, which this outline may ideally inform and inspire. Figure 1 outlines the issues and will serve as a point of reference for the discussion that follows.

Justice Frameworks

Sources	Standards	Scope
Theological/spiritual (e.g., Catholic, Protestant, Judaic, Islamic, Eastern, Native American spirituality, feminist theology, revitalization)	universalism/absolutism	human-centered (e.g., exclusion/inclusion based on class, race/ethnicity, gender, sexual orientation, age, ability, religion, and nationality)
Political (e.g., Nationalist, Democratic/Pluralist, Socialist/Communist, Anarchist, international accords)	particularism/relativism	eco-centered (e.g., earth-based religious/political movements, animal rights and green movements, Gaiai hypothesis)
	distributive	
	commutative	
	retributive	
	restorative	
Philosophical/Cosmological (e.g., idealism, materialism, utilitarianism, libertarian, communitarian, existentialism, feminist philosophy, post-modernism, Eastern philosophies, Afrocentric cosmology)	merit	
	need	
	liberty/freedom	
Natural/Social Scientific (e.g., ecological, biological, psychological, anthropological, sociological, economic, demographic)	equality/equal rights/equal access	

Figure 1. Justice Frameworks and Action Parameters

Action Parameters

Goals	Conditions	Strategies
• Macro/Micro-Level Change (e.g., global, international, national, local, personal)	• use of existing social, legal, or political channels/civil disobedience (e.g., failure to comply with law, active violation of law)	• individual/collective/coalitions
• General/Specific Change (e.g., changes in law/custom)	• nonviolent/militant (e.g., violence in self-defense or offensive actions, property damage, attacks on persons)	• hierarchical/grass roots leadership (e.g., community organizing and mobilizing)
• Reform/Radical transformation/revolution	• overt/covert (e.g., use of publicity and media, secret planning and implementation)	• indirect/direct action (e.g., speaking out, group consciousness-raising, public awareness, campaigns, symbolic protest through art, music, literature, and theater, creation of alternative schools, economies, political institutions and communes, community building through mobilizing/organizing, lobbying, legal actions/lawsuits, marches, boycotts, strikes, sit-ins and occupations, tax evasion, draft resistance, economic sabotage, armed self-defense, armed offensives)
• inclusion/self-determination/equal rights/equal access/political and/or economic separation		

Figure 1. Justice Frameworks and Action Parameters

Justice Frameworks

In general, discourses on justice share common features: All emerge from specific sources that frame the nature of the discussion; all identify standards by which justice/injustice is measured and meted out, and all, in varying degree, address the scope of justice—the range of Beings to which the standards apply. And finally, all, directly or indirectly, suggest actions appropriate for achieving justice. Each will be considered in turn.

Sources

Justice frameworks may be most immediately analyzed with reference to their inspirational sources. Perspectives on justice or, conversely, injustice began with a particular worldview, a vantage point from which to gauge and assess. Historically and currently, justice has been defined from several vantage points: religious/spiritual, philosophical, political, and scientific. Historically and currently, these sources continue to frame most discussions of justice.

The world's religions provide some of the oldest and most diverse perspectives on justice. Here justice is a divinely revealed absolute. All of the major world religions, as well as nature-based perspectives of indigenous peoples, include notions of duties, rights, and standards of conduct. These outline just relationships between humans, the divine, and nature. Often, religious perspectives on justice have both sacred and secular implications. Divinely inspired justice should pervade this world as well as the next. (Catholic social teaching provides an excellent example of this and is discussed in detail in Dr. Connors' article in this text.) Indeed, for much of human history, sacred justice was synonymous with secular justice; it was "on Earth as it is in Heaven" (Klass; Lehman and Meyers; Gudorf).

Philosophy is an equally significant source regarding justice. From the early Greeks to the present day, explicit discussions of justice remain a central topic of philosophical debate. Indeed philosophical views of the common good, universal rights and ethics, and just distribution and retribution have shaped both political and scientific views of justice (Isnay; Shute and Hurley). More recent philosophical treatments of justice have rejected the notion of absolute justice that is the trademark of the modern era. Justice here is situated, relative, and subject to change (Kaufman).

Political theorists, governmental legal systems, and international bodies offer secular views of justice in treaties, constitutions, documents, and accords. These are often the source of common sense understandings that many hold regarding justice and the relationship between citizens and the state, civil rights and liberties, access to resources and just law and punishment. Originally, political notions of justice were most often discussed relative to the nation state. Many current political discussions of justice, however, are global; these emerge from international bodies such as the United Nations or transnational nongovernmental organizations (NGOs) (United Nations, Amnesty International, Human Rights Watch).

The sciences, both natural and social, are less explicit sources on the topic of justice. Like political sources, earlier philosophical perspectives often inform these views. Although the term itself is rarely used, rudimentary perspectives on justice are embedded in their analyses of the social institutions and arrangements, the psyche, and the natural world. The conflict paradigm in sociology, for example, presents a clear commentary on structured inequality and its correlation with classism, racism, sexism, heterosexism, and ageism (Collins, 1975, 1994). Similarly, ecology incorporates mechanistic models of science into a holistic view that emphasizes balance, biodiversity, and sustainability (Naess; Miller). All the previous justice questions regarding distribution, rights, responsibilities, and equity are implicit in these approaches.

It is crucial to note that these sources do not provide unified perspectives on justice. These sources of justice, in fact, are neither internally consistent nor mutually exclusive. There are vast disagreements within categories as well as points of congruence between them. Philosophers, for example, have debated for centuries over the nature of justice—is it an absolute ideal or constructed relative to material circumstances? Is justice best represented by "the greatest good for the greatest number" or "from each according to his/her ability to each according to his/her need"? Is liberty, equal treatment, or equal opportunity the standard (Ishay; Lebacqz)? Such is also the case with religious, political, and scientific sources; they share a certain starting point for framing justice, but diverge on its precise meaning.

There are, on the other hand, many similarities that exist between the different sources. Although emanating from religious and scientific sources respectively, Native American spirituality and deep ecology arrive at strikingly similar views of environmental justice and a balanced relationship between humans and nature. Whether other species are perceived to be our spiritual kin or other species within the ecosystem, the resultant definition of justice is the same. Perhaps one of the most striking examples of this congruency can be found in the life and work of Dr. Martin Luther King Jr. As a minister, president of the Southern Christian Leadership Conference, and a leader in the struggle for civil rights, he moved with ease from framing justice religiously and politically. Full civil rights for African Americans, he argued, must be granted for moral reasons and constitutional reasons. The Bible and the Bill of Rights both spoke to the issue and, for King, were completely compatible sources on justice (Carson, et al.; Washington).

Sister Helen Prejean, CSJ, provides another excellent example of drawing upon the congruencies among justice frameworks. The author of *Dead Man Walking* and presenter at a CSC Core convocation in the fall of 1999, Sister Helen opposes the death penalty on several grounds: moral/theological, philosophical, and political. As honorary chair of Moratorium 2000, a global grassroots campaign that aims towards the ultimate abolition of capital punishment, Sister Helen Prejean eloquently opposes the death penalty, first on the basis of Catholic social teaching on life. She also notes high financial and political costs as well as race and class disparities. All suggest U.S. constitutional violations of due process and equal protection as well as violations of standards set by the U.N. Commission on Human Rights. Still other views draw upon common themes from disparate sources to create hybrid perspectives on justice.

Liberation theology is a prime example here. Grounding Catholic social teachings' preference for the poor in a Marxist critique of capitalism, liberation theology imbues faith with political implications. The liberation is spiritual, economic, and political (Hennelly). Similar fusion is found in the revitalization movements of other oppressed peoples past and present: the Handsome Lake Revival of the Iroquois Nations, Ghost Dance movements among North American Plains Tribes, and the Rastafarians of Jamaica. Rastafarians, for example, fuse Biblical prophecy with Pan-African political ideology to create a critique of Western culture, a vision of African Liberation and an entire lifestyle (Brown; Lewis; Campbell). In all these cases, mergers of native religions, Christianity, and political ideologies shape the view of justice.

These interconnections among seemingly disparate sources closely relate to questions of justice standards and scope. What constitutes justice? Who is justice for? Thinkers from all the sources have grappled with the many dimensions of this issue, and their tentative answers are explored in the ensuing sections.

Standards

As the foregoing discussion implies, the sources for framing justice arguments are only a starting point. The issue of how justice might be measured—what are the standards for justice—is at the heart of all discussions. Again, there are many questions and no definitive answers.

Two general dimensions will be considered here. First of all, justice standards may be construed as universalist or particularist. Proponents of the universalist position argue that justice standards are universally applicable, transcending time, culture, and social context—and often absolute.

Until recently, the universalist approach has characterized most theological, philosophical, political, and scientific views of justice. Discussions of divine and natural law, "the inalienable rights of citizens," and universal human rights as set forth by the United Nations all suggest universalist standards (Declaration of Independence, United Nations). (See Appendix B.) The majority of explicit theological, philosophical, and political justice tracts are grounded in universal standards. So, too, are many of the more implicit justice perspectives that emerge from the sciences and the humanitarians as well as indigenous religions and grassroots social movements.

Others argue that justice standards emanate from particular historical circumstances, perspectives, or situations of oppression. This perspective is frequently associated with the post-modern, post-colonial critique of what bell hooks calls "the white supremacist capitalist patriarchy" (hooks, 1992, p. 22). This perspective is often rooted in a critique of supposedly universalistic standards as non-inclusive and proceeds from the perspective of excluded groups. Particularistic standards of justice are explicitly expressed in strands of existential and feminist philosophy, in some variations of identity politics of racial/ethnic minorities, women, GLBT persons, and Third World nationalists; and in the religious/political agendas of revitalization movements (Brown, Collier, Cruikschank; Fanon; Hennelly; Kaufman; Lewis). Perhaps, the anthropological debate over "cultural relativism" represents one of the clearest expositions of particularistic views of justice in the social sciences. In addition, particularist perspectives of justice are implicit in the standpoint critiques of theory in the social sciences, the interdisciplinary approaches of women's, multicultural, and GLBT studies and some local-level grassroots movements whose initial impetus is often very specific situations of injustice (Collins, Patricia, 1990; Fisher, 1994; hooks, 1984; Kendall; Merchant; Rothenberg).

One of the most heated debates over universal/particular justice standards is centered on the practice of female genital mutilation (FGM), which involves the removal of all or part of the external female genitalia without anesthetic. While FGM is practiced in other regions of the world, it is most widely practiced in Northern Africa, where over 100 million women have undergone the procedure. First brought to Western attention in the work of Alice Walker (i.e., *Possessing the Secret of Joy* and *Warrior Marks*), FGM clearly illustrates the tension between universalist and relativist views of justice. Proponents contend that it is a cultural tradition that can only be understood and addressed from within (El Saadawi). Opponents cite a long list of physical complications (e.g., infection, pain-induced shock, urine and menstrual retention, damage to the urethra, painful intercourse, greater risk of STD infection, and obstructed labor) and maintain that FGM is a human rights violation and, perhaps, grounds for asylum (Noble, Covetz and Janagishita; Seager, pp. 52–53). As Alice Walker so succinctly puts it, "Torture is not culture" (Walker and Parmar, p. 95).

Discussions of the general or specific applicability of justice standards are closely intertwined with the universalistic/particularistic debate. Here, the debate centers on the extent to which justice standards apply to all areas of social life or are limited to certain select concerns. Philosophers and political theorists have provided most of the explicit discourse, here often dividing justice into four areas: distributive (i.e., distribution of rewards and resources), commutative (i.e., justice in exchange), retributive (i.e., justice in punishment), and restorative (i.e., justice in compensation) (LeBacqz, pp. 9–10). Perspectives on justice may encompass some or all of these. Many theological and political perspectives often encompass all four, as part of divinely sacred and secular justice (Thompson; Ishtay). Certain political perspectives and grassroots movements, on the other hand, narrow the focus. Libertarians, for example, emphasize commutative justice in exchange, arguing that the only just government intervention involves minimal regulation of the economy to insure equitable exchange (Nozick). In contrast, civil rights movements of disenfranchised groups often argue for distributive justice. Globally, for example, women perform over 65% of the world's unpaid labor, are more likely than men to live in poverty, and earn less than 70% than men make for comparable work. Women are over-represented in the lower wage sectors of economies and are disproportionately employed in the unprotected enterprise zones of the global economy (Seager). These are clearly issues of distributive justice. Retributive and restorative justice are concerns for groups who focus on issues related to the criminal, civil, and administrative law, such as racial profiling, incarceration, capital punishment, political prisoners, calls for compensation and reparations (Amnesty International, Feagin). The post-apartheid hearings on Truth and Reconciliation in South Africa as well as calls for reparations for the descendants of slaves in the U.S. are both examples of restorative justice.

The final dimension relative to justice standards is the hallmark, the ultimate measure of justice. This is the subject of much debate within and between all the perspectives on justice and is at the heart of much theological, philosophical, and political literature on justice. In general, discussions of justice often make reference to central concepts: merit and/or need, liberty/freedom, equality, and rights. Again, these are illusive concepts, which are defined in disparate ways in religious documents, philosophical tracts, and the constitutions of nation states (Ishtay; Shute and Hurley).

Most national constitutions, for example, enumerate the rights and freedoms available to all or particular groups of citizens. The United Nations' Universal Declaration of Human Rights, however, lists rights that seem applicable to everyone regardless of nationality; ". . . recognition of the inherent dignity and of the equal and inalienable rights of all members of the human family is the foundation of freedom, justice and peace in the world" (United Nations, p. 21). (See Appendix A.)

More important, however, is the prioritizing of these standards. Liberals, particularly those in Western democracies, tend to hold freedom and liberty central to justice. The rights of individuals, then, especially those safeguarding freedoms, take precedent over equality. The rights of free speech, to keep and bear arms, to own/accumulate private property, to pursue happiness, are supposedly universal standards of justice. In the U.S. however, their primacy in law and public opinion leads to constricted definitions of equality. Equal access to all social resources, in most liberal analyses of justice, is a lesser hallmark of justice that is limited by individual merit, rights, and liberties (LeBacqz, pp. 10–11; Howard and Donnelly). Equality, then, is frequently defined in the most minimal of terms as equal protection under the law. It has rarely meant equal access to rewards and resources, a point that is painfully clear to the poor, people of color, and women.

Marxists/socialists, on the other hand, regard economic equality and freedom from economic oppression as the preconditions for justice. Need, not merit, is the measure; a longstanding Marxian dictum speaks directly to this point—"from each according to their ability to each according to their need" (Marx). Further, individual freedoms, especially those related to material accumulation, are defined as lesser considerations subject to restraint in pursuit of the higher standard and the communal good (Marx and Engels, 1948; Feuer; Kautsky; Trotsky; Shiva). Indeed, much historical conflict over the ideologies of capitalism and socialism/communism revolve around the standards of justice and the value of freedom vs. equality, merit vs. need, the right to accumulate wealth vs. the right to basic necessities of survival.

Finally, the definitions of justice standards such as freedom, equality, and rights are shaped by considerations of the scope of justice, i.e., justice for whom and why.

Scope

The scope of justice is one of the most significant elements that shape justice perspectives. Scope, here, refers to the range of persons and/or beings to which justice standards apply. It includes considerations of inclusivity and discrimination, as well as human-centered and eco-centered claims.

The majority of explicit and implicit justice frameworks focus on justice as a concept that is applicable and available to humans. On closer examination, however, it is clear that historical and contemporary perspectives have frequently narrowed the concept of justice, which permits the exclusion of certain categories of persons.

Prior to the twentieth century, the classical philosophical, theological, and political perspectives of the West have limited justice to those who were deserving by nature of either nationality or morality. Almost invariably, this led to the dehumanization and subsequent oppression of persons who failed to meet the standards of "reason" or "morality." As Richard Rorty notes, "For most white people, until very recently, black people did not so count. For most Christians, up until the seventeenth century or so, most heathens did not so count. For the Nazis, Jews did not so count. For most males, in countries where the average annual income is under $4000, most females still do not so count. Whenever tribal and national rivalries become important, members of rival tribes and nations will not so count" (p. 263).

Philosophically and theologically, such a narrow scope of justice allowed seemingly "righteous" and "reasonable" men to endorse slavery, conduct inquisitions, colonize, and exterminate indigenous peoples globally, brutalize women and children in the name of discipline and property rights, and execute anyone who deviated from proscribed norms of sexual conduct (Golden, et al.).

Politically, this constricted view of personhood allowed even the "enlightened" Western democracies to limit those so-called universal and "inalienable" rights to white men who owned property. At the time of its writing, the rights and freedoms enumerated in the U.S. Constitution were only available to white, adult, property-owning males. Native Americans—the only indigenous Americans—are mentioned in the Declaration of Independence as the "merciless Indian savages, whose known rule of warfare, is an undistinguished destruction of all ages, sexes, and conditions" (Declaration of Independence, p. 7). African Americans, then enslaved, were counted as three-fifths of a person for purposes of determining state population size and subsequent representation. They remained property (a point reinforced by several Supreme Court decisions) until the ratification of the Thirteenth Amendment in 1865 (The Constitution of the United States, pp. 14, 42). Women, of course, were not citizens either and were, for all intents and purposes, the property of their parents or husbands. Full constitutional rights were finally extended to women with the passage of the Nineteenth Amendment in 1920 (*Ibid.*, p. 48).

Constricted views of personhood and, consequently, justice are not limited to the past. In the U.S., federal law did not prohibit discrimination against racial/ethnic minorities, women, the differently abled, and senior citizens until the mid-1960s. GLBT persons and those under eighteen still do not have the full rights of citizenship here, and GLBT persons, in particular, are denied federal civil rights protections against discrimination in several areas including employment, housing, family relationships, the military, security clearances, and matters of the criminal law (Hunter, Michaelson, and Stoddard). In addition, many contend that the theoretical inclusion of formerly disenfranchised groups in constitutional claims of justice does not necessarily translate into justice in practice. As noted before, equal protection under the law does not translate into equal access to social resources. The persistence of institutionalized classism, racism, sexism, heterosexism, and ageism is well documented and continues to be regarded as just by certain groups of religious and political conservatives (Doob, Kendall, Rothenberg).

Globally, the scope of justice also continues to be narrowly construed. Despite the broadly based universal human rights outlined in a series of international accords, a variety of explicit theological and political views and implicit socio-political perspectives exclude certain persons from the purview of justice. Race/ethnicity, gender, sexual orientation, age, and religion remain the source of devalued status in many regions of the world. The system of apartheid in South Africa remained legal until 1992, and the ill effects are still felt by the black majority (Bratton). Similarly, post-colonial religious and ethnic conflict rages from Bosnia to Indonesia. Women are still denied social and legal rights in many areas of the world. They remain the property of men, are denied access to education, restricted in their movements, are bought, sold, beaten, mutilated, forced to labor, raped, and killed at will. In many of the Middle Eastern Islamic theocracies, the movement and dress of women are also restricted (Seager). Prior to its collapse in 2002, the Taliban in Afghanistan "banned employment for women, halted formal female education pending the development of an 'appropriate' curriculum, imposed strict dress codes, and introduced strict controls on the movement of women outside the home" (Marsden, pp. 88–89). Similarly draconian policies persist in many other countries in the Middle East.

So, too, in most of the world, GLBT persons and children are often excluded from the scope of justice. Same-sex activity is still illegal in most nations of the world, and GLBT persons continue to be religiously and politically persecuted. Children are parental property and, in spite of international standards to the contrary, over 75 million children under fifteen labor, often in sweatshop conditions. Female children, particularly in areas of Central and East Asia, are viewed as economic and social liabilities and are disproportionately subject to abortion, infanticide, and abandonment (Seager; Noble, Cover, and Janagishita).

The scope of justice is not always so narrow. More inclusive perspectives flourish as well. Historically, these can be found in some strands of early Greek philosophy, the nature-based religions of many indigenous peoples, the universal tenets of Buddhism which extend to all sentient beings, and the informal, non-stratified political arrangements of foraging bands (Barnes; Ishtay; LaDuke; Ward). Some of these perspectives are supported by extensive writings, others are reported in the anthropological and historical literature. All, however, limit social differentiation and inequality and extend the scope of justice at minimum, to all humans.

Several Western-based theological, philosophical, and political perspectives also broaden the scope. Progressive interpretations of Christianity include all people and often advocate for secular justice for all as well. Many Catholic and Protestant theologians have been involved in the struggle for civil rights, economic justice, and women's rights on religious as well as political grounds. Catholic social teaching holds up the dignity of every person and the preference for the poor as key tenets (Thompson). Feminist theology has also expanded traditional interpretations of Christianity to be more inclusive of the role(s) of women, both spiritually and in institutional roles on the church (Plaskow and Christ; Johnson, Sallie).

In the past 150 years, the identity politics of disenfranchised groups have staked both explicit and implicit claims for inclusion within justice frameworks. The poor, racial/ethnic minorities, women, religious sects, senior citizens, the differently abled, and GLBT persons through social action and interdisciplinary writings have continued to push the margins of justice debates. Much of this work is rooted in a critique of the narrow Eurocentric, patriarchal view of justice held by many Western political and philosophical frameworks. A vast array of work is included here: socialist critique of capitalism ranging from Marx to the present; feminist and postcolonial philosophy, political theory; critical conflict and standpoint theory in sociology; multicultural and feminist perspectives in a variety of disciplines, and political demands for inclusion that range from abolition and Seneca Falls, to the Civil Rights era and beyond (Carson, et al.; Collins, Patricia; Feuer; Marx and Engels; Kendall; Rothenberg; Wallace; Weitz; Wallace and Wolf). The common feature of all is a broad-based scope of justice that seeks to include all persons within existing socio-political parameters of justice or create new non-discriminatory alternatives.

At the heart of all these claims are several key points. Oppressions intersect; class, race, gender, sexual orientation and age are sources of interrelated disadvantages and subsequent injustice. Further, justice is not a commodity that can be parceled out to some and not all. It is an all or nothing proposition. As Martin Luther King Jr. so aptly noted in "Letter from a Birmingham Jail": "Injustice anywhere is a threat to justice everywhere. We are caught in an inescapable network of mutuality tied in a single garment of destiny" (p. 85). Whatever affects one directly affects all indirectly.

Finally, the scope of justice may be extended to non-human species and, in fact, the entire planet. Eco-centered perspectives in justice contend that classical configurations limit the scope of justice to human centered concerns, thus overlooking a range of beings who may also be entitled to rights, freedoms and equality. While some of these justice arguments are centuries old, many have emerged in the late 20th century in conjunction with the ecology and animal rights movements (Merchant; Finsen and Finsen).

Historically, eco-centric views of justice are found in non-Western religions such as Native American spirituality. In fact, according to anthropological evidence indigenous animistic religions are the oldest in the world. Many still persist and, in the U.S., Native American spirituality continues to inform both the religious and ecological positions of many Native Americans. In *All Our Relations*, Winona LaDuke quotes Anishinabe elder Eddie Benton, "There are two separate roads to choose from— the road to technology and the other road to spiritualism. The elders feel that the road of technology represents a continuation of headlong rush to technological development. This is the road that has led to modern society, to a damaged and scorched earth. . . . The other road represents the slower path that traditional native people have traveled and are now seeking again. The earth is not scorched on this trail. The grass is still growing there" (p. 198). Buddhism also extends the scope of justice to non-humans. Buddhism has long held that the utmost earthly goal is to "Bear the burden of all beings. . . . Make the vow to save all beings, to set free all beings. . . . As long as the world remains, as long as sentient beings remain, then so too shall I remain and ease the suffering of the world" (Ishtay, p. 6). Similar notions are also found in the teachings of several other religions including Taoism and Hinduism.

More recently, eco-centered conceptions of justice have begun to be included in Western theological thought. Feminist theology in particular is a key contributor here. Elisabeth Johnson, CSJ, in *Women, Earth, and Creator Spirit* argues for an ecofeminist reconsideration of "hierarchical dualism" which has relationships between God/Man, Man/Woman, and Man/Nature. Johnson writes, "Hierarchical dualism . . . places the privileged, so-called rational man apart from and above other persons such as the poor and people of color. . . . Feminist analysis insists that the devastating ecological consequences of this two-tiered vision cannot be fully addressed until we face it as a whole. . . . We need to realize that the natural environment is oppressed, manipulated, and abused in ways analogous to the patriarchal use of women" (pp. 11–12).

Eco-inclusive perspectives on justice extend beyond theology. Philosophy has made significant contributions including further development of eco-feminist ideas. Perhaps, most important, philosophy paved the way for continued challenges to human-centered views of justice on several fronts. Norwegian philosopher Arne Naess coined the term deep ecology in 1972 (Naess). As Carolyn Merchant notes, deep ecology "has now become the legitimating framework for an array of ecological movements from spiritual greens to radical EarthFirst!ers" (p. 86). Philosophers were also among the first to critique speciesism and make the case for animal rights. In particular, Peter Singer and Tom Regan inspired the contemporary animal rights movement with their respective works, *Animal Liberation* and *The Case for Animal Liberation* (Finsen and Finsen).

Several perspectives found in the natural and social sciences comparably widen the scope of justice. Physicists, biologists, and chemists have begun to question the predominance of the Western mechanistic view of science (Naess; Sheldrake, 1981, 1985; Shiva, 1997, 2000, 2002). Holistic approaches, which view the earth as an ecosystem or a complex organism itself, imply that balance, equality, and in fact, justice, require a consideration of non-human nature. In fact, one scientific approach—the Gaia hypothesis—contends that the entire earth itself is a complex organism that should receive consideration as such (Miller).

The social sciences and interdisciplinary areas of study have also begun to expand their scope of inquiry to the environment and other species. Increasingly, sociology, psychology, women's studies, and multicultural studies have considered the relationship between social and environmental inequality. Eco-psychology and the study of environmental racism, sexism, and classism are all cases in point (Bullard; Roszak; Roszak, Gomes, and Kanner). Similarly, the sociological interest in social movements has provided analyses of the green and animal rights movements as well as exposés of animal abuse in a variety of settings (Kunkel; Catton and Dunlap).

Finally, more inclusive, eco-centered views of justice have emerged from political thought and practice. Rudimentary notions of eco-justice can be found in the socialist writings of Marx and Engels as well as the early anarchists (Merchant, pp. 134–144; Runkle). Both critique economic and political relations as oppressive and exploitive to humans as well as the environment. These ideas find contemporary manifestation in the writings and activism of the socialist ecologists, socialist ecofeminists, and anarchist social ecologists (Chase; Shiva). These perspectives have informed much of the green movement in the U.S. as well as indigenous efforts globally to maintain ecologically sound practices.

National legislation and international treaties have also begun to reflect more expansive views of justice. Animals and the environment have limited legal protection here, and there is continued lobbying and political pressure to expand our legal notions of animal and environmental rights. Political proponents are for a variety of changes in our legal system including enhanced penalties for animal cruelty, the abolition of animal experimentation and factory farming, and moratoria on nuclear energy, urban sprawl, and the use of fossil fuels (Bullard; Merchant; Newkirk; Saign; Wise).

In addition, international bodies and agencies are increasingly called upon to consider the environment and other species in political treaties and agreements. Pressures from indigenous peoples and environmental groups globally have led to agreements on sustainable development, pollution reduction, and endangered species protection. Examples include the inaugural Earth Summit held in Rio de Janeiro in 1992 and the United Nations Declaration of Indigenous People's Rights (Saign; Ewen). While many such documents are motivated by human-based concerns, they do nonetheless extend the concept of justice, rights, and protections to non-humans as well.

Justice frameworks, then, provide an analytical basis from which to identify and evaluate justice arguments. Justice frameworks may be characterized by their implicit or explicit definitions of justice—its source, standards and scope. As the foregoing suggests, even this rudimentary classification schema quickly becomes complicated with comparisons and caveats and, at best, serves as a rough guide to the intricacies of justice.

And yet, this is only half the story. Once justice has been conceptualized, its realization inevitably comes into question. Justice without action is merely an intellectual exercise; the circumstances of everyday life demand much more. Consequently, justice frameworks are inextricably linked with action parameters, the subject we now turn to.

Action Parameters

Justice and action inform and reinforce each other. Particular justice frameworks often directly shape action. Indeed, many philosophical, theological, political, and scientific discussions of justice also specifically address action as well. Conversely, grassroots action—both spontaneous and organized—often suggests justice frameworks. As we shall see, many activists, initially guided by the specific injustices at hand, then find that their particular concerns may be linked to more far-reaching justice issues.

Action, as justice, is also shaped by general considerations. Seemingly disparate approaches to action share common themes: Action parameters include goals or desired outcomes of action, conditions and contingencies which shape the course action may take, and specific strategies implemented to bring attention or resources to the justice issue at hand. These dimensions of action, as well as their links to justice frameworks, will now be discussed in detail.

Before proceeding, a point of clarification here is in order. The flow of the discussion might imply that justice frameworks are formulated first, that the goals and conditions, and strategies of action are carefully contemplated before strategies are employed. Sometimes, that is, in fact, the case. Karl Marx's praxis (i.e., theory and action) is based on years of study and scholarly analysis that is then translated in practical programs of action (Feuer; Marx and Engels). The justice framework does give rise to action parameters.

But Marx's own epitaph—"The philosophers have merely described the world—the goal, however, is to change it"—points to another possibility. Sometimes action comes first, the connections to justice frameworks later. Many grassroots activists don't know or care about Marx, Gandhi, political theory, or philosophical constructs. They know they must respond to a situation of injustice. Gabriel, a compañero quoted in Jennifer Harbury's *Bridges of Courage* makes just this point. "Karl Marx was a fine man, but he died in industrialized Germany over a hundred years ago, without ever setting foot in Guatemala. What did he know of our history, our conditions, our people? What did he know of our indigenous population? Do you think all those people are up in the mountains because of some nineteenth century European? Please, tell all your friends, tell them to think of us as what we are, as Guatemalan citizens and revolutionaries" (pp. 78–79). Let us keep this in mind, then, as we enter the final section of our discussion. While the dimensions of action are the end point here, they may, in reality, serve as the beginning.

Goals

Goals are essential to any course of action; they are the end to be achieved, the outcome to be attained. In general, goals often emanate from justice frameworks and additionally shape the nature and type of action. The goals of action vary along several dimensions.

First of all, the goal of action may be micro- or macro-level change (i.e., global, international, national, local, or personal). In other words, the goal may be changing one's mind or changing the world. Often movements for justice have as their goal change that spans all levels. The feminist movement is illustrative here. Feminists recognize many justice issues for women—"the personal is political"—and consequently have multiple goals. These include personal transformation through consciousness-raising; local provision of health care, legal services, shelters for battered women and counseling for victims of sexual assault; national efforts to pass the Equal Rights Amendment (ERA) and other legislation to protect the rights of women; and improvements in the economic, political, social, and medical status of women globally (Ferree and Hess; Rowbotham).

For many activists, recognition of justice issues and related goals on one level may lead to broader justice frameworks and goals. Much grassroots action emerges at the local level only to uncover links with global goals. Consider Julia "Butterfly" Hill and Luna. Hill did not come from a family of activists, nor was she involved with environmental organizations. But, in 1997, when she saw the ancient redwoods of the Pacific Northwest and witnessed their destruction via logging, she was immediately transformed into an activist. What began as a temporary tree-sit in a 180 foot high, 1,000 year old redwood that became known as Luna, turned into a 738 day stay. Hill's immediate goal was to save just one tree, but in the process, she helped raise public awareness of the threats to deforestation and was as she puts it, "dumped in the deep-end of the entire movement—not just tree-sitting, not just forest movements, but the whole social, environmental and consciousness movement" (Welton and Wolf, p. 224).

The second dimension of goals is related to the breadth of change. Goals may be general (i.e., overall societal or global change) or specific (i.e., change in particular laws or circumstances.) Movements for justice may be very specific in their focus. The anti-abortion movement, for example, has as its specific goal the abolition of abortion and the repeal of Roe v. Wade (Blanchard). Similarly, supporters of Fauziya Kasinga were not generally seeking to change all U.S. policies on refugees and asylum seekers. The Kasinga case specifically focused on the availability of asylum status for women seeking to escape genital mutilation (Kausinga sought asylum in the U.S. in 1995; she fled her native Togo to avoid FGM. After two years in INS detention and several asylum requests that were denied, she was finally granted asylum in a landmark decision. The INS now recognizes female genital mutilation as a form of persecution whose victims are entitled to international protection.) (Martin and Midgey; Kasinga; Amnesty International,1997).

Many justice movements, however, have both general and specific goals that seek to change specific laws and situations of injustice and generally transform larger social and/or cultural arrangements. Frequently, action may originate with specific goals that are ultimately linked to general justice frameworks and goals. CODEPINK and the anti-war movement provides an example. In response to the threat of a U.S. invasion of Iraq, millions of people around the world took to the street in protest, and a plethora of anti-war groups sprang up. CODEPINK, a group founded by women on the following premise was one of them: "We call on women around the world to rise up and oppose the war in Iraq. We call on mothers, grandmothers, sisters, and daughters, on workers, students, teachers, healers, artists, writers, singers, poets and every ordinary outraged woman willing to be outrageous for peace. Women have been the guardians of life—not because we are better or purer or more innately nurturing than men, but because the men have busied themselves making war. Because of our responsibility to the next generation, because of our own love for our families and communities and this country that we are a part of, we understand the love of a mother in Iraq for her children and the driving desire of that child for life" (www.codepink.org). CODEPINK continues to oppose the occupation of Iraq and has expanded its' network and goals. In addition to peace, CODEPINK is now engaged in initiatives on fair elections, civil rights and a repeal of the USA PATRIOT ACT, environmental sustainability, economic issues and media responsibility and fair reporting. What was initially a very specific response to perceived injustice has now become linked with general justice issues and broader goals.

Thirdly, the goals of action may vary according to the extent of change desired to achieve justice—reform, radical transformation or revolution. The connection between justice frameworks and the goals of action is particularly strong here. Liberal political perspectives on justice almost always imply reformist goals; injustice can be remedied by changes in laws or policies. Leftist perspectives, such as Marxism/socialism and anarchism, often have far-reaching radical transformation and even revolution as their goals. Various factions of feminism exemplify these differences. Liberal feminists advocated reform of existing laws and policies regarding women's rights, especially those offering reproductive rights, employment opportunities and institutional access as expressed in the Equal Rights Amendment (ERA). Cultural feminists, on the other hand, contend that our culture must be radically transformed, and deeply rooted concepts of gender, femininity, and beauty must be challenged. And finally, socialist feminists hold that sexism is a consequence of capitalist class structure. Further, the liberation of women is contingent upon the collapse of capitalism, and may require revolution (Ferree and Hess; Stan). (See Dr. Doherty's, Dr. Hilden's, and Dr. Konchar Farr's article for a detailed discussion of feminist perspectives.)

The final dimension of goals to be considered here concerns the outcome sought by those taking actions. Those who fight against perceived injustice may seek inclusion, equal rights, and access to the social order. Justice movements may consciously strive for self-determination and economic and/or political separation. Different strands of the civil rights movement are indicative of these variations in goals. Martin Luther King Jr. and the Southern Christian Leadership Conference (SCLC) sought integration, inclusion, and ultimately, the color-blind society exemplified in King's "I Have a Dream . . ." speech (Carson, et al.; King, pp. 101–106). The Student Non-violent Coordinating Committee (SNCC) also sought inclusion, but emphasized Black self-determination and equal access to social/political/economic institutions (Carson, et al.; Payne). Other aspects of the movement were less interested in integration and more concerned with Black Power, reparations, and Black controlled institutions. Included here are early Malcolm X and the Nation of Islam, who advocated religious, political, and economic separation from white America (Malcolm X). The Black Panther Party also outlined goals in their Ten-Point Program that centered around Black self-determination politically, economically, legally, and culturally (Foner; Jones).

The goals of action, then, may vary in several respects. In many ways, justice frameworks shape goals. Justice frameworks often implicitly suggest acceptable outcomes. Liberal, human-centered environmentalists, for example, may be inclined to have reformist goals that include new legislation, more recycling and expanded Environmental Protection Agency enforcement powers. Eco-centered anarchists, conversely, are likely to have goals that are directed towards general, macro-level radical transformation of existing economic and political relations.

Justice frameworks also help us understand why those who agree on a situation of injustice (e.g., racism, sexism) may disagree on the goals of action. As the foregoing discussion suggests, justice frameworks separate liberal feminists from socialist feminists and SCLC from the Black Panther Party. In fact, differences in the framing of the justice issue at hand are the source of factionalization in many justice movements. As we shall see, justice frameworks may also contribute to the creation of coalitions with regard to the other two dimensions of action-conditions and strategies.

Conditions

Once the goals of action have been identified, the conditions for proceeding come into play. The conditions of action help shape specific strategies and include considerations of civil disobedience, nonviolence and militancy, and visibility. Justice frameworks and goals both inform decisions regarding the conditions of action. Indeed, much of the literature on justice also addresses the dimension of action. The conditions of action, however, are also constrained by existing cultural, social, and political arrangements. The global variations are too vast to fully address here.

Nonetheless, it is important to keep in mind that certain conditions can be met only in select socio-political contexts. Overt organizing, peaceful protests and public pressure for social change are more available as options in societies that recognize the rights of assembly, free speech, and petitioning the government for redress. Repressive socio-political arrangements limit the options for action and may contribute to undercover organizing and extra legal action.

The question of legal action versus civil disobedience is central to any discussion of action. Are there any conditions under which the law should be violated, or should action proceed only within the boundaries of the law? Movements for justice have responded in a variety of ways. Resistance to injustice, globally and nationally, has frequently relied on both existing legal channels and civil disobedience.

On occasion, use of existing legal channels is successful in bringing about change. Years of legal challenges to segregation by the NAACP, for example, led to the historic 1954 Supreme Court victory, *Brown v. Board of Education*, which declared "separate but equal is inherently unequal" (Carson, et al., pp. 22–25). Years of lobbying by NOW led to expanded powers for the Equal Employment Opportunity Commission (EEOC) and increased protection against discrimination against women in the workplace (Ferree and Hess). Most recently, after years of lobbying, Congress approved a bill that relaxes citizenship requirements for Hmong refugees. In recognition of their contributions to U.S. involvement in the Vietnam War, Hmong veterans and their spouses are exempted from the regular language requirements and "given special consideration on the civics section" of the U.S. citizenship test (Doyle and Madigan, p. A4).

The list of examples could go on. Many issues of justice have been at least partly resolved through law-abiding means. Nearly every movement cited throughout has relied to some degree on existing political/legal channels. Others contend that often this is not enough—unjust laws must be disobeyed. Civil disobedience, what Henry David Thoreau called "resistance to civil government" has a long and storied history as a means to justice (Thoreau). As the discussion of action strategies will illustrate, civil disobedience may take shape in several ways. In general, however, civil disobedience includes both failure to comply with the law (e.g., Thoreau's refusal to pay taxes in objection to slavery and the Mexican War; Rosa Parks' refusal to give up her bus seat to a white man as required by Montgomery, Alabama, city ordinance) or active violation of the law (e.g., Sister Rita Steinhagen's crossing of the line into Federal property at Fort Benning, GA, in protest of the School of the Americas (SOA), which has long been a training school for Latin American dictators and military leaders, who have been linked to brutal attacks on civilians and clergy) (Thoreau; Carson, et al.; Harvey, Nelson-Pallmeyer).

Currently, allies of the GLBT community, most notably the mayor of San Francisco, have sparked large-scale civil disobedience by approving marriage licences for gay and lesbian couples in defiance of prohibitive state laws.

In contemporary times, the theoretical underpinnings of civil disobedience are most clearly associated with Mahatma Gandhi's campaigns of "non-cooperation" with the British colonial government in India, and the civil rights movements' noncompliance with U.S. segregationist policies in the 1950s and 1960s. Both these efforts succeeded in bringing about significant political change (i.e., Indian independence and Federal civil rights legislation) through a variety of non-violent resistance efforts.

The question of civil disobedience is intertwined with the question of nonviolence. Indeed, some contend that once civil disobedience is accepted as a possible condition of action, the issue of nonviolence or militancy is raised. This is the second significant condition of action—is the use of force and/or violence ever legitimate and, if so, under what conditions?

This issue is at the heart of a lengthy debate over the relationship between justice (i.e., ends) and action (i.e., means). It is one of the few areas of the justice literature that expressly addresses action. The connections between justice frameworks and action parameters will be clarified in the course of the discussion.

Movements for justice have staked out divergent positions on the issue of nonviolence/militancy. Many adhere to the principle of strict nonviolence. This was the position of Gandhi, who argued that nonviolent resistance was required to achieve a just end. For Gandhi, satyagraha (clinging to truth) was the means and the end. "Means and ends are convertible terms in my philosophy of life . . . They say, 'means are after all means.' I would say, 'means are after all, everything; as the means, so the end'" (Ishay, pp. 353–354). Gandhi's nonviolent action has had a profound influence on other justice movements throughout the U.S. The impact of his thought and action on Martin Luther King Jr. and Cesar Chavez, the United Farm Workers founder known as the "Gandhi of Grapes" (Levy). Nonviolent action is currently the preferred mode of protest for an array of justice movements ranging from Women Against Military Madness (WAMM) to the Catholic Worker Movement (Cornell, Ellsberg and Forest).

Action may also take a more militant direction. This may include the destruction of property, armed self-defense, and armed offensives. Proponents of militant action contend that ends sometimes justify the means. A variety of movements hold that property can be destroyed to protect life and may, in fact, be termed nonviolent since no living beings are harmed.

EarthFirst! for example, argues that the sort of economic sabotage, known as monkey wrenching, constitutes "nonviolent resistance to the destruction of natural diversity and wilderness. It is never directed against human beings, or other forms of life. It is aimed at inanimate machines and tools that are destroying life" (Foreman and Haywood, p. 11). Often this type of action is predicated upon the notion that property is being destroyed in pursuit of the higher goal of preserving life. An oft-quoted statement from the Animal Liberation Front (ALF) sums up this position: "If we are trespassing, so are the soldiers who broke down the gates of Hitler's death camps; if we are theives, so were the members of the Underground Railroad who freed the slaves of the South; and if we are vandals, so were those who destroyed forever the gas chambers of Buchanwald and Auschwitz" (X). A variety of leftist political movements, some peace activists, and segments of the green and animal rights movement have taken comparable positions (Burns; Finsen and Finsen).

Militant action may also mean armed self-defense. It is sometimes the recourse of people who feel that a situation of injustice is life threatening. Such was the case with the Black Panther Party (BPP) and the American Indian Movement (AIM). Each organization had as its initial purpose, the protection of the Black and Native American communities respectively, from violent attacks and police brutality (Ironically, each group's attempt at self-defense led in each case to escalating local and federal law enforcement violence.) (Foner; Jones; Mathiessen). Regardless of the efficacy of this approach, the right to self-defense is widely recognized by a variety of philosophical and political justice frameworks, including the U.S. government.

The most dramatic form of militant action involves armed offensive action directed towards others. Those who feel that revolutionary struggle represents the only recourse for change advocate violent action; some who are willing to seek justice, as Malcolm X "by any means necessary" (Malcolm X, p. 21). Frequently, this response arises when the perceived injustice is so great, the alternatives so constrained, that other options seem ineffective.

Armed resistance may occur in several ways. It may take shape as spontaneous, unorganized, collective disruption, or riots. Frustration over continued injustice may erupt in anger. Some would argue that a majority of post-1960 urban riots in the U.S. fit this description. From Watts in 1965 to L.A. in 1992, smoldering frustration over persistent poverty, discrimination and police harassment was ignited into riot by specific incidents of perceived injustice. In most cases, police violence against citizens and lack of response by the criminal justice system served as the spark (Madhubuti, 1994; Smith, 1993).

Armed resistance may also involve individuals or organizations that engage in acts of sabotage or terrorism. Domestically, these unannounced, often random attacks have been carried out by radical antiwar activists, leftists factions of the labor movement, militant members of the anti-abortion movement, anti-industrialist Theodore Kaczynski, a.k.a. the Unabomber, and the right wing militia movement, most notably Oklahoma City bomber Timothy McVeigh (Blanchard; "FC"; Corcoran; Burns; DeBenedetti). Prior to September 11, 2001, acts of international terrorism occurred primarily outside of the U.S. mainland. Internationally, however, terrorist activities have accompanied many longstanding struggles for land and independence. Included here are the activities of the Irish Republican Army (IRA), the Palestinian Liberation Organization (PLO), Hamas, and the Shining Path of Peru (revolutionary Maoists who are seeking land redistribution). Perhaps the most famous examples come from the Middle East, where the daily round of suicide bombers have become commonplace in the struggle for a Palestinian homeland, and the Al Qaeda organization of Osama bin Laden has declared a "holy war" on the secular West.

Finally, armed resistance may manifest itself as organized military action against imperial or national governments. Those struggles often utilize "guerrilla warfare" (i.e., warfare techniques which rely on a series of surprise attacks, then retreats, to wear down the opponents) (Guevara, 1963). This method was used to revolutionary advantage in China, Vietnam, and Cuba (Mallin, 1969).

Latin America struggles for land and life—in Chiapas, El Salvador, Nicaragua, Bolivia, and Guatemala—also come to mind here. Decades of governmental terror have taken their toll. As Salvadoran Democrat Rubén Zamora notes, "People turn to armed struggle when they do not see an alternative. Of all the people I have known who went down that path, none did it because they wanted to. They didn't spend time debating the ethics of it because to them it was obvious. Ending violence means ending the situation that gives rise to it" (Harbury, p. 2).

Justice frameworks are closely tied to the consideration of nonviolent and/or militant action. Most theological frameworks advocate nonviolence. Gandhi and King's aforementioned commitment to nonviolence was informed by their respective beliefs in Hinduism and Christianity. Similarly, Catholic social teachings' emphasis on the dignity of every person is central to the official position on nonviolence and commitment to peace. Subsequently, the official Church advocates nonviolent opposition to cultural, social, and political practices deemed threatening to life. This includes abortion, capital punishment, euthanasia and "unjust war" (Gurdorf; Thompson).

Conversely, varying degrees of militant action are most often associated with philosophical and political justice frameworks. The literature here is replete with discussions of just war and revolution as acceptable and, perhaps inevitable, courses of action. Although revolution is often associated with socialist and anarchist positions, it is also an option for proponents of liberal democracy. Indeed, one of the most famous expositions is found in the Declaration of Independence, "We hold these truths to be self-evident that all men are created equal; that they are endowed . . . with certain inalienable rights; that among these are life, liberty and the pursuit of happiness. That to secure these rights, governments are instituted among men, deriving their just powers from the consent of the governed; that whenever any form of government becomes destructive of these ends, it is the right of the people to alter or abolish it. . . . It is their right, their duty to throw off their government . . . " (Declaration of Independence, p. 3).

Despite these connections, justice frameworks are not always predictors of the propensity for non-violence or militancy. On occasion, theological perspectives on justice inspire militant action ranging from property destruction to armed insurrection. Examples abound. Religious opposition to the Vietnam War resulted in several cases of self-immolation and dramatic destruction of property by the Berrigan Brothers and others (Burns; DeBenedetti). Philip and Daniel Berrigan, both Jesuit priests, poured their own blood in draft files and, in another action, burned draft files with homemade napalm while declaring "we believe that some property has no right to exist" (Burns, p. 103).

Theological perspectives have also endorsed militant action. Certainly, the Islamic concept of *jihad* (holy war) is a case in point. Some interpretations (but, it should be noted, not all) of this concept suggest that the killing of civilians is justified here, and that suicide missions in pursuit of jihad will result in martyrdom. Advocacy of violent action is by no means limited to Islam. Christianity has had its share of violent adherents as well. In addition to the aforementioned anti-abortion and IRA actions, Christian religious calling inspired some of the most notable slave revolts and abolitionist actions, including Nat Turner's rebellion and John Brown's attack on Harper's Ferry (DuBois; McKissack and McKissack).

Similarly, philosophical and political positions may also propose strictly nonviolent action. Socialists such as Kautsky advocated reform, not revolution; Leo Tolstoy, an avowed anarchist, was one of the most eloquent proponents of pacifism (Kunkle; Kautsky, pp. 328–338). Many of the political grassroots movements previously discussed strictly adhere to principles of nonviolence. The Navdanya (Nine Seeds) Movement, led by socialist ecofeminist Vandana Shiva, provides an excellent example.

Although the movement targets globalization, agricultural monocultures, and the WTO, Navdanya is based on the principles of Gandhi and nonviolent resistance. As Shiva notes, "an intolerance of diversity is the biggest threat to peace in our times; conversely, the cultivation of diversity is the most significant contribution to peace—peace with nature and between diverse peoples" (Shiva, 1997, p. 119).

The final condition of action is related to visibility—should action be overt or covert? Again, this dimension of action is related to goals and the other conditions of action. Overt action is designed to increase awareness of a justice issue, win public support, and increase political pressure for change. In contemporary times, this requires skillful use of the media. Strategic use of the media may include selective framing of the justice issue. The congruency between various justice frameworks allows for interchangeability and the subsequent ability to pick and choose the presentation relative to the audience. The aforementioned example of Martin Luther King Jr. illustrates this point. He could argue for civil rights from a Biblical basis, a justice framework he often used to inspire Black congregations and sympathetic white believers. King also advocated for civil rights with political frameworks, using secular arguments to appeal to politicians and the general public. King strategically tailored his message and his choice of justice frameworks to maximize their impact (Carson, et al.; King; Burns, pp. 237–239).

Other social movements have also benefited from careful consideration of justice frameworks. The efforts of the Farm Animal Reform Movement (FARM) are well documented in this regard (Kunkel). FARM, founded in 1981, is devoted to the eradication of factory farming (i.e., large-scale meat/dairy production that treats animals as product units). There are a number of justice issues related to factory farming—environmental (e.g., the role of cattle/hogs in global warming, deforestation, and water pollution), animal rights (e.g., animal confinement and abuse from the farm to the slaughterhouse), and human health concerns (e.g., the use of antibiotics, hormones, and pesticides in meat production). In other words, this issue can be framed philosophically or politically in either human-centered or eco-centered ways. FARM's original campaigns emphasized animal rights as the central issue. As opinion polls indicated, this argument failed to resonate with the public. FARM then began to focus on the human health concerns related to consumption of mass-produced meat. Shortly thereafter, FARM also began to address the justice issues related to environmental destruction. FARM expanded the justice frameworks used to garner opposition to factory farming, and subsequently expanded their potential base of support as well.

A variety of justice movements have publicized their causes through media campaigns, and some would contend that strategic publicity is crucial for success (Shaw; Burns). The changes brought about by the civil rights movements, for example, are partly attributable to widespread media coverage. Public outrage over police treatment of peaceful protesters in Birmingham and Selma, Alabama coalesced national support for civil rights legislation (Burns). Currently, PETA and the AIDS Coalition to Unleash Power (ACT-UP) are examples of organizations that have used the media to their advantage. PETA's relentless publicity campaign against animal testing was instrumental in creating the growing market for cruelty-free products. And, ACT-UP's carefully staged demonstrations resulted in increased public awareness of the AIDS crisis, relaxed FDA drug trials and reduced costs for AIDS drugs and protocols (Shaw; Finsen and Finsen; Cruickshank).

Much overt action occurs within legal boundaries. Civil disobedients, however, often use overt action and subsequent arrest to dramatize their position. The images of Martin Luther King Jr. languishing in the Birmingham jail and 70-year-old Sister Rita Steinhagen serving federal prison time for trespassing at the SOA protest did much to stir up public sympathy for these causes (Burns; Harvey).

Covert, undercover action is often utilized when illegal actions bear serious consequences (e.g., long-term incarceration or capital punishment) or when the political circumstances are extremely repressive. Groups such as ALF (Animal Liberation Front) and ELF (Earth Liberation Front), which advocate "economic sabotage," are so covert that membership consists of anonymous, autonomous cells which act first and claim responsibility later (Finsen and Finsen). In other situations, any dissent is not tolerated. The South African government, for example, banned anti-apartheid organizations, forcing Nelson Mandela and the other members of the African National Congress underground (Harwood; Clark).

Justice frameworks and action goals, in part, shape the conditions of action. All these in turn influence the specific implementation of action, the topic to which we now turn.

Strategies

This final action parameter focuses on the practical implementation of action, the selection of strategies. At this level, the discussion is the most concrete and tactical. Issues of individual and/or collective action, leadership style, and specific actions are central to action strategies.

Action may be individual, collective, or based on coalitions. This is a key strategic question. Much action is individual and includes a range of legal/illegal, nonviolent/militant, and overt/covert options from letter writing to sabotage. Although many discussions of action focus on collective responses, the role of the individual should not be discounted. As Robert Fisher notes, "'the personal is political'—first articulated by radical feminists in the late 1960s—guides people to organize around aspects of daily life most central to them, while keeping in mind that struggles over personal issues and relationships . . . are inextricably tied to collective struggles of the constituency group and the larger society" (1993, pp. 335–336).

Individual action is thus often connected to collective efforts towards change. Collective action occurs in many and varied ways. Groups may be loosely organized and connected only by shared goals and tactics (e.g., EarthFirst! and ALF) or they may be highly structured and organized with identified members and planned agendas (e.g., NOW, NAACP, and the Urban League). Group efforts may focus on justice issues at the local, state, national, or international level. Examples include Mothers of East Los Angeles (MELA), the Minnesota Public Interest Research Group (MPIRG), Women's Health Action Mobilization (WHAM), United for Justice and Peace (a coalition of over 800 anti-war groups in the U.S.) and GreenPeace (Shaw; Fisher, 1993, 1994). The distinctions here are not always so clear. Local grassroots initiatives often develop into national or international organizations. The Association of Community Organizations for Reform Now (ACORN) provides an illustration. ACORN, now a multi-issue community organizing initiative, began in Little Rock, Arkansas, in 1970. Initially targeting racial discrimination in housing locally, ACORN gradually evolved into an organization with a nationwide base. As it expanded, so did its focus, swiftly moving from neighborhood issues to electoral politics on the state and national levels (Fisher, 1994, pp. 147–153).

Group action on a justice issue may be enhanced by the formation of coalitions. Groups with seemingly different issues and agendas may find they actually share much common ground. The aforementioned congruency among justice frameworks contributes to the possibility of coalitions. Groups which frame a justice issue in different ways may come together in joint action. Several examples illustrate this point. Nationally and globally, there is a growing partnership between green groups and human rights organizations. The environmental racism movement in the U.S. consists of a variety of religious, civil rights, women's, and green organizations including the United Church of Christ, the NAACP, the SCLC, MELA, GreenPeace, and the National Toxics Campaign (Bullard pp. 24–29)

Globally, Amnesty International has joined forces with GreenPeace, the World Wildlife Fund, the Sierra Club and others to fight for environmental protection and human rights. The joint effort dates back to the mid-1980s and carries on the legacy of Chico Mendes, who was murdered in his attempts to stop Amazon deforestation. "Chico Mendes . . . considered himself solely a social justice activist. His principle aim was to protest his fellow rubber tappers' right to earn a livelihood from the forest. Once he encountered the environmental movement in 1985, however, Mendes realized that the international struggle to save the rainforest and his local struggle to save the rainforest and his local struggle to empower its inhabitants amounted to nearly the same thing. . . . He showed that human rights and environmental issues are inextricably linked together" (Sachs, p. 3).

Recently, a broad based coalition came together in Seattle to protest at World Trade Organization (WTO) meetings. These seemingly unlikely allies also joined forces in Washington, DC at protests over the World Bank and International Monetary Fund and again at the 2003 protest against the FTAA (Free Trade of the Americas Agreement) meeting in Miami. Opposition to the effects of the global economy has united former adversaries who have decidedly different justice issues. Included in this coalition are anarchists (anti-technology, corporate hierarchy and consumerism), Confédération Paysanne (French farmers who oppose U.S. hormone-fed beef), Médécins Sans Frontiéres (opposed to high cost prescription drugs for AIDS patients), Public Citizen (generalized opposition to multinational corporations), Sea Turtle Restoration Group (environmental concerns), Seattle Lesbian Avengers (anti-bovine growth hormone), Sierra Club (anti-genetically modified food and rainforest logging), and the Teamsters (opposed to loss of U.S. jobs). The mass actions in Seattle, Washington, DC, and Miami are indicative of how seemingly disparate organizations can join together. The common threads found among different justice frameworks can be the basis for coalitions and joint action (Elliott, pp. 36–39; Harris, pp. 21–25).

Leadership style is a strategic decision that every justice movement must contemplate. Should there be a clearly defined leader or should what Ella Baker calls "group-centered leadership" prevail? (Payne, p. 893). The issues of leadership style have been the subject of much debate among both activists and academicians (Fisher, 1993, 1994; Alinsky, 1946, 1971; Boyte, Rivera and Evlich, eds.; Shaw). On one end of the spectrum are those who favor a hierarchical leadership model; at the other, are advocates of grassroots, community-based organizing.

Although many justice movements here and elsewhere have used both approaches, the U.S. civil rights movement is often used as the example of different leadership models. The approach of SCLC emphasized well-known leaders, most notably Martin Luther King Jr. This approach is especially effective in mobilizing, i.e., "involving large numbers of people for relatively short periods of time and probably for relatively dramatic activities" (Payne, p. 894). Certainly the Montgomery bus boycott and the historic marches in Birmingham, Selma, and Washington, DC are examples of successful mobilizing.

In sharp contrast, the strategies employed by SNCC emphasized organizing, i.e., creating on-going groups that are mass-based and claimed by the community itself. SNCC's voter registration campaigns in Mississippi, Alabama and Georgia, for example, required long-term commitments to the development of local community organizations that could be sustained without SNCC's presence. "Let the people decide" became a SNCC slogan, one that captured its concern with decentralization and grassroots participation (Burns, p. 13).

In some respects, this dichotomy—mobilizing vs. organizing—is a false one. Many justice movements rely on both approaches. This has been the case with the Civil Rights, feminist, GLBT and green movements both globally and nationally (Ferree and Hess; Cruickshank; Merchant). Further, strong leaders frequently emerge from grassroots organizing. In fact, some models of community organizing require the leadership of trained organizations. This is indicative of the approach of Saul Alinsky and his contemporary followers. Alinsky, known for his labor organizing in Chicago, continually stressed the significance of professional organizers in community-based action (Alinsky; Fischer, 1994).

Issues of leadership style are not always resolved via careful pre-planning. It is important to recognize the spontaneity that characterizes many justice movements. Grassroots action often just happens, without the presence of outside organizers or mobilizers. The gang truce and alliance, United for Peace, which sprang from the ashes of the L.A. riots is a case in point (Madhubuti, 1993). The Bloods/Crips initiative to address issues of economic and educational access in the inner city was truly grassroots, in this sense. It, like many other movements around the world, emerged without the benefit of trained organizations or theoretical models for change.

Finally, action may be indirect (i.e., focused on increasing awareness of the justice issue or resolving it by creating alternative institutions) or direct (i.e., focused on the perceived source of injustice). Again, these approaches are not mutually exclusive. Justice movements may simultaneously engage in both types of action. The feminist movement, for example, indirectly sought change through consciousness-raising groups, women's presses, and the creation of women's collectives. At the same time, many feminists were involved in lobbying for legislative change, marching and other mass demonstrations (Ferree and Hess). Indeed, many justice movements engage in both indirect and direct actions, relying on a combination of specific tactics.

Action, both direct and indirect, may take shape in a number of ways. Specific tactics may be used alone or in conjunctions with other actions. Again, justice frameworks and the goals/conditions of action influence decisions regarding specific actions. A partial list of options includes speaking out; group consciousness raising; the creation of alternative schools, economies, political groups, and communes; legal actions/lawsuits; community and internet organizing; marches; boycotts; strikes; sit-ins; occupations; jail-ins; tax evasion; draft resistance; economic sabotage; armed street patrols; guerrilla warfare and armed offensives.

Certainly this list is not exhaustive. Variations on all these general action options currently exist. And, today, tomorrow or the day after, someone will imagine and enact a new tactic. Most of these actions have been discussed or alluded to throughout. Many have been used to great effect here and elsewhere. Mass actions such as boycotts, strikes, sit-ins and marches have become staples of protest globally.

From sit-ins at the segregated lunch counters in Greensboro, NC, to student sit-ins in Tiananmen Square, from Gandhi's Great Salt March to the Million Man and Million Mom marches, from boycotts of grapes to boycotts of the Gap, action is adapted to address an assortment of justice issues. Most of the action options listed are well known and familiar. Special attention, however, should be paid here to two that are rarely discussed—symbolic protest and speaking out.

The role of symbolic protest—through art, music, literature, poetry and theater—is often overlooked. Justice movements have been sparked and sustained by well-chosen words, song, and paint. As Bertolt Brecht so aptly put it, "Art is not a mirror held up to reality, but a hammer with which to shape it" (Felshin, p. 34).

All the justice movements referred to in this discussion have been supported by symbolic protests. Indeed, the role of symbolic protest in justice movements is so far-reaching that it is another treatise unto itself. For now, however, the key point is this—action for justice may take sometimes surprising symbolic shape. The feminist art of Judy Chicago and the street theater of the Guerilla Girls, the revolutionary murals of the Sandanistas, the poems of Pablo Neruda and Sonia Sanchez, the freedom songs of the Civil Rights movements and the South African struggle, Anna Deavere Smith's plays on urban unrest, the songs of labor and anti-war protest, Faith Ringgold's paintings and the novels of Toni Morrison and Rosa Guy, the Rainbow flag and the Names Project's AIDS Quilt, the reggae of Rastafarianism, the provocative posters of ACT-UP and PETA, Black/Red/Green Power fists, the political rap of Public Enemy and Tupac Shakur, the prison writings of Leonard Peltier and Mumia Abu Jamal, Michael Moore's cinematic lampoons of corporate greed and gun culture, Maya Lin's memorials of the Vietnam War and the Civil Rights struggles, and anonymous graffiti written on somebody's wall, are all actions for justice in a more symbolic form (Broudz and Garrad; Cockraft, Weber and Cockraft; Fine; Jacobs, and Heller; Cooper and Chalfant; Jones; Neruda; Morrison, 1970, 1987; Lewis; Campbell; Rose; Sakolsky and Wei-Han Ho; Carson, et al.; Cruikschank; Ferree and Hess; Wilson, 1999; Smith, 1993, 1994; Denisoff; Sturken; Aldaraca, Baker and Zimmerman; Walker, 1982, 1983).

Finally, the significance of speaking out must not be underestimated. All this discussion of marches and mass movements may create the impression that action must be dramatic, perhaps dangerous, that one must go to jail or die in the street to effect change.

This is certainly not the case. Simply speaking out is one of the most important actions towards justice that one can take. In the *Transformation of Silence into Language and Action*, Audre Lorde urges us to overcome our fears and speak. "I began to recognize a source of power within myself that comes from the knowledge that while it is most desirable not to be afraid, learning to put fear into perspective gave me great strength. I was going to die, if not sooner then later, whether or not I have ever spoken myself. My silences had not protected me. Your silence will not protect you. . . . Because the machine will grind you into dust anyway, whether or not we speak. We can sit in our corners mute forever while our sisters and ourselves are wasted, while our children are distorted and destroyed, while our earth is poisoned; we can sit in our safe corners mute as bottles, and we will still be no less afraid" (pp. 41–42).

We will still be afraid and we will still live without justice. It can be argued, perhaps, that all our actions are contingent upon this one, that speaking out is the necessary precondition for all other actions related to justice. There are others who contend that our silence must be broken for ourselves as well as others. Perhaps Pastor Martin Niemöller, who was imprisoned by the Nazis, puts it best in the quote that opens this chapter, "First they came for the socialists, and I did not speak out because I was not a socialist. Then they came for the trade unionists, and I did not speak out because I was not a trade unionist. Then they came for the Jews, and I did not speak out because I was not a Jew. Then they came for me and there was no one left to speak for me" (Ishay, p. 452).

Action parameters—goals, conditions, and strategies—guide the direction towards social change. As we have seen, justice frameworks and action parameters are intertwined in complex ways. Sometimes justice frameworks point directly towards certain modes of action. At other times, the congruence among justice frameworks allows for action coalitions and strategic framing of justice issues. And finally, spontaneous grassroots action may later find links with existing justice frameworks.

The relationship between justice and action is complicated and often unpredictable, yet always present in sometimes obvious, sometimes subtle ways.

Concluding Remarks

Justice and action. We end as we began, perhaps a bit closer to capturing the complexities of these concepts. As the discussion and examples indicate, these words do indeed have many different dimensions, many different meanings. The foregoing descriptive overview is an initial attempt to locate the common threads among various perspectives; to synthesize the insights provided by a multiplicity of disciplines and experiences.

It is hoped that this more general consideration of justice frameworks, action parameters, and the connections between them aids us in understanding and analysis. If we can recognize the central elements of justice frameworks (i.e., sources, standards, scope) and action parameters (i.e., goals, conditions, strategies), we should be able to use these analytical tools to understand any specific issue of justice/action. Perhaps, we can better evaluate and empathize with the perspectives and actions of others. In the process, we might also critically analyze our own perspectives. We might, in fact, come to realize our own positions on issues of justice and uncover our own propensities to act. In the oft-quoted words of JFK, "If not us, who? If not now, when?"

Questions for Discussion

1. Select an issue related to your GSJ course topic (i.e., Environmental Justice, The Immigrant Experience, Latin America, Voices of Dissent, Women's Health Issues, Women and Work). Choose two perspectives on this issue and compare/contrast using the elements of justice frameworks (i.e., sources, standards, and scope). What are the similarities and differences between these two approaches? What are the strengths and weaknesses of each? With the same example, choose two actions for change, and compare/contrast using the variations in action parameters (i.e., goals, conditions, and strategies). What are the similarities and differences between the two courses of action? What are the strengths and weaknesses of each approach? Which justice perspective and action approach most closely corresponds with your own views? Explain.

2. Identify your own perspective on justice. What are the sources, standards, and scope of your definition of justice? What actions would you recommend in pursuit of justice? Address the goals, conditions, and strategies of action. What factors have influenced your view of justice and action?

3. Review the United Nation's Universal Declaration of Human Rights. Does this list adequately capture the rights that should be available to all people? Is anything or anyone missing? Is it even possible to claim or identify universal standards of justice? Why/why not?

4. Discuss your views of civil disobedience. Is violation of the law ever acceptable? Why/why not? If so, under what circumstances? Discuss your views of nonviolence vs. militancy. Is the use of violence ever acceptable? Why/why not? If so, under what circumstances?

5. Why should women be particularly concerned about justice? What justice issues do women face globally? Nationally? Locally? What actions can you take to address the issues cited here?

Note

[1] My own analytical struggle with the issues of justice and action began as I prepared to teach this course. I searched, in vain it seems, for course materials that would capture the range of interdisciplinary perspectives and positions relative to justice and action. Discipline specific material seemed too limiting—the philosophers had a lot to say about certain views of justice, but little that spoke of action. The political theorists, on the other hand, discussed justice and action in the context of governments and official documents, but often ignored the grassroots activists. And, the activists, well, they were activists who often engaged the issues of justice without much analysis or theorizing. None of the existing writings on justice and action seemed to provide a larger framework for comparison and critical analysis. The interdisciplinary literature I sought was not there. The possibility of creating such an analytic scheme to critically compare justice perspectives and action options occurred to me as I was examining factions of the Civil Rights Movement in detail. The Southern Christian Leadership Conference (SCLC), the Student Non-violent Coordinating Committee (SNCC), the Nation of Islam (NOI), Malcolm X and the Black Panther Party (BPP) all emerged from the same struggle, but they had diverse goals and tactics. The ways in which these groups varied, however, could be systematically analyzed and discussed. Their justice arguments emanated from different sources; they applied varying standards, and also diverged regarding the scope of these justice standards. In addition, the proposed course of action for all these groups varied markedly. SCLC, SNCC, NOI and the BPP differed with respect to goals, positions on the appropriateness of nonviolence vs. militant action, leadership styles and strategies. If, then, we could identify variables that provided a framework for comparing and contrasting elements of the Civil Rights Movement, couldn't we also utilize that framework to compare justice and action across disciplines and movements? This was where I began; this article is the result.

Appendix A

Liberal Arts: Disciplines, Subject Matter, and Methods

Humanities

- The Fine Arts, Foreign Languages, History, Literature in English, Philosophy, Theology

- Emphasis on symbolic communication and expression, interpretation, and questions of meaning, experience, existence, metaphysics and cosmology

- Rules and norms of grammar, logic and composition; multiple paradigms and schools of theory and practice; qualitative methods—reliance on critical thinking and a degree of methodological "subjectivity" in interpretation of historical, philosophical and religious texts, works of art, literature and music

Social Sciences

- Anthropology, Economics, Geography, Political Science, Psychology, Sociology

- Emphasis on empirical examination of human interaction with the environment, culture, economic and political arrangements and activity, the self and society

- Standard methodologies that span disciplines; multiple paradigms within disciplines with common historical and theoretical roots; use of both qualitative and quantitative methods—emphasis on empirically measurable variables, correlation, and a degree of "objectivity" in examining human activity

Natural Sciences

- Biology, Chemistry, Physics, Mathematics and all related sub-fields of study

- Emphasis on the observable, empirical underpinnings and unchanging principles of the physical world, including human existence

- Standard methodologies that span disciplines; tendencies towards single paradigms that stand until "disproved"; use of quantitative methods—emphasis on mathematical formulas, theorems, the experiment, causation, "proof" and "objectivity" in the examination of empirical data

Appendix B

Universal Declaration of Human Rights

Adopted and proclaimed by General Assembly
Resolution 217 A (III) of 10 December 1948

On December 10, 1948 the General Assembly of the United Nations adopted and proclaimed the Universal Declaration of Human Rights the full text of which appears in the following pages. Following this historic act the Assembly called upon all Member countries to publicize the text of the Declaration and "to cause it to be disseminated, displayed, read and expounded principally in schools and other educational institutions, without distinction based on the political status of countries or territories."

Article 1.

All human beings are born free and equal in dignity and rights. They are endowed with reason and conscience and should act towards one another in a spirit of brotherhood.

Article 2.

Everyone is entitled to all the rights and freedoms set forth in this Declaration, without distinction of any kind, such as race, colour, sex, language, religion, political or other opinion, national or social origin, property, birth or other status. Furthermore, no distinction shall be made on the basis of the political, jurisdictional or international status of the country or territory to which a person belongs, whether it be independent, trust, non-self-governing or under any other limitation of sovereignty.

Article 3.

Everyone has the right to life, liberty and security of person.

Article 4.

No one shall be held in slavery or servitude; slavery and the slave trade shall be prohibited in all their forms.

Article 5.

No one shall be subjected to torture or to cruel, inhuman or degrading treatment or punishment.

Article 6.

Everyone has the right to recognition everywhere as a person before the law.

Article 7.

All are equal before the law and are entitled without any discrimination to equal protection of the law. All are entitled to equal protection against any discrimination in violation of this Declaration and against any incitement to such discrimination.

Article 8.

Everyone has the right to an effective remedy by the competent national tribunals for acts violating the fundamental rights granted him by the constitution or by law.

Article 9.

No one shall be subjected to arbitrary arrest, detention or exile.

Article 10.

Everyone is entitled in full equality to a fair and public hearing by an independent and impartial tribunal, in the determination of his rights and obligations and of any criminal charge against him.

Article 11.

(1) Everyone charged with a penal offence has the right to be presumed innocent until proved guilty according to law in a public trial at which he has had all the guarantees necessary for his defence.

(2) No one shall be held guilty of any penal offence on account of any act or omission which did not constitute a penal offence, under national or international law, at the time when it was committed. Nor shall a heavier penalty be imposed than the one that was applicable at the time the penal offence was committed.

Article 12.

No one shall be subjected to arbitrary interference with his privacy, family, home or correspondence, nor to attacks upon his honour and reputation. Everyone has the right to the protection of the law against such interference or attacks.

Article 13.

(1) Everyone has the right to freedom of movement and residence within the borders of each state.

(2) Everyone has the right to leave any country, including his own, and to return to his country.

Article 14.

(1) Everyone has the right to seek and to enjoy in other countries asylum from persecution.

(2) This right may not be invoked in the case of prosecutions genuinely arising from non-political crimes or from acts contrary to the purposes and principles of the United Nations.

Article 15.

(1) Everyone has the right to a nationality.

(2) No one shall be arbitrarily deprived of his nationality nor denied the right to change his nationality.

Article 16.

(1) Men and women of full age, without any limitation due to race, nationality or religion, have the right to marry and to found a family. They are entitled to equal rights as to marriage, during marriage and at its dissolution.

(2) Marriage shall be entered into only with the free and full consent of the intending spouses.

(3) The family is the natural and fundamental group unit of society and is entitled to protection by society and the State.

Article 17.

(1) Everyone has the right to own property alone as well as in association with others.

(2) No one shall be arbitrarily deprived of his property.

Article 18.

Everyone has the right to freedom of thought, conscience and religion; this right includes freedom to change his religion or belief, and freedom, either alone or in community with others and in public or private, to manifest his religion or belief in teaching, practice, worship and observance.

Article 19.

Everyone has the right to freedom of opinion and expression; this right includes freedom to hold opinions without interference and to seek, receive and impart information and ideas through any media and regardless of frontiers.

Article 20.

(1) Everyone has the right to freedom of peaceful assembly and association.

(2) No one may be compelled to belong to an association.

Article 21.

(1) Everyone has the right to take part in the government of his country, directly or through freely chosen representatives.

(2) Everyone has the right of equal access to public service in his country.

(3) The will of the people shall be the basis of the authority of government; this will shall be expressed in periodic and genuine elections which shall be by universal and equal suffrage and shall be held by secret vote or by equivalent free voting procedures.

Article 22.

Everyone, as a member of society, has the right to social security and is entitled to realization, through national effort and international co-operation and in accordance with the organization and resources of each State, of the economic, social and cultural rights indispensable for his dignity and the free development of his personality.

Article 23.

(1) Everyone has the right to work, to free choice of employment, to just and favourable conditions of work and to protection against unemployment.

(2) Everyone, without any discrimination, has the right to equal pay for equal work.

(3) Everyone who works has the right to just and favourable remuneration ensuring for himself and his family an existence worthy of human dignity, and supplemented, if necessary, by other means of social protection.

(4) Everyone has the right to form and to join trade unions for the protection of his interests.

Article 24.

Everyone has the right to rest and leisure, including reasonable limitation of working hours and periodic holidays with pay.

Article 25.

(1) Everyone has the right to a standard of living adequate for the health and well-being of himself and of his family, including food, clothing, housing and medical care and necessary social services, and the right to security in the event of unemployment, sickness, disability, widowhood, old age or other lack of livelihood in circumstances beyond his control.

(2) Motherhood and childhood are entitled to special care and assistance. All children, whether born in or out of wedlock, shall enjoy the same social protection.

Article 26.

(1) Everyone has the right to education. Education shall be free, at least in the elementary and fundamental stages. Elementary education shall be compulsory. Technical and professional education shall be made generally available and higher education shall be equally accessible to all on the basis of merit.

(2) Education shall be directed to the full development of the human personality and to the strengthening of respect for human rights and fundamental freedoms. It shall promote understanding, tolerance and friendship among all nations, racial or religious groups, and shall further the activities of the United Nations for the maintenance of peace.

(3) Parents have a prior right to choose the kind of education that shall be given to their children.

Article 27.

(1) Everyone has the right freely to participate in the cultural life of the community, to enjoy the arts and to share in scientific advancement and its benefits.

(2) Everyone has the right to the protection of the moral and material interests resulting from any scientific, literary or artistic production of which he is the author.

Article 28.

Everyone is entitled to a social and international order in which the rights and freedoms set forth in this Declaration can be fully realized.

Article 29.

(1) Everyone has duties to the community in which alone the free and full development of his personality is possible.

(2) In the exercise of his rights and freedoms, everyone shall be subject only to such limitations as are determined by law solely for the purpose of securing due recognition and respect for the rights and freedoms of others and of meeting the just requirements of morality, public order and the general welfare in a democratic society.

(3) These rights and freedoms may in no case be exercised contrary to the purposes and principles of the United Nations.

Article 30.

Nothing in this Declaration may be interpreted as implying for any State, group or person any right to engage in any activity or to perform any act aimed at the destruction of any of the rights and freedoms set forth herein.

References

Abu-Jamal, Mumia. *Live from Death Row*. Reading, MA: Addison-Wesley, 1995.

———. *Death Blossoms: Reflections from a Prisoner of Conscience*. Farmington, MA: The Plough Publishing House, 1996.

Adam, Barry. *The Rise of a Gay and Lesbian Movement*. Rev. ed. New York: Twayne, 1995.

Alexander, A. *The Farrakhan Factor*. New York: Grove Press, 1998.

Alexander, Ewan, ed. *Voice of Indigenous Peoples*. Santa Fe, NM: Clear Light Publishers, 1994.

Amnesty International. *United States of America: Rights for All*. New York: Amnesty International, 1998.

———. *Amnesty Report 2001*. New York: Amnesty International, 2001.

———. *Broken Bodies, Shattered Minds: Torture and Ill-treatment of Women*. New York: Amnesty International, 2001.

———. *Refugees*. New York: Amnesty International, 1997.

———. *Torture Worldwide*. New York: Amnesty International, 2000.

Anderson, M. and Patricia Hill Collins, ed. *Race, Class, and Gender: An Anthology*. Belmont, CA: Wadsworth, 1998.

Arden, Harvey, ed. *Prison Writings: My Life Is a Sundance: Leonard Peltier United States Prisoner # 89637–132*. New York: St. Martin's Press, 1999.

Bell, Derrick. *Faces at the Bottom of the Well: The Permanence of Racism*. New York: Basic Books, 1992.

Bloods and Crips. "Bloods/Crips Proposal for L.A.'s Face-Lift." *Why L.A. Happened*. Ed. H. Madhubuti. Los Angeles, CA: Third World Press, 1993.

Bové, Jose and Francois Dufour. *The World Is Not for Sale: Farmers against Junk Food*. New York: Verso, 2001.

Boyte, Harry. *Commonwealth: A Retur.. io Citizen Politics*. New York: Free Press, 1989.

Branch, Taylor. *Parting the Waters: America in the King Years, 1954–63*. New York: Simon and Schuster, 1988.

———. *Pillar of Fire: America in the King Years, 1963–65*. New York: Simon and Schuster, 1998.

Bratton, M. "After Mandela's Miracle in South Africa." *Current History* 97 (1998): 214–219.

Breitman, G., ed. *Malcolm X Speaks: Selected Speeches and Statements.* New York: Grove Press, 1965.

Broude, Norma and Mary D. Garrard, ed. *The Power of Feminist Art.* New York: Harry Abrams, Inc., 1994.

Brown, Dee. *Bury My Heart at Wounded Knee.* New York: Holt, Rinehart and Winston, 1971.

Bullard, Robert. *Confronting Environmental Racism: Voices from the Grass-roots.* Boston, MA: South End Press, 1993.

Burgos-Debray, E., ed. *I, Rigoberta Menchú: An Indian Woman in Guatemala.* London: Verso, 1984.

Burns, Stewart. *Social Movements of the 1960s: Searching for Democracy.* New York: Twayne, 1990.

Campbell, H. *Black Noise: Rasta and Resistance: From Marcus Garvey to Walter Rodney.* Trenton, NJ: Africa World Press, 1987.

Carmichael, Stokley and Charles Hamilton. *Black Power: The Politics of Liberation in America.* New York: Random House, 1967.

Carson, Claybonne, David J. Janow, Gerald Gill, Vincent Hardy, and Darlene Clark Hines, ed. *The Eyes on the Prize Civil Rights Reader: Documents, Speeches and Firsthand Accounts from the Black Freedom Struggle.* New York: Penguin Books, 1991.

Chinosole, ed. *Schooling the Generations in the Politics of Prison.* Berkeley, CA: New Earth Publications, 1996.

Chomsky, Noam. *Secrets, Lies and Democracy.* Tucson, AZ: Odonian Press, 1994.

———. *The Prosperous Few and the Restless Many.* Tucson, AZ: Odonian Press, 1994.

———. *9–11,* New York: Seven Stories Press, 2001.

Chuck D. with Y. Yah. *Fight the Power: Rap, Race and Reality.* New York: Delacorte Press, 1997.

Clark, Steve, ed. *Nelson Mandela Speaks: Foraging a Democratic Nonracial South Africa.* New York: Pathfinder, 1993.

Cleaver, Eldridge. *Soul on Ice.* New York: Random House, 1968.

Cockcraft, Eva, John Weber and James Cockcraft. *Toward a People's Art: The Contemporary Mural Movement.* New York: E. P. Dutton, 1977.

Collins, Patricia Hill. *Black Feminist Thought: Knowledge, Consciousness and the Politics of Empowerment.* Boston, MA: Unwin Hyman, 1990.

Cone, James. *Martin and Malcolm: A Dream or a Nightmare.* Maryknoll, NY: Orbis, 1991.

———. *Black Theology and Black Power.* Maryknoll, NY: Orbis Books, 1997.

Cooper, Martha and Henry Chalfant. *Subway Art.* New York: Henry Holt and Company, 1984.

Cornell, T., R. Ellsberg and J. Forest, ed. *A Penny a Copy: Readings from the Catholic Worker.* Maryknoll, NY: Orbis, 1995.

Cose, Ellis. *Color-Blind: Seeing Beyond Race in a Race-Obsessed World.* New York: Harper Perennial, 1997.

Cruikshank, M. *The Gay and Lesbian Liberation Movement.* New York: Routledge, Chapman and Hall, 1992.

Dalton, H. *Racial Healing: Confronting the Fear between Blacks and Whites.* New York: Anchor, 1995.

Davis, Angela. *Women, Race and Class.* New York: Random House, 1981.

Declaration of Independence and the Constitution of the United States, The. New York: Penguin, 1995.

Deloria, Vine, Jr. *Custer Died for Your Sins.* New York: Macmillan, 1969.

———. *Behind the Trail of Broken Treaties.* New York: Delacorte, 1974.

Denisoff, R. Serge. *Sing a Song of Social Significance.* Bowling Green, KY: Bowling Green University Press, 1972.

Doob, C. B. *Racism: An American Caldron.* New York: Longman, 1999.

Draher, Patricia and John P. Pierce, ed. *Compassion and Protest.* New York: Cross River Press, 1991.

Duberman, Martin. *Stonewall.* New York: Plume, 1993.

Due, L. *Joining the Tribe: Growing Up Gay and Lesbian in the '90s.* New York: Anchor, 1995.

Ehrenreich, Barbara. *Nickled and Dimed.* New York: Metropolitan Books, 2001.

Elliott, M. "The New Radicals." *Newsweek* 13 (1999) Dec. 21–25.

Faludi, Susan. *Backlash: The Undeclared War Against American Women.* New York: Crown, 1991.

Fanon, Franz. *The Wretched of the Earth.* New York: Grove Press, 1963.

Feinberg, Leslie. *Transgender Warriors.* Boston: Beacon Press, 1996.

Felshin, Nina, ed. *But Is It Art? The Spirit of Art as Activism.* Seattle, WA: Bay Press, 1995.

Feree, M. and B. Hess. *Controversy and Coalition: The New Feminist Movement Across Three Decades of Change.* Rev. ed. New York: Twayne, 1995.

Fletcher, J., T. Jones and S. Latringer. *Still Black, Still Strong: Survivors of the War Against Black Revolutionaries.* New York: Semiotext(e), 1993.

Foner, P., ed. *The Black Panthers Speak.* Philadelphia: J. B. Lippincott.

Friedan, Betty. *The Feminine Mystique.* New York: Dell, 1963.

Golden, R., M. McConnell, P. Mueller, C. Popper, and M. Turkovic. *Dangerous Memories: Invasion and Resistance Since 1492.* Chicago, IL: Chicago Religions Task Force on Central America, 1991.

Gomez-Quinones, J. *Mexican Students Por la Razda: The Chicano Student Movement in Southern California, 1969–1977.* Santa Barbara, CA: Editorial la Causa, 1978.

Hacker, Andrew. *Two Nations: Black and White, Separate, Hostile, Unequal.* New York: Ballantine Books, 1992.

Hampton, H. and S. Fayer, ed. *Voices of Freedom: An Oral History of the Civil Rights Movement from the 1950s through the 1980s.* New York: Bantam, 1991.

Harris, B. "The Scoop on the WTO." *Mother Jones*, Nov. 30, 1991: 21–25.

Harris, D. "WTO Watch: Explaining the Mess." *Mother Jones*, Dec. 7, 1999: 14–17.

Harwood, R. *Mandela.* New York: Plume, 1987.

Hennelly, A., ed. *Liberation Theology: A Documentary History.* Maryknoll, NY: Orbis, 1990.

Hill, Julia "Butterfly." *The Legacy of Luna.* San Francisco: HarperSanFrancisco, 2000.

hooks, bell. *Black Looks: Race and Representation.* Boston, MA: South End Press, 1992.

———. *Feminist Theory from Margin to Center.* Boston, MA: South End Press, 1984.

———. *Killing Rage: Ending Racism.* New York: Henry Holt, 1995.

———. *Where We Stand: Class Matters.* New York: Routledge, 2000.

Hunter, N., S. Michaelson and T. Stoddard. *ACLU Handbook: The Rights of Lesbians and Gay Men.* 3rd ed. Carbondale, IL: Southern Illinois University Press, 1992.

Ishay, M., ed. *The Human Rights Reader: Major Political Essays, Speeches and Documents from the Bible to the Present.* New York: Routledge, 1997.

Jacobs, Karrie and Steven Heller. *Angry Graphics: Protest Posters of the Reagan/Bush Era.* Layton, Utah: Gibbs-Smith, 1992.

Jacobson, D., ed. *The Immigration Reader: America in Multidisciplinary Perspective.* Malden, MA: Blackwell, 1998.

James, J., ed. *The Angela Y. Davis Reader.* Malden, MA: Blackwell, 1998.

Jencks, Christopher. *Rethinking Social Policy: Race, Poverty and the Underclass.* New York: Harper Perennial, 1992.

Jones, Charles, ed. *The Black Panthers Reconsidered.* Baltimore, MD: Black Classics, 1998.

Joseph, A., Jr., T. Thomas and J. Eden. *Wounded Knee: Lest We Forget.* 2nd ed. Cody, WY: Buffalo Bill Historical Center, 1993.

Kendall, D. *Race, Class and Gender in a Diverse Society.* Needham Heights, MA: Allyn and Bacon, 1997.

Klass, M. *Ordered Universes: Approaches to the Anthropology of Religion.* Boulder, CO: Westview, 1995.

Kotlowitz, Alex. *There Are No Children Here.* New York: Anchor, 1991.

Kozol, Jonathan. *Amazing Grace: The Lives of Children and the Conscience of the Nation.* New York: Harper Perennial, 1995.

———. *Savage Inequalities: Children in America's Schools.* New York: Harper Perennial, 1992.

LaDuke, Winona. *All Our Relations: Native Struggles for Land and Life.* Cambridge, MA: South End Press, 1999.

Levy, J. *Cesar Chavez: Autobiography of a La Causa.* New York: W.W. Norton, 1975.

Lewis, W. *Soul Rebels: The Rastafari.* Prospect Heights, IL: Waveland Press, 1993.

Lorde, Audre. *Sister Outsider: Essays and Speeches.* Freedom, CA: Crossing Press, 1984.

Lubiano, W., ed. *The House That Race Built.* New York: Vintage Books, 1988.

Madhubuti, H., ed. *Why L.A. Happened.* New York: World Press, 1993.

Malcolm X. *Malcolm X Speaks.* New York: Grove Press, 1965.

———. *Two Speeches by Malcolm X.* New York: Pathfinder, 1965.

Mandela, Nelson. *Nelson Mandela Speaks: Forging a Democratic Nonracial South Africa.* New York: Pathfinder, 1993.

Marcus, E. *Making History: The Struggle for Gay and Lesbian Equal Rights, 1945–1990.* New York: HarperCollins, 1992.

Martin, P., and E. Midgey. "Immigration to the United States." *Population Bulletin.* 54, June 1999: 12.

Matthiessen, Peter. *Sal Si Puedes: Cesar Chavez and the New American Revolution.* New York: Dell, 1969.

———. *In the Spirit of Crazy Horse: The Story of Leonard Peltier and the FBI's War on AIM.* New York: Vintage, 1991.

McCarthy, Timothy Patrick and John McMillian. *The Radical Reader.* New York: The New Press, 2003.

McChesney, Robert W. *Rich Media, Poor Democracy.* New York: New Press, 1999.

McCloud, B. *African American Islam.* New York: Routledge, 1995.

McKissack, Patricia and Frederick L. McKissack. *Rebels Against Slavery: American Slave Revolts.* New York: Scholastic, 1999.

Millman, M., and R. Moss Kanter, ed. *Another Voice: Feminist Perspectives on Social Life and Social Science.* New York: Octagon, 1976.

Mooney, Patrick H. and Theo J. Majka. *Farmers' and Farm Workers' Movement: Social Protest in American Agriculture.* New York: Twayne, 1995.

Moraga, C. and G. Anzaldua, ed. *This Bridge Called My Back: Writings by Radical Women of Color.* Watertown, MA: Persephone Press, 1981.

Morrison, Toni. *Beloved.* New York: Plume, 1987.

———. "Home" *The House That Race Built.* Ed. W. Lubiano. New York: Vintage, 1997.

———. *The Bluest Eye.* New York: Holt, Rhinehart & Winston, 1970.

Munoz, C. *Youth, Identity and Power: The Chicano Movement.* New York: Verso, 1989.

Murton, Thomas. *Gandhi on Non-Violence.* New York: New Directions, 1965.

Nelson-Pallmeyer, Jack. *School of the Assassins: Guns, Greed, and Globalization.* Maryknoll, NY: Orbis Books, 2001.

Noble, J., J. Cover and M. Janagashita. *The World's Youth.* Washington, DC: Population Reference Bureau, 1996.

Novick, G. *Genocide Against the Indians.* New York: Pathfinder, 1970.

Patterson, Orlando. *The Ordeal of Integration: Progress and Resentment in America's Racial Crisis.* New York: Civitas/Counterpoint, 1997.

———. *Rituals of Blood: Consequences of Slavery in Two American Centuries.* New York: Basic Civitas, 1998.

Patton, Susan. *African-American Art.* New York: Oxford University Press, 1998.

Payne, Charles. "Ella Baker and Models of Social Change." *Signs* 14:4 (1989): 885–899.

Plaskow, J. and Carol P. Christ, ed. *Weaving the Visions: New Patterns in Feminist Spirituality.* San Francisco, CA: Harper and Row, 1989.

Powell, Richard J. *Black Art and Culture in the 20th Century.* London: Thames and Hudson, 1997.

Reagan Johnson, Bearnice. "Coalition Politics: Turning the Century." *Homegirls: A Black Feminist Anthology.* Ed. B. Smith. New York: Kitchen Table Press, 1983.

Roediger, D., ed. *Black on White: Black Writers on What It Means to Be White.* New York: Schocken, 1998.

Rose, Tricia. *Black Noise: Rap Music and Black Culture in Contemporary America.* Middletown, CT: Wesleyan University Press, 1994.

Rothenberg, P., ed. *Race, Class and Gender in the U.S.: An Integrated Study.* 4th ed. New York: St. Martin's Press, 1998.

Rowbotham, S. *Women in Movement: Feminism and Social Action.* NY: Routledge, Chapman and Hall, 1992.

Sakorsky, R. and F. Wei-Han Ho., ed. *Sounding Off! Music as Subversion/Resistance/Revolution.* Brooklyn, NY: Autonomedia, 1995.

Schlosser, Eric, *Fast Food Nation,* Boston: Houghton Mifflin, 2001.

Seager, Joan. *The State of Women in the World Atlas.* New York: Penguin, 1997.

Shakur, Sanyika. *Monster: The Autobiography of an LA Gang Member.* New York: Penguin, 1993.

Shaw, Randy. *The Activists Handbook: A Primer for the 1990s and Beyond.* Berkeley: University of California Press, 1996.

Shilts, Randy. *And the Band Played On: People, Politics and the AIDS Epidemic.* New York: Penguin, 1988.

Shiva, Vandana. "Staying Alive: Development, Ecology and Women." *The Human Rights Reader: Major Political Essays, Speeches and Documents from the Bible to the Present.* ed. M. Ishay. New York: Routledge, 1997: 253–263.

———. *Biopiracy.* Boston, MA: South End Press, 1997.

———. *Stolen Harvest.* Boston, MA: South End Press, 2000.

———. *Water Wars.* Boston, MA: South End Press, 2002.

Shute, S. and S. Hurley, ed. *On Human Rights: Oxford Amnesty Lectures.* New York: Basic Books, 1993.

Signorile, M. *Queer in America: Sex, Media and the Closets of Power.* New York: Anchor, 1993.

Smith, Anna Deavere. *Fires in the Mirror.* New York: Anchor, 1993.

———. *Twilight: Los Angeles, 1992.* New York: Anchor, 1994.

Smith, Dorothy. *The Everyday World as Problematic: A Feminist Sociology.* Boston, MA: Northeastern University Press, 1987.

Stan, Adele. *Debating Sexual Correctness.* New York: Anchor, 1994.

Sturgeon, Noel. *Ecofeminist Natures: Race, Gender, Feminist Theory and Practical Action.* New York: Routledge, 1997.

Sturken, Marita. *Tangled Memories: The Vietnam War, the AIDS Epidemic, and the Politics of Remembering.* Berkely, CA: University of California Press, 1997.

Taylor, R. *Sweatshops in the Sun: Child Labor on the Farm.* Boston, MA: Beacon Press, 1973.

———. *Chavez and the Farmworkers: A Study in the Acquisition of Power.* Boston, MA: Beacon Press, 1975.

Thompson, B. and S. Tyagi, ed. *Names We Call Home: Autobiography of Racial Identity.* New York: Routledge, 1996.

Thomas, Janet. *The Battle in Seattle,* Golden, CO: Fulcrum, 2000.

United Nations. *Human Rights: A Compilation of International Instruments.* Vol. 1. New York: United Nations Publications, 1999.

Upchurch, C. *Convicted in the Womb: One Man's Journey from Prisoner to Peacemaker.* New York: Bantam, 1997.

Walker, Alice. *In Search of Our Mothers' Gardens.* New York: Harcourt Brace Jovanovich, 1983.

———. *Possessing the Secret of Joy.* New York: Harcourt Brace Jovanovich, 1992.

————. *The Color Purple.* New York: Harcourt Brace, 1982.

Walker, Alice and P. Parmar. *Warrior Marks: Female Genital Mutilation and the Sexual Blinding of Women.* New York: Harcourt Brace Jovanovich, 1993.

Walker, S., C. Spohn and M. Delone. *The Color of Justice: Race, Ethnicity and Crime in America.* 3rd ed. Belmont, CA: Wadsworth, 2000.

Wallace, R., ed. *Feminism and Sociological Theory.* Newbury Park, CA: Sage, 1989.

Ward, Martha C. *A World Full of Women.* 2nd ed. Boston, MA: Allyn and Bacon, 1999.

Washington, J., ed. *I Have a Dream: Writing and Speeches That Changed the World/Martin Luther King Jr.* New York: HarperCollins, 1992.

Weitz, R., ed. *The Politics of Women's Bodies: Sexuality, Appearance and Behavior.* New York: Oxford, 1998.

Welton, Neva and Linda Wolf. *Global Uprising,* Gabriola Island, BC: New Society, 2001.

West, Cornell. *Race Matters.* New York: Vintage, 1993.

Whelehan, I. *Modern Feminist Thought.* New York: University Press, 1995.

Wilson, William Julius. *The Truly Disadvantaged: The Inner City, the Underclass and Public Policy.* Chicago: University of Chicago Press, 1987.

————. *When Work Disappears: The New World of the Urban Poor.* New York: Alfred A. Knopf, 1996.

Wilson, S. K., ed. *The Crisis Reader: Stories, Poetry and Essays from the NAACP's Crisis Magazine.* New York: Random House, 1999.

————. *The Opportunity Reader: Stories, Poems and Essays from the Urban League's Opportunity Reader.* New York: Random House, 1999.

Wolf, Naomi. *The Beauty Myth.* New York: Anchor, 1991.

Yanker, Gary. *Prop Art: Over 1000 Contemporary Political Posters.* New York: Darien House, Inc. 1972.

Russ Connors is associate professor and chair of the theology department here at the College of St. Catherine. He came to St. Kate's in 1995, after teaching for 12 years at St. Mary Seminary in Cleveland, Ohio, his hometown. He earned a doctoral degree in Christian ethics in 1983 and since then has developed some special interest and expertise in medical ethics. He was awarded a fellowship in the bioethics program of the National Institutes of Health in Bethesda, Maryland from 1990–1991, and has served as a consultant to a variety of health care institutions. Russ is the author or co-author of three books, the most recent of which (with Pat McCormick of Gonzaga University) will be published this summer by Paulist Press, Facing the Issues: Dimensions of Character, Choices, and Community. *This will explore many current ethical issues in medical, sexual, environmental, and social ethics. In addition, Russ has published a host of articles in scholarly journals and on a wide variety of topics related to Christian ethics. He is married to Patricia Cahalan Connors, associate professor of music at St. Catherine's, and together they have two (great!) children, Elizabeth, age 5 and Patrick, age 2.*

Catholic Social Teaching— Convictions and Connections

Russell B. Connors, Jr., S.T.D.

Introduction: Vignettes

As a state senator, Adam's positions on two issues have been clear and consistent: he has been strongly in favor of state-supported quality health care for all, and he has been opposed—just as strongly—to recent cut-backs in social services for the poor. In an interview in the local newspaper, the senator was quite forthright about the connections between his faith and his political life. "Some of my deepest convictions about justice," he explained, "have long been grounded in Catholic social teaching."

• • •

One of the students asked Sister MaryAnn how, given her feminist convictions, she remained part of a church that seems so riddled with sexism. Quickly and candidly she replied, "It's largely because of Catholic social teaching that I remain a Catholic, much less a sister. And besides," she went on, "it's my church too."

• • •

They were there every Saturday morning, the busiest time at the local grocery store. Their signs marked a protest of the store's continued policy of selling fruits and vegetables grown and picked by non-union farm workers. When asked why they were there each week, some of them referred to Catholic social teaching in their answer.

• • •

The pastor, Fr. Jordan, has "taken some heat" from some in the parish for the welcoming things he has been saying in recent Sunday homilies regarding gay and lesbian persons. And he has made church meeting rooms available for a prayer and study program sponsored by a group of gay and lesbian Catholics. As he said in the church bulletin, "There is a direct link between Catholic social teaching and our embrace of gay and lesbian persons."

• • •

"In the U.S.," Martina says, "we approach immigration from the point of view of the stresses on our own country. I understand that, but it is wrong. We must see this from the point of view of those who often suffer. The stresses on us are minor compared to the suffering of many who desire to come here." Martina has been called naïve by some of her colleagues at the University, but she does not flinch in her views. A convert to Catholicism, Martina says that one of the most attractive things about the Catholic Church to her was its social teaching, especially its notion of the "option for the poor."

• • •

Sheila has enough to do. But several weeks ago she found the time to distribute fliers about her nursing association's opposition to the state initiative to legalize physician-assisted suicide. A member of her church's "Peace and Justice Commission," next week she will be part of a panel discussion at the local public high school on capital punishment. She is similarly opposed to the death penalty. When asked to explain her convictions about these issues, Sheila refers to Catholic social teaching.

• • •

"I need to be clear with you, however, before I accept the position as principal of this school. The salaries of our teachers are simply unjust. I will not stop bringing this up until the situation improves dramatically." This is what John had said to the pastor and members of the finance commission as he accepted the position as principal of the Catholic elementary school. And it came to pass. For the past four years, at budget time, John has battled for more just wages for the teachers, grounding a strong and convincing argument in Catholic social teaching.

• • •

People make connections between Catholic social teaching and an amazing spectrum of issues, often doing so (as these vignettes make clear) in startlingly diverse ways, in ways that defy categorization as conservative or liberal, Republican or Democrat.

The phrase "Catholic social teaching," refers to the sum total of teachings provided by Catholic leaders—popes, bishops, and sometimes theologians—concerning the social issues of the day, especially over the last 100 years. Christian faith does not shield believers from difficult social issues, but rather, impels them to try to contribute to their solutions. In that spirit, the popes and bishops do not presume to offer simple answers to complex questions, but try to show what the relationship might be between Christian faith and social issues. Catholic teachings are put forth in various types of documents, as the Works Cited pages of this article illustrate. Invariably, those documents include both *convictions* and *connections*. By *convictions* I mean the fundamental presuppositions that ground Catholic involvement in social issues. And by *connections* I mean the way those convictions might be applied to specific questions and concerns. The purpose of this article is to uncover those key *convictions* and to examine how the *connections* get made.

It seems right to state four things very clearly at the start. The first is a bias: I am a Roman Catholic and I am proud of Catholic social teaching (henceforth, CST). As others have observed, it is sadly one of Catholicism's "best kept secrets" (Henriot). To say this is not to claim that it is a tradition that is perfect, completely consistent, or without blind spots. CST is a work-in-progress. Indeed, that is one of its virtues. Secondly, it is important not to reduce Catholicism to its teachings about justice. As important as those are, Catholicism also stands for other things, things like the phenomenon of sacramentality (our experience of the created universe as a medium through which we have contact with the divine), its confidence in humanity's pursuit of truth and wisdom wherever it is to be found, the sacredness and inviolability of conscience, the importance of community, etc. As we proceed I will look for ways to show the connections between CST and some of these other important features of Catholicism. Thirdly, extolling the virtues of CST is not my way of attempting to gloss over the faults and sins of the Catholic Church itself. As we will see, CST is not about what *everyone else* should do. The convictions of justice that are the heart of CST *apply to the church itself.* Gratefully, the church is gradually getting better at acknowledging its own injustice and sinfulness and its ongoing need of reformation. Fourthly, this is an overview, an introduction. I will have accomplished my goal if, at the end, the reader feels she has tasted of some of the primary flavors of CST. The works cited at the end will point to a fuller menu.

The remainder of this article is in two unequal parts. After a brief historical introduction, Part One will present what I think are the key *convictions* that are the heart of CST. I will first state the convictions themselves and then elaborate on their sources and their significance. Part One will close with a word about the interpretation and application of the seven major convictions to concrete issues, and with a reflection on the purposes of CST. More briefly, Part Two will explore the *connections* between CST and specific issues. We will do this by focusing simply on two of the key convictions of CST—the dignity and rights of every human being and the option for the poor—seeing how those convictions *connect* to some contemporary questions and concerns.

Part One: Catholic Social Teaching—Convictions

History.[1] Modern CST is commonly thought to have begun with the encyclical letter "Rerum Novarum" ("The Condition of Labor") of Pope Leo XIII in 1891. In that letter the pope faced squarely the conditions of workers in what had become industrialized and urbanized Europe. In a word, conditions were miserable. Many workers (including children) worked long hours in sometimes horrific environments for shockingly small wages—nothing close to a wage that would support a family. Housing and living conditions in the large industrial cities of Europe were equally miserable. Poverty was rampant.

The approach of Leo XIII's letter of concern was new in that rather than simply call for a renewed effort at works of *charity* to assist those in need (although that was indeed part of his message), he called for *social justice.* He called for a change in the social structures and institutions of the day that were the causes of the poverty and misery of the workers. He called for a just and living wage, for working conditions that were safe, and for laws that would prevent the abuse of children in the workforce. Fundamental to all of this was his insistence on the dignity of all people as children of God. He insisted that human dignity must be recognized and respected in the workers of the world.

Since Leo XIII, the Church has taken it to be its responsibility to address the issues of the day that concern the human community—sometimes matters of hunger and poverty, sometimes matters of prejudice and discrimination, sometimes matters of war and peace. Christian faith, the pope and bishops have argued, should not lead us to try to escape these difficult problems, but to try to contribute to their solution in light of the Gospel of Christ. This has given rise over the last 100 years to Catholic social teaching.

Convictions. Many people who discuss CST do so by naming and analyzing some basic moral *principles.* I think it is more helpful to state *con-*

victions. The word *principles* may suggest to some that what we are dealing with here is theory, philosophically precise but abstract moral principles that await application in the real world. The word *convictions* is better, I think, because it suggests that CST is not only about ideas, but about *passions*, the emotions, attitudes, and dispositions that fuel action on behalf of justice. That is the goal. If there were time for it here (there is not), history would demonstrate that the convictions to follow are not the result of someone's doctoral dissertation; rather, they are the result of the church's reflection on what (in its better moments) it has been *doing*.

At the heart of CST we find seven important convictions:

- *Human Dignity*. The life and dignity of every human being is of incalculable worth and must be recognized, respected, and reverenced. Human rights, "the minimum conditions for life in community," (U.S. Catholic Bishops, "Economic Justice for All" par. 17) must be protected and promoted in order for human dignity to be respected and for human beings to flourish.

- *Community*. Human beings, social by nature, flourish in association with others in community. Everyone has a need, a right, and a responsibility to participate in community life. "Society as a whole, acting through public and private institutions," (U.S. Bishops, "Economic Justice for All," par. 18) is responsible for protecting and promoting not only the good of individual persons, but also the common good of the society as a whole.

- *Equality*. All human beings are fundamentally equal, regardless of race, creed, gender, sexual orientation, and educational or economic status. Every "-ism" that alienates and oppresses people must be opposed and overcome.

- *Work*. Work is critically important for human flourishing. Accordingly, the dignity of work and the rights of workers are the foundation of economic justice.

- *Option for the Poor*. "All members of society have a special obligation to the poor and vulnerable" (U.S. Bishops, "Economic Justice for All," par. 16)—not only in our own country, but also around the world.

- *Peace*. As history sadly demonstrates, war and other forms of violence are the enemies of human well-being. There must be a presumption against war and every other use of force.

- *Care for the Earth*. With increasing conviction, CST calls for the care of the earth itself, for the protection and promotion of the well-being of the natural environment not only for the sake of human beings (including future generations), but also for the earth itself and *all* its inhabitants.

Elaboration. Let us explore the significance of these seven convictions, paying attention not only to their sources, but also to some of the issues to which they have been connected over the years.

Human Dignity. Authors who write about the central convictions of CST invariably enumerate and describe them differently. Whether there are seven or nine or nineteen convictions and how they should be stated and described are matters of some opinion. But virtually everyone familiar with this tradition agrees that however many convictions there are, the first and most basic one is about the dignity of human beings. In the introduction to their 1983 pastoral letter on war and peace, the U.S. Catholic Bishops explained the reason for their concern about war and peace by referring to a central conviction about human beings:

> At the center of the Church's teaching on peace and at the center of all Catholic social teaching are the transcendence of God and the dignity of the human person. The human person is the clearest reflection of God's presence in the world; all of the Church's work in pursuit of both justice and peace is designed to protect and promote the dignity of every person. For each person not only reflects God, but is the expression of God's creative work and the meaning of Christ's redemptive ministry. Christians approach the problem of war and peace with fear and reverence (U.S. Catholic Bishops, "The Challenge of Peace: God's Promise and Our Response," par. 15).

With this passage as a starting point, three comments concerning Catholicism's emphasis on human dignity are in order. First, as the statement from the bishops makes clear, the source of CST's emphasis on human dignity is religious in nature. That source is the Christian belief (found also in Judaism and Islam) that each human being is created by God and is a unique reflection of God's holy presence in the world. It is also part of Christian faith that the entire universe, as created by God, is somehow "charged with the grandeur of God," as Gerard Manley Hopkins once put it. CST affirms this, but without embarrassment emphasizes that in a preeminent way *human beings* reflect God's presence in the world. Surely one can be convinced about the dignity of human beings for many reasons. Human intelligence and freedom—our abilities to think and to choose (perhaps especially to love)—as well as some of the amazing accomplishments of humankind (scientific, artistic, altruistic) are certainly good enough reasons to respect human life. CST affirms those reasons. But its deepest convictions about human dignity are rooted in the Christian belief about humanity's relation to God. *In and through* our contact with God's creation—especially (but not exclusively) other human beings—we come into contact with God. Theologian Richard McBrien refers to this as the principle of *sacramentality*. He suggests that it is one of the distinguishing characteristics of Catholicism: the Creator is encountered through the creation (McBrien, pp. 9–11). If this is right, then so too are the bishops: human life is not simply to be respected, but reverenced.

Let us return to the quote above from the U.S. Bishops for a second observation about CST's emphasis on human dignity. As we have seen, the quote is from a pastoral letter on war and peace. But as a matter of fact, one could very easily take out the words *on war and peace* in the opening line and make a wide variety of substitutions. Thus, the sentence could read, "At the center of the Church's teaching [*on economic justice* or *on abortion and euthanasia*, or *on health care reform*, or *on capital punishment*, or *on domestic abuse*, or *on global poverty and hunger*, etc., etc., etc.] and at the center of all Catholic social teaching are the transcendence of God and the dignity of the human person." You get the idea. This emphasis on human dignity grounds CST's interest and involvement in *all* social issues. CST offers no recipe for simple answers to complex questions; it has no formula for ensuring universal agreement on social issues. (It is wise to be suspicious of anyone who does.) What CST does offer is a starting point and a central conviction. Whether one is a liberal democrat or a conservative republican, CST proposes a broad but exceedingly important criterion for moral discernment: the protection and promotion of the dignity of human beings.

Third, CST's conviction about human dignity shows itself in its emphasis on *human rights*. Flowing directly from the dignity of the human person, Catholic tradition calls for the recognition of and respect for fundamental *human rights*. Unlike some philosophical approaches to human rights, CST insists that human rights are not conferred upon an individual because they are citizens of a given society. No, the origin of human rights is found in the nature of the human person as such; they are neither given to persons nor (legitimately, at least) taken away from persons by society.

What exactly do we mean by "rights"? Theologian J. Milburn Thompson described human rights as *those basic human goods that are due to human beings so that they can develop themselves fully as persons living in community* (Thompson, pp. 94–97). Some like to think of human rights as the minimum that we have "coming to us" simply because we are human beings. Protection and promotion of human rights is important not simply so that we can survive or "get by" in life, but so that we can strive to flourish as human persons.

It is important to flesh out Catholicism's view of human rights with some examples. Let us consider Pope John XXIII's list of human rights in his 1963 encyclical letter "Pacem in Terris":

- The right to life and a worthy standard of living. These rights include the right to bodily integrity, to food, clothing, shelter, healthcare and necessary social services.

- Rights pertaining to moral and cultural values. These include the right to one's good reputation, the right to search for truth, the right to be informed about public matters of concern, etc.

- The right to worship God according to one's conscience.

- The right to choose one's state in life.

- Economic rights. These include a right to work, to work in a safe environment, and to receive a just wage. Economic rights include a right to private property (and other sources of wealth) as long as this does not interfere with more basic rights of others.

- The right to meet and associate with others.

- The right to emigrate and to immigrate. These rights are especially necessary given the injustices and oppression that exist in some places and countries.

- Political rights. These involve one's ability to take an active part in the civil and political life of one's community.

Obviously a lot of detail is left for interpretation and application—such as what one means by "necessary social services," or what exactly a right to healthcare includes. In our own country, for example, it would not be hard to imagine both Democrats and Republicans espousing this list of human rights, but disagreeing on how minimally or maximally the government should become involved in seeing to it that they are secured. Even so, by any standard this exposition of human rights sets an agenda for what every society should be concerned about. Flowing from human dignity, CST insists, human rights are important so that we can strive to develop ourselves fully as human beings, in keeping with our common vocation to live as creatures fashioned in the image of God.

Community. If an emphasis on the dignity and rights of every human being is the right hand of CST, emphasis on the importance of community is the left hand. It is only for the sake of simplicity that we discuss them separately here. If Richard McBrien is right, another distinguishing characteristic of Catholicism is its emphasis on the importance of community for human flourishing (McBrien, pp. 12–14). Far different from those aspects of our culture that display a particularly stubborn form of rugged, competitive, and isolating individualism (Bellah), CST insists that the good of the individual is essentially bound up with the good of the community. Following the lead of Catholic social ethicist Thomas Massaro, let us look briefly at three elements of CST's stress on community: *solidarity, common good, and participation* (Massaro, pp. 119–124).

Solidarity is a word that is easier to describe than it is to define. It refers both to an inner conviction and to an outer commitment. The inner conviction involves both the intellectual insight and the affective appreciation of the reality of interdependence: we are all connected; we need one another. CST invites us to believe that at our best moments, simply as human beings, we are able to recognize within ourselves a deep sense of care for one another. When we see the suffering of others (I am thinking especially of the suffering that results from oppression and injustice) it is our sense of solidarity that moves us to "feel for" them and, in some elusive but real way, to share in their suffering. Solidarity enables us to "feel for" others not only because "it could have been me," but because of the nearly mystical conviction that when one person is denied her rights, in some way we all are; when one group is enslaved, none of us is free; when one group suffers from violence and oppression, we are all diminished. Solidarity begins with this kind of conviction of the heart, but it does not end there. The test of genuine solidarity is that it moves to committed action. Action may vary greatly depending on one's closeness to the situation at hand, as well as one's resources (often more extensive than we think). But real solidarity manifests itself in action on behalf of others, caring, committed action—frequently in the social, political arena—that is aimed at dismantling oppression and building justice.

As is obvious, solidarity presumes an appreciation of the *common good*. Pope John Paul II has written about the connection between these two ideas as follows:

> This then [solidarity] is not a feeling of vague compassion or shallow distress at the misfortunes of so many people, both near and far. On the contrary, it is a *firm and persevering determination* to commit oneself to the *common good*, that is to say to the good of all and of each individual, for we are *all* really responsible for *all* (John Paul II, "On Social Concern," par. 38).

Those with a sense of solidarity, CST suggests, are convinced that one's own individual good is woven into the fabric of the good of others. The common good is "the good of all and of each individual." It presumes that one's individual good must not come at the expense of others: the good of management must not be at the expense of labor, the thriving of the wealthiest must not involve the suffering of the poorest, the well-being of men must not be built upon the oppression of women, the welfare of human beings must not involve the mistreatment of other creatures on the planet. When such inequities exist, CST suggests, we not only have a lack of the common good, but a caricature of individual good. Individual "good" that is the fruit of injustice bears within it the seed of its own destruction.

This understanding of the relationship between the individual good and the common good logically includes an emphasis on the importance of *participation* in social life. CST insists that we all have the right and the responsibility to participate in the life of community. Precisely because of our solidarity with one another, our interdependence, we are called to participate in community life, as much as our abilities enable us to do so. Not only because it is important for us to "speak up on our own behalf," but also because of the contributions we can make to other individuals and to society at large, every human being must be given the opportunity to participate fully in the social institutions and communities. When it is only a powerful few who exercise authority, when it is only the wealthy whose voice is heard, when it is only the men who hold positions of influence (whether in our halls of government or in our places of worship), something is terribly wrong with the picture. Calling the church itself to examine its own conscience, CST suggests that the ability of all to participate and contribute fully in the life of community is very simply a matter of justice.

Equality. The first two convictions of CST that we have just described are on virtually every list of the "basic principles" of Catholic social thought. Equality is not. Nevertheless, it is an important aspect of contemporary Catholic social thought. The following passage from the bishops at the Second Vatican Council (1962–1965) displays well, I think, the church's view on equality:

> Since all . . . possess a rational soul and are created in God's likeness, since they have the same nature and origin, have been redeemed by Christ, and enjoy the same divine calling and destiny, the basic equality of all must receive increasingly greater recognition.

> True, all . . . are not alike from the point of view of varying physical power and the diversity of intellectual and moral resources. Nevertheless, with respect to the fundamental rights of the person, every type of discrimination, whether social or cultural, whether based on sex, race, color, social condition, language, or religion, is to be overcome and eradicated as contrary to God's intent ("Pastoral Constitution on the Church in the Modern World," par. 29).

The phrase "must receive increasingly greater recognition" should be seen for what it really is: an acknowledgment that not only in society at large but within the church itself, recognition of the fundamental equality of all human beings as persons has been slow in coming. Historically, most of the major institutions of Western Civilization have not been democracies; they have not been grounded in a conviction about the fundamental equality of all people, and they have been slow to recognize those various "isms" that constitute sins against equality. For instance, as Marvin Mich has documented well in his recent book, until fairly recent times, the church (along with other institutions) did not see any great difficulty with slavery, at least not enough to lead the way in dismantling it: ". . . it was common for Catholic laity, bishops, priests, and religious orders to be slaveholders" (Mich, p. 135). In a similar vein, Catholicism's struggle to recognize the equal dignity of women and men and its resistance to allow that recognition to show itself in its own structures displays the fact that whatever equality might mean in Catholic thought, it has not meant (and does not now mean) equal access to all positions of leadership within the church itself. Bishop Ray Lucker from New Ulm, Minnesota, has called for the church to own up to its own sins of racism and sexism, insisting that equality must indeed receive "greater recognition" within the church itself (Lucker). Equality, as one of the key convictions of CST, is a work in progress.

Work. During the last hundred years, the theme of work has received important attention in CST. Catholic social thought looks at work not simply from the perspective of what workers do, but what work does to and for workers. Pope John Paul II has written much about this, especially in his 1981 encyclical letter "Laborem Exercens" ("On Human Work"). Obviously work is important both because many of us spend a high percentage of our lives at our work, and also because it is essential for our livelihood. But CST suggests something more. It is through work that we fulfill a part of our human nature. Work is one of the ways we develop ourselves as persons. It is through our work that we are able to express ourselves, to fulfill ourselves, and to contribute to the human community (Pope John Paul II, "On Human Work," par. 6). These ideas may strike some of us as unrealistic, as ideals that are a long way from reality. Sadly, for too many people that is the case. Work for many is routine, burdensome, and even oppressive. CST argues that that is not as it should be. Workers ought to be given an opportunity to take responsibility for what they do, to make their work their own. The more that happens, the more work can become an opportunity for self-expression, for personal fulfillment, and for the satisfaction that comes from making a genuine contribution, even if a small one, to the well-being of other people. Put differently, if work is for people, and not the other way around, then those responsible for the work that other people do should be looking for ways in which that work can both express and promote human dignity.

Lest all this seems to be too lofty a goal to have in mind regarding human work, the recent *Catechism of the Catholic Church* names several more concrete things that relate to justice for workers. Men and women, first of all, should have *access to employment* in ways that are fair. The professions and the workforce should be ". . . open to all without discrimination" (#2433). Secondly, workers are entitled to a *just wage* for the work that they do. This means a wage that allows one to provide a reasonable and dignified quality of life for oneself and one's family materially, socially, culturally, and spiritually (#2434). The *Catechism* notes that it is not morally sufficient that a contract has been reached between employers and workers. A just wage must meet more stringent criteria; it must take into account the quality of life it allows a person and his or her family to enjoy (#2434). Thirdly, workers should have *recourse to a strike* when it becomes morally legitimate (#2435). Reasons that might warrant strikes (which, hopefully, can be carried out in nonviolent ways) include not only unjust wages, but also unsafe or burdensome working conditions. The dignity and rights of persons call for safe working environments. Finally, workers have a right to *social security contributions*, which (in countries like our own) are required by legitimate authority (#2436). The *Catechism* does not include healthcare benefits with this, largely because in many countries healthcare is provided by the state and not linked to employment. But in countries where access to healthcare (which Pope John XXIII listed as a human right) is linked to employment, an argument could surely be made from CST that employers should be required to see to it that their workers are provided with healthcare benefits. In exchange for all of this, workers indeed have serious obligations to fulfill their own responsibilities to their employers with honesty and integrity. Though it seems accurate to say that the emphasis in CST is clearly on the rights of workers, it is also true that rights and responsibilities go together.

Option for the Poor. One of the most celebrated and controversial of the key convictions of CST is what has become known as "the option for the poor." Thomas Massaro is right in noting that there is something both new and old about this idea. It is new in that the phrase appears in no official church documents until the 1970s; it is old in that the idea seems evident in Christian tradition from the beginning. Just as in the Old Testament book of Exodus God seemed to intervene in human history to "take the side of" the enslaved Hebrews (Exodus, chapters 3–15), leading them (*in and through* Moses) from oppression to freedom, so too in our day, God is "taking the side of" the poor and oppressed *in and through* all those people (Christians and others) who commit themselves to the social struggle for justice and liberation. And just as Jesus of Nazareth liberated all people from the bondage of sin and the sting of death, and called his followers to commit themselves, as he had, to "proclaiming glad tidings to the poor" and bringing "liberty to captives" (Luke 4: 18–19), so too, the followers of Jesus are true to their real mission to the extent that they commit themselves to the ongoing work of liberation, the work of helping to fashion God's reign of justice, love and peace (Gutierrez, Boff, Schubeck).

The contemporary emphasis on an option for the poor emerges from a very specific historical, political situation: the situation of poverty and injustice in Latin America, poverty and injustice that was/is essentially linked to social and political structures. Beginning in the 1960s and '70s, Christian theologians in those countries began to make connections between their social/political situation and the essential message of Christianity. What does God want, these theologians asked, in situations of structural poverty and injustice? God wants nothing less than the liberation of all people from any and all things that are the cause of oppression and injustice.

In a fresh and challenging way liberation theology has reminded the Christian community that even though it is true that God loves all people (rich and poor alike, and yes, not only the oppressed, but the oppressors as well), and even though we should try not to pit one group against another or to involve ourselves in violence, Christian faith does call us to make a special option for the poor. Not unlike a parent who loves all her children, but whose love is poured out regularly on behalf of the child most in need, so too "the heart of God" and the passionate care and commitment of Christian people needs to be directed regularly to those most in need, to those who suffer.

If there is something new and fresh about the theme of option for the poor, as it emerged from liberation theology, there is something ancient about the theme as well. Latin American liberation theologians helped the church across the world to recognize that God's option for the poor and our call to make a similar option is implicit in the scriptural stories about God's involvement with humankind, including God's involvement with us through Jesus Christ. By the mid-'70s the option for the poor began to be spoken about directly and forcefully by popes and bishops, enough that today virtually no one writing about CST would leave it off the list of key principles or convictions. (Pope John Paul II, "On the Hundredth Anniversary of 'Rerum Novarum,'" par. 11).

Although liberation theology—and its call for an option for the poor—originated in a specific social situation in Latin America, since the 1980s it has undergone a variety of transformations. The general theme of liberation and the specific call for an option for the poor have been taken up by Christian theologians around the world as they have considered a host of other instances of structural injustice and oppression in society and in the church itself. Drawing on these themes, African-American theologian James Cone has helped to pioneer "black theology," spelled out especially in his influential A Black Theology of Liberation (1970). And of course many (not all) feminist theologians have welcomed these same themes and have drawn out their implications for patriarchal cultures, including the Catholic Church. Anne E. Patrick's Liberating Conscience (1996) is a fine recent example of a Catholic feminist theology of liberation. The collection of articles called *Liberation Theology*, edited by Curt Cadorette, et. al., displays the wide variety of ways in which liberation theology and its option for the poor have made their mark not only on CST but on Christian theology around the world

Peace. It should come as a shock to no one: CST is decidedly in favor of peace. But who isn't? Hopefully Christians take it to be part of their responsibility, both as citizens of the earth and as followers of Christ, to do all in their power to eliminate (or at least to minimize) violence in the world and to work for peace.

But there are two things about CST's convictions regarding peace that are distinctive and that deserve attention here: its theology of peace and, for lack of a better phrase, its contributions to "the politics of peace."

Catholicism's theology of peace is captured briefly but clearly in the following two passages from the U.S. Catholic Bishops' pastoral letter on peace in 1983:

> Because peace, like the kingdom of God itself, is both a divine gift and a human work, the Church should continually pray for the gift and share in the work. We are called to be a Church at the service of peace, precisely because peace is one manifestation of God's word and work in our midst. ("The Challenge of Peace," par. 23).

> Let us have the courage to believe in the bright future and in a God who wills it for us—not a perfect world, but a better one. The perfect world, we Christians believe, is beyond the horizon, in an endless eternity where God will be all in all. But a better world is here for human hands and hearts and minds to make ("The Challenge of Peace," par. 337).

By the phrase "kingdom of God" or "reign of God" Christians believe that God is "up to something" in the world. Especially through the life, teaching, and dying and rising of Jesus Christ, God has inaugurated a victory of grace over sinfulness, justice over oppression, peace over violence and, most dramatically, life over death. In this way, Christian faith provides believers with a view of history, a very hopeful one. God has been and remains "up to" the transformation of the human race and all of creation. Christian faith daringly insists that God is fashioning a new heaven and a new earth, one which will be characterized by justice, love, and peace. This is what God wants; this is what God is doing.

But how? So far this theology of peace is all about what *God* is doing; it is God's gift, with only glimpses of it on the horizon of human existence. But part of Christian faith concerning the "reign of God" is that we are called to participate in what God is doing through the way in which we live our lives, through the ways in which we work for love and justice and peace. There is not only *discontinuity* between this real world and what lies "beyond the horizon," there is *continuity* as well. A "perfect" world, a *perfectly peaceful* world, Christian faith suggests, is beyond us. But a better world, a more peaceful world, is ours to fashion. *In and through* our peacemaking efforts the "reign of God" is being fashioned. This, I think, is the heart of CST's theology of peace.

But we must speak also (and less poetically) of "the politics of peace." I have two things in mind here: CST's convictions about non-violence and its espousal of just-war theory. These two seemingly conflicting traditions are two different threads woven into the one fabric of Catholicism's approach to peace.

History is important here. In the earliest centuries of Christianity the followers of Jesus were faced with questions concerning how deeply they should become involved in the social, political, and military structures of the culture in which they found themselves, the Roman Empire. Many scholars believe that in the earliest decades after Christ—the decades in which the writings of the New Testament were being formulated—Christians believed that the return of Christ and the end of the world as we know it was on the immediate horizon. In such a context, some of the "hard sayings" attributed to Jesus in the New Testament, particularly the radical call to non-violence (". . . I say to you, offer no resistance to one who is evil. When someone strikes you on your right cheek, turn the other one to him as well" [Matthew 5: 39]) seem to be more palatable. If the world is ending tomorrow, endurance may be an easier pill to swallow. In fact, many of the earliest Christians suffered persecution because of their faith, and so the "hard saying" about non-violence may well have reflected the actual experience of some of Jesus' first followers. All of this contributed to the fact that not only in the first few decades, but also for the first several centuries of the life of the church, non-violence was taken to be the way of Jesus and the way for his followers to live.

Lisa Sowle Cahill (whose book on this topic is a masterful analysis of this part of Catholic tradition) is among those who suggest that once Christianity became "mainstreamed" in the time of Constantine (fourth century), Christians' involvement in the military and justification of the use of force (including killing) on behalf of the state became more widely accepted (Cahill, p. 40). Although peace remained the ideal, justification of the use of force in this less-than-perfect world became widespread. Under the leadership of Augustine (354–430), criteria were developed for determining a just war, and as Massaro notes, "The just-war theory came to form the mainstream of Christian reflection on violence for many centuries" (Massaro, p. 152).

Over the centuries the criteria for determining a just war and for determining just actions within war have evolved. In a contemporary way the 1983 pastoral letter of the U.S. Bishops stated the criteria as follows:

- just cause (protecting innocent persons, securing human rights, etc.)

- competent authority (war must be declared by those with authority for the public order; leaving ambiguous the status of revolutions)

- comparative justice (a criteria that calls for an analysis of which side is sufficiently "right" in a dispute)

- right intention (only the reasons that provide the just cause can be intended, not revenge or violence for its own sake)

- last resort (all possibilities for non-violent resolutions have been tried and exhausted)

- probability of success (there should be some prospect that the use of force will accomplish the goals identified in the just cause)

- proportionality (the damage done to all parties must be proportionate to the good that is hoped for) (U.S. Bishops, "The Challenge of Peace," pars. 86–99).

In addition to these seven criteria for determining when it may be *just to go to war,* the Bishops also provided two criteria for determining what would and would not constitute *just actions within the war* itself:

- proportionality. There must be a proper proportion between the damage one's actions (e.g., bombing) cause to opposing forces, to civilian populations, and to the environment and the good that is likely to be achieved by such actions (103).

- discrimination. "The response to unjust aggression must be discriminate; it must be directed against unjust aggressors, not against innocent people caught up in a war not of their making" (104).

If taken seriously these two criteria are very stringent. Think for a moment of what was done in Hiroshima and Nagasaki at the end of World War II. In a world in which the weapons of war have become capable of ever more massive destruction, not only of opposing forces, but of civilian population centers and the natural environment itself, meeting the criteria of proportionality and discrimination in the conduct of war is very difficult, some think virtually impossible.

It should be obvious that these criteria are far from some simple checklist for determining a just war or for determining just actions within war.

Each criterion calls for analysis, and relative to specific situations (e.g., the War in the Gulf) each one is open to a variety of interpretations and opinions. As a result, in many circles there is an understandable degree of cynicism about the usefulness of the just war theory itself.

The two traditions of non-violence and just war theory have existed side by side as part of Catholic social thought for centuries. In truth, however, the just-war tradition came to overshadow the tradition of non-violence. Although there have always been challenging, prophetic voices within Catholicism that have attempted to remind the church of the universal call to peace and even the "hard sayings" about non-violence, mostly they have been individual, lonely voices. Today, however, there is a good deal of evidence that that may be changing (Mich, 275–312). CST has given increasing attention to non–violence in recent years. Perhaps as the flaws and the limits of the just war theory become more and more evident (especially in this nuclear age), the presumption against war and the promotion for peace have received greater and greater emphasis. CST still struggles with difficult political situations in which the human rights of innocent people are trampled upon; in such situations, in this sin-riddled world, is violence a regretful but necessary evil? Or does the use of force and violence simply breed more violence? There are no easy answers (Himes).

Care for the Earth. Twenty years ago it would have been unthinkable that someone would list "Care for the Earth" as one of the key convictions of CST. If any of the convictions being described here are evidence that CST is a work-in-progress, this one is. But with increasing strength in its voice, CST proclaims that that we are all charged to care for the earth. What exactly this means, however, and how precisely this conviction is related to most of those that have been described above, is less clear. To explore this, let us look at Catholicism's approach to "care of the Earth" in three ways (to some extent in historical fashion) by examining three concepts laid out well by Catholic "ecofeminist" theologian Elizabeth A. Johnson: *kingship, stewardship,* and *kinship* (Johnson, pp. 29–40).

Kingship. The idea of kingship is based upon what Johnson describes as hierarchical dualism:

"It is based on hierarchical dualism that sees humanity separated from the earth and placed in a position of absolute dominion over all other creatures who are made for us. In this view, the creatures of the world are ranked . . . with greater value being assigned to those up on the great chain of being. At the lowest level is inorganic matter; next comes vegetative matter, followed by animals, human beings, and non-physical spirits or angels. In the progression from the pebble to the peach to the poodle to the person, with women somewhere between the latter two, the higher order of creatures has the right to use and control the lower . . . This is the patriarchal pyramid again, resulting in a top-down domination of nature by man" (Johnson 29).

From the perspective of kingship, the world has been created for us and awaits our dominion and control. Related to this is a 1967 article published by Lynn White, a widely respected historian who taught at Princeton, Stanford and UCLA. It was entitled "The Historical Roots of Our Ecological Crisis," and it argued that the Judeo-Christian tradition— which claimed, with biblical authority (Genesis 1:28), that humans are to subdue the earth and have dominion over all things—is largely to blame for the ecological crisis in which we find ourselves. White's argument corresponds a great deal with Johnson's idea of kingship. At our worst, these thinkers claim (and I would agree), not only has "care of the Earth" not predominated in Catholic thought, but in the past Catholic teaching has contributed to an attitude of dominion that has been part of humanity's irresponsibility and recklessness in regard to the earth.

Stewardship. But Christian tradition has also espoused stewardship as a way of viewing of humanity's relation to the earth. In Johnson's view, stewardship ". . . keeps the structure of hierarchical dualism but calls for human beings to be responsible caretakers or guardians of the earth and all its creatures. . . In this model humanity is still at the top of the pyramid of being but has the duty to protect and preserve what seems weaker and more vulnerable" (Johnson, p. 30). Stewardship is often found in the writings of the pope and bishops. In 1991, for example, the U.S. Catholic bishops wrote that we must be "faithful stewards" of the gift of God's creation. Stewardship, they suggested, means that ". . . we must both care for creation according to standards that are not of our own making and at the same time be resourceful in finding ways to make the earth flourish."(U.S. Catholic Bishops, "Renewing the Earth," 429).

When combined with several of the key convictions we have already discussed—especially convictions about human rights, equality, and the option for the poor—the idea of stewardship can generate and motivate very strong convictions and actions directed to care for the earth. The idea of stewardship, in combination with the human rights tradition, is compatible with the idea that all persons (including future generations of people) have a right to a safe and healthy environment. A commitment to stewardship, combined with CST's conviction that racism is a crime against human dignity and equality, would also lead one to be deeply concerned about "environmental racism"—the phenomenon that people of color are regularly and systematically exposed to a disproportionate degree of environmental harm and hazard (Bullard). To be sure, not all are satisfied with stewardship as the appropriate way to think about our charge to care for the earth. But it is a long way from kingship or dominion. As I see it, stewardship is the predominant way that CST currently calls for environmental responsibility.

Kinship. But for Johnson and others, stewardship does not go far enough. The idea of kinship, she argues, takes us where we must go: "If separation is not the ideal but connection is; if dualism is not the ideal but the relational embrace of diversity is; if hierarchy is not the ideal but mutuality is; then the kinship model more closely approximates reality. It sees human beings and the earth with all its creatures intrinsically related as companions in a community of life. . . . This kinship attitude does not measure differences on a scale of higher or lower ontological dignity but appreciates them as integral elements in the robust thriving of a whole" (Johnson, p. 30).

Two comments about kinship are important. First, it is an attempt to recognize and celebrate the diversity of all creatures in a way that steadfastly avoids the pattern of "higher" and "lower," or what Johnson has called "hierarchical dualism." The idea of kinship is not that there are no "distinctions between human beings and other forms of life": a rock is not a tree, and a tree is not a person. Instead, the conviction of kinship is that it is both unnecessary and irresponsible to assign "greater" and "lesser" value to diverse creatures. The relation of humanity to the rest of creation should be marked not by superiority, but by the recognition of interconnectedness and mutuality.

The second thing that should be said about Johnson's idea of kinship is that the idea is not entirely new. Although some version of the stewardship model has usually been at the center of Catholic thinking, traces of the kinship model have been part of Catholic social thought all along. In "Creation and an Environmental Ethic," Michael and Kenneth Himes demonstrate how the idea of kinship (they prefer *companionship*) was part of the thinking of St. Augustine, St. Thomas Aquinas, and above all St. Francis of Assisi and is part of a "sacramental vision" that sees ". . . every creature, human and non-human, animate and inanimate" a sign of the love and presence of God (Himes, 112).

To espouse kinship as the right way to envision humanity's relation to the rest of the universe would be a stretch for CST. At first glance it might seem that the first six convictions of CST that we have discussed are so centered on the dignity of human beings that there is little room for the rest of creation in the energy of CST. Admittedly, Catholic social thought—to date at least—has focused on the well-being of human beings. But perhaps scholars like Elizabeth Johnson are helping the Christian community appreciate in fresh ways the intimate connections between the welfare of people and the welfare of the earth and all its inhabitants. It may well be that one of the contributions feminist, non-dualistic, and non-hierarchical thought patterns are starting to make for CST is the ability to emphasize the dignity and sacredness of humankind without compromising the dignity and sacredness of the earth and all its creatures. We are in this together. That conviction, I believe, is "going forward" in many places in our world today, including in CST.

Principle of Application and Purposes of CST. We have come to the end of this reflection on seven key convictions of CST. By way of conclusion, and before seeing how these convictions might *connect* with some specific issues, it is important to do two things: first, to take note of a principle of application regarding these convictions, and secondly, to say a word about the purposes of Catholic moral teachings, including CST.

A Principle of Application. In their 1986 pastoral letter on economic justice, the U.S. Bishops spoke first about general *principles* and then went on to make *applications* to specific issues of economic policy. I have followed this line of thought as I have named general *convictions* of CST and, shortly, will make *connections* to some concrete issues. CST recognizes important differences between principle and application (conviction and connection), acknowledging that the movement from one to the other is neither easy nor obvious. The bishops describe this movement as follows. It is important to quote at some length.

> In focusing on some of the central economic issues and choices in American life in the light of moral principles, we are aware that the movement from principle to policy is complex and difficult and although moral values are essential in determining public policies, they do not dictate specific solutions. They must interact with empirical data, with historical, social, and political realities, and with competing demands on limited resources. The soundness of our prudential judgments depends not only on the moral force of our principles, but also on the accuracy of our information and the validity of our assumptions.

> Our judgments and recommendations on specific economic issues, therefore, do not carry the same moral authority as our statements of universal moral principles and formal church teaching; the former are related to circumstances which can change or which can be interpreted differently by people of good will. We expect and welcome debate on our specific policy recommendations. Nevertheless, we want our statements on these matters to be given serious consideration by Catholics as they determine whether their own moral judgments are consistent with the Gospel and with Catholic social teaching. We believe that differences on complex economic questions should be expressed in a spirit of mutual respect and open dialogue (U.S. Bishops, "Economic Justice for All," pars. 134–135).

In a church with a reputation for its emphasis on authority, these words from the bishops have a refreshing humility about them, indeed realism (which, in the end, is what humility really is). Keenly aware of the complexity of the economic issues they were addressing, the bishops proceeded by naming some general, but admittedly somewhat abstract moral principles that should govern economic policy choices. Two examples suffice: "Every economic decision and institution must be judged in light of whether it protects or undermines the dignity of the human person" (par. 13); "All members of society have a special obligation to the poor and vulnerable" (par. 16).

The bishops acknowledged that there is a difference between general principles and specific recommendation regarding economic policy. People of good will—Catholic or otherwise—may agree that we have special obligations to the poor, but disagree profoundly regarding which revisions in, say, a taxation plan would best meet the needs of the poor. And yes, (as much as it might pain me at times to admit this) both Democrats and Republicans can espouse the convictions of CST, but disagree about many matters of public policy. This doesn't mean that CST means nothing, only that it may mean more than one thing. CST provides critical criteria for assessing public policy. Does a proposed taxation plan help or hinder the quality of life of the poor and vulnerable? CST is convinced that that is the right question, even as it admits that the answer is far from obvious.

Purposes of CST. I think it can be said that the purposes of CST—and of all of the church's moral teachings—are twofold. First, they are intended to lift up the moral dimension of important issues of the day and in that way to contribute to public discussion of issues that effect the common good. Second, they exist to help form the consciences of Catholic people so that they might make judgments and choices that are not only wise, but which bear the mark of Christian faith convictions.

In the introduction to their pastoral letter on economic justice the bishops noted that they intended to speak both because they were Americans and also because they were pastors. As Americans, they strove to address public issues in ways that would make sense to all Americans. Groups as diverse as the National Organization for Women and the National Rifle Association do the same: they address public issues, attempting to persuade others concerning their values and convictions. So too, CST is often addressed to "the public," attempting to lift up the moral dimensions of important social issues.

As pastors, the bishops addressed members of the Catholic Church. As part of their teaching office, it is the responsibility of the pope and bishops to make connections between Catholic faith and important moral issues in order to guide the consciences of Catholics. In the pastoral letter quoted above, the bishops stated that they hoped both their general principles and their specific policy applications would be "given serious considera-tion by Catholics as they determine whether their own moral judgments are consistent with the Gospel and with Catholic social teaching" (par. 135). That captures well what Catholic teaching is concerning the respon-sibilities of Catholics regarding the moral teachings of the church. In the words of the bishops at Vatican II, in forming their consciences, Catholics are to "pay careful attention to" the moral teachings of the church ("Dec-laration on Religious Liberty," par. 14). Catholicism is not "in the busi-ness" of assuming moral responsibility for others; or at least it ought not be. But it is "in the business" of naming the moral aspects of important social issues and contributing to consciences that are wise and just.

Part Two: Catholic Social Teaching—Connections

In the concluding part of this article (much more brief than Part One) it is neither possible nor necessary to try to even touch on the wide array of social issues that have commanded the attention of CST in recent years. My purpose here is simply this: I would like to show how some of CST's key convictions—especially about human dignity and the option for the poor—*connect* to three specific issues: capital punishment, immigration, and the place of gay and lesbian persons in the church. What should emerge is the fact that CST is not simply a matter of general or vague con-victions, but includes the drive to make connections with the important issues of the day.

Capital Punishment: Does Every Life Count? *Catholic Social Teaching is opposed to the use of the death penalty as a legitimate means of punishment.* That simple sentence captures the way CST's conviction about the dig-nity of every human being connects with this perennially difficult issue. Having said that, however, it is also true that there is nothing simple about Catholic teaching on capital punishment. As James Megivern's recent 600-page history on this issue illustrates, Catholic convictions have changed dramatically on this issue. In what follows let us simply take note of some of the historical features of this issue, examine the "why" of current Catholic opposition to capital punishment, and see how CST's contemporary stance on the death penalty connects with other issues in which human life is at stake.

Toward the end of his historical treatment of Catholicism's view of the death penalty, Megivern quotes from a 1960 article by Jesuit theologian Antonio Messineo as a way of summarizing the predominant stance of the church on this issue:

> The Church, from the Fathers to St. Thomas Aquinas down to our own day, with unswerving unanimity, taught the legitimacy of capital punishment, and that therefore it could confidently be affirmed that the death penalty was in perfect accord with Christian thought (Megivern, p. 460).

As Megivern chronicles, the *reasons* for the church's predominant approval (there were always "voices of dissent") of the legitimacy of the death penalty evolved over the centuries. In the fourth and fifth centuries, as Christianity became the "established" religion of the Roman Empire, it was virtually unthinkable that the state could not exercise lethal force, including the exercise of capital punishment (3). From the eleventh through the seventeenth centuries the church invoked various arguments to explain why the death penalty could be seen as a justifiable way of dealing with heresy, more precisely with heretics (3–4). This period saw the establishment of the Inquisition, which involved both the torture and death of heretics. And it was during this period that St. Thomas Aquinas invoked the image of a "diseased organ" to explain the justifiability of capital punishment: just as a surgeon removes a diseased organ for the welfare of the total body, so too the state may "remove" a "diseased member" for the overall good of the community (Megivern, pp. 115–116). In more recent centuries the argument tended to move toward just defense: the state may exercise capital punishment as a necessary way of defending itself against those prone to heinous crimes against the state and its citizens. As recently as 1952, Pope Pius XII, attempting to uphold both the inviolability of the right to life and the justifiability of the death penalty, argued that the state, in exercising capital punishment, does not/can not take away the right to life from an individual. Instead, through the death penalty the state deprives the criminal of the *good* of life "after he by his crime has already been dispossessed of his right to life" (Megivern, p. 459).

Given this history, why is it that the church *today* is opposed to the use of capital punishment? Pope John Paul II's words from "The Gospel of Life" (1995) are important here. After affirming the rightful place of punishment the pope argued as follows:

> . . . the nature and extent of the punishment must be carefully evaluated and decided upon, and ought not go to the extreme of executing the offender except in cases of absolute necessity: in other words, when it would not be possible otherwise to defend society. Today however, as a result of steady improvements in the organization of the penal system, such cases are very rare, if not practically non-existent ("The Gospel of Life," par. 56).

Noteworthy is the fact that the pope did not quibble with the state's theoretical right to capital punishment. Instead, his argument focused on the rightness of the *use* of capital punishment in ordinary circumstances today. Under normal circumstances, he argued, capital punishment is not right precisely because it is not necessary; the rightful purposes of punishment can be served otherwise. This argument, essentially that of the U.S. Bishops in a 1980 statement on the issue, expresses current CST on the matter.

For some, more important and more convincing than the pope's argument for the non-use of the death penalty, is the fact that the church's current teaching emphasizes the conviction that every human life is sacred, yes, even the life of those whose actions have violated life. For many, our call to recognize the dignity of every human being and the value of every human life is upheld in a powerful way through CST's stand against the death penalty. Perhaps no one has dramatized this conviction more effectively than Helen Prejean, CSJ, in her book (and later the film) *Dead Man Walking: An Eyewitness Account of the Death Penalty in the United States.* She and others like her argue that there are a host of things wrong with the death penalty: judicial errors *do* take place that result in the execution of innocent people; there is evidence of racial bias at work in the disproportionate way people of color are sent to their death; and the notion that capital punishment deters others from violent crime seems largely unsubstantiated. But beyond these arguments there is something more. Does not capital punishment simply continue a senseless circle of violence? Does it not make us killers ourselves? And do we not deaden a voice within us that calls us to mercy, even for those who have offended us so terribly? Prejean and others answer yes to these questions. They think that yes, part of the core of Christian faith, is also accessible to all people of good will. I believe they are right.

A final word about CST's current stance on capital punishment is this: it is part of what the late Cardinal Joseph Bernardin (Chicago) called "a consistent ethic of life." This is the idea that there is fundamental value that grounds Catholic teaching on all issues related to life: the dignity and inviolability of the life of every human being. Put differently, the fundamental value CST is attempting to protect and promote in its teachings on abortion, euthanasia, assisted-suicide and capital punishment is the value of every human life. Even more precisely, as the teaching on abortion makes explicit, we ought not discriminate or "cut corners" on the dignity of human life because of its stage of development (Congregation for the Doctrine of the Faith, "Declaration on Procured Abortion," par. 11). To be sure, CST recognizes the value of the life and well-being of a mother in an unplanned and unwanted pregnancy; it embraces the virtue of compassion that motivates those who propose assisted-suicide or euthanasia as a way to respond to the suffering of a loved one; and it stands in awe in the face of the rage and devastation of those who have lost a loved one through violent crime. But with all that, CST suggests that the taking of life through abortion, assisted-suicide or euthanasia, or through capital punishment pits values and even human lives against one another in ways that cause us not to flourish, but to diminish. On these issues CST constitutes "hard sayings." That is obvious. But the "consistent ethic of life" is not simply about what CST opposes; it is about a conviction it wishes to celebrate: every life counts.

Immigration: Who Is a Neighbor? *Catholic Social Teaching, seeing immigration from the point of view of those whose social condition of poverty or oppression leads them to emigrate, argues that such persons have a right to emigrate and that countries that are able have a responsibility to provide residence, indeed welcome.* This sentence captures the way CST makes a *connection* between its convictions about human dignity and the option for the poor and the issue of immigration.

There are religious roots for the concern about immigration in both Judaism and Christianity. Perhaps the most important of all the stories in the Hebrew Scriptures is the story of the Exodus (Exodus, chapters 3–15). In the story, God heard the cries of the Jews suffering from slavery and oppression in Egypt and God did something about it. In and through the leadership of Moses, the story goes, God enabled the Jews to flee from oppression and led them safely (eventually!) to their own land. The "moral lesson" is that God cares for those who suffer, God cares for migrants and refugees. God's people should do the same.

By almost anyone's standard, the story of the Good Samaritan in the New Testament is one of the classic texts in all of literature. I won't do justice to it here. But among other things, the story is about an encounter between two people who are "set up" to be enemies, to despise one another. The one who has been beaten, presumably a Jew, is ignored by his own religious leaders. And then a Samaritan (stereotypically a bitter enemy of the Jews) enters the scene. In a remarkably grace-filled moment, he is "moved with pity" and proceeds to go out of his way, to inconvenience himself, to take practical steps to tend to the man's needs. In Luke's Gospel, after Jesus' instructions to love our neighbor as ourselves, this story is told in response to the question "And who is my neighbor?" (Luke 10: 25–29). So among the "moral lessons" of the story there is this one: we should consider carefully what it means to be a neighbor. "Neighbor" is not simply about living close to someone else; and it is not simply about "feeling comfortable" with others. In the Good Samaritan story "neighbor" is more of a verb than a noun. The word "neighbor," the story suggests, describes the way we respond to the "the other," "the stranger," particularly the stranger who suffers.

What this faith tradition provides for CST is not a detailed set of proposals regarding immigration policies. Rather, it provides a perspective, a starting point. CST enters discussions about immigration from the perspective of those whose poverty or oppression causes them to leave their home, suggesting that when it is necessary the ability "to emigrate to other countries and to take up residence there" is a matter of human rights (Pope John XXIII, "Peace on Earth," par. 25). Motivated by a conviction about the dignity of *all* persons and, even more, by its option for the poor, CST argues that the right to emigrate calls for a corresponding responsibility for those who are able to provide a safe haven for those who need it, and indeed to provide the social services that may be necessary to secure a quality of life that befits human dignity. Put more simply, we are to be "neighbor" to those who suffer. And as in the New Testament story, "being neighbor" may involve overcoming racism and other forms of discrimination that are often at work in our personal attitudes toward refugees and migrants as well as in our institutional and national policies (Pope John Paul II, "On Human Work," par. 23).

None of this is to say, as Catholic theologians William O'Neill and William Spohn have noted, that there should not be a fair distribution of both the burdens (which countries should offer asylum) and benefits (which countries should benefit from immigration of skilled workers) of immigration policies internationally (O'Neill and Spohn, 100–101). Indeed, there may be reasons to limit immigration. However, CST suggests that such limitation has a condition: "Efforts to stem migration that do not effectively address its root causes are not only ineffectual, but permit the continuation of the political, social, and economic inequities that cause it" (U.S. Bishops Committee on Migration, "One Family Under God," 13).

It should be clear that CST does not offer a detailed proposal regarding immigration policies nationally or internationally. What it does offer is a perspective we might adopt regarding migrants and refugees. Who are these people? They are our brothers and sisters. Their ability to flee from poverty and oppression is a matter of human rights. Our call to provide welcome, to "be neighbor," is a matter of human responsibility. Many questions remain, but that is a start, a challenging one.

Gay and Lesbian Persons in the Church: Who Belongs at the Table?
Catholic Social Teaching recognizes that gay and lesbian persons, created in the image and likeness of God and brothers and sisters to us all, unfortunately often suffer from discrimination and violence, even murder. Every form of prejudice or oppression directed against gay and lesbian persons—whether in society at large or within the Christian community itself—is an offense against human dignity and human rights and should be eradicated. Gay and lesbian persons should receive a particular welcome in the church—not only because of what the Christian community may offer them, but also because of the way their particular experiences can enrich the church.

I am well aware of the complexity and the controversy of the issue at hand. Had I asked, I know there are many who would have suggested that I conclude with something else. But the issue is important, very important. And as the italicized paragraph above suggests (a paragraph that belongs well within the bounds of official Catholic teaching on the connections between homosexuality and justice), some of Catholicism's most important convictions relative to homosexuality are more about justice than they are about sex. Knowing that many questions will remain when I have finished, let me offer just two comments on the place of gay and lesbian persons within the church.

As we have seen, two of the most important convictions of CST are about human dignity/human rights and an option for the poor and vulnerable. The words italicized above make it clear, I think, that the Christian community has special obligations to gay and lesbian persons. There is no need to document the ways in which gay and lesbian persons often suffer from discrimination (or something worse) precisely because of their sexual orientation. Gay and lesbian persons have experienced everything from raised eyebrows to laughter to ridicule to marginalization to the denial of human rights to violence to murder. Without question, their human dignity has often been defaced. And they remain "vulnerable" in a variety of ways. CST's convictions about the dignity of *all* persons and the desire to "take the side" of the poor and vulnerable are the reason the church should muster its best energies to help eradicate such discrimination both in society and in the Christian community. That should begin by providing a special degree of welcome in the church itself, as the U.S. Bishops put it, "a special degree of pastoral understanding and care" ("To Live in Christ Jesus," par. 4; Peddicord). To say this differently, gay and lesbian persons belong at *all* our tables. As the pastor in one of this article's opening vignettes seems to understand, the church must do much better extending hospitality toward gay and lesbian persons, especially at the nourishing table of the Eucharist.

But there is another, equally important reason for such hospitality. To put it simply, the Catholic Church has unfinished business regarding its own teaching on homosexuality. The unfinished business will not be attended to well without the voice of gay and lesbian persons themselves. Now there are many who think that the church's current teaching about homosexuality (briefly, that a homosexual orientation does not involve any moral fault, but that homosexual relations *do* precisely because *all* sexual relations, for *all* people, belong exclusively within the context of heterosexual marriage) is just right. But of course there are many who do not. Some think that the church's teaching on this needs to be expressed better, more cogently, more compassionately. Others think that the teaching is so riddled with "heterosexism" that we must "erase the board and start over." The tensions, indeed divisions, within the church on this issue are more pronounced than ever. In my view, the experience—especially the moral experience—of gay and lesbian persons must be "factored in" to Catholic theological reflection about homosexuality more than it ever has before. If, as I believe, Christian ethics is reflection on moral experience in the light of Christian faith, then Christian ethical reflection about homosexuality cannot help but be well served by paying particularly close attention to the experience and narratives of gay and lesbian persons themselves.

As I hope this article has made clear, CST—indeed Catholic teaching on all matters of morality—is an evolving reality. In my view, that is not a weakness of Catholic teaching, but one of its strengths. Good teaching requires good listening. So, as CST urges, let us make sure that gay and lesbian persons know their welcome at our table. And let us not only speak, let us listen.

Works Cited and Recommended Sources

Bellah, Robert N., Madsen, Richard, Sullivan, William M., Swindler, Ann, Tipton, Steven M. Habits of the Heart: Individualism and Commitment in American Life. New York: Harper & Row, 1985.

Bernardin, Joseph Cardinal. *Consistent Ethic of Life.* Thomas G. Fuechtmann, Ed. Kansas City, MO: Sheed & Ward, 1988.

Boff, Leonardo. *Jesus Christ Liberator.* Maryknoll, NY: Orbis Books, 1978.

Bullard, Robert D., Ed. *Confronting Environmental Racism: Voices from the Grassroots.* Boston, MA: South End Press, 1993.

Cadorette, Curt, Giblin, Marie, Legge, Marilyn J., Snyder, Mary H. *Liberation Theology: An Introductory Reader.* Maryknoll, NY: Orbis Press, 1992.

Cahill, Lisa Sowle. *Love Your Enemies: Discipleship, Pacifism, and Just War Theory.* Minneapolis, MN: Fortress Press, 1994.

Catechism of the Catholic Church. English Ed., United States Catholic Conference, Inc.- Libreria Editrice Vaticana, 1994.

Congregation for the Doctrine of the Faith. "Declaration on Procured Abortion" (1974). Excerpts. *Medical Ethics: Sources of Catholic Teachings.* Kevin D. O'Rourke, OP, and Philip Boyle, OP., Eds. St. Louis, MO: Catholic Health Association. 1989, 37–39.

Gutierrez, Gustavo. *A Theology of Liberation.* London: SCM Press, LTD, 1974.

Henriot, Peter J., DeBerri, Edward P., Schultheis, Michael J. *Catholic Social Teaching: Our Best Kept Secret.* Maryknoll, NY: Orbis Books, 1992.

Himes, Kenneth R., OFM. "The Morality of Humanitarian Intervention." *Theological Studies.* March 1994 Vol. 55, No. 1. 82–105.

Himes, Michael J. and Himes, Kenneth R., OFM. "Creation and an Environmental Ethic." *Fullness of Faith: The Public Significance of Theology.* Mahwah, NJ: Paulist Press, 1993 104–124.

Hopkins, Gerard Manley. "God's Grandeur." *The Norton Anthology of English Literature,* Revised, Vol. 2. New York: W. W. Norton & Co., 1968, 1433.

Johnson, Elizabeth A. *Women, Earth, and Creator Spirit.* Mahwah, NJ: Paulist Press, 1993.

Lucker, Raymond A. "Justice in the Church: The Church as Example." *One Hundred Years of Catholic Social Thought: Celebration and Challenge.* John A. Coleman, SJ, Ed. New York: Orbis Books, 1991, 88–100.

Massaro, Thomas, SJ. *Living Justice: Catholic Social Teaching in Action.* Franklin, Wisconsin: Sheed & Ward, 2000.

McBrien, Richard P. "What is Catholicism?" *Catholicism.* Revised ed. New York: Harper, 1994, 3–17.

Megivern, James J. *The Death Penalty: An Historical and Theological Survey.* Mahwah, NJ: Paulist Press 1997.

Mich, Marvin L. Krier. *Catholic Social Teaching and Movements.* Mystic, CT: Twenty-Third Publications 1998.

O'Neill, William R., SJ, and Spohn, William C. "Rights of Passage: The Ethics of Immigration and Refugee Policy." *Theological Studies.* March, 1998. Vol. 59, No. 1 84–106.

Patrick, Anne E. *Liberating Conscience: Feminist Explorations in Catholic Moral Theology.* New York: Continuum 1996.

Peddicord, Richard, OP. *Gay and Lesbian Rights-A Question: Sexual Ethics or Social Justice?* Kansas City, MO: Sheed & Ward, 1996.

Prejean, Helen, CSJ. *Dead Man Walking: An Eyewitness Account of the Death Penalty in the United States.* New York: Random House 1993.

Pope John XXIII. "Pacem in Terris" ("Peace on Earth") (1963). *Catholic Social Thought: The Documentary Heritage.* Ed. David J. O'Brien and Thomas A. Shannon. Maryknoll, NY: Orbis Books, 1997.

Pope John Paul II. "Centesimus Annus" ("On the Hundredth Anniversary of 'Rerum Novarum'") (1991). *Catholic Social Thought: The Documentary Heritage.*439-488.

Pope John Paul II. "Evangelium Vitae" ("The Gospel of Life") (1995). Vatican City: Libreria Editrice Vaticana 1995.

Pope John Paul II. "Laborem Exercens" ("On Human Work") (1981). *Catholic Social Thought: The Documentary Heritage* 352–392.

Pope John Paul II. "Peace With All Creation" (January 1, 1990). *Origins,* Vol. 19 465–468.

Pope John Paul II. "Sollicitudo Rei Socialis" ("On Social Concern") (1987). *Catholic Social Thought: The Documentary Heritage* 395–436.

Pope Leo XIII. "Rerum Novarum" ("The Condition of Labor") *(1891)*. *Catholic Social Thought: The Documentary Heritage* 14–39.

Schubeck, Thomas L., SJ. *Liberation Ethics: Sources, Models, and Norms.* Minneapolis, MN: Fortress Press 1993.

Thompson, J. Milburn. *Justice & Peace: A Christian Primer.* Maryknoll, NY: Orbis Books, 1997 179–205.

U.S. Catholic Bishops. "The Challenge of Peace: God's Promise and Our Response" (1983). *Catholic Social Thought: The Documentary Heritage* 489-571.

U.S. Catholic Bishops. "Economic Justice for All" (1986). *Catholic Social Thought: The Documentary Heritage* 572–680.

U.S. Catholic Bishops. "Renewing the Earth" (November 14, 1991). *Origins,* Vol. 21, 425–432.

U.S. Catholic Bishops. "Statement on Capital Punishment." Washington, DC: U.S.CC 1980.

U.S. Catholic Bishops. "To Live as Christ Jesus." Washington, DC: U.S.CC 1976.

U.S. Catholic Bishops. Committee on Migration. "One Family Under God." Washington, DC: U.S.CC, 1998.

Vatican II, Catholic Bishops. "Dignitatis Humanae" ("Declaration on Religious Liberty") (1965). Documents of Vatican II. Ed. Austin P. Flannery. Grand Rapids, MI: Eerdmans, 1975).

Vatican II, Catholic Bishops. "Gaudium et Spes" ("Pastoral Constitution on the Church in the Modern World") (1965). *Catholic Social Thought: The Documentary Heritage* 166–237.

Questions for Reflection and Discussion

1. The author named seven central convictions of Catholic Social Teaching (CST). He tried to show the relationship between those convictions and Catholic Christian *faith*. And yet the convictions themselves are stated in a way (in the list on pp. 46–47, at least) that does not make explicit reference to Christian faith. Connors seems to think that these convictions could be held by people who are not Christian. What do you think of that? Are these convictions (all of them? some of them?) accessible to all people? Is this important?

2. Which of the seven convictions seems most important or valuable to you? Why? Identify the conviction about which you have the most questions or concerns. What are those questions and concerns?

3. Connors says these convictions are not about "what everyone else should do," but that they also "apply to the church itself (p. 45). In several places Connors seems to acknowledge that the church itself—in some of its policies and practices—has failed to live according to its own teachings. What do you make of this?

4. In the last part of the article Connors tried to make some connections between the seven convictions of CST and three specific issues. What are some of the things you found helpful or not-so-helpful about the way he made those connections?

5. Here is an assignment. Look through the opening section of today's newspaper. Identify what seems to you to be some issue of justice. As Connors did, try to make some connections between the seven convictions of CST (or at least some of them) and the issue of justice you have identified. What do you learn as you do this?

Note

[1] As is the case with several sections of this article, this history is drawn from my *In the Breath of God: Christian Morality*, Ch. 7 "Christian Morality and Social Responsibility" (Chicago: Loyola Press, 2000).

Sharon Doherty is assistant professor of anthropology and women's studies, and director of Abigail Quigley McCarthy Center for Women, B.A., M.A., Ph.D., University of Minnesota. Amy B. Hilden is assistant professor of philosophy, B.A., Ph.D., University of Minnesota. Cecilia Konchar Farr is associate professor of English and women's studies at the College of St. Catherine and a former director of the Core Curriculum. Professor Farr earned her Ph.D. at Michigan State University and her B.A. at Slippery Rock State College in Pennsylvania. She teaches, studies and writes about modernism, American literature, feminist theory and contemporary U.S. culture.

Creativity in Chaos:
Feminist Social Justice

*Sharon Doherty, Ph.D., Amy Hilden, Ph.D.,
and Cecilia Konchar Farr, Ph.D.*

As we write this, activists from around the world are meeting at the Beijing+5 Conference on Global Feminism to assess progress toward feminist justice goals worldwide. Movement leaders are addressing the need for more education for girls, for equitable political representation in the world's councils, for access to health care and family planning, for prevention of domestic violence and the abuse of women and girls. These activists share a vision of a better world, a world where women would enjoy dignity, opportunity, and equality. To share this feminist vision of an end to oppression is one thing. To agree on the details, the "whys" or "hows," is another thing altogether.

Feminist approaches to social justice are as diverse as the feminists who engage them, as the many agendas and actions of Beijing Declaration on Women's Rights attests. As Nancy Heitzeg points out in her essay in this volume, activists for social change can begin with particulars or universals, with the commitment to changing certain oppressive practices, or with the belief that everyone should be treated fairly—or just about anywhere in between. The Beijing Declaration reflects that diversity, with language about particulars (education, representation) and principles (dignity, opportunity, and equality).

In this essay you will read about particulars, about feminist social change movements in the U.S. and about how American feminism has connected with various other justice movements, as well as (in shaded boxes) about individual feminists and their visions for change. You will also read about universals, about theories of justice that both embrace and critique Western justice theories. Feminism in the U.S. works within these differences in philosophical foundations and in chosen courses of action. At its best, U.S. feminism also embraces a global feminist vision, embodied in the agreements of the Beijing document.

We three feminists—a philosopher, a cultural anthropologist and community worker, and a literary critic—embody a small part of the diversity that women's movements embrace. We purposefully chose the challenging task of co-authoring to reassert this aspect of feminist work. We do not attempt to represent all feminist perspectives, but instead consider a range of activists' ideas and experiences. While we take on the topic of "Feminist Social Justice" with some trepidation, our hope is to begin a conversation with you about feminist theories and strategies for ending oppression, and about the potential for coalitions between those engaged in feminism and those engaged in related justice work.

In this article, we focus on the U.S. to give you a foundation of the complexities—cultural as well as political—of feminism here. But we three also espouse global feminist goals that would reach beyond national borders in the work to end oppression. We find hope as activists in working together, despite women's cultural, racial, political, religious, and moral differences, in the U.S. and around the globe. In meetings like Beijing+5 and in movements for social change around the world, women committed to justice sift through the chaos to locate shared goals. As American Civil Rights leader Septima Clark wrote, "I have great belief in the fact that whenever there is chaos, it creates wonderful thinking. I consider chaos a gift" (Lanker, 164). The results of that creative thinking are the topic of this essay.

Feminism, Justice, and the College of St. Catherine

As you engage in the ideas of the Global Search for Justice course, students with different information and opinions about feminism surround you. Feminism can be a point of stress at the College of St. Catherine, a Catholic women's college with commitments to justice. Some of us associated with the college are dedicated feminists—with inevitably different definitions of what that means. Others are wary of feminism, or consider it a perspective distant from them. Still others believe feminism is in conflict with the college's Catholic identity. Our president, Andrea Lee, IHM, addressed the potential conflict in her inaugural address on April 30, 1999. Some see a Catholic women's college as a paradox, she said, but she sees great potential in what seems to be contradictory: "[T]he women of St. Catherine stand firmly at the vortex of that paradox . . . at the intersection of risk and caution; at the juncture of tradition and discovery. The intersections are electric with possibility; energy spins off in multiple directions, subject only to our intentional harnessing" (18).

Like Septima Clark, Sister Andrea finds a call to creativity in the challenge of paradox. Her address also included a multimedia piece, in which the faces of Sisters of St. Joseph who made contributions to the college over the years were displayed on a screen, accompanied by the song "Breaths" by the African-American *a cappella* women's group Sweet Honey in the Rock (Diop). Audience members were moved as we looked at the faces of sisters living and dead and listened to the words:

> Those who have died have never never left;
> The dead are not under the earth.
> They are in the rustling trees;
> They are in the groaning woods;
> They are in the crying grass;
> They are in the moaning rocks;
> The dead are not under the earth; . . .
> Those who have died have never never left;
> The dead have a pact with the living.

Our new president put her ideas into practice as she placed the song, rooted in ancient ideas of the sacred, together with the images of those mostly-Irish sisters. She demonstrated that it is possible to be different and to make sense to each other—it is possible to employ the art of one tradition to honor the pioneers of another.

In this course, we embrace the social justice tradition of our founders and sponsors, the Sisters of St. Joseph, and work to understand the diversity of feminist traditions globally. However, to consider justice for women, we also must engage with other social change movements that affect women. From Women's Suffrage to labor organizing to indigenous women's community building, to civil rights to women's liberation to academic feminism to Third Wave calls to action, feminist justice thinking offers a fascinating range of perspectives for further exploration.

First Wave U.S. Feminism

The notion that women develop moral reasoning skills in the context of a web of relationships with others is a staple of contemporary feminism, one that you will read more about later in this essay. A study of U.S. women's movements demonstrates that this web exists in justice work as well. The U.S. women's movement, characterized historically as First Wave, encompassing the Suffrage Movement of the nineteenth and early twentieth centuries, and Second Wave, including the Women's Liberation Movement of the mid-twentieth century, found its roots in activist work in other movements. For the Suffrage Movement, that work was Abolition. Activists Susan B. Anthony and Elizabeth Cady Stanton, Angelina Grimké and Lucy Stone, Sojourner Truth and Harriet Jacobs found their public voices in the abolition movement and began to strain at the limitations on the participation of "ladies" in the work. Arguing against slavery, both black and white women began to make connections between their rhetoric of freedom and rights and the limitations of that rhetoric when it came to women. Angelina Grimké, in 1837, called for equality within the movement: "I am persuaded that woman is not to be as she has been, a mere second-hand agent in the regeneration of a fallen world, but the acknowledged equal and co-worker with man in this glorious work" (Sklar, viii).

Equality, however, was a more dangerous concept than it may first appear. The idea of "separate spheres" dominated nineteenth century thinking in the newly established United States. Privileged white men, mainly property-owners, operated in the public sphere, as citizens and moral agents, as we shall see later in this essay. Accordingly in this way of thinking, slaves, lower-class and indigenous men and all women were limited to private spheres. Early calls for women's rights were calls not for equality but for more respectful attention to the domestic sphere of influence and to women's unique role as Republican Mothers of the next generation of Americans.

Thus, when suffragists began their relentless quest for the vote with the first women's rights convention in Seneca Falls, New York, in July of 1848, their statement that "all men and women are created equal," was a radical departure. While today we hear their words as the inevitable fulfillment of the promise of democracy, then it was widely taken as a call to social disintegration and was met with years of opposition and derision. The first wave feminist movement, led by Susan B. Anthony, "a brilliant organizer," and Elizabeth Cady Stanton, "a charismatic speaker and writer," took more than 70 years to achieve its goal of full citizenship for women (Evans, 103). By the time the Nineteenth Amendment was ratified in 1920, granting women the right to vote, both Stanton and Anthony had been dead for years.

What seems natural to us now, the enfranchisement of all citizens of a democratic society, was a justice agenda hard won by the activists of the Abolition and Women's Suffrage movements. And what started as a powerful coalition of men and women, both black and white, was lost in the struggle over limited access to power. When post–Civil War political alliances forced abolitionists to side with white men of the Republican Party who were trying to assert control over the defeated Confederacy, women who had worked side-by-side for the vote were disregarded:

> Women's rights advocates within the abolitionist movement such as Susan B. Anthony, Elizabeth Cady Stanton, and Sojourner Truth expressed horror at

the inclusion of the word "male" in the Fourteenth Amendment to the Constitution; this amendment imposed penalties on states that denied the right to vote to male citizens over 21. Another group of women's rights activists led by Lucy Stone, Henry Blackwell, and Frederick Douglass agreed that "this hour belongs to the negro," fearing that debate about women suffrage at the federal level would introduce additional controversy and endanger [its] . . . passage. To this Elizabeth Cady Stanton hotly replied: "My question is this: Do you believe the African race is composed entirely of males?" (Evans, 122).

This impasse ended a dream of "universal suffrage" and split the movement into two groups, one dominated by mainly professional and privileged white women who saw women's suffrage as their primary cause, and the other dedicated to black male suffrage and the belief that women's suffrage would follow naturally from it. As we will discuss later in this essay, this attempt at broad-based coalition building was revisited in the 1960s, as was the effort to rise above a feminist agenda that privileged white women and their concerns.

Sojourner Truth

That man over there says women need to be helped into carriages, and lifted over ditches, and to have the best place everywhere. Nobody ever helps me into carriages, or over mud-puddles, or gives me any best place! And ain't I a woman? Look at me! Look at my arm! I have ploughed, and planted, and gathered into barns, and no man could head me! And ain't I a woman? I could work as much and eat as much as a man—when I could get it—and bear the lash as well! And ain't I a woman? I have borne thirteen children, and seen them most all sold off to slavery, and when I cried out with my mother's grief, none but Jesus heard me! And ain't I a woman?[1]

Women in the Labor Movement

Women's engagement with justice issues hasn't always led them to what our culture defines as "women's issues." Almost two centuries ago, about the same time women began organizing for universal suffrage, women in the newly developing U.S. labor movement began organizing for justice that was not defined within a feminist movement. Working class women and men, both together and separately, became involved in organizing for workers' rights as the factory economy gained momentum in the northeastern U.S. in the early nineteenth century. Before that time, farming and family-based crafts had been the primary contexts for the production of goods among the white non-affluent population. The Factory economy—particularly in the textile mills—changed people's relationship to work. Oppressive circumstances emerged for both women and men, including long hours (mandatory twelve-hour days were common-place), dangerous working conditions, and low pay. In circumstances comparable to the international sweatshops of our time, the wealthy classes who owned the factories in the 1800s used working women and men's labor to build their empires.

The situation at that time was particularly bad for women, as historian Alice Kessler-Harris describes:

> Whereas for men it was at least possible to enter factories as skilled workers exercising their craft, no such possibilities existed for women. From the beginning the transition from household manufactures for personal use, to domestic production for a merchant, and then to factory production was predicated on breaking down the labor process into ever smaller parts. In sharp contrast to the independent woman who sewed or knitted at her own pace and then sold what her craft had produced, women who spun for a market or bound shoes for a factory had little control over what they were doing . . . . Where their labor at home had been highly skilled and self-regulated, the condition of employment outside it required leaving their skills behind and obeying another's clock. Thus women quickly and very early confronted a de-skilling process that would occur later for men. The result was to leave them wholly at the mercy of labor market forces—dependent on others for jobs and wages (28–9).

> Some comparisons are revealing. Starting wages in the least skilled men's jobs paid more than those earned by highly skilled and experienced women. Lowell women (women in the textile mill in Lowell, Massachusetts) made about $1.90 per week plus board, which amounted to another dollar per week, while the men in the plants averaged 80 cents per day (37).

Anthropologist Karen Sacks argues that it is important to look at both class and race in analyzing women's activism around issues like labor organizing, because the societal expectations always have varied for different groups of women. She writes:

> In both the colonial period and after independence, the only woman whose place was in the home was the woman of property. Neither slave women nor free property-less women "belonged" there . . . [F]or free as well as slave women, work outside the home was not looked down upon as unfeminine; rather, it was demanded as the only virtuous activity of property-less women (485–6).

In considering the relationship between nineteenth century labor union activism and the middle-class movement usually identified as *the* women's rights movement of that time, it is important to consider both connections and differences. For example, some analysts have underestimated working-class women, considering them less aware of their oppression than middle-class women's rights activists, usually more highly educated women. Nineteenth century movement activities indicate that is not the case. While their activities generally were not defined in the same way, many women in factories were fully engaged in working for justice. As Sacks points out:

> Collective action by textile-mill women preceded that of middle-class women. . . . The first factory strike took place in 1824, just after the birth of the factories themselves, and involved both men and women. The 1830s saw a large number of strikes and the beginnings of many labor organizations, labor parties and papers, all short-lived. In this context, the record is full of male-female labor cooperation and independent women's actions and organizations" (487).

Some branches of the working class movement also were engaged in the abolition movement and the struggle for women's right to vote. The Association of Working People of New Castle, Delaware, for example, "demanded the vote for women in 1831," according to Sacks (488). The Lowell factory women, in 1832, "formed a Female Anti-Slavery Society, and by 1845 they were fund-raising and circulating anti-slavery petitions, despite hostility on the part of the mill owners." Sacks explains: "The mill women argued that a labor force in slavery degraded free labor as well as slave labor, and that all labor had a two-faced enemy: The lord of the loom and the lord of the lash" (488).

The rhetoric of nineteenth century women's labor activism, like that of contemporary unions, often focused on their patriotism and their expectation that they be respected community members. Kessler-Harris notes that metaphors of liberty were common in strike situations of that period. The strikers at a Lowell textile mill declared in a resolution of the Factory Girls Association in 1836, "As our fathers resisted unto blood the lordly avarice of the British ministry, so we, their daughters, never will wear the yoke which has been prepared for us" (41).

Mary Harris Jones (Mother Jones)

In Coaldale, in the Hazelton district, the miners were not permitted to assemble in any hall. It was necessary to win the strike in that district that the Coaldale miners be organized.

I went to a nearby mining town that was thoroughly organized and asked the women if they would help me get the Coaldale men out. This was in McAdoo. I told them to leave their men at home to take care of the family. I asked them to put on their kitchen clothes and bring mops and brooms with them and a couple of tin pans. We marched over the mountains fifteen miles, beating on the tin pans as if they were cymbals. At three o'clock in the morning we met the Crack Thirteen of the militia, patrolling the roads to Coaldale. The colonel of the regiment said "Halt! Move back!"

I said, "Colonel, the working men of America will not halt nor will they ever go back. The working man is going forward."

"I'll charge bayonets," he said.

"On whom! . . . We are not enemies," said I. "We are just a band of working women whose brothers and husbands are in a battle for bread. We want our brothers in Coaldale to join us in our fight. We are here on the mountain road for our children's sake, for the nation's sake. We are not going to hurt anyone and surely you would not want to hurt us."

They kept us there until daybreak and when they saw the army of women in kitchen aprons, with dishpans and mops, they laughed and let us pass. An army of strong mining women makes a wonderfully spectacular sight. Well, when the miners in the Coaldale camp started to go to work they were met by the McAdoo women who were beating their pans and shouting, "Join the union! Join the union!"

They joined, every last man of them, and we got so enthusiastic that we organized the street car men who promised to haul no scabs for the coal companies. As there were no other groups to organize we marched over the mountains home, beating on our pans and singing patriotic songs.[2]

Justice and Indigenous Women

While women labor activists could call on a still-young tradition of freedom and patriotism in the U.S., women activists among North America's indigenous peoples, who had experienced the dark side of U.S. nation-building, call on an older tradition in their work for social justice. As Winona LaDuke, of the Mississippi Band of Anishinaabeg, writes:

> There is nothing quite like walking through a small field of hominy corn,
> corn you know your ancestors planted on this same land a thousand years
> ago. Corn is in the recipes and memories of elders. That inherited memory is
> the essence of cultural restoration and the force that grows with each step
> toward the path—"the lifeway"—as some of the Anishinaabeg call it (130).

LaDuke, the Green Party's candidate for vice president of the United
States in 1996 and 2000, leads the the White Earth Land Recovery Project
(WELRP), established in 1989, which addresses "the crisis of land tenure
on White Earth" reservation in northern Minnesota. Like other indigenous groups, the Anishinaabeg originally had millions of acres of land-
holdings in the Midwest. Through various legal and illegal methods,
most of that land passed into the hands of the U.S. government, and from
there to individual European immigrants and their descendants. The traditional land of the White Earth band was especially wanted for its tim-
ber, and lumber families such as the Weyerhausers built their fortunes by
logging it. In 1867, a portion of that traditional land was set aside as the
White Earth reservation. In 1889 the U.S. government passed the Nelson
Act, which "opened up the White Earth reservation to allotment" and set
the stage for individual ownership and a clear path to selling off land
piece by piece. After this, reservation land rapidly changed hands from
Anishinaabeg to whites. As LaDuke reports,

> Mechanisms were set in place to pry land from children at boarding school,
> blind women living in overcrowded housing, soldiers at war, veterans, and
> those who could not read or write English. A common saying describing
> what happened sprung up in nearby Detroit Lakes: "Fleec[ing] the Indian"
> (118–119).

The WELRP's goal is to return as much of the reservation land to the
Anishinaabeg as possible. Mechanisms for recovering the land include
"supporting the transfer of public lands back to the White Earth tribal
government, [and] buying land from willing sellers" (126).

WELRP has purchased more than 1,300 acres of land and works to foster
the stability of endangered ecosystems. The land is held in a conservation
trust, and the project leads efforts to "preserve Native languages and culture, restore traditional seed stocks, and reinstate self-determination and
self-reliance" (126–127). LaDuke explicitly links the preservation of biodiversity in the forests and in traditional farming to the potential for the
Anishinaabeg culture to survive. LaDuke's perspective on justice
involves the integration of environmental and cultural preservation.

Women of indigenous North American groups such as LaDuke's Anishinaabeg have faced situations quite distinct from women of other cultural
traditions on this continent. While some outsiders have seen indigenous
women as particularly oppressed, often in native cultures women have

had recognized leadership roles important to the group. In cultures based on horticultural economies, clans and other groups are key social and political units. The communal character of decision-making in such cultural groups at the time of white contact often led outsiders from the more individually-focused European traditions to misunderstand or not even see women's leadership when it was present. Among some indigenous nations, women's councils and women's work groups have had serious power in important areas of community life.

Among the Seneca of northeastern North America, for example, before white contact the land traditionally "belonged" to the women, although they did not have a concept of land ownership like that of the Euro-Americans (Rothenberg, 68). Women also owned the tools of agricultural production and food preparation. Women raised crops together in cooperative work groups. They determined the distribution of cooked food and surpluses. Women "could make significant determinations for or against military action by refusing provisions" (69).

Wilma Mankiller, who recently completed her service as chief of the Cherokee nation, explains in her autobiography that women's leadership was integral to Cherokee society in traditional times, but was not always visible to those who wrote the histories:

> [I]t is certain that Cherokee women played an important and influential role in town government. Women shared in the responsibilities and rights of the tribal organization. Our Cherokee families were traditionally matrilineal clans. In general, women held the property, including the dwelling and garden. Women also maintained family life and farmed, while the men spent much of their time away on the hunt or in warfare.
>
> . . . Precious few non-Indian people are aware of the role native women played in ancient tribal societies. Written records of tribal people have been taken from the notes and journals of diplomats, missionaries, explorers, and soldiers—all men. They had a tendency to record observations of tribal women through their relationships to men. Therefore, tribal women have been inaccurately depicted, most often as drudges or ethereal Indian princesses (19).

In many indigenous societies women "had the liberty to dispose of their property and the fruits of their own labor as they saw fit" (Albers, 136). That control over use and distribution is a key component of equality for many activists. Among many groups, including LaDuke's Anishinaabeg (sometimes called Ojibway) both women and men's work had prestige, and there was flexibility in gender roles. Such flexibility is another characteristic linked to egalitarian patterns within societies. In Ojibway and other societies, women could gain both prestige and wealth for their work, whether that was work usually performed by women or usually performed by men. Men, too, could gain prestige for work usually done by women. "Thus, when women excelled in warfare, they achieved the same kinds of prestige as their male warrior counterparts. . . . Importantly, when people achieved prestige through channels most often utilized by the opposite sex, it was not perceived as a threat to established notions of femininity or masculinity" (Albers, 136).

Those patterns of gender relations and women's leadership are important to consider when thinking about justice as it relates to indigenous women. The justice priorities of many indigenous women center on cultural issues, including survival of their groups. While issues of gender are important, the dominant culture's frequent underestimation of women's status in indigenous groups complicates the prospect of coalitions. Native women's responses to feminism range from "[t]he belief that Indian women do not need the feminist movement" (Bataille and Sands, 129) to Paula Gunn Allen's statement that "To survive culturally, American Indian women must often fight the United States government, the tribal governments, women and men of their tribe or their urban community who are virulently misogynist or who are threatened by attempts to change the images foisted on us over the centuries by whites" (47).

Allen points out that oppression of women in indigenous groups exists today. Sexual abuse and other violence against women "are powerful evidence that the status of women within the tribes has suffered grievous decline" since contact with the dominant white culture:

> Often it is said that the increase of violence against women is a result of various sociological factors such as oppression, racism, poverty, hopelessness, emasculation of men, and loss of male self-esteem as their own place within traditional society has been systematically destroyed by increasing urbanization, industrialization, and institutionalization, but seldom do we notice that for the past forty to fifty years, American popular media have depicted American Indian men as bloodthirsty savages devoted to treating women cruelly. While traditional Indian men seldom did any such thing—and in fact among most tribes abuse of women was simply unthinkable, as was abuse of children or the aged—the lie about "usual" male Indian behavior seems to have taken root and now bears its brutal and bitter fruit (45–46).

In the face of this complex situation, contemporary indigenous women are creating alternative models of leadership, rooted in traditional values. Rayna Green suggests that indigenous women's leadership "can help take American history back from the dark swamp into which it has fallen." She posits that "our notions of leadership could help in taking our own history back if in fact our traditions for leadership were acknowledged, understood, and appreciated, in their differences, in the conventional role models for leadership that we have now" (63). Green warns that traditional leadership models should not be viewed as generic Indian categories, "because there ain't no such thing. There is no such thing as 'Indians,' of course." She explains that among the "many, many native people of this world" are leadership models that apply to the roles of women—mythic female leaders from different North American groups, for example, including Grandmother Spider, White Buffalo Calf Woman, and Corn Mother.

The leadership models Green focuses on will echo with models of contemporary feminist thinking later in this essay. She writes, "I'm talking here about models of kinship: mother, sister, grandmother, aunt. And it is those models that universally are used by Indian women to measure their capacity for leadership and to measure the success of their leadership. I want to talk about that in contrast with achievement models, which in fact are somewhat uncomfortable for us" (65).

Green offers several cautions to those who will think about these leadership models. First, it is important that the kinship relationships are not necessarily biological or even literal, because it can be "liberating" to believe that "the community of humankind is our community and our family"—liberating but also burdensome to realize that we can fulfill all of those roles to our fellow human beings" (65–66). She also emphasizes that she is not calling for a return to women being only in roles based on home and family. This kinship model is not about limitations; it is about ways of relating in the public world. Family responsibilities and public responsibilities both are important and expected. Finally, Green points out that indigenous women are "not thoughtless communitarians. We are individuals. We do take personal pride and personal pleasure in things." But these individuals, she explains, are "evaluated and understood in the context of our community. Our power and our leadership has to be for those communities, because they need us for their survival" (71).

Women in the Civil Rights Movement

Coalition building to save communities has also been a tactic of women working in the twentieth century Civil Rights Movement. Like the abolitionists and union organizers before them, women were key activists in the Civil Rights Movement, and especially in the community organizing that characterized the movement in the 1950s and 60s. Also like abolition, the Civil Rights Movement was, as Bernice Johnson Reagon says, a "borning" movement (Payne, 891). The second-wave feminist movement and other justice movements emerged from it.

One memorable woman activist, Ella Baker, focused her justice efforts primarily on civil rights, working against both race discrimination and economic inequality. As an organizer, her approach was centered on what she called "group-centered leadership." As Charles Payne explains, "From her perspective, the very idea of leading people to freedom is a contradiction in terms. Freedom requires that people be able to analyze their own social position and understand their collective ability to do something about it" (893).

Ella Baker was a power player in the civil rights movement. She insisted, however, on defining power in her own way and often was in conflict with the men who more publicly led the movement. Unlike most African American women of her time, she had the opportunity to attend college and was valedictorian of her class at Shaw University. After graduation she moved to New York City and began to become involved in justice activities. Baker had key leadership roles in several civil rights organizations, including service in the 1940s as the NAACP Assistant Field Secretary and then its National Director of Branches. She worked with the SCLC, and helped found SNCC and the Mississippi Freedom Democratic Party, key activists groups.

With her focus on "group-centered leadership" rather than leader-centered groups (Payne, 892), Baker asked good questions and created contexts in which leaders emerge. She strategically nurtured the potential of those with whom she worked, particularly the young activists in the SNCC. Because she was a college-educated organizer, experienced in working with people in power, Baker was a different kind of threat to the status quo than many women activists. She worked in paid jobs in the movement. She debated strategies with the ministers in the SCLC, who by virtue of their position and their gender expected to be in control. Her refusal to bow down to that expectation led her to shift her efforts to working with the young people in SNCC, a grassroots element of the movement and the seedbed of the later anti-war and women's movements.

While her own emphasis was on civil rights, Baker also engaged in analyses of issues related to gender within the movement. When she worked with the SCLC, as Payne explains:

> [s]he tried to get the leadership to go into some of the rural counties where Blacks were not voting at all. Prophetically, she tried, also without success, to get the organization to place more emphasis on women and young people, the constituencies that would soon carry much of the movement. Miss Baker's emphasis on women reflected her sense of how southern Black organizations worked. "All of the churches depended, in terms of things taking place, on women, not men. Men didn't do the things that had to be done and you had a large number of women who were involved in the bus boycott. They were the people who kept the spirit going [the women] and the young people." Being ignored was hardly a surprise to her: "I had known . . . that there would never be any role for me in a leadership capacity with SCLC. Why? First, I'm a woman. Also, I'm not a minister. . . . The basic attitude of men and especially ministers, as to . . . the role of women in their church setups is that of taking orders, not providing leadership" (890).

Baker intentionally built the leadership of both women and men in SNCC. She influenced African-American women activists like Eleanor Holmes Norton, who later was elected to Congress, as well as white activists Casey Hayden and Mary King, who played key roles in the early second wave feminist movement (Burns, 116–117).

Patricia Williams from *The Alchemy of Race and Rights: Diary of a Law Professor*

Buzzers are big in New York City. Favored particularly by smaller stores and boutiques, merchants throughout the city have installed them as screening devices to reduce the incidence of robbery: if the face at the door looks desirable, the buzzer is pressed and the door is unlocked. If the face is that of an undesirable, the door stays locked. Predictably, the issue of undesirability has revealed itself to be a racial determination. . . . The installation of these buzzers happened swiftly in New York; stores that had always had their doors wide open suddenly became exclusive or received people by appointment only. I discovered them and their meaning one Saturday in 1986. I was shopping in Soho and saw in a store window a sweater that I wanted to buy for my mother. I pressed my round brown face to the window and my finger to the buzzer, seeking admittance. A narrow-eyed, white teenager wearing running shoes and feasting on bubble-gum glared out, evaluating me for signs that would put me against the limits of his social understanding. After about five seconds, he mouthed, "We're closed," and blew pink rubber at me. It was two Saturdays before Christmas, at one o'clock in the afternoon; there were several white people in the store who appeared to be shopping for things for their mothers.

I was enraged. At that moment I literally wanted to break all the windows of the store and take lots of sweaters for my mother. In the flicker of his judgmental gray eyes, that saleschild had transformed my brightly sentimental, joy-to-the-world, pre-Christmas spree to shambles. He snuffed my sense of humanitarian catholicity, and there was nothing I could do to snuff his, without making a spectacle of myself.[3]

Second Wave Women's Movement

The decade of the 1960s opened with the increasing visible activism of the Civil Rights Movement in the U.S. and became a decade of protest. Oppressive institutions and practices were challenged by those who had been left out of the center of American life; left out of decision making, power, and liberation. The Civil Rights Movement, the Anti-Vietnam War Movement, and the Women's Liberation Movement were three of these central movements of protest. At the core of each of these movements was a recognition of the injustice of some fundamental state of affairs—

racial discrimination, unjustifiable international aggression and violence, and sex/gender discrimination. Each of these movements sought to right the wrong of that injustice.

The U.S. Women's Movement, as we have seen, arose out of the Civil Rights Movement and the Anti-Vietnam War Movement. Within these movements for social justice and change, women worked side by side with men for their causes, but, as with Ella Baker, did not always receive respect and equal consideration for the struggles of their own liberation from oppressive forces. As Robin Morgan describes in *Sisterhood Is Powerful*, a focus on women within these other protest movements was not always well received:

> In 1964, Ruby Doris Smith Robinson, a young black woman who [with Ella Baker] was a founder of SNCC (then the Student Non-violent Coordinating Committee) wrote a paper on the position of women in that organization. It was laughed at and dismissed. In 1965, Casey Hayden and Mary King, two white women who had been active in SNCC and other civil rights organizations for years, wrote an article on women in the Movement for the now-defunct journal *Studies on the Left*. Women began to form caucuses within the Movement organizations where they worked; men's reactions ranged from fury to derision. In 1966, women who demanded that a plank on women's liberation be inserted in the SDS resolution that year were pelted with tomatoes and thrown out of the convention. But the caucuses went on forming, and gradually became small groups all on their own, as women more and more came to see the necessity of an independent women's movement, creating its own theory, politics, tactics, and directing itself toward goals in its own self-interest (which was also the self-interest of more than half the world's population) (xxiv).

In 1966, NOW, the National Organization for Women, was founded, as an organization that pledged to "bring women into full participation in the mainstream of American society . . . exercising all the privileges and responsibilities thereof in truly equal partnership with men" (xxiv). NOW's early membership was made up mostly of professional, middle-aged, middle- and upper-class white women (it also allowed male members). NOW's objective at its founding was, like Anthony and Stanton's, to fight within the system, to open doors for the inclusion of women in what were traditionally male-dominated and male-controlled institutions and sectors of society. As Morgan says, NOW was "essentially an organization that wants reforms about the second-class citizenship of women" (xxv). The institutions of society were not fundamentally problematic or corrupted, in this view; the problem was simply the exclusion of women from them. NOW lobbied legislators, called attention to discrimination against women in education, worked for women's reproductive rights and fought job discrimination. NOW activists, in the tradition of Mother Jones, worked to improve women's access and opportunities in the workplace—

for example, they worked to challenge the mandatory retirement of female flight attendants when they married or turned 35.

Such reform of the existing structures was characterized by some within the women's movement as "add women and stir." The assumption by movements of reform such as NOW was that the institutions themselves were basically good ones and that the issue facing women was simply access to those otherwise worthy institutions. Access would be improved, they believed, by 1) pointing out the injustice of excluding qualified women from positions traditionally held exclusively by men just because they are women, and 2) increasing/improving opportunities for women to be successful in a "man's world" by increasing women's access to education and reproductive control, developing high quality childcare, and raising women's self-esteem and self-confidence through "consciousness raising" groups (groups where women met to share their experiences of oppression and to find solidarity with other women experiencing similar obstacles to their fullest personal development). These women came to speak out against the arrangements and institutions of society that kept them where they were—traditionally in the domestic sphere, raising children, keeping house, caretaking their husbands and communities, disproportionately bearing the burden of nurturing everyone else except themselves. These women began to situate themselves as individuals within the larger context of a society that systematically privileged men and defined women as second-class citizens. The injustice of this was clear. There was no good reason to treat women as less than fully capable of choosing their own life and participating fully in the social and political sphere that they had been restricted from. Furthermore, they sought change in the structure of the division of labor within the home—men were asked to participate in caring for the children and the home and to become partners in their wives' personal development projects.

In the theorizing and activism that followed this phenomenon in the U.S. in the late 1960s and '70s, gender held central importance. Women were discriminated against on the basis of gender (the social/cultural/political/historical expectations of what a woman is and what she ought to do) they argued, and such a discrimination was not done for any good reason, and was therefore arbitrary and indefensible. Since it was the case, they argued, that all women are discriminated against in this way, all women could become a potentially powerful coalition to resist gender discrimination and bring about authentic social change.

However, not all women involved in the second-wave women's movement in the U.S. agreed that gender was the sole, or even fundamental, form of discrimination against women. Many feared that the women's movement of the 1960s would, they said, "fall into the same trap as did our foremothers, the suffragists: creating a bourgeois feminist movement that never quite dared enough, never questioned enough, never really reached out beyond its own class and race" (Morgan, xxv–xxvi). The emphasis on gender as the fundamental form of oppression, these more radical women suggested, reflected middle-class values, especially the liberal view that if you have equal opportunity, the outcomes of social inclusion, success and influence will follow. Other groups within the larger women's movement, more radical than NOW, spoke out against the fundamentally oppressive natures of many social practices, arrangements, and institutions—the family, marriage, racism, classism, compulsory heterosexuality, religious institutions, cultural institutions, the media, government, the military, capitalism, education, and so on. These women called for a radical overhauling of mainstream American society, one that would remedy the injustices inherent within male dominated, white supremacist, heterosexist institutions. Their entry into this commitment was recognition of the fact that women's lives are frequently marked by lack of choices, violence (physical, mental, psychological, and spiritual), poverty, enforced dependency through marriage and childbearing, compulsory heterosexuality, lack of access to education, etc., and that the experiences of these by women differed depending upon a woman's race, ethnicity, class, sexuality.

For example, a middle-class white woman's fundamental obstacle to personal freedom and participation in American society might be the sexist attitudes that exist at higher levels in the corporate world or the availability of safe and effective means of controlling reproduction. A woman who is a recent immigrant from Mexico, on the other hand, would find these kinds of concerns far from her own experience of what makes her life difficult (though, of course, not ultimately irrelevant). She might be searching out adequate and safe housing for her family, safe and successful schools for her kids, and bilingual translation for her trips to the doctor or social services agencies, or ways to confront racist, anti-immigrant attitudes in her encounters with mainstream white American society. Her experience of forces in place that work to exclude her from participation in society will be vastly different from the middle-class white woman's fighting for acceptance in corporate America and adequate reproductive control. This is not to diminish the difficulty of the former woman's struggles, but to highlight the way that the differences that exist among women inform their experiences of injustice and therefore must inform our theorizing and activism to remove the injustices.

Gloria Steinem from *Outrageous Acts and Everyday Rebellions*

In my first days of activism, I thought I would do this ("this" being feminism) for a few years and then return to my real life (what my "real life" might be, I did not know). Partly, that was a naïve belief that injustice only had to be pointed out in order to be cured. Partly it was a simple lack of courage. But like so many others now and in movements past, I've learned that this is not just something we care about for a year or two or three. We are in it for life—and for our lives.[4]

Women's Entry into Academia

One of the notable and continuing successes of the second-wave women's movement (and one that may directly affect you) was the increase in the number of women in higher education. These women, many the working-class or poor recipients of generous post–World War II federal tuition aid, others the beneficiaries of Affirmative Action, changed the nature of academic institutions in what at first seemed just the way reformist feminists had hoped. But it soon became clear that "add women and stir" would not work in academia. The critiques of the institutions of higher learning that feminist professors and students engaged in moved activism into new territories and challenged fundamental assumptions of Western thought.

Academia is, of course, one of the central places where knowledge is created in our society—it is not the only one, but it has traditionally been the *privileged* one. Only those vested with the credentials of higher degrees have been seen as credible "creators of knowledge," as credible and respected articulators of the "way the world really. is." This is highly problematic on a number of fronts. There has been limited access to those positions. The grooming of those who eventually obtain those positions begins in early childhood, and those who can access high-quality education and resources through positions of race and class privilege generally predominate in higher education. Also, what "counts" as real knowledge derives from certain "legitimized" procedures, such as the scientific method, detached and "neutral" observation and conclusion-drawing, impartiality, and deductive reasoning.

When white women and women of color entered academia in greater numbers, and especially when they brought with them a feminist understanding of the sexist and patriarchal forces that have traditionally excluded women from positions of influence and power, the kinds of questions being asked about "how the world really is" changed. Gender was introduced as a central theoretical construct, with an emphasis on the recognition that women's reality had in large part been defined or constructed under white patriarchal (male-controlled/male-dominated) norms. Questions about how women and men are different—biologically, psychologically—led to reformulations of human nature ("human nature" had previously been deduced from study of and consideration of male nature alone). Literary and artistic frameworks were expanded by the inclusion of the different ways that women express themselves creatively in language and images. Traditional methods carried out within the scientific enterprise were challenged by new methodologies and epistemologies. The research on maize by the geneticist Barbara McClintock, outlined in an essay by Evelyn Fox Keller and reprinted in *The Reflective Woman* reader, exemplifies this challenge. McClintock conceptualized herself in relationship to the corn she studied rather than as radically separate from it. The way that she came to "know" the corn was through situating herself in relationship to the corn; she let the corn "speak to her" rather than simply observing the corn through her own assumptions.

McClintock's research is an example of one of the most influential and important changes that women brought to traditional theorizing about the world: the approach of situating oneself in relationship to the thing being studied, as opposed to the detached methodology of modern science. Feminist academics took this concept to the classroom as well, in ways you may have experienced at the College of St. Catherine. Sandra Shullman explains:

> I do not consider work as a feminist scholar a job or a career. I see it from the perspective of being a way of life. The professional is the political. And to try to separate out myself as an intellectual feminist from a living feminist is a very, very difficult process—one that I see a lot of my colleagues struggle with. I don't think you can just think about feminism for periods of time without the fundamental process of recognizing that you are part of what you are studying. It is naïve to believe that you can be a feminist scholar and not be an activist, a supporter, and a political advocate for women.

In this approach to education, professors don't check their politics at the door for a version of objectivity that feminist scholars began to find objectionable. In feminist pedagogy, or teaching methods, students and faculty are viewed as connected in a learning process. This plays out in classrooms without lecterns, chairs arranged in circles and students working with one another as well as with the professor in a process of discovery. Feminist professors (such as the three of us) see themselves not as authoritative deliverers of truth but as mentors and co-learners, as advocates for students and as active participants in the movement to end oppression. To understand what a radical departure this theory and pedagogy represent, it is important to situate contemporary feminist thinking in the context of the Enlightenment, of Enlightenment-inspired notions of the individual, and of its conceptualizations of justice.

> ## Gloria Anzaldúa from *Borderlands/La Frontera*
>
> I still feel the old despair when I look at the unpainted, dilapidated, scrap lumber houses consisting mostly of corrugated aluminum. Some of the poorest people in the U.S. live in the Lower Rio Grande Valley, an arid and semi-arid land of irrigated farming, intense sunlight and heat, citrus groves next to chaparral and cactus. I walk through the elementary school I attended so long ago, that remained segregated until recently. I remember how the white teachers used to punish us for being Mexican.[5]

Early Enlightenment Articulations of Justice

The Enlightenment is the revolution in thinking that occurred during the seventeenth and eighteenth centuries in Europe and that still today underpins much of Western culture. It is characterized by individuals affirming themselves as independent thinkers and knowers, as well as as separate, detached observers of the natural and social world (the foundational structure of the scientific method) and autonomous individuals pursuing their own self-interest (the foundational structure of liberal political society). Early enlightenment thinking views the individual as independent and basically unattached to other individuals (the ideal conceptualization of the self).

In science the result of such thinking was that scientists could place themselves at a distance from the thing being studied (be it a seashore, a rainforest, fruit flies, rhesus monkeys, molecules, solar systems, social groups, or human infants), allowing the thing studied to be known by observation of it alone by the trained scientists. The scientist, if carrying out the scientific method properly, would neutrally receive the object and draw conclusions about it in a supposedly value-free way.

In traditional epistemological (theory of knowledge), moral and political theory, the individual became the center of theorizing the form of our social lives together. Descartes, Hobbes, and Kant are significant contributors to this line of thinking, which, it should be noted, was challenged by some classical and contemporary philosophical perspectives, including Marxism, existentialism, and feminism, as we shall discuss later. The entity that is often called the hero of the Enlightenment was an individual that could be thought of as independent of others (Code).

In his *Meditations*, for example, René Descartes literally isolated himself from others and from the distractions of everyday social life to engage in thinking, whereby he had an epiphany. He came to understand that he was an independent thinking being; he could come to know the truth of the world by himself. Understanding the social and cultural context of

Descartes' project is important. At the time of his life, knowledge and truth generally came down to the people from those at the top of the hierarchical structures of the monarchy and the church. The people, the masses, were seen as a part of an organic whole, each with a particular function to serve in the society—raising the food, creating the objects of daily life, bearing and rearing children, selling wares, governing, guiding spiritually, ruling. The truth of how the world is (what is real), of what is expected of us, of what we are obligated to do, or what God requires of us—these "truths" were derived from those at the top levels of society and they were handed down to the people.

Descartes challenged this. In brief, he argued that the body (or specifically sensation) was an unreliable source of knowledge. Our senses frequently deceive us; for example, when we hear the phone ringing while using a hand-held hair dryer. We must, therefore, suspend our reliance on the body as a source of knowledge, because what we believe to be true through the body is frequently doubtful. He sought another source of reliable knowledge. What could he know for sure? In a world of so much uncertainty and doubt, he came to realize that the only thing he knew with certainty to be true was that he was aware of himself thinking. What is real? What is certain? I exist as a thinking thing. And thus an individual, isolatable, separate (from the organic whole that characterized the pre-Enlightenment social structure), epistemological (knowing) agent was conceptualized.

The political and social implication of Descartes' metaphysics is that if you are a thinking being, you can come to know what is true, regardless of anything else. This "regardless" was most importantly regardless of the body and the way it is situated or given meaning in society—for example, as a woman, as a male laborer with callused hand and sun-parched skin, as a person with brown skin. Our knowing the truth is not dependent, he argued, on appealing to the knowledge-creation process of others (and those others were, in his day, those in power).

Descartes' conclusion, which substantially informed the understanding of the modern person in Western thought, was at the time a profoundly radical metaphysical shift. He put forth a new understanding of what it means to be a human person. Importantly, however, he postulated an individual human knower in isolation from other human beings. Such a move was, of course, essential to his project of removing the knower from the nexus of dependent knowing that characterized his culture at the time of his life, dominated as it was by those in power. Knowledge came to be dependent upon a particular way of situating oneself as a knower—in separation and isolation from that which was known one could come to know the truth. The mind became the privileged vehicle of knowledge and the body (or objects without minds) became the thing to be known.

In Enlightenment moral and political theory, the isolated, abstract (because essentially disembodied) individual was adopted as the central character in theorizing about our social lives. We do not live our lives alone. We live with and are dependent upon others for not only our well-being, but our survival as well. But for whatever reason, doing this well is not easy (history attests to this). Just why this is the case, just why human beings have so frequently found living harmoniously and peacefully with others difficult is beyond the scope of this essay. Are we naturally self-centered? Are we naturally cooperative, caring, and compassionate, and other forces impinge on that tendency? It's hard to know how we would answer a question about the fundamental nature of human beings.

The political philosopher Thomas Hobbes postulated that we are essentially egotistical, self-interested beings, and that we will act in ways that promote our own self-interest. Establishing bonds between others—giving us reasons to work together cooperatively—is the objective of moral and political theory, he argued. Within the intervention of rules of civil society, we would be trapped, according to Hobbes, in a state of nature that is a state of war. This, he argued, is how we are naturally inclined. Since we are self-interested essentially, and will therefore naturally fend for ourselves and our intimates only, we must establish a society that artificially structures a system of cooperation for mutual benefit (it is in one's self-interest, Hobbes argued, to cooperate with each other). I'll farm for you, you make shoes for me. I'll raise your barn, if you'll raise mine. I'll share my food with you, if you share your food with me. I won't kill you, if you won't kill me.

The essentially isolated, separate individual is the starting point of Hobbes' theory of society. The task of moral and political theory, then, is to articulate ways that justify the establishment of bonds of interaction for mutual benefit, reciprocity, and cooperation. Coming together in this way is not natural to us; it must be constructed out of our understanding that society would work better in this way. That is, the state of war that is natural to human beings can be managed for the benefit of all.

Immanuel Kant adopts a similar starting point of the isolated, separate individual in his Enlightenment-era moral theory. In brief, the moral agent of Kant's ethics is a rational being who possesses free will. For Kant, an action has moral worth only if it is done out of this free will and for the sake of duty. Inherent in this, of course, is the freedom to choose not do it. Morality requires that we do the former, but often, by our own free will, we fall short. Kant understood that doing something good or right when you are inclined to do it is easy—such as helping a friend because you love her. It is doing something good or right for someone when you don't want to, or when you are not inclined to, that is hard. This latter action, then, is the only one that has moral worth in Kant's view. Acting out of love or friendship is not a moral act in Kant's conceptualization of morality. It is valuable, of course, in its own right, but it is not moral in that it is easy. Morality, doing the right thing when one doesn't want to do it, is hard. This is the essence of Kant's duty-based ethics.

Kant's ethics also establish the idea that because we are rational and free beings, we can come to know moral law and act on it. If we are called upon to put our personal inclinations and wants aside in order to act for the sake of the moral law, we are capable of transcending our own lives in order to think universally. It follows that we cannot justifiably make ourselves or our group morally special. I can't—if I am acting rationally—argue that I may lie whenever I want to if it benefits me, and yet demand that you never lie to me. I cannot justify arguing that I deserve a good and safe school for my kids while you do not. I cannot argue that my race deserves social privilege. Kant's ethics require us to see every other person as 1) another rational being, 2) autonomous, and 3) morally equal. Out of this view, Kant derives what is probably the most important articulation of his (and any) ethics: We may not use a person, whether ourselves or another, as a mere means to an end, but must treat them as an end in themselves. Kant's formulation of the moral law establishes a requirement of respect that is foundational to Western culture.

Building on this foundation, the contemporary moral and political philosopher John Rawls sets forth a useful mechanism to help us establish rules to live by that are consistent with this ethic. Imagine that there is an "original position" (prior to the formulation of social rules) whereby we (any collection of rational, self-interest individuals) are being a "veil of ignorance." Behind the veil, no one knows anything about themselves other than that they are rational and self-interested. We know nothing of our social position, race, ethnicity, sex/gender, sexuality, economic class, able-bodiedness, age, talents, or aptitudes. Nothing. Behind that veil we must come up with principles that will guide our lives together to bring about the fairest society for its members. Behind the veil we will articulate, first, Rawls contends, principles of justice that maximize the greatest amount of freedom to all members equal to everyone else (that is, everyone is similarly free to pursue the goods of the society). Second, if there are inequalities in the society, they must be consistent with the advantage of the least advantaged (that is, if some have obtained wealth, they must use that wealth to benefit those who are least economically advantaged).

As we can see from this cursory exploration of traditional Western moral and political theory, articulations of justice and of a just (good, moral, ethical) society have depended upon a conceptualization of the separate, isolatable, autonomous, abstract individual as the essential characterization of the human being. Such a move seemed necessary because justice is fundamentally a notion of universality—what we owe any human being regardless of any other considerations. The requirement of universality and its inherent abstraction does important moral work. No matter what nation, race, gender, ethnic group, religious group, subculture, etc., a person belongs to, justice requires that we treat that person fairly and with respect. Justice in this way serves as a powerful constraint on our conduct towards others. No matter what we might feel or want, justice in these particular Western view obligates us to treat others with respect and just consideration.

In the 19th century, however, Karl Marx articulated a different view of the foundation of justice. Marx rejected the notion of an abstract conceptualization of the individual or of justice, and instead, located justice within the material (actual or concrete) lives of human beings. In his "historical materialism," Marx argued that ideas or concepts are interwoven within, and arise out of, the material (physical) lives and interactions of human beings. All complex forms of human intelligence, including an understanding of justice, are determined by the material (and for Marx, this meant fundamentally, economic) conditions of a given society. An implication of this view is that there is no absolute moral norm; that is, there is no concept of justice that is universally applicable. The material conditions of the lives of actual, situated human beings determine what a just arrangement would look like.

Within capitalism, Marx argued, it is those in power who determine which conceptions will prevail in that society. Since it is the material conditions of one's life that establishes the foundation of ideas and concepts, the context within which one is situated, and for Marx, this meant economically, will determine what one believes to be true about the world. For example, the "truth" or validity of the unequal distribution of wealth in capitalist societies. Employing this notion of "historical materialism" as a theory of the creation of ideas and concepts, Marx argued for the revolutionary potential of the oppressed to articulate their own conceptions of a just arrangement of society.

From the perspective of the oppressed, a perspective inextricably interwoven and embedded within particular material conditions, a different view of equality and justice can be known. A materialist perspective allows us to see how economic, political, Marx's historical materialism established a way to counter the Western Enlightenment notion of the abstract individual. With materialism, the particularity of individual experience is the center of our theorizing. This notion was indispensable to the feminist critiques of the theories of the Enlightenment.

Rebecca Walker

The complex, multi-issue nature of our lives, the instinct not to categorize and shut oneself off from others, and the enormous contradictions we embody are all fodder for making new theories of living and relating. This continuing legacy of feminism, which demands that we know and accept ourselves, jettisoning societal norms that don't allow for our experiences, is a politically powerful decision . . . Rather than allowing ourselves and others to be put into boxes meant to categorize and dismiss, we can use the complexity of our lives to challenge the belief that any person or group is more righteous, more correct, more deserving of life than any other.[6]

Feminist Critiques of Enlightenment Theories of Justice

In the late 1960s, as we noted, there was a groundswell of theorizing about justice (and ethics in general) from feminist academics. This theorizing took two forms. First, it paid attention to contemporary social problems that surround the lives of women, such as reproductive choice, work and wage equality, domestic violence and rape, childcare deficiencies, and women's health. Second, it critiqued the traditional Western Enlightenment approaches to ethics and justice. Feminists began to demonstrate white male bias in the theories of justice. You will recall that these theorists took as their starting point, ironically, a non-attached, non-situated (that is, genderless, raceless, classless) rational being. How could such a conceptualization involve male bias?

As Alison Jaggar points out, in order to understand the history of theorizing around justice we must recognize that women were excluded from the category of full rational being, and thus were incapable of being full moral agents. Aristotle, Rousseau, and Kant, among others, endorsed this claim of women's moral inferiority. For these theorists, the virtues that women were capable of were lesser virtues than the virtues of men. For example, the women of the privileged economic class of these male theorists were expected to be silent, demure, obedient, and faithful. They were seen as deficient in the ability to reason and to see the world in an abstract, impartial way. Women were stuck in the emotional world, unable to transcend it to achieve the abstract, reason-based realm of justice.

Another form that male bias took in traditional theorizing about justice is that justice was a norm of interaction that applied in the public sphere only. It was seen as a framework to understand and negotiate relationships among essentially equal individuals (remember all particularity within individual persons had been vacuumed out, and only rationality and self-interest remained). The domestic realm, where women were situated, was seen as outside the jurisdiction of the demands of justice, as Jaggar points out, and therefore it was "beyond the scope of legitimate political regulation" (81). Theorizing that restricted its focus to public life was clearly inadequate to address many of the injustices of women's (and girls') lives. As Jaggar explains:

> Feminist philosophers began early to criticize this conceptual bifurcation of social life. They pointed out that the home was precisely the realm to which women had historically been confined and that it had become symbolically associated with the feminine, despite the fact that heads of households were paradigmatically male. These feminists argued that the philosophical devaluation of the domestic realm made it impossible to raise questions about the justice of the domestic division of labor (Okin, 1989), obscured the far-reaching social significance and creativity of women's work in the home (Jaggar and McBridge, 1985), and concealed, even legitimated, the domestic abuse of women (as well as children, especially girls) (Jaggar, 1983; MacKinnon, 1987) (81).

A third form of white male bias within traditional theorizing around justice was the growing awareness of a distinctive moral experience or sensibility in women that had gone unnoticed. Many women started to claim that the view of the social and moral person as abstract, free, equal, independent, disinterested, and essentially disconnected from both other people and the natural world was contrary to women's experience and to the experience of many people of color. Out of recognition of these inadequacies of traditional theories of justice, feminists adopted a materialist perspective, and a new ethic developed. Yet, this feminist critique was itself limited in that it was articulated almost exclusively by women who had the racial and class privilege to enter the academy, where the language of justice was taught and spoken. Their critique centered, for the most part, on gendered bias, and neglected to take serious account of the other forms of bias that comprise traditional theorizing—the biases of racial, ethnic, and class privilege.

The Confrontation of the Second Wave's Privilege

Clearly, the movements for social change we have explored used appeals to justice to motivate, justify, and drive their calls to action. In each of these movements, some group was unjustifiably excluded from full participation in society and denied equal access to the goods of society, including the individual and social good of defining oneself. Each movement fought against the tendency among others to make themselves morally special—an outright violation of the requirement of justice. When feminist activists struggled for women's freedom to define ourselves, to have access to education, work, and other spheres of influence, to make choices around childbearing and childrearing, to escape cycles of violence and poverty, they were appealing to justice. They sought an explanation of what was wrong in how society treated women, and they called for action to change that treatment. Our gender should not situate us outside of the obligations of justice, they argued. In traditional Western terms, justice requires the fair treatment of women.

But more than that, justice requires the fair treatment of all persons. Early second-wave feminist theory that centralized gender as the fundamental theoretical construct neglected to take into account the fact that all women do not experience being a woman in the same way. White, middle-class feminism that held gender as the fundamental form of oppression were theorizing from their own experience as women who were otherwise privileged by race and class. For them, the obstacle to their full participation in society was gender discrimination alone. If they could just reveal the injustice of gender exclusion and convince those in power to dismantle the structures that stood in the way of (white) women's progress, justice for women would be achieved. Indeed, when the obstacles to higher education for white, middle-class women were removed, they were able to enter the ranks of the creators of knowledge, as we have demonstrated. However, gender discrimination is not the only form of discrimination many women experience. As bell hooks writes about the white, middle-class women's movement and theorizing:

> Although the impulse towards unity and empathy that informed the notion of common oppression was directed at building solidarity, slogans like "organize around your own oppression" provided the excuse many privileged women needed to ignore the differences between their social status and the status of masses of women. It was a mark of race and class privilege, as well as the expression of freedom from the many constraints sexism places on working class women, that middle class white women were able to make their interests the primary focus of feminist movement and employ a rhetoric of commonality that made their condition synonymous with "oppression." Who was there to demand a change in vocabulary? What other group of women in the United States had the same access to universities, publishing houses, mass media, money (6)?

Audre Lorde (an African-American, lesbian, poet, and theorist) makes a similar argument in her letter to Mary Daly (a white, lesbian, philosopher/theologian), regarding Daly's book *Gyn-Ecology*, a history of the oppression of women:

> [T]o imply that all women suffer the same oppression simply because we are women, is to lose sight of the many varied tools of patriarchy. It is to ignore how those tools are used by women without awareness against each other. . . . I ask that you be aware of how this serves the destructive forces of racism and separation between women—the assumption that the herstory and myth of white women is the legitimate and sole herstory and myth of all women to call upon for power and background, and that non-white women and our herstories are noteworthy only as decorations, or examples of female victimization. I ask that you be aware of the effect that

this dismissal has upon the community of black women, and how it deval-
ues your own words (67–69).

Maria Lugones affirms:

> I am particularly interested here in those many cases in which white/Anglo
> women do one or more of the following to women of color: they ignore us,
> ostracize us, render us invisible; stereotype us, leave us completely alone,
> interpret us as crazy. All of this *while we are in their midst*. The more inde-
> pendent I am, the more independent I am left to be. Their world and their
> integrity do not require me at all. There is no sense of self-loss in them for
> my own loss of solidity. But they rob me of my solidity through indiffer-
> ence, an indifference they can afford and that seems sometimes studied. . . .
> Many times white/Anglo women want us out of their field of vision. Their
> lack of concern is a harmful failure of love that leaves me independent from
> them (423).

Reflecting upon these words and considering the requirements of justice,
we are faced with an apparent paradox. Justice requires that we treat all
people the same, that we give them their due and that we treat them with
respect. By ignoring differences among women, second-wave privileged
feminism seems to have been acting in a way consistent with the requirements of abstract, universalizing justice. Treat everyone the same, the
doctrine of justice says; don't see difference. Yet, in philosophically, psychologically, socially and politically important ways, we are not the same.
Women experience the world, themselves and power differently depending upon how they are marked racially, ethnically, economically, sexually.
We are not treating everyone equally and with respect when we ignore
them and their needs, experiences, and concerns. We are not treating
everyone equally and with respect when we put our own particular
needs, experiences, and concerns at the center of the world. This characterizes the world under patriarchy, the world that second-wave feminism
critiques. Using the tools of Western thinking, feminism has had to struggle with this tendency to place the experience of some at the center of
claims made about the world.

The experiences that women of color in the U.S. describe of being
excluded from feminist theorizing and activism can be approached two
ways. First, white feminism has, perhaps, failed to get justice right. That
is, it has carried on its theorizing and activism within the context of
treating a particular group (white, privileged women) as morally special
or privileged. Or, second, there may be another moral value that feminists need to make clear and to take seriously, an ethics not traditionally
Western, a way of coming to know the needs and experiences of others
in a non-detached, personal way.

Nellie Wong

. . . . when I was growing up, I was proud
of my English, my grammar, my spelling
fitting into the group of smart children
smart Chinese children, fitting in,
belonging, getting in line

when I was growing up and went to high school,
I discovered the rich white girls, a few yellow girls,
their imported cotton dresses, their cashmere sweaters,
their curly hair and I thought that I too should have
what these lucky girls had

when I was growing up, I hungered
for American food, American styles,
coded: white and even to me, a child
born of Chinese parents, being Chinese
was feeling foreign, was limiting,
was unAmerican . . . [7]

The Ethic of Care

The "failure of love" that Lugones speaks of points us in the direction of another way of orienting ourselves to others in the world—through love, care, and compassion. These moral values come from a different capacity in human beings than the disinterested ethic of justice; however, some have argued that it is the capacity to care that motivates justice in the first place. While justice may compel us to see each person as the same, as worthy of moral respect and fair treatment, care and compassion compel us to see each person as an individual. Each individual has unique experiences and needs arising from her particular, concrete ways of being oriented in the world.

The abstract conception of the person in traditional Western theories of justice explicitly ignores individual difference. It is individual difference, as well as certain feelings and emotions, such theory asserts, that get in the way of moral and just treatment of others. However, such theory tends towards a profound level of abstraction; in this way it can be seen as a cold and detached way of orienting ourselves to the lives of others. As the feminist philosopher Annette Baier argues:

> [T]he main complaint about the Kantian version of society with its first virtue justice, construed as respect for equal rights to formal goods such as having contracts kept, due process, equal opportunity including opportunity to participate in political activities leading to policy and law-making, to basic liberties of speech, free association, and assembly, religious worship, is that

none of these goods do much to ensure that the people who have and mutually respect such rights will have any other relationships to one another than
the minimal relationship needed to keep such a 'civil society' going (51).

As Baier admits, there is "little disagreement that justice is a social value
of very great importance, and injustice an evil"(47). Yet, justice doesn't
seem to do all of the moral work that needs doing. Its requirement of a
detached approach to our interactions with others flies in the face of what
many of us find most compelling and essential in our lives—our being
particular persons and our being in relationships with particular others.
This context is often marked by our being called upon by another to come
forward and care for them. As Annette Baier points out, the theoretical
and activist movements that arose as a counter to the assumed
supremacy of justice as a social and moral virtue had men of color and
women as their members, even, as we have seen, as their leaders. They,
who have only recently seen some remedy to the long history of racist
and sexist oppression in the U.S., were among the first to argue that justice is only one social/moral value among others. Furthermore, they
insisted that justice's undeniable value could not be fully manifested
without other human capacities being present.

Nel Noddings, one of the first theorists explicitly to articulate the framework that became known as the ethic of care, offered this explanation of
theories of justice:

> [T]his doctrine yields no real guidance for moral conduct in concrete situa-
> tions. It guides us in abstract moral thinking; it tell us, theoretically, what to do,
> "all other things being equal." But other things are rarely if ever equal. A and
> B, struggling with a moral decision, are two different persons with different
> factual histories, different projects and aspirations, and different ideals (14).

One major theory that attempted to fill in this missing piece was the
moral development research of the feminist psychologist Carol Gilligan.
In a ground-breaking, dominant-moral-theory-shattering book, *In a Different Voice*, Gilligan proposed that care, compassion, and personal
responsibility to others have enormous moral virtue and that women
have greater ease with caring attitudes and practices than men. Women,
she wrote, speak "in a different voice" (at least at times) from the voice of
justice. The radical nature of Gilligan's work is best understood in the
context of its development. In her research into moral development, or
the process by which we come to see ourselves as moral decision-makers
and actors, Gilligan strove to explain the phenomenon that her colleague
Lawrence Kohlberg had described in his research. Studying, at least initially, only privileged undergraduate male students at Harvard University, Kohlberg concluded that when faced with moral dilemma scenarios,
the most accomplished moral reasoners were those who appealed to
abstract, universal principles to guide their decisions. For example, in the

famous "Heinz Dilemma" Heinz must decide whether or not to steal a drug that will save his wife's life, a drug that the druggist has refused to sell to him at a price that Heinz can afford (the druggist wants $2000 for the drug (he developed it for $200), and Heinz has been able to collect only $1000). Should Heinz steal the drug? For Kohlberg, the sophisticated moral (read "Kantian") judgment would conclude that Heinz ought to steal the drug, for human life is more valuable than money for the druggist. The general principle not to steal is overriden by the more compelling universal respect for human life.

When Kohlberg gave these dilemmas to female subjects, they often concluded that it was not clear that Heinz should steal the drug at all. They often expressed concern for the relationships involved—Heinz's broken trust with the druggist, the question of who would care for Heinz's wife if he were arrested for stealing the drug and possibly imprisoned. Because of this tendency to take more into consideration than a basic, abstract principle, Kohlberg concluded that women did not develop a very sophisticated sense of moral reasoning; that they tended to get "stuck" in consideration of the relationships involved and the responsibility that one had to those relationships. (Kohlberg's conclusions about this gender difference were, of course, consistent with Sigmund Freud's view that girls/women never develop a strong superego, or moral conscience).

Gilligan hypothesized that perhaps Kohlberg's female subjects were not making unsophisticated, inadequate, or immature moral judgments, but that perhaps they were tuning into a different component of moral decision-making—compassion for the particular people in the dilemma and for their particular circumstances. Such an approach, attention to particularity rather than universality, was unlike traditional justice thinking.

Gilligan sought to explain and confirm her hypothesis by conducting moral dilemmas research on women. She found a tendency among women to emphasize care and responsibility in their moral deliberations. She found, also, that women turn to justice concerns in their moral deliberations, but that they tend to weigh more heavily the personal, individual, and particular dimensions of troublesome decision-making situations. (Importantly, Gilligan also found that boys and men appeal to care as well as justice concerns, but that boys and men tend to weigh more heavily the more impersonal components that make up justice decisions.) Gilligan concluded that women aren't inadequate in moral reasoning, but that we reason in a "different voice" than men. The ethic of care, a framework of considering another and his/her needs, found its origins in Gilligan's articulation of this phenomenon. Furthermore, it was seen, at least initially, as an ethical framework with strong gender components, that women seem to find greater ease with turning to care, compassion, emotion, and relationships than boys and men.

Feminism found a powerful theoretical framework in care as an ideal of human interaction, as well as a guide to the creation of good personal and social interactions. One of its strengths clearly was its commitment to attention to particularity, to all that makes up a person—her history, her community, her culture, her personality, her talents, her needs, her wants. When one cares for another person, one cannot do this in a detached, abstract way. Caring is a personal interaction; if one cares out of a sense of duty alone, it seems clear that something important is missing. If I tell my son that I will read to him before bed because it is my parental duty, he would be justified in being angry and quite hurt. Of course, he wants me to read to him before bed because I care for and love him, and because our relationship and time together is important to me as well. My behavior toward him is informed by something different from duty.

As Patricia Hill Collins writes in "Toward an Afro-centric Feminist Epistemology," the ethic of care is a fundamental element of knowing the world well and acting responsibly within it. The ethic of care emphasizes three things: individual uniqueness, the appropriate emotions in our interactions with others, and the development of the capacity for empathy. When we are caring, we are present with the other; our lives are concretely joined. This recognition of our lives being concretely intertwined, and the way that this interconnection calls upon us to act in particular ways towards each other, is what Maria Lugones appeals to in explaining her pain at being ignored by, and seen as irrelevant to, white women. White women "fail to love" women of color, fail to take their particularity into account. This failure does not, it seems on the surface, detract from the integrity of white women, for their world is not recognized as incomplete without women of color in it. It is a failure, however, that keeps the world incomplete.

Argentinean Mothers of the "Disappeared"

Once in power [in Argentina in 1976], the military systematized and accelerated the campaign of terror, quickly annihilating the armed organizations of the Left and the unarmed ones, as well as many individuals with little or no connection to either. The indiscriminate nature of the kidnapping campaign and the impunity with which it was carried out spread terror—as intended. Relationships among friends and relatives were shattered by unprecedented fear. Perfectly decent individuals suddenly became afraid even to visit the parents of a kidnap victim, for any such gesture of compassion might condemn the visitor to a terrible fate. In a terrorized society, a small organization of women, mothers and other relatives of kidnapped Argentines staged a stunning act of defiance. One Thursday afternoon they gathered in the Plaza de Mayo, the main square in Buenos Aires and the site of countless historic incidents beginning in 1810 with the events that led to Argentina's separation from the Spanish Empire. In the center of the Plaza de Mayo, within clear sight of the presidential palace, the national cathedral and several headquarters of ministries and corporations, the Mothers paraded in a closed circle.

. . . When they marched, the Madres [Mothers] wore white kerchiefs with the names of the disappeared embroidered on them. Often they carried lighted candles and almost always they wore or carried photographs of the disappeared. . . . The Latin American women's movements are clearly politics of resistance. The women who engage in them court imprisonment and torture and in some cases have become "disappeared" themselves. . . . The women talked among themselves about their terrors, found others who shared their fears, and marched with them in affinity groups. And thus they brought their bodies to bear against the state.[8]

Tension between Justice and Care

Many care theorists and critics of the ethic of care point out, with Kant, that caring for those you love is easy. You do for them because you care for them. Caring for those we don't know, and even clearly do not care about is harder. You will recall that it was this difficulty that led Kant to his more general, universal approach in the first place. How do feminist thinkers address this question?

You may remember Sister Helen Prejean, in her 1999 visit to St. Catherine's, telling of her experience with Patrick Sonnier, the death-row inmate at Louisiana State Penitentiary that she developed a relationship with in the period prior to his execution. She recounts how hard it was to reconcile her abhorrence for his crime (the murder of a young woman and man after raping the woman) with her care for him as a person. "We soon become steady correspondents, and I begin to think of him as a fellow human being, though I can't for a moment forget his crime, nor can I reconcile the easy-going Cajun who writes to me with the brutal murderer of two helpless teenagers" (13). Clearly, as for Sister Helen, there can be tension between caring and our demand for justice, tension between understanding the complexity of a particular, concrete human with the understanding that sometimes none of that matters. At times caring is hard and we turn to justice (or the abstract law) to answer our questions. As Prejean reveals, however, we are often called upon to care when caring is hard and justice is easy. Justice can keep us at a distance from each other. It can, on the other hand, provide essential constraints on our interactions with others.

Remember the feminist critique that traditional theories of justice were for the public sphere only, not applicable to interactions within the home? Justice was, undoubtedly, conceptualized to establish limits and constraints on how individuals may treat each other in the public domain, the place where male theorists in the past faced the greatest challenges in preserving their own self-interests. Individuals, as essential equal persons, deserve respect, bear certain rights. As the feminist theorist Marilyn Friedman points out, however, justice also has a place in our most intimate relationships. Caring for those we love is easy; however, this isn't the whole story. In our intimate interpersonal relationships, there can be failures of care and love. Friedman writes:

> Justice, at the more general level, is a matter of giving people their due, of treating them appropriately. Justice is relevant to personal relationships and to care precisely to the extent that considerations of justice itself determine appropriate ways to treat friends or intimates. Justice as it bears on relationships among friends or family, or on other close personal ties, might not involve duties, which are universalizable, in the sense of being owed to all persons simply in virtue of shared moral personhood. But this does not entail the irrelevance of justice among friends or intimates . . . Thus, in a close relationship among persons of comparable moral personhood, care may degenerate into the injustices of exploitation, or oppression. Many such problems have been given wide public scrutiny recently as a result of feminist analysis of various aspects of family life and sexual relationships. Women-battering, acquaintance rape, and sexual harassment are but a few of the many recently publicized injustices of "personal" life (68).

As Friedman argues and as we have posited, there are at least two different moral orientations—justice and care. Neither does all of the moral work that needs doing. At times care will motivate us to do good and right to another, as well as to work to dismantle an entire system of social or political life that is inconsistent with caring. On the other hand, at times a more abstract and impartial approach will be necessary. Traditional conceptualizations of justice, contrary to many current critiques of it, provide the framework for concluding that privileging of oneself or one's group is unjustifiable. As Friedman argues, we have a duty (a justice term) not to harm our intimates; our intimates deserve equal and respectful treatment. And if care doesn't motivate us not to harm them, then the justice requirement ought to. That many of the traditional theorists did privilege themselves and others like them does not render their theory inadequate to establish this kind of essential constraint on individuals and groups. One could argue that they simply made fundamental category mistakes about who could be full moral agents. That women, people of color, colonized groups, and less privileged classes were seen as unworthy of equal and respectful treatment was a failure, at least in part, of application of justice (the philosopher among us would argue), not a failure of the theory itself.

Clearly, care and compassion are not enough. Feminists have been clear about this. One might articulate the "constraint" function of justice with the following: If you don't care, then be fair. Kant knew caring for those we love is easy; caring for and doing the right thing for those we don't love is hard. And if we can't pull up the care and compassion strong enough to motivate us to do good and right to others, then justice can be appealed to as a guide and limit to our actions and the actions of others. Care has further limitations, at least in some of its articulations. Nell Noddings points out that:

> Our obligation [to care] is limited and delimited by relation. We are never free, in the human domain, to abandon our preparedness to care; but practically, if we are meeting those in our inner circles adequately as ones-caring and receiving those linked to our inner circles by formal chains of relation, we shall limit the calls upon our obligation quite naturally. We are not obliged to summon the "I must" [care] if there is no possibility of completion in the other. I am not obligated to care for starving children in Africa, because there is no way for this caring to be completed in the other unless I abandon the caring to which I am obligated. I may still choose to do something in the direction of caring, but I am not obliged to do so (15).

This may strike many of us as hardly acceptable. If personal care doesn't motivate us to care for starving children in Africa, what does? If our doing good and right for someone arises solely out of our relationship to them, then do we owe nothing to those we aren't intimately involved with? Some feminist theorists have found Noddings' conclusions inadequate, her extension of the obligation of care too limited. One can imagine that we would be excused from an obligation to care for folks in our own communities if they were far enough outside our "formal chains of relations." In a society such as ours that is so profoundly segregated, this is easily imaginable. When care as a motivator loses its force because we are outside of the personal context required for care to make sense, then justice kicks in.

Feminism and Justice Today

Such consideration of care and justice strengthens contemporary feminism. Feminists will be most inclusive and most effective if we engage other connections, even those that may at first seem paradoxical. With gender no longer standing alone at the center of analysis, feminists look at connections between, for example, pacifism and feminism, spirituality and freedom, or ecofeminism and indigenous rights. These connections help us to understand the complexities of women's lives and women's approaches to justice. They also contribute to the strategy of building coalitions to work for a more just world.

For Catholic feminist Char Madigan, CSJ, for example, pacifism and feminism are connected, and both are related to her activism for economic justice. In all those areas, Madigan works to end domination and build community. In 1977 Madigan, with two other sisters, founded St. Joseph's House, which began as a shelter for homeless women and children. She explains:

> I think the shelter work turned me into a flaming radical feminist and that work turned me into a flaming radical pacifist. . . . Working with the homeless women and women who had been abused, I got mad. I was mad at men. And then I realized that men were trapped in the same way that women were by economic domination. . . . Domestic violence involves somebody trying to dominate and exploit somebody else, and countries were doing that economically. Economic violence is domestic violence written in capitalism letters, justifying dominance and exploitation.

Like her mentor Dorothy Day, the co-founder with Peter Maurin of the Catholic Worker Movement, Madigan "wanted to put an end to this domination, this lordship—I don't even want a God who lords it over creation. I think the main thing is that we are all part of one another. I wanted to replace [domination] with community and the nonviolence that supports it."

This is consistent with the perspectives of Rosemary Radford Ruether and other feminist theologians. For Reuther:

> [g]ender hierarchy is seen as central to a total system and ideology of patriarchy. Feminism sees patriarchy as a multilayered system of domination, centered in male control of women but including class and race hierarchy, generational hierarchy, and clericalism, and expressed also in war and in domination of nature. . . . Redemption means overcoming all forms of patriarchy. . . . Spirit and matter, God and body need to be reintegrated, locating the divine power of renewal of life-giving and loving relations in mutual relationality between all beings, not dominating control from outside (274).

Winona LaDuke makes similar connections in her vision of a world in which we see all creation as our relations. She takes the idea of kinship beyond humans, to consider our relationships to all living beings and to the earth itself.

> Native American teachings describe the relations all around—animals, fish, trees, and rocks—as our brothers, sisters, uncles, and grandpas. Our relations to each other, our prayers whispered across generations to our relatives, are what bind our cultures together (2).

These and similar ideas are central to current feminist thinking about justice. In fact, making connection across differences could be said to characterize the work of young feminists today, the work that is often identified as Third Wave feminism.

Third Wave feminism aimed early on to "fill a void in young women's leadership and mobilize young people to become more involved socially and politically in their communities," according to Third Wave Direct Action founders, Rebecca Walker and Shannon Liss (Third Wave Foundation, Who We Are/History). Third Wave activists have mobilized against sexism, but they have also mobilized for issues beyond those traditionally addressed by Second Wave feminism. From opposing private prisons to campaigning for living wage legislation with initiatives such as Third Wave ROAMS (Reaching Out Across Movements), the Third Wave Foundation is committed to making real links between justice movements and to advancing young women's leadership in those efforts.

Third Wave feminism as a phenomenon is not easy to define, and that is promising in our context of creative thinking arising from chaos. Young women seeking justice and meaningful lives are making many paths, some recognizable to older feminists as movement work, and others emphasizing individual expression in areas like popular music and media. In the recent *Third Wave Agenda: Being Feminist, Doing Feminism*, editors Leslie Heywood and Jennifer Drake call for "languages and images that account for multiplicity and difference, that negotiate contradiction in affirmative ways, and that give voice to a politics of hybridity and coalition" (9). Where some Third Wave feminists focus on their disagreements with the Second Wave, the contributors to *Third Wave Agenda* explore both continuities with and differences from the activism and theorizing of earlier eras. While noting, for example, that anti-racist work is central to the Third Wave, Heywood and Drake recognize their debt to U.S. feminists of color who were active early on in challenging white middle class domination within Second-Wave feminism. That work helped to set the stage for Third-Wave approaches to justice across lines of race and class, globally and within the United States. Like many feminist and queer theorists, some Third-Wave feminists also think in multiple terms about sexuality and gender, refusing to be placed in dualistic categories, even questioning traditional ideas about "woman" as an identity.

There has been debate (even among us three) about whether or not the Third Wave will be seen historically as a movement distinct from the Second Wave. As Cathryn Bailey says, it is difficult to know where one wave ends and another begins when one is in the water; distance over time will help people to see the distinctions more clearly. At the very least, the Third Wave must be recognized as a space for young women to enter into feminist thinking and action on their own terms. Beyond that, Third Wave commitment to deep engagement with issues of racism and multiple differences helps create links to other contemporary women's movements. Indigenous women working for cultural continuity, women in union movements, women in a range of civil rights movements, even second wave feminists can build their own visions of justice apart from and in coalition with the ideas and activism of the Third Wave.

As we do, we will continue to struggle with the integrity of our theorizing. [Note that we use the term "theorizing" here to denote an active process, a work in progress, rather than "theory," which implies a finished product.] Feminism is an internally self-monitoring and self-critical movement that must assuage the tendency to conclude that it has arrived at a definitive conclusion. There are many voices that need to participate in this discussion, many perspectives that need representation, if we would come closer to getting this thing right. Then, perhaps, in negotiating the ensuing chaos creatively, we'll open ourselves to more of what Septima Clark described as "wonderful thinking"—thinking that can inspire genuine feminist social change.

Sharon Doherty
Amy Hilden
Cecilia Konchar Farr

Notes

[1] Sojourner Truth's quotation is taken from Loewenberg Bert J., and Ruth Bogin, eds. *Black Women in Nineteenth-Century American Life*, (University Park: Pennsylvania State University Press, 1976) as quoted in Patricia Hill Collins' *Black Feminist Thought*. Collins' explication follows:

> Rather than accepting the existing assumptions about what a woman was and then trying to prove that she fit the standards, Truth challenged the very standards themselves. Her actions demonstrate the process of deconstruction—namely, exposing a concept as ideological or culturally constructed rather than as natural or a simple reflection of reality (Alcoff, 1988). By deconstructing the concept *woman*, Truth proved herself to be a formidable intellectual. And yet Truth was a former slave who never learned to read or write.

[2] This Mother Jones quotation from her autobiography is excerpted from *In Our Own Voices: Four Centuries of American Women's Religious Writing*, pp. 42–43.

3 Patricia J. Williams from *The Alchemy of Race and Rights: Diary of a Law Professor*, p. 44.

4 Gloria Steinem from *Outrageous Acts and Everyday Rebellions*, p. 392.

5 Gloria Anzaldúa from *Borderlands/LaFrontera*, p. 89.

6 Rebecca Walker in her introduction for *To Be Real*, pp. xxxviii–xxxix.

7 Nellie Wong from "When I Was Growing Up" in Anzaldúa's *This Bridge Called My Back*, p. 7.

8 This quotation from Nathan Laks is excerpted from Sara Ruddick's "A Women's Politics of Resistance."

Works Cited

Albers, Patricia. "From Illusion to Illumination: Anthropological Studies of American Indian Women." *Gender and Anthropology: Critical Reviews for Research and Teaching*, Sandra Morgen, ed. Washington, DC: American Anthropological Association, 1989: 132–149.

Allen, Paula Gunn. "Angry Women Are Building: Issues and Struggles Facing American Indian Women Today" in *The Sacred Hoop: Recovering the Feminine in American Indian Traditions*. Boston: Beacon, 1986. Reprinted in *Race, Class, and Gender: An Anthology*, 3rd ed. Margaret L. Andersen and Patricia Hill Collins, eds. Belmont, CA: Wadsworth, 1998: 43-47.

Anzaldúa, Gloria and Cherrie Morago, eds. *This Bridge Called My Back: Writings by Radical Women of Color*. New York: Kitchen Table, 1983.

Anzaldúa, Gloria. *Borderlands/LaFrontera: The New Mestiza*. San Francisco: Aunt Lute, 1987.

Baier, Annette. "The Need for More than Justice," *Justice and Care: Essential Readings in Feminist Ethics*. Virgina Held, ed. Boulder, CO: Westview, 1995: 47–58.

Bailey, Cathryn. "Making Waves and Drawing Lines: The Politics of Defining the Vicissitudes of Feminism," *Hypatia* 12:3, 1997:17–28.

Bataille, Gretchen and Kathleen Mullen Sands. *American Indian Women: Telling Their Lives*. Lincoln: Nebraska Univ. Press, 1984.

Burns, Stewart. *Social Movements of the 1960s: Searching for Democracy*. New York: Twayne, 1990.

Code, Lorraine. *What Can She Know?: Feminist Theory and the Construction of Knowledge*. Ithaca and London: Cornell Univ. Press, 1991.

Collins, Patricia Hill. *Black Feminist Thought: Knowledge, Consciousness, and the Politics of Empowerment*. New York and London: Routledge, 1990.

Daly, Mary. *Gyn-Ecology: The Metaphysics of Radical Feminism*. Boston: Beacon, 1978.

Descartes, René. *Meditations on First Philosophy,* translated by Donald A. Cress Indianapolis: Hacket, 1979.

Diop, Birago. "Breaths." Music by Ysaye Barnwell for Sweet Honey in the Rock. *Good News.* Flying Fish, 1981.

Evans, Sara. *Born for Liberty: A History of Women in America.* New York: Macmillan, 1989.

Friedman, Marilyn. "Beyond Caring: The De-moralization of Gender." *Justice and Care: Essential Readings in Feminist Ethics,* Virginia Held, ed. Boulder, CO: Westview, 1995. 61–77.

Gilligan, Carol. *In a Different Voice.* Cambridge, MA: Harvard Univ. Press, 1982.

Green, Rayna. "American Indian Women: Diverse Leadership for Social Change." *Bridges of Power: Women's Multicultural Alliances,* ed. Lisa Albrecht and Rose M. Brewer. Philadelphia: New Society, 1990.

Held, Virginia, ed. *Justice and Care: Essential Readings in Feminist Ethics.* Boulder, CO: Westview, 1995.

Heywood, Leslie and Jennifer Drake. "Introduction." *Third Wave Agenda: Being Feminist, Doing Feminism.* Leslie Heywood and Jennifer Drake, ed. Minneapolis, MN: University of Minnesota Press, 1997.

Hobbes, Thomas. *Leviathan.* New York: Collier, 1962.

hooks, bell. *Feminist Theory: From Margin to Center.* Boston: South End, 1984. (2nd ed. 2000)

Jaggar, Alison. "Feminist Ethics: Projects, Problems, Prospects." *Feminist Ethics,* Claudia Card, ed. Lawrence, Kansas: Univ. Press of Kansas, 1991: 78–104.

Jones, Mary Harris. *The Autobiography of Mother Jones.* Chicago: Charles H. Kerr, 1990. Reprinted in *In Our Own Voices: Four Centuries of American Women's Religious Writing,* Rosemary Radford Ruether and Rosemary Skinner Keller, eds. New York: HarperCollins, 1995.

Kant, Immanuel. *Grounding for the Metaphysics of Morals,* Indianapolis: Hackett, 1981.

Kessler-Harris, Alice. *Out to Work: A History of Wage-Earning Women in the United States.* New York: Oxford Univ. Press, 1982.

LaDuke, Winona. *All Our Relations: Native Struggles for Land and Life.* Cambridge, MA: South End, 1999.

Lanker, Brian. *I Dream a World: Portraits of Black Women Who Changed America.* New York: Stewart, Tobori and Chang, 1989.

Lee, Andrea, IHM. "Moving to Music Not Yet Written: Inaugural Thoughts from within the Paradox." *Scan: St. Catherine Alumnae News*, Volume 74, Number 3, 1999: 9–29.

Lourde, Audre. "An Open Letter to Mary Daly." *Sister Outsider*, Trumansburg, New York: The Crossing Press, 1984.

Lugones, Maria. "Playfulness, 'World'-Travelling and Loving Perception." *Women, Knowledge, and Reality*. Ann Garry and Marilyn Pearsall, eds. New York: Routledge, 1996. 419–433.

Madigan, Char, CSJ. Interview with Sharon Doherty. 14 June 2000.

Mankiller, Wilma and Michael Wallis. *Mankiller: A Chief and Her People*. New York: St. Martin's, 1993.

Mills, Kay. *This Little Light of Mine: The Life of Fannie Lou Hamer*. New York: Dutton, 1993.

Morgan, Robin, ed. *Sisterhood Is Powerful: An Anthology of Writings from the Women's Liberation Movement*. New York: Vintage, 1970.

Noddings, Nel. *Caring: A Feminine Approach to Ethics and Moral Education*. Berkeley, CA: University of California Press, 1984. Segment reprinted as "Caring" in *Justice and Caring: Essential Readings in Feminist Ethics*, Virginia Held, ed. Boulder, CO: Westview, 1995:. 7–30.

Payne, Charles. "Ella Baker and Models of Social Change." *Signs: Journal of Women in Culture and Society* 14:4, 1989: 885–899.

Prejean, Sister Helen. *Dead Man Walking*. New York: Vintage, 1993.

Rawls, John. *A Theory of Justice*. Cambridge, MA: Harvard Univ. Press, 1971.

Reflective Woman, The. College of St. Catherine, Meade, et al., eds. Acton MA: Copley Custom Publishing Group, 2000.

Rothenberg, Diane. "The Mothers of the Nation: Seneca Resistance to Quaker Intervention." *Women and Colonization: Anthropological Perspectives*, Mona Etienne and Eleanor Leacock, eds. New York: Praeger, 1980: 63–87.

Ruddick, Sara. "A Women's Politics of Resistance." *Applied Ethics: A Multicultural Approach*, Larry May and Shari Collins Sharratt, eds. New Jersey: Prentice Hall, 1994.

Ruether, Rosemary Radford. *Women and Redemption: A Theological History*. Minnepolis: Fortress, 1998.

Sacks, Karen. "The Class Roots of Feminism." *Monthly Review 27*, Number 9, 1976. Reprinted in *Issues in Feminism: An Introduction to Women's Studies*, 2nd ed, Sheila Ruth, ed. Mountain View, CA: Mayfield, 1990: 485–495.

Sklar, Kathryn Kish. *Women's Rights Emerges within the Antislavery Movement 1830–1870: A Brief History with Documents*. Boston: Bedford, 2000.

Steinem, Gloria. *Outrageous Acts and Everyday Rebellions*. New York: Holt, 1983.

Third Wave Foundation. 29 April 2002. <http://www.thirdwavefoundation.org/

Walker, Rebecca, ed. *To Be Real: Telling the Truth and Changing the Face of Feminism*. New York: Anchor, 1995.

Williams, Patricia. *The Alchemy of Race and Rights: A Diary of a Law Professor*. Cambridge, MA: Harvard Univ. Press, 1991.

Discussion of "Creativity in Chaos: Feminist Social Justice" by Doherty, Hilden, and Konchar Farr

Several key issues shaped our approach to the article:

1) feminist ideas and actions are important to consider in the search for justice, even as feminism is a point of resistance for some of our students,

2) it is important to engage with multiple differences (race, class, gender, etc.) and with women's lives across cultures and subcultures,

3) feminist perspectives can help us to understand women's contributions and struggles in justice movements beyond those movements that have been named feminist,

4) such understanding can broaden our view of how feminism relates to building a more just world.

With those issues in mind, we made a commitment to dislodging the idea of feminism as monolithic. We see this article as beginning a conversation, engaging diverse women's visions "of a better world, a world where women would enjoy dignity, opportunity, and equality." Students do not have to claim a feminist identity to engage in study that draws on feminist work.

Following are some sample discussion questions related to the article.

1. What have been key sources of information in your life about feminism? Why do you think the word creates such intense reactions from people?

2. What were some connections and tensions between the following justice movements in the 19th century: abolition, suffrage, and the women's labor union movement?

3. Why might obtaining the political right of voting have been a lower priority to many nineteenth century working class women than it was

to the middle class leaders of the suffrage movement? Do you think the women who were involved in the union movements of that era were feminists? Why or why not?

4. Why did so many Europeans misunderstand women's power and contributions in the Seneca, Cherokee, and other indigenous North American societies? How, in this case, was cultural misunderstanding connected to injustice? What are some components of the historical legacy of that misunderstanding?

5. How can an analysis of Ella Baker's social position as a middle class African American woman help us to understand (a) the barriers to her work and to her recognition as a leader, and (b) her particular contributions to justice through the Civil Rights Movement?

6. What are some limitations of Enlightenment views of universal justice based on "an individual, isolatable, separate . . . , epistemological (knowing) agent?" Does the idea of relatedness to all creation, as expressed by Winona LaDuke and Char Madigan, CSJ (Doherty, Hilden, and Konchar Farr, 107–108), challenge Descartes' perspective (92–94)? Why or why not?

7. Discuss the following passage:

   [N]ot all women involved in the second-wave women's movement in the U.S. agreed that gender was the sole, or even fundamental, form of discrimination against women. Many feared that the women's movement of the 1960s would, they said, "fall into the same trap as did our foremothers, the suffragists: creating a bourgeois feminist movement that never quite dared enough, never questioned enough, never really reached out beyond its own class and race" (Morgan, xxv–xxvi).

   What challenges are involved in avoiding such a trap?

8. What difference does it make that Aristotle, Rousseau, and Kant considered women to be morally inferior to men? How did Carol Gilligan's work on moral development change the terms of the conversation about justice and moral deliberation?

9. What did/do Audre Lorde and Maria Lugones consider to be key consequences of some white feminists' lack of attention to differences among women?

10. In what ways has the intellectual focus on an "ethic of care" been a challenge to traditional western conceptions of justice? How might the effort to consider an ethic of care and an ethic of justice together be useful?

11. Rebecca Walker, co-founder of the organization Third Wave, is committed to a feminist justice approach that accounts for multiple differences. "Rather than allowing ourselves and others to be put into boxes meant to categorize and dismiss," she argues, "we can use the complexity of our lives to challenge the belief that any person or group is more righteous, more correct, more deserving of life than any other" (xxxviii–xxxix). In your view, does this Third Wave approach help to link feminism to other justice traditions?

Works Cited

Doherty, Sharon, Amy Hilden, and Cecilia Konchar Farr. "Creativity in Chaos: Feminist Social Justice," *The Global Search for Justice*, The College of St. Catherine. Acton, MA: Copley, 2000.

LaDuke, Winona. *All Our Relations: Native Strugles for Land and Life.* Cambridge, MA: South End, 1999.

Morgan, Robin, ed. *Sisterhood Is Powerful: An Anthology of Writings from the Women's Liberation Movement.* New York: Vintage, 1970.

Walker, Rebecca, ed. *To Be Real: Telling the Truth and Changing the Face of Feminism.* New York: Anchor, 1995.

John Pellegrini is associate professor of biology, B.A., Vassar College; Ph.D., State University of New York—Stony Brook.

Poster/Project Assignment

John Pellegrini, Ph.D.

All students taking Global Search for Justice are required to compose a presentation on a justice issue pertaining to the theme of their class. Students in the Day College present their work at an all-campus poster session on the St. Paul campus. Students in Weekend College and Summer School share their work by posting it on the CORE Projects Blackboard Web site.

To create your poster or project, research your topic thoroughly and compose an informative and attractive presentation. Remember that this is a justice course. Like the course, your presentation should start by defining the justice issue and end with a description of the best strategies for positive action. The body of your poster should review the most significant research related to your topic (cite the work of others) and use compelling visual images to make your points. As you begin your work and again later as you finalize it, consider the following checklist as a guideline. Below the Checklist, refer to the appropriate section heading— WEC/Summer online project or Day College poster—for further format-specific suggestions.

Poster/Project Checklist

Title

_____ Does the title clearly state the justice issue?

_____ Are all authors' names listed below the title?

Content

_____ Does the introduction put your topic in the context of your course's theme?

_____ Is the justice aspect of the issue clearly articulated?

_____ Does the body of the text present enough material to educate the viewer about the problem you have investigated and what is currently known about it?

_____ Do you use scholarly sources and properly cite the work of others?

_____ Have you included compelling pictures and graphs that demonstrate important ideas?

_____ Do you discuss action strategies for change (at the individual and
community levels)?

_____ Have you critically analyzed the effectiveness of different action
strategies?

_____ If you undertook community work on this project, do you
describe it and reflect on it?

_____ Is there a clear conclusion suggesting an action strategy and
rationale to the reader?

Organization, Clarity and Style

_____ Are concepts explained clearly and at a level appropriate to the
audience?

_____ Have you used correct grammar and spelling?

_____ Is the presentation easy to read (uses large font sizes)?

_____ Have you used space wisely?

_____ Is the presentation visually interesting?

_____ Is there a logical flow within and between sections (Introduction,
Body, Conclusions, References Cited)?

Day College Poster Session

A poster is often thought of as a concise version of a research paper. It
should include a thesis statement, a history of the issue, and a description
of action strategies for change. Be sure the justice issue is clearly stated
and thoughtfully analyzed. The following are style suggestions:

- Overall approach for a 36" x 48" poster

  - **Traditional:** Copy individual pages of your content onto card-
  stock (heavy paper) and mount them onto a self-standing
  poster board with rubber cement

  - **Single-sheet:** Create a PowerPoint file and choose the
  File/Page Setup menu. Select a Page Width of 48 inches and a
  Page Height of 36 inches. Then import all of your text and
  graphics into the file while using the View/Zoom menu for on-
  screen viewing. When finished, copy the file to a disk and bring
  it to a professional printing service (e.g., Kinko's) for print out.
  It may take them a day, and it will be more expensive than the
  traditional option described above, but it is easier and cleaner.

- Text content: Include a significant body of text that names issues, players, solutions.

- Image content: Include at least five relevant images (pictures, graphs) with legends.

- Font size: Title of 60 point type, Body of text at 20 point or larger.

- Margins of at least one inch; line spacing of 1.5 for text.

- Provide an obvious sequence for pages/sections of the poster.

WEC/Summer PowerPoint Project

Your presentation must "give itself" to online viewers. Since you will probably not be adding audio narration to the file (though you could if you were very ambitious), you need to include your research findings clearly and thoroughly in text and images. Your graphics will require explanatory figure legends.

- Sequence your slides thoughtfully in a logical progression for the reader.

- Most viewers will see your presentation within the frame of a Web browser, so keep font sizes and images large and clear.

- Consider including links to relevant Web pages that interested viewers can follow.

- Post your presentation on the CORE Projects Blackboard Web page as an attachment to a New Thread on your class' discussion board. This Blackboard page is a password-protected site for WEC and Summer Core students and faculty. It should appear on your Courses page at http://eclipse.stkate.edu.

- After you post your presentation on the discussion board, post a provocative question related to your topic to begin an exchange of ideas within the Core community.

Supplemental Readings

Lynne Gildensoph teaches biology at the College of St. Catherine. She has a masters degree in plant physiology from Rutgers University and a Ph.D. in crop biochemistry from the University of Illinois. Her research interests include the structure of plant membrane ATPases and pond and wetland ecology. As a lifelong peace activist, Lynne serves on the boards of several organizations and participates in hands-on work. "I truly believe that people working in community can accomplish a great deal . . ., and there is a synergistic energy that is generated through this process."

Karen Harris grew up in the Washington, DC area. She did her undergraduate work at Georgetown University, obtaining a degree in history and diplomacy in developing regions from the School of Foreign Service. She will soon complete a masters degree at the College of St. Catherine in Organizational Leadership. Karen is passionate about furthering understanding and respect between people from diverse cultures and promoting social justice, and has made a commitment to always work for organizations that promote justice. She has utilized her skills in training, facilitation and organizational leadership both domestically and internationally. At the College of St. Catherine, she helped to develop several courses that raise awareness about justice by giving students an opportunity to experience pressing social issues. This is done by embedding service-learning and other community action components into courses and building mutually beneficial community partnerships, thereby empowering students to become leaders grounded in social responsibility.

A Call to Action
GSJ and Community Partnerships

Lynne Gildensoph, Ph.D. and Karen Harris

Never doubt that a small group of thoughtful committed citizens can change the world. Indeed, it is the only thing that ever has.

—Margaret Mead

The Role of Community Action in GSJ

Our objective in writing this chapter is to stimulate your interest in using your Global Search for Justice course as a means for learning outside the classroom, which will, hopefully, reinforce what you are learning in the classroom. We are both activists, and have found that working against injustice, and addressing the complex power issues that so often accompany it, has allowed us to grow in ways that are important. Taking action helps us to counter a sense of powerlessness, and keeps us hopeful that change can and does happen. We have found that we *can* make a difference; and so can you, if you want to. Engaging in community work brings clarity to the questions of what is injustice and why should I care? In this chapter, we intend to provide you with information and ideas for getting involved in the broader community outside our gates, recognizing that meeting even one community member or hearing one personal story would probably have a greater impact than anything we could write on these pages. In addition, this chapter is meant as a companion to Chapter 1 in this text titled "Justice and Action: Frameworks and Foundations for Social Change" by Nancy Heitzeg where a broader discussion of social justice frameworks and action parameters exists. Please read Chapter 1 prior to reading this chapter.

To understand social justice, we need to look at social injustice. Social injustice is an institutionalized system of unequal resources and power resulting in some people who are privileged and benefit at the expense of those who are not. Social injustice is not a random event, but is systematic and evolves over time.[1] This results in an increasing concentration of wealth and power unless challenged by people at the grass roots level.

What is an institutionalized system of unequal resources? The following statistics help illustrate this concept. "The richest 5% of the world's people have incomes 114 times those of the poorest 5%. Every day more than 30,000 children around the world die of preventable diseases."[2] Even more illustrative is the fact that these income figures do not include the potential income that is not paid to all the women who work in the home. When a maldistribution of wealth and resources exists, society ends up with a maldistribution of priorities (legislative, legal, societal, etc.) leading to the creation of some of the pressing social injustices facing our global society today. Social justice is a commitment to a re-distribution of these resources and a reordering of the world's priorities. Social justice is also the belief that the freedom to vote is not enough, although it is a start, even in countries where the majority of people do not exercise this right (such as the United States). We also need freedom from hunger, freedom from all forms of violence, freedom from discrimination and freedom from pollution. Social justice is an obligation that we have to the planet and to future generations.

As the Global Search for Justice course was being developed, faculty recognized that it would not realize its full potential without addressing the ability of people to take action against injustice. Reading and talking about injustice is a good way to start, but more is needed. It is just too difficult to hear about the crushing problems that are facing so many people without knowing that there are ways that people can join together to redress wrongs. The faculty committee that developed the GSJ course also considered the action piece to be a legacy of the Sisters of St. Joseph of Carondelet, the order that founded the College of St. Catherine. These women have been dynamic promoters of Catholic social teachings and have taken action with their ministries whenever they have observed injustice, especially in the areas of health care, education, and housing. Back in 1905 when they founded the College of St. Catherine, the Sisters of St. Joseph knew the answer to the question of what one or two people, or a group working together, can do to counter injustice. It is precisely their commitment to justice that opened the door to higher education for women in the upper Midwest.

In 1905, mainstream society believed in teaching women needlework and manners, not philosophy and literature. Reverend John Todd, a Protestant Minister, absolutely denounced the idea of women's education saying *"as for training young ladies through a long intellectual course, as we do young men, it can never be done. They will die in the process . . . . the poor thing has her brain crowded with history, grammar, arithmetic, geography, etc. . . . she must be on the strain all the school hours, study in the evening til her eyes ache, her brain whirls, her spine yields and gives way, and she comes through the process of education enervated, feeble, without courage or vigor, elasticity or strength."*[3] But the sisters of St. Joseph had a vision, they had commitment, and they did not concern themselves with what other people thought of women's education, and so they founded The College of St. Catherine.

Catholic social teachings form one of the underpinnings of the GSJ course. (For a thorough discussion of the history and practice of CST, please read Chapter 2 of this text "Catholic Social Teaching—Convictions and Connections" by Russ Connors.) J. Milburn Thompson, a Catholic scholar, says that "increasingly Catholic social thought has understood social justice in terms of *participation*. Social justice implies that persons have an obligation to be active and productive participants in the life of society and that society has a duty to enable them to participate in this way."[4] Pope Paul VI, in his encyclical *A Call to Action* stated, "It is not enough to recall principles, state intentions, point to crying injustice and utter prophetic denunciations; these words will lack real weight unless they are accompanied for each individual by a livelier awareness of personal responsibility and by effective action."[5]

Faculty who teach GSJ are each charged to develop a course that "links the students' academic experiences with meaningful and effective participation in society" one that allows students to "create public associations through which one can join with others to exercise influence" and to "develop a public role in creating social change in their immediate communities as part of larger contexts . . . [to] respond to global issues through a lived understanding of justice."[6] As you can see, the call to action is critical to the learning in GSJ courses. This action piece is integrated in different ways, depending upon the topic, the faculty member facilitating the course discussion, and the student participants. The range of action types is broad, encompassing educating oneself and others about a particular injustice, letter writing (for example to legislators and corporations), service-learning, action-research, boycotts, and protests, among others. With this chapter we would like to invite both faculty and students to think about getting out into the community and joining with others working to make the world a more livable place for everyone. This article will address both self-directed actions taken by students and the GSJ courses in which faculty incorporate a community action component. Either way, we believe that ongoing reflection facilitated by the faculty throughout the course is **critical** to this process. The actions you take as a student may be directly linked to your GSJ topic (or they may not be), but the learning about action that occurs out in the community is directly linked to the goals and objectives of this course. As an added benefit, you will be interacting with people who will enrich your world—and vice-versa. Working with community partners helps fulfill another goal of this course, which is "to listen to others' diverse interests and articulate a common, larger goal. . ."[6]

Justice Requires Education

How can ordinary citizens begin to confront an unequal power structure? The first thing we can do is educate ourselves. The Global Search for Justice course seeks to counter the tide of the information we receive from the mainstream media by adding the critical question of justice to the equation. Actually, there have been a number of surveys that show that the people who consume the most commercial-TV news know the least about the subjects covered in those newscasts.[7] The research shows that the coverage today is so skewed toward the official version of the story (like the U.S. government version of the war in Iraq) that we never learn anything of critical importance. In fact, the more commercial news we consume, the more we are spoon-fed the party line, and the less we are able to raise the difficult questions. Do we rely on the mainstream media for our information or do we seek out alternative perspectives like *Mother Jones, Utne Reader, Z* magazine, the *Nation, Sun* or *Ms. Magazine* to learn another version of what is happening in the world? For example, when we seek out alternative sources of information, we learn that the proposed FY2004 budget would have the federal government giving $399 billion to the Pentagon. That is 2½ times the expenditures on Housing and Urban Development, the Department of Education, the Environmental Protection Agency, food and nutrition, and job training combined.[8] In this context, how can it be argued that we don't have enough money for basic human needs like health care, education, food, and housing? Is it a money problem or a problem of priorities and political will?

After educating ourselves, the next step we need to take is action. Civil rights leader Martin Luther King Jr. pinpointed the connection between the two when he wrote "education without social action is a one-sided value because it has no true power potential. Social action without education is a weak expression of pure energy."[9]

The Role of Action in a Participatory Democracy

In his book *Soul of a Citizen: Living with Conviction in a Cynical Time,* Paul Rogat Loeb, a scholar connected to the Center for Ethical Leadership in Seattle, discusses the fact that solving common problems with a community helps people to overcome the powerful sense of cynicism that appears to infect our culture and to act as an "antidote to powerlessness."[10] As members of a participatory democracy, we need to engage with others in the act of public work. He says "We've all but forgotten that public participation is the very soul of democratic citizenship, and how much it can enrich our lives." We've become so used to just sitting back and letting others solve our problems, that this idea of a participatory democracy seems to be all but dead in our culture. Although we know that each of you will have different issues to which you will be drawn over the course of your lives, we hope that you will take the risk of working with people, many of whom you will not know when you start, to address issues that engender injustice. Loeb, himself a long-time activist who has associated with others who have devoted their lives to activism, says about those who engage in this fashion, "Social activism gives them a sense of purpose, pride, and service; teaches them new skills; shows them how to confront daunting obstacles; lets them experience new worlds. It offers a sense of camaraderie and helps them build powerful friendships, partnerships . . ."

The mission statement of The College of St. Catherine[11] asks students to develop leadership skills grounded in social responsibility. In her book *Dismantiling Privilege: An Ethics of Accountability,* Mary Elizabeth Hobgood, citing Beverly Harrison, says "Power is good when democratically shared in the service of the commonweal. Democratically shared power promotes self-awareness, self-management, and responsible interdependence. Democratically shared power promotes justice and the flourishing of the whole creation."[12] Harry Boyte (co-Director of the Center for Democracy and Citizenship at the Humphrey Institute at UMN) and Nan Kari (a CSC faculty member for many years and a co-founder of the Jane Addams School for Democracy in St. Paul) state, in their book *Building America. The Democratic Promise of Public Work,* that citizenship "emphasizes a democracy of shared values and understandings achieved through a deliberative process."[13] They promote the idea that the commonwealth (or public good) is best served by active citizens who, through their work, learn the difficult lessons that working in community can teach. They state:

> For people to come to a view of themselves as active, effective citizens means most importantly realizing that civic action is simply hard work that can produce results. It is unpredictable. It means dealing with people who make us uncomfortable. It involves learning to think strategically, taking into account dynamics of power, interest, and the long-range consequences of one's action. Civic action on public questions rarely comes out entirely as we imagine, nor does it produce all the results we might hope for. At the same time, it can have a catalytic effect, generating new sources of energy that are anticipated.

In many cases, over the course of life, the issues we become involved with are ones that are close to our own hearts. Mostly, but not always, they are issues that affect us directly. For example, say you have just discovered that you are living in a neighborhood that has a very high lead level in the soil. You know that lead is toxic to humans, and could affect the development of your children. What do you do? Well, you could write letters on your own behalf to the MN Department of Health, but think of how much more effective your action would be if you knocked on your neighbors' doors and enlisted them to work with you. A hundred letters, and possibly some media action, might get the attention of those who would not necessarily be attentive to your one letter. The skills learned in this kind of action are myriad: how to critically analyze information and write effective letters, how to interact positively with your neighbors, how to engage with media sources, how to organize yourself and others, how to successfully determine who holds the power in a particular situation and how to keep people excited and moving forward in the face of inaction on the part of those whom you would like to move. These are skills that will benefit you at home and at work—for the rest of your life. Working in this manner allows people to connect to power. This is especially true when local groups are able to link to each other and to national groups such that they develop strategic connections so that social change work can occur. Later in this chapter we provide some specific examples of effective action to whet your appetite for getting out there and doing something yourselves. Our hope is that the Global Search for Justice course will enhance the critical thinking and analysis skills necessary to thoughtfully discuss an issue and research and write a good paper which articulates an argument about a particular justice issue, and that you will also gain the skills necessary to make you a committed, effective citizen, one who feels a call to action. Innovative Brazilian educator Paulo Freire, in *Pedagogy of the Oppressed*[14] states:

Students, as they are increasingly posed with problems relating to themselves in the world and with the world, will feel increasingly challenged and obliged to that challenge. Because they apprehend the challenge as interrelated to other problems within a total context, not as a theoretical question, the resulting comprehension tends to be increasingly critical and thus constantly less alienated. Their response to the challenge evokes new challenges, followed by new understandings: and gradually the students come to regard themselves as committed.

You, the student, will access the type of learning that comes through experiences outside of the classroom. Hopefully you will not be the only party to benefit by this interaction. Community organizations and the community members they represent are also beneficiaries. Whether self-initiated by the student or developed by the faculty, our experience has shown us that the service or action performed is a catalyst to building relationships. It is an avenue through which we can explore strategies for justice and realize the critical role of building respect between cultures in this process. It is the process of building relationships that is key to challenging the status quo regarding social justice issues. That is precisely why it is essential to the work, and the resultant learning, that community partnerships be built and maintained. These partnerships, to be effective, are based on mutual respect and a desire to accomplish agreed-upon goals. There are examples of individual collaborations as well as community partnerships throughout the history of The College of St. Catherine. Students and faculty have worked with Hmong adults to prepare for their citizenship exams, provided English language lessons to Hispanic adults on the west side of St. Paul, celebrated Halloween with Somali children in the Cedar-Riverside neighborhood, lent a hand with prairie restoration, visited Somali women at home so that they could learn English, coached adolescents to become active on an issue (Public Achievement), and much, much more.

Community Action: Charity Model vs. Community Partnerships

An essential component of the mission for the Office of Community Work and Learning at St. Kate's (which coordinates classroom-community interactions) is to challenge traditional notions of service and charity, which for many of us, is the most familiar way of making a difference. This kind of critical analysis can be effectively done within the context of service-learning—"a pedagogical model that intentionally integrates academic learning and relevant community service."[15] In *Addams, Day, and Dewey: The Emergence of Community Service in American Culture*,[16] Keith Morton and John Saltmarsh explore the three "paths" of service influenced by Jane Addams (an activist who founded Hull House in Chicago to work with recent immigrants), John Dewey (an educator and philosopher of education who advocated for strong federal government and active citizenship supported by democratic and experiential education) and Dorothy Day (the founder of the Catholic Worker Movement who supported the creation of alternative communities which reject many of the values of capitalism and democracy in favor of more humane or spiritual values). These three contemporaries shared in the political movements and social struggles of their time (late 1890s to mid 1900s) and to greater or lesser degrees, "shared political sympathies, activist commitments, social responses, and spiritual searching in determining life choices of how one behaves morally for a more just existence." They shared a profound sense of the crisis of community and the "unavoidable questions raised about equality, justice, and citizenship in a democratic culture." The central experience that most forcefully and directly clarified the crisis of community for each of them was the practice of charity.

As John Dewey wrote in his 1908 version of *Ethics*:

> "Charity" (conceived as conferring benefits upon others, doing things for them). . . . assumes the continued and necessary existence of a dependent and "lower" class to be the recipient of the kindness of their superiors; a class which serves as the passive material for the cultivation in others of the virtues of charity, the higher class acquiring "merit" at the expense of the lower, while the lower has gratitude and respect for authority as its chief virtue.[16]

Addams, who anguished over what she referred to as the 'charitable relation' claimed that "there is no point of contact in our modern experience which reveals more clearly the lack of that equality which democracy implies." Yet throughout her work at Hull House for more than a decade, she retained an optimistic faith in democracy and consolation that "the painful condition of administering charity is the inevitable discomfort of a transition into a more democratic relation."

In 1932 Dewey restated his position even more forcefully. "Charity" he wrote "may even be used as a sop to one's social conscience while at the same time it buys off the resentment which might otherwise grow up in those who suffer from social injustice. Magnificent philanthropy may be employed to cover up brutal economic exploitation."

For Day, the question of charity is understood on a more humanistic level, "we have learned that the only solution is love and that love comes with community."[16] From her perspective, charity distorted one's ability to know others, and thus endangered community. Distancing herself from the Catholic Church, Day wrote that "there was plenty of charity" but "too little justice."[17]

Despite their disdain for the concept of charity, all three identified "service" as a way to understand the larger, systemic issues that lead to poverty. Dewey viewed service as the path to becoming more educated and effective citizens and Day viewed it as the vehicle to developing our own ability to love more completely. We share their views and believe that charity is needed as a short-term approach for people in crisis but that justice is the long-term solution. We now pose these central questions to you as a student of social justice: What does it mean to be truly of service to others? Does service, with all its contradictions, contain an antidote to the modern crisis of capitalism and community? Can just relationships be developed while performing some of the critical acts of service needed by so many struggling today? In what ways can service lead to justice? Do you need to experience the suffering of others in order to respond thoughtfully to these questions? By engaging in the complex and invigorating process of community work and learning, we believe you will find the answers to these questions and discover a few more questions of your own.

Guidelines for Reflecting on Your Community-based Experience

At the College of St. Catherine, we believe that building collaborative partnerships with diverse community organizations is key to building an inclusive and just process. Thus far, we have developed a handful of community partners with whom we seek to address larger social issues. Students and faculty are invited to get involved with these organizations and others through the Office of Community Work and Learning. A list of current partnerships is available in the office, but it is also possible that you can develop a new connection that reflects your interests. You may be able to use what you learn to inform your final research paper, which asks you to consider and report on how effective action can be used to remedy a social injustice. In the praxis of social justice, taking action and reflecting on your experience are fundamental. We strongly recommend that you keep a self-reflection journal where you can record and develop your personal thoughts and feelings throughout the experience.

In some situations, the faculty member may have already established a community action component for this course and in other situations, you may be asked to self-initiate your community involvement. Either approach can be meaningful for both you and the community organization and its members if you approach the experience with the following points in mind:

1. Do some preliminary reading about the issues, people, or community you will be working with and then think about how useful this information is to your experience. It is important to understand some background and history before you get

involved. In particular, what is the history of injustice and what kind of progress has been made on the issue or in the community?

2. Identify a community organization and/or type of action you'd like to be involved with by speaking with your professor or contacting the Office of Community Work and Learning at ext. 8718.

3. Examine your ideas about what your role will be in the community and whether or not you intend to help or serve others. Is there a difference for you? In order to nurture a partnership with others, we ask that you view yourself as an outsider and not the expert. What does this mean to you? What can an outsider do to assist others?

4. Identify some of your goals or objectives for the experience. If your goals are focused more on doing, try to add specific learning objectives to your list, including, but not limited to, what you might learn about yourself. Throughout the experience, think about whether your role is to accomplish something or learn about the process of building a just relationship.

5. Examine your pre-conceived notions about the people with whom you will be working. What kind of differences and similarities do you think you will experience if you'll be working with people from different socio-economic or cultural backgrounds? At the end of the experience, go back and compare the reality of your experience with your initial ideas.

6. View your first few on-site assignments as building trust and rapport with the people with whom you will work. Nothing can be accomplished without a relationship. Throughout the experience, continue to ask yourself whether you are focusing more on the task or more on the relationship. Ask yourself which is more valuable in the long run. Where does social change occur?

7. Reflect on the role of the community in the organization. Are community members strictly clients or do they also play a leadership role in the organization? What does the organization do to empower or disempower the community?

8. What are the specific social justice issues being addressed by this organization and which approaches are being used to create more justice? Does the organizational approach perpetuate injustice in any way? If you are acting independently of an organization, ask yourself these same questions.

9. Finally, what more can be done to seek justice on this issue within this particular community or group? What is your role in work-

ing for justice on this issue? Do your decisions or actions in any way perpetuate the injustice you are examining?

Working with your faculty member, reflect upon the above questions in writing. What have you learned about this organization, about taking action through partnerships, and about yourself, as you move through the process of engaging in the community.

Some Examples of Effective Action at the Local, National and Global Levels

Can one person really make a difference?

Jane Addams founded the first major settlement house for immigrants (Hull House) in a poor area of Chicago. This house served as a model for social justice and reform—it was a place where poor people in the community could learn about home economics, childcare, health education, and employment. It also became a training ground for social workers. Jane Addams has been credited with helping to pass the first factory inspection act, establishing the first juvenile court, formulating child labor laws, streamlining welfare, and initiating compulsory school attendance. She also co-founded the American Civil Liberties Union and helped to organize the Women's International League for Peace and Freedom. She was the first woman to win the Nobel Peace Prize. That's what one woman can do! Remember that, although Jane Addams was an incredible force for getting social change accomplished, she worked within a community, which she helped pull together. It was this community that was necessary for the nurturance and training of all who passed through Hull House.

In honor of her memory, the College of St. Catherine partnered with Neighborhood House (established in St. Paul's West Side in the 1880s to work with immigrants), the Center for Democracy and Citizenship at the Humphrey Institute of the University of Minnesota, and the College of Liberal Arts at the University of Minnesota to found the *Jane Addams School of Democracy* located on the West Side of St. Paul. The stated values of this school are[17]:

- Everyone is a teacher and everyone is a learner
- We honor all cultures
- Citizenship means making contributions to the community
- Adults and children learn together
- Changes can happen when people work together

The philosophy that underpins the work at Jane Addams is that "every member of our community has something of value to offer and that, through hard work; ordinary people can accomplish the extraordinary and improve our society and the world. Work with public purpose is a source of democratic power, requiring knowledge of a practical 'citizen politics.' The Jane Addams School, with its attention to democratic space and processes has become a vehicle through which people can exercise their collective power or 'civic muscle'." One hundred years after her life, the community work of Jane Addams continues to have a ripple effect, highlighting what kind of impact one woman can have in her community. This is an amazing legacy.

In West Harlem, New York, two women, Peggy Shephard and Vernice Miller, created West Harlem Environmental Action (WHEA) to confront the City of New York's decision to place the North River Sewage Treatment Plant in their community.[18] This was the fourteenth environmentally hazardous facility to be put in this predominantly African-American community, and they were sick of being used as a dumping ground. Around this time, a study called "Toxic Waste and Race in the U.S." reported that locating hazardous waste sites in communities of color was not a coincidence. The authors of the study found that higher income communities of color were more likely to be chosen for dumpsites than low-income white communities. West Harlem Environmental Action filed a lawsuit against the City of New York and won $1.1 million for a community fund and, even better, their organization was empowered to decide if the NY Department of Environmental Protection was doing a good job of monitoring the sewage treatment plant. If it was not, WHEA was given the power to shut down the plant's operations! That's what two women, working to form a community of people with similar concerns and the desire to take action, can do! Our country is full of stories like these. Women are making an impact, in ones, twos and groups, all over the world, even if we don't hear about their actions in the mainstream media. The work accomplished by grass roots groups (large and small) is incredibly important in our democratic society, for it helps foster change.

The Challenge

Hopefully you are now thinking about how you can make your mark as an active citizen of our democracy by engaging in public work. This work is exciting and challenging, and will give you a small taste of what people working together can accomplish. Many groups that start as small partnerships among people addressing similar concerns grow to become national and global movements. This taste of community action may stimulate some of you to become lifelong activists, since you will acquire many of the skills and tools you will need to affect action. Whether you become a lifelong activist or get involved only once in your lifetime, you will touch upon the pulse of democracy.

Remember that this work is not always easy, but that the learning that takes place is invaluable, and, you'll be following in the footsteps of some amazing women. As Paul Rogat Loeb says: "You begin to find out who you really are. The implication is clear enough: we become human only in the company of other human beings. . . . Community involvement, in other words, is the mirror that best reflects our individual choices, our strengths and weaknesses, our accomplishments and failures. It allows our lives to count for something."[10]

For a current listing of our current community partners and the type of engagement possible, please visit the Office of Community Work & Learning, located in #233 Coeur de Catherine. Or, you can call us at extension 8718 and visit our website at http://minerva.stkate.edu/offices/administrative/cwl.nsf.

The Low Road

Marge Piercy

Two people can keep each other
sane, can give support, conviction,
love, massage, hope, sex.
Three people are a delegation,
a committee, a wedge. With four
you can play bridge and start
an organization. With six
you can rent a whole house,
eat pie for dinner with no
seconds, and hold a fund raising party.
A dozen make a demonstration.
A hundred fill a hall.
A thousand have solidarity and
    your own newsletter;
ten thousand, power and your own paper;
a hundred thousand, your own media;
ten million, your own country.

It goes on one at a time,
it starts when you care
to act, it starts when you do
it again after they said no,
it starts when you say *We*
and know who you mean, and each
day you mean one more.

What can they do
to you? Whatever they want.
They can set you up, they can
bust you, they can break
your fingers, they can
burn your brain with electricity,
blur you with drugs till you
can't walk, can't remember, they can
take your child, wall up
your lover. They can do anything
you can't stop them
from doing. How can you stop
them? Alone, you can fight,
you can refuse, you can
take what revenge you can
but they roll over you.

But two people fighting
back to back can cut through
a mob, a snake-dancing file
can break a cordon, an army
can meet an army.

Notes

[1] Cruz, Nadine. 2001. *National Society for Experiential Education Conference, pre-conference workshop on social justice* (San Antonio).

[2] *UN Human Development Report 2002.* United Nations Development Programme.   Retrieved   on-line   from   http://hdr.undp.org/reports/global/2002/en/ November 21, 2003. p. 13.

[3] Rosalie Ryan, CSJ and Wolkerstorfer John Christine, CSJ. 1992. *More than a Dream.* The College of St. Catherine. (St. Paul). p. 1–2.

[4] Thompson, J. Milburn. 1997. *Justice & Peace. A Christian Primer.* Orbis Books (Maryknoll, NY). p. 276.

[5] Pope Paul VI. 1971. *A Call to Action.* The Vatican (Rome).

[6] *Core 399: Global Search for Justice Concept Paper.* 1995. The College of St. Catherine. (St. Paul). pp. 1–5.

[7] Schechter, D. 1998. *The More You Watch, the Less You Know.* Seven Stories Press. New York.

8 Speeter, Greg. (2003). *How the U.S. Military is a Local Issue.* National Priorities Project. Retrieved from http://www.nationalpriorities.org/issues/military/MilitaryLocal.html December 3, 2003.

9 King, M. L. Dr. 1967. *From Where Do We Go From Here: Chaos? or Community?* Harper & Row (New York). p. 182.

10 Loeb, P. R. 1999. *Soul of a Citizen: Living with Conviction in a Cynical Time.* St. Martin's Griffin (NY). pp 1–11.

11 College of St. Catherine. 2002. Mission Statement. (St. Paul). Retrieved from http://minerva.stkate.edu/president.nsf/pages/visionmission December 3, 2003.

12 Hobgood, M. E. 2000. *Dismantling Privilege. An Ethics of Accountability.* The Pilgrim Press (Cleveland). p. 172.

13 Boyte, H. and Kari. N. 1996. *Building America. The Democratic Promise of Public Work.* Temple Univ. Press (Philadelphia). p. 255.

14 Freire, P. 1972. *Pedagogy of the Oppressed.* Harmondsworth: Penguin.

15 Howard, Jeffery P. F., Ed and Rhoads, Robert A, Ed. Spring, 1998. "Academic Service-Learning: A Pedagogy of Action and Reflection" in *New Directions for Teaching and Learning.* Jossey-Bass Publishers. (Indianapolis). Abstract.

16 Morton, K. and J. Saltmarsh. Fall, 1997. "Addams, Day, and Dewey: The Emergence of Community Service in American Culture." In *Michigan Journal of Community Service Learning* (Ann Arbor). pp. 137–149.

17 The Jane Addams School for Democracy website. www.publicwork.org/jas accessed November 5, 2003.

18 Rocheleau, D., B. Thomas-Slayter, et al. (1996). *Feminist Political Ecology: Global Issues and Local Experiences.* Routledge. (New York). pp. 62–85.

Sherry Tousley teaches in the Business Administration Department at the College of St. Catherine. Over the past years, she has trained and consulted with Fortune 500 companies in the U.S. as well as abroad on a variety of intercultural and management issues and has worked with executives and managers from all over the world. As well, she has provided diversity training for U.S. Customs in Canada and several locations in the U.S. Tousley has taught a variety of international and intercultural graduate courses in Taiwan each year for the past five years and has worked with Taiwanese CEOs, executives, and politicians. She has lived abroad and traveled extensively, most recently throughout Asia, and has been actively involved with human rights issues in Tibet and Tibetan freedom. Sherry teaches both TRW and GSJ.

Eastern Perspectives: A Contrasting View of Justice and Action

With a Buddhist Commentary on
The Ones Who Walk Away from Omelas

Sherry Tousley

Understanding justice and action through traditional values prevalent in the Far East requires one to consider the interconnection of all things. One begins by viewing the world as a web of relationships. Common in this part of the world is the value of collectivism, that is, group membership constitutes a fundamental state of being and harmonious membership is a life long pursuit. In this cultural context, the individual thinks in terms of "we," of honoring the group and its members.

Underlying this existential state of group membership is, in many Eastern countries, the value of face maintenance, also referred to as giving and saving face (Hofstede, 1984; Hu and Grove, 1991; Ting-Tomey, 2001). In such cultures, life is a series of interactions and maneuvers in which an ultimate goal is to avoid embarrassing others as well as one's self. Overt expression of contrasting opinions is generally discouraged in such cultures because such expressions could, however inadvertently, cause another to feel embarrassment and thus experience loss of face. In addition, conflict is generally perceived to be negative and dealing with conflict directly is traditionally considered a sign of weakness. This uncertainty avoidance response to conflict is related to the desire to avoid interpersonal risks and manifests itself in an array of other cultural characteristics such as high context communication and indirectness.

High context communication is common in much of Asia and is a means of delivering meaning with minimal or no use of words (Hall). By using nonverbal signals, communication is less direct and the risks of disrupting the harmony or causing loss of face are further minimized. Silence, body language, facial expressions, sighs, and even the setting or context provides meaning far beyond what is normally conveyed by such means in the West. The Chinese language, for example, is structured in such a way that a variety of meanings can frequently be inferred by any one statement, thus further facilitating indirect communication.

The Thai term *kreng cai* refers to the desire to be self effacing, respectful, courteous and careful not to intrude or impose on others. Similar to face maintenance, *kreng cai* also involves the sincere effort not to cause embarrassment to anyone. Anger is generally handled indirectly. If an employee is greatly angered by a co-worker (generally due to face related issues) for example, rather than speak directly to the individual, the offended party may write a letter to the co-worker's supervisor expressing dissatisfaction with the individual (Fieg).

Establishing harmony within the group involves blending with others and avoiding calling special attention to oneself. "The nail that protrudes gets hammered down" is one of many Asian expressions that admonishes against standing out in the crowd. This value is so pronounced in Japan that decisions in the work environment are often made with the use of *ringi-sho*, a time consuming and rather laborious method (by Western standards) whereby many managers meticulously and repeatedly review and then sign their agreement to endorse a new idea before it is implemented. In so doing, if the idea fails, no one person is to blame and thus no one becomes the protruding nail (Moran).

Web thinking refers to the inclination of people to think in terms of the network of people of which they are part in an on going manner (Beamer). The focus with web thinking is on context. This orientation includes providing the history of a situation, putting information in a historical context, and looking for hidden meanings behind what is actually stated. A web thinker might answer the question, "Are we going by bus or by train tomorrow?" as follows—"We will leave early tomorrow morning." To the Western mind, the question asked has not been answered. To the Eastern mind, a search for the *real* intent of the question, the hidden agenda, results in an answer based on her or his guess as to what the asker actually wanted to know. In many parts of Asia, one might not readily ask what he or she wants to know but may ask a question indirectly, hoping that the real intent of the question will be understood and thus answered.

The desire for indirectness can be observed in what Koreans refer to as *nunch'i*, which translates as 'eye measured.' *Nunch'i* refers to the effort to read another person's mind, to probe another's motives, to study another's face to such an extent that one grasps a situation without the use of words. It amounts to using one's eyes to read the hidden agenda behind all social interactions. The ultimate form of *nunch'i* is to sense what another wants and to deliver it without the other ever having to express that want. This kind of behavior is by no means unique to Koreans but manifests itself in varying degrees throughout many parts of Asia (Robinson in *Samovar and Porter*, 74–81).

In some Far Eastern countries, the word "no" is not used. Japan is a case in point. To use the word "no" is considered rude because it is abrupt and might cause loss of face or disturbance of the harmony. One of the values of *nunch'i* is that when used properly, one is not required to directly ask or respond with a negative. Typically in such countries as Japan, rather than say no, one might say, "It is very difficult." while sucking in air. The word "yes" does not have the same meaning in such contexts as it does in the West either. "Yes" means, "I have heard you" or "I understand you" but not "I agree with you" or "I agree to take an action."

What do all of these examples have to do with justice? Each represents what would be considered in the West to be a profound valuing of subtlety, indirectness, and carefulness in approaching others. The concept of fighting for justice in the West is often by no means subtle or indirect but is frequently a head-on confrontation. Gandhi in his pursuit of justice through nonviolence used a model much more harmonious with Eastern ways of thinking and perceiving the world. Further examination of related beliefs and philosophies can help elucidate further the nature of Eastern thinking and its relationship to justice and action.

The origins of hierarchy in the East are frequently associated with Confucius who lived from 551 to 479 B.C. Confucian values continue to have a profound impact on many Eastern societies. An example of his enduring influence is Taiwan, where one must pass a test on Confucian values in order to graduate from high school. Confucius believed that certain power relationships should be maintained within a society. He identified five such relationships, father and son, older brother and younger brother, husband and wife, teacher and students, and national leader and citizens. In each of these paired relationships, the second, according to Confucius, should honor and obey the first. Confucius did not address directly the relationship between sisters. Clearly his perception was that males should dominate (Jiayin). Secondarily, the elder member of any relationship should dominate. Other influential values associated with Confucius are moral cultivation, the valuing of interpersonal relationships, orientation toward the family, and the previously discussed values of avoiding conflict, maintaining harmony and face maintenance (Fang).

The historical deference and obedience of women to men that has been prevalent in Asia is generally associated with Confucius. Scholars Sun Xiao and Pan Shaoping state in *The Chalice and the Blade in Chinese Culture*, "Confucius despised women indiscriminately and placed women and '*xiaoren*' (mean persons) into the same category"(Sun and Pan, 220). However considerable evidence exists that the subservience of women long preceded Confucius. Historians have found evidence that patriarchy came to China in 2000 B.C., for example, when women became male "possessions" (Du Jinpeng and Min Jiayin).

In China today, female infanticide continues due to the strong preference for male children. As well, "kitchen fires," a phenomenon that occurs when husbands and their families are not satisfied with the dowries brought by their new wives, are reported daily in the newspapers of India. Thus while the role of women is changing in parts of Asia, the position of women in the hierarchical order remains in many countries, significantly lower than that of men.

Filial piety is a key cultural value that has emerged from Confucian thought. It consists of honoring and obeying one's parents (Hofstede and Bond). The extent of this relationship to parents may include bowing to one's father, consulting parents on major life decisions, and avoiding the slightest hint of disrespect even where significant disagreement exists. The question of religious conversion, for example, might be handled by asking one's parents permission to convert to another religion and refraining from doing so if it meets with disapproval by parents even when the son or daughter is well into adulthood.

A common phenomenon among lesbian and gay members of Taiwanese society today, for example, is the avoidance of any direct acknowledgement of their sexual orientation with parents. Many feel that to do so would violate filial piety, risk showing disrespect, disrupt the harmony, and could cause loss of face (Chang-Ling, Huang is one of various Taiwanese scholars that believes that homosexuality will ultimately have less difficulty being accepted in Asian societies than in Western countries because unlike some Christian groups that have interpreted scripture as denouncing homosexuality, use or interpretation of Asian sacred texts to denounce homosexuality is uncommon. As well, the key Eastern values of loving kindness and compassion tend to encourage acceptance).

In summary, filial piety promotes the maintenance of hierarchy, harmony, indirectness, and risk avoidance. While Far Eastern cultures are particularly associated with Confucian values, this honoring and obedience to parents as well as the other power dynamics he advocated are common throughout most of Asia.

A cultural concept closely related to filial piety and the Confucian ordering of power relationships is power distance. This term refers to the extent to which a society tolerates and accepts the uneven distribution of power among its members. In many Western societies, small power distance is the norm, that is, the desire for equality and fairness. In many Eastern societies, large power distance is common, meaning that a high degree of acceptance of inequality exists. Part of this belief is that there is an existential ordering of power in the universe and that this is how life *should* be. Large power distance includes the belief that the powerful have special privileges and even that the powerful are a different kind of people, so much so that less powerful members of such societies would likely not even think of talking with someone with power (Hofstede, 1997). In the most traditional Thai settings, for example, people often do not talk with their bosses at work. The boss exists at an entirely different level and should not be approached for conversation (Fieg).

In parts of the East today, particularly China, Confucian values have taken a significant twist regarding perceptions and use of power. In the People's Republic of China, by virtue of the fact that an individual has power, that individual is perceived to have the right to act and the individual's actions preclude judgment as to the rightness or wrongness of the action. This orientation is beginning to change subtly as China moves toward compliance with international trade standards but remains prevalent in many sectors of Chinese society. This absence of correlation between use of power and ethical considerations has significant implications for concepts of justice in China. Western perceptions of justice and the right to fight for justice are not common themes in mainland China today. Generally the powerful are political figures and government officials in China. Their right to use power as they wish regardless of the ethicality of its use and the expectation that citizens comply without complaint are the norms. In fact, survival for the powerless generally depends upon this kind of response.

Falon Gong, a recently emerging philosophy and religion in the People's Republic of China, has demonstrated Eastern justice in action by making use of subtlety as well as high context and indirect expressions to communication with the Chinese government. Key beliefs of this religion involve taking care of the body and mind by engaging in Tai Chi-like exercises, engaging in good works and various other generally non-provocative and peaceful practices. Falon Gong has been so threatening to the Chinese government in recent years however that thousands of followers have been rounded up and imprisoned or killed and practicing the religion is now banned in China. Before the ban, practitioners would gather together in public locations and engage in group Tai Chi exercises, a quiet, innocuous activity. However the locations and dates they chose to do this were locations where the Chinese government had committed unjust acts and atrocities upon the citizens of China and on the anniversaries of these occasions. An additional perceived threat to the Chinese government was that practitioners communicated their meeting places and dates through the internet, a medium that is frightening to the government because communication flows so freely through the system and cannot be entirely controlled by the government. While Falon Gong practitioners engaged in these physical exercises, they were using time and place to make a political statement without any use of words, calling the government into question in the most subtle, high context, non-violent ways. However even this was much too confrontational for the Chinese government.

The philosophy of Taoism is yet another influence in Asia. The central concepts of Taoism are Tao, Yin Yang, and Wu Wei. Tao refers to the Oneness that shapes the universe out of which rises the multitude, the diversity of all being. Yin Yang refers to that great diversity in terms of the duality of the universe and is a key influence particularly in Far Eastern thought. Stated in other terms, the universe is comprised of opposites, which form the whole. Just as day changes to night, weak can become strong which can once again grow weak, and good can change to evil which can change back to good and so on. This awareness of the ever-changing nature of the universe is said to have given Chinese, in particular, great forbearance and strength in the face of hardship as well as caution during periods of prosperity (Fang, 32).

Fang describes Wu Wei by stating, " Wu Wei nurtures a calmness of mind that empowers one to swallow all the confronting forces and then become their master in the end." Wu Wei is a kind of persistent passivity that over comes by letting go and enduring. Lao Tzu, the founder of Taoism, captured this attitude and state of being in his statement, "The softest things in the world overcome the hardest things in the world." In summary Fang states, "Taoism denotes simplicity, contentment, spontaneity, tranquility, weakness, and most important, Wu Wei" (Fang, 29, 30).

Other values prevalent in much of Asia are integration, human heartedness, moral discipline, and Confucian work dynamism (Hofstede and Bond). Among the values associated with integration are interpersonal harmony, tolerance, noncompetitiveness, and group solidarity. A noncompetitive approach is tied closely to face maintenance and harmonious relations since significant triumph over another could cause damage to solidarity and accord as well as loss of face. The popularity of total quality management and in particular, continuous improvement in parts of

Asia is understandable in terms of these values. Continuous improvement allows individuals and organizations to compete with themselves toward continual excellence and in a variety of ways side steps the perception of the head-on competitive approach common to businesses in the West. From a Western perspective, such Asian organizations are definitely competing in the international arena. However, the emphasis on self-improvement toward greater levels of excellence shifts the focus. Japan, Korea, and to some extent Taiwan have all developed major groups of collective, interlocking companies that share expertise and a wide range of benefits, a model harmonious to Asian cultural values but very difficult to establish in individualistic societies such as the United States.

Human-heartedness refers to behaving in a gentle and compassionate manner. Included in this orientation are the values of patience, courtesy, and kindness toward other people (Hofstede and Bond). This cultural dimension is often perceived and mislabeled by Westerners as "Asian hospitality." While these values play a role in the experience of hospitality in Asia, human-heartedness extends far beyond the arena of hospitality and has implications in every day life. Kindly, generous, and gracious treatment is at the core of human-heartedness.

In many Asian countries, in-groups and out-groups play a significant role. In Chinese culture, for example, people who share a common last name may perceive each other as members of an in-group even if they do not personally know each other. Membership within an in-group means that courtesy and consideration are extended. However out-groups are often not afforded this same kind of consideration. Behaviors associated with human-heartedness may not be readily apparent when individuals are interacting with out-groups. The shoving and pushing that take place in Japanese subways may be, in part, an example of treatment toward out-groups.

Moral discipline refers to restraint and moderation in daily living and, in several ways, stands in perhaps greatest contrast to values held in the West. For example, an aspect of moral discipline involves the perception that having personal desires is a negative attribute (Payutto, Hofstede, 1998, 1997). Another aspect of this cultural dimension is the goal of keeping oneself disinterested and pure in relationships and activities and "following the middle way." Often misunderstood in the West, these values refer to finding balance and exercising moderation (Hofstede and Bond). The impact of Western materialism on Asia has, to a significant extent, diminished the perception that personal desires are negative. However, in various Asian cultures, girls, in particular, are taught to have few personal desires. As well, keeping oneself "disinterested and pure" does not mean being apathetic or uncaring. Rather it refers to a value prevalent in

Buddhism, Taoism, and to some extent Hinduism, that of nonattachment, not clinging to anything or any outcome.

The concept of *karma*, common in some Asian religions and closely linked to belief in reincarnation, is the idea that we are all responsible for our lives, that the collection of positive and negative acts and behaviors in which we have engaged determine the circumstances of our present and future lives. If one has lived a cruel, mean spirited life, then that individual's next life is likely to contain numerous challenges and opportunities to learn the lessons that were not learned in previous lives. If one responds to such experiences with even-tempered willingness to learn and actually integrates the learning, one spiritually evolves and also enhances the possibilities of better circumstances in future lives (Adhe, 1997; Sogyal Rinpoche, 1992; Dalai Lama, 1990; Blofeld, 1970).

Karma suggests that outcomes will unfold based on one's past and current actions. If a friend is involved in some personal difficulty, a compassionate response is appropriate. However, attempts to intervene may be meaningless because *karma* is at work. The cause and effect mentality in the West, in which people believe they can intervene to affect outcomes may be perceived in India, for example, as occasions to respond with kindliness but nonintervention because the *karma* of the individual involved will play itself out.

The idea of *karma* has implications for perceptions of justice. Through the lens of *karma*, hardships generally emerge because one has lessons yet to learn in life. In the West we might respond to unfair treatment or injustice with a pursuit of justice in the outer world. One who sees the world through the influences of *karma* may be inclined to focus on the inner world, engaging in introspection, personal growth and spiritual evolution as a response to adversity. Seen in this light, difficulty in life is not a result of injustice but rather an opportunity to transcend one's *karma* and to evolve spiritually.

Confucian work dynamism is an orientation toward life and work. On one end of the continuum of this value, persistence and thriftiness are appreciated. A sense of shame and strong awareness of status differences within personal relationships are also part of this worldview (Hofstede and Bond). Traditional Thai culture exhibits such an acute awareness of status differences that traditionally, one of the first questions two people ask each other upon initially meeting is, "When did you graduate from high school?" Each is attempting to determine which is older. Once one has been designated as older, the younger, for the duration of their relationship, speaks to the elder with terms of greater respect and honor (Fieg).

On the other end of the Confucian work dynamism continuum is a deep appreciation for tradition and personal steadiness and stability. This orientation is closely associated with face maintenance, "balance or reciprocity when greeting others, giving and receiving favors, and giving gifts" (Hofstede and Bond). Giving gifts is an important dimension of relationship building in many Asian countries. The Chinese word *guanxi* refers to the maintenance of an extended network of relationships often sustained through the on going exchange of gifts and the reciprocation of favors. This kind of behavior is crucial to the successful development of business relationships and opportunities in many parts of Asia. Within such relationships, both parties seek each other out for exchange of personal favors. This is yet another way that people in the East go out of their way to look after and maintain relationships.

T. Parson identified various motivations for relationship development from culture to culture, among them, relationships for the sake of what one may personally gain from others and relationships as ends in themselves. Prevalent in countries such as the United States is the tendency to seek relationships for the personal benefit that one may derive from the connection. Relationships formed through *guanxi* share this orientation to some extent. In much of Asia, however, people also tend to perceive relationships as ends in themselves to an extent that may be quite unfamiliar in much of the U.S. In the West, people often say that they simply do not have time for relationships. In Asian, relationship-based cultures, time is simply available to become closely acquainted with others. The traditional greeting in India, *namaste*, is an expression of deep reverence and is a powerful symbol of the value placed on the other and the implied worth of the relationship.

Yet another value dimension that contrasts the East and the West is the Truth and Virtue continuum (Bond and Hofstede). Christianity, Judaism, and Islam, that is, religions originating in the Middle East, advocate the pursuit of Truth as an ultimate goal, that is, knowing and understanding the Truth. Buddhism, Hinduism, Taoism and other religions originating primarily in Eastern Asia pursue Virtue or virtuous behavior. This difference in orientations has several implications. Truth orientation generates a missionary or conversion mentality because part of the pursuit of Truth is to come to *know* the Truth and in knowing Truth, the desire is to share the Truth and to convince others of the Truth. Virtue orientation, on the other hand, focuses on behaviors that are kindly and beneficial to others. The belief in reincarnation is common in many Virtue-oriented cultures. If one lives a kindly life, showing generosity and virtuous behavior on behalf of others, one is believed to evolve spiritually and as well, improve the circumstances into which she or he will be born in the next life.

Those who live by Virtue orientation generally do not perceive that Truth is knowable. Such individuals might hold several different beliefs from several different religious traditions. Some of these beliefs might contradict each other yet the person of Virtue orientation will likely not be concerned about the apparent contradictions. In this worldview, humans are finite beings who cannot know or understand the ultimate Truths of the universe and therefore if some personal convictions contradict one another, it is the result of the finite nature of the human mind. For the Virtue-oriented person, loving, kind, virtuous behavior is the goal.

In summary, efforts to characterize Eastern concepts of justice entail understanding that just behavior begins with respectful treatment of others, with acknowledgement of the group and its importance, with courtesy and maintenance of harmony in relationships, and with subtlety (although in some contexts, such as mainland China, if one is sufficiently powerful, these behaviors are not an expectation.).

To be unjust in traditional Eastern circles is not only to be cruel but also to show disregard for another's face or image, to ignore ancient standards of hierarchy and to disrespect elders, to be blunt or confrontational, to directly argue a point. Many eastern philosophies and religions maintain that any kind of adversity is an opportunity for personal spiritual evolution, not an occasion to fight for justice. As well, several of these philosophies acknowledge the endless role of opposites in the workings of the universe; when life is difficult, a matter of time will make it pleasant again. Thus hardship and even what we call "injustice" in the West may merely be life continuing on its path of perpetual change. Fighting for justice in the West may, in more traditional circles in the East, be addressed by enduring, searching the soul, and transcending past internal limitations.

The extent to which an Eastern culture embraces the role of women as low in the hierarchy, for example, will affect the extent to which people within that culture perceive harsh treatment of women as any cause for notice or action. The subservience and low status of women may be so imbedded in the perceptions of the citizens of a culture that what Westerners perceive as unjust is merely the kind of treatment that women naturally experience or perhaps deserve in life because of the *karma* of being a woman.

The Eastern value of human heartedness and the Virtue Orientation are two concepts that do inspire action. However, the motivating factors come primarily from a spiritual orientation to treat others with compassion and loving kindness, generally not so much from a call to fight for justice. In daily life, and especially when others are suffering, these two orientations call for consideration, care, and generosity. Spiritual evolution occurs through such treatment. As well, one's *karma* can be improved. Such behaviors are good and make a better person of the practitioner while simultaneously benefiting others. Ultimately several Eastern philosophies suggest that compassionate response leads to enlightenment.

Clearly Western concepts of justice have had a significant impact throughout the world and battles for justice are fought regularly in many Eastern countries. However, to see beyond what is, in the West, often misunderstood as Eastern passivity or acceptance of injustice and to see the East with greater clarity, one must understand the ancient and often very subtle orientations that have molded much of the East and learn to rethink some of the most basic premises of the West.

Applying Buddhist Values to "The Ones Who Walk Away from Omelas"

[To be read after the Le Guin piece]

An examination of how the Dalai Lama, a Buddhist and the spiritual and political leader of the Tibetan people, might respond if he were suddenly placed in Ursula K. Le Guin's community of Omelas in "The Ones Who Walk Away from Omelas" will serve to illustrate several of the above mentioned Asian values. Le Guin's dynamic piece serves many purposes, one of which is a conduit for debate as to what constitutes an ethical response to a deeply unethical situation. Applying Asian values to this context is intended to bring their use and application into greater focus and light.

The Dalai Lama embodies many of the values prevalent in the East, in particular, human heartedness, integration, moral discipline, and Virtue Orientation. His concern is not with saving his own face but rather with giving face to others. His focus is on the evolution of all living beings toward greater loving kindness, compassion, and enlightenment. He is also clearly an advocate for helping others understand dependent arising, that is, the interconnection of all things.

Careful observation of the Dalai Lama and his past behaviors would indicate that he would remain in Omelas. He would likely begin by talking with the people of Omelas, by communicating that to leave the child abandoned in its prison is not demonstrating loving kindness and compassion. Then he would thank the people of Omelas, that is, all of those who were maintaining the status quo and keeping the child in these inhumane and cruel conditions. He would thank them for being his teacher, for teaching him to transcend his anger and deepen his compassion.

In time, he would attract a following, people who wanted to be like him, people who wanted to be near him. These people would, in time, join him in taking objects of comfort to the child such as food, diapers, and blankets. Before long they would bring the child out of its prison and would provide comfort and care.

A brief examination of Buddhism will further clarify the actions of the Dalai Lama. According to Buddhist philosophy, the true nature of reality is total Oneness. When we are born into the physical world, we are given the five senses. These five senses in effect splinter reality. They give us the perception of separateness, of this desk and that chair, of your eyes, my hands and so on and so on. Thus Buddhist philosophy contends that the true nature of reality is total Oneness.

Therefore this entire context that Westerners have construed to be reality, the material realm of technology and materialism, ego, and acquisition are all only illusions. In the same manner, all of the bells and the joys, the parades and the smiles that the people of Omelas stand to lose once this child comes out of imprisonment are also really only an illusion. Only after this child is brought out through loving kindness and compassion can the real bells and the real joys of Omelas emerge at last.

For the Dalai Lama, unlike many Eastern contexts, there are no in-groups or out-groups. He would respond in a loving manner to all of the members of this story. He has, in the past, commented that all human beings have been profoundly good in past lives, that entering life in human form is very difficult and indicates that we have all lived previous lives of great goodness. Without such goodness in one's past, human form is not accessible according to this philosophy. He further has concluded that as humans, we should recognize that profound goodness in each other and should treat each other with loving kindness in response to that past goodness. As well, we should treat all life forms in a kindly fashion. Thus no out-groups exist for the Dalai Lama.

He demonstrates classic Asian values in his commitment to human heartedness, his response of tolerance and noncompetitiveness. He does not attempt to triumph over the people of Omelas but to respond by thanking them for teaching him to become more compassionate. In so doing, he demonstrates his commitment to maintaining the community harmony as well.

He also exemplifies moral discipline in his approach. He does not become enraged with the people of Omelas or stage a revolt in the town square nor does he attempt any personal gain from his interactions. He quietly finds balance and sets a tone of moderation in his gradual efforts to free the child.[1] Finally, his approach of compassion and loving kindness in the face of adversity echo the Taoist concept of Wu Wei. Once again, in the words of Taoist founder Lao Tzu, "The softest things in the world overcome the hardest things in the world."

Note

[1] This account of the Dalai Lama's response to Omelas serves as a metaphor for
his actual behaviors and responses to the Chinese government over the past
fifty years. He won the Nobel Peace Prize in 1989 for his tireless response of
loving kindness and compassion toward a government that has murdered over
a million Tibetans, imprisoned and tortured countless Tibetan nuns and monks,
forced abortions and sterilizations on Tibetan women, destroyed six thousand
Tibetan Buddhist monasteries and has made the practice of Tibetan Buddhism
virtually illegal in Tibet.

References and Works Cited

Adhe, Ama. *The Voice that Remembers*. Boston: Wisdom Publications, 1997.

Avedon, John F. *In Exile in the Land of Snows*. New York: HarperPerenniel, 1997.

Bates, Chris and Ling-li. *Culture Shock! Taiwan*. Portland: Graphic Arts Center Publishing Company, 1995.

Beamer, Linda. "Web Thinking," *The Bulletin of the Association for Business Communication*. Volumn LVII, Number 1, March 1994: 13–18.

Blofeld, John. *The Tantric Mysticism of Tibet*. New York: E.P. Dutton, 1970.

Blofeld, John. *Taoism*. Bolder: Shambala, 1978.

Condon, John C. *With Respect to the Japanese*.Yarmouth: Intercultural Press, 1984.

Dorgan, Michael, "Abduction Crackdown," *St. Paul Pioneer Press*. April 18, 2000.

Fadiman, Anne. *The Spirit Catches You and You Fall Down*. New York: Noonday Press, 1997.

Fang, Tony. *Chinese Business Negotiating Style*. Thousand Oaks: Sage Publications, 1998.

Fieg, Paul, John. *A Common Core—Thais and Americans*. Yarmouth: Intercultural Press, 1989.

Gochenour, Theodore. *Considering Filipinos*. Yarmouth: Intercultural Press, 1990.

Gudykunst, William B. and Young Yun Kim. *Communicating with Strangers*. New York: McGraw-Hill, 1992.

Hall, Edward T. *Beyond Culture*. New York: Anchor Books, 1981.

Hall, Edward T. *The Dance of Life*. New York: Anchor Books, 1989.

Hall, Edward T. *The Hidden Dimension*. New York: Anchor Books, 1982.

Hall, Edward T. *The Silent Language*. New York: Anchor Books, 1981.

Harris, Phillip and Robert T. Moran. *Managing Cultural Differences*. Houston: Gulf Publishing, 2000.

Hartzell, Richard W. *Harmony in Conflict—Active Adaptation to Life in Present-day Chinese Society*. Taipei: Caves Books, 1993.

Hofstede, Geert. *Cultures and Organizations—Software of the Mind*. New York: McGraw Hill, 1997.

Hofstede, Geert and Michael Bond. "The Confucian Connection: From Cultural Roots to Economic Growth," *Organizational Dynamics*. New York: American Management Association, 1988: 19–20.

Hofstede, Geert. *Culture's Consequences: International Differences in Work-Related Values*. Beverley Hills, CA: Sage Publications, 1984.

Hu, Wenzhong and Grove, Conrelius. *Encountering the Chinese*. Yarmouth: Intercultural Press, 1991.

Hsiung, Ping-Chun. *Living Rooms as Factories*. Philadelphia: Temple University Press, 1996.

Jandt, Fred and Paul B. Pedersen. *Constructive Conflict Management—Asia-Pacific Cases*. Thousand Oaks, CA: Sage Publications, 1996.

Jiayin, Min. ed. *The Chalice & the Blade in Chinese Culture*. Beijing: China Social Sciences Publishing House, 1995.

Le Guin, Ursela K. "The Ones Who Walk Away from Omelas." In *The Global Search for Justice*. Acton, MA: Copley Custom Publishing Co., 2000.

Lama, Dalai, *Awakening the Mind, Lightening the Heart*. San Francisco: HarperCollins, 1995.

Lama, Dalai, *Ethics for the New Millennium*. New York: Penguin Putnam Inc., 1999.

Lama, Dalai, *Freedom in Exile*. San Francisco: HarperCollins, 1990.

Lama, Dalai, *A Policy of Kindness*. Ithaca, NY: Snow Lion Publications: 1990.

Lui, Pilip H. P., *Taiwan's Presidential Election 2000*. Washington, DC: Center for Strategic and International Studies, 2000.

Lustig, Myron W. and Koester, Jolene. *Intercultural Competence—Interpersonal Communication Across Cultures*. Third edition, By, New York: Longman, 1999.

McInnis, Kathleen M., Helen E. Petracchi, and Mel Morgenbesser. *The Hmong in America*. Dubuque: Iowa: Kendall Hunt Publishing Company, 1990.

Moran, Robert T. *Getting Your Yen's Worth*. Houston: Gulf Publishing, 1985.

Parson, T. & E. Shils. *Towards a General Theory of Action*. Cambridge, MA: Harvard University Press, 1951.

Payutto, P.A. *Buddhist Economics*. Bangkok: Buddhadhamma Foundation, 1998.

Rinpoche, Sogyal. *The Tibetan Book of Living and Dying*. San Francisco: HarperCollins, 1992.

Robinson, James H. "Communication in Korea: Playing Things By Eye," In Larry A. Samovar and Richard E. Porter's *Intercultural Communication—A Reader*. Belmont, CA: Wadsworth Publishing Co., 2000.

Samovar, Larry and Porter, Michael. *Intercultural Communication—A Reader*. Belmont, CA: Wadsworth Publishing Co., 2000.

Scarborogh, Jack. *The Origins of Cultural Differences and Their Impact on Management*. Westport, Connecticut: Quorum Books, 1998.

Solomon, Richard H. Chinese *Negotiating Behavior*. Washington, DC: United States Institute of Peace Press, 1999.

Ting-Toomey, Stella. *Managing Intercultural Conflict Effectively*. Thousand Oaks, CA: Sage Publications, 2001.

Tzu, Sun. *The Art of War*. Singapore: Graham Brash (Pte) Ltd., 1982.

Wang, Jianguang, ed. *Westerners through Chinese Eyes*. Beijing: Foreign Language Press, 1995.

Wangyal, Geshe. *The Door of Liberation*. Boston: Wisdom Publications, 1995.

Ursula K. Le Guin (b. 1929), a feminist science fiction writer, is author of numerous poems, plays, short stories and novels for adults and children. She has been the recipient of numerous Nebula and Hugo Awards for her work, including her popular Earthsea *trilogy.* The Birthday of the World: And Other Stories *(2002) is her latest book.*

The Ones Who Walk Away from Omelas

Ursula K. Le Guin

With a clamor of bells that set the swallows soaring, the Festival of Summer came to the City of Omelas, bright-towered by the sea. The rigging of the boats in harbor sparkled with flags. In the streets between houses and red roofs and painted walls, between old moss-grown gardens and under avenues of trees, past great parks and public buildings, processions moved. Some were decrous: old people in long stiff robes of mauve and grey, grave master workmen, quiet, merry women carrying their babies and chatting as they walked. In other streets the music beat faster, a shimmering of gong and tambourine, and the people went dancing, the procession was a dance. Children dodged in and out, their high calls rising like the swallows' crossing flights over the music and the singing. All the processions wound towards the north side of the city, where on the great water-meadow called the Green Fields boys and girls, naked in the bright air, with mud-stained feet and ankles and long, lithe arms, exercised their restive horses before the race. The horses wore no gear at all but a halter without bit. Their manes were braided with streamers of silver, gold, and green. They flared their nostrils and pranced and boasted to one another; they were vastly excited, the horse being the only animal who has adopted our ceremonies as his own. Far off to the north and west the mountains stood up half encircling Omelas on her bay. The air of morning was so clear that the snow still crowning the Eighteen Peaks burned with white-gold fire across the miles of sunlit air, under the dark blue of the sky. There was just enough wind to make the banners that marked the racecourse snap and flutter now and then. In the silence of the broad green meadows one could hear the music winding through the city streets, farther and nearer and ever approaching, a cheerful faint sweetness of the air that from time to time trembled and gathered together and broke out into the great joyous clanging of the bells.

Joyous! How is one to tell about joy? How describe the citizens of Omelas?

They were not simple folk, you see, though they were happy. But we do not say the words of cheer much any more. All smiles have become archaic. Given a description such as this one tends to make certain assumptions. Given a description such as this one tends to look next for the King, mounted on a splendid stallion and surrounded by his noble knights, or perhaps in a golden litter borne by great-muscled slaves. But there was no king. They did not use swords, or keep slaves. They were not barbarians. I do not know the rules and laws of their society, but I suspect that they were singularly few. As they did without monarchy and slavery, so they also got on without the stock exchange, the advertisement, the secret police, and the bomb. Yet I repeat that these were not simple folk, not dulcet shepherds, noble savages, bland utopians. They were not less complex than us. The trouble is that we have a bad habit, encouraged by pedants and sophisticates, of considering happiness as something rather stupid. Only pain is intellectual, only evil interesting. This is the treason of the artist: a refusal to admit the banality of evil and the terrible boredom of pain. If you can't lick 'em, join 'em. If it hurts, repeat it. But to praise despair is to condemn delight, to embrace violence is to lose hold of everything else. We have almost lost hold; we can no longer describe a happy man, nor make any celebration of joy. How can I tell you about the people of Omelas? They were not naïve and happy children—though their children were, in fact, happy. They were mature, intelligent, passionate adults whose lives were not wretched. O miracle! but I wish I could describe it better. I wish I could convince you. Omelas sounds in my words like a city in a fairy tale, long ago and far away, once upon a time. Perhaps it would be best if you imagined it as your own fancy bids, assuming it will rise to the occasion, for certainly I cannot suit you all. For instance, how about technology? I think that there would be no cars or helicopters in and above the streets; this follows from the fact that the people of Omelas are happy people. Happiness is based on a just discrimination of what is necessary, what is neither necessary nor destructive, and what is destructive. In the middle category, however— that of the unnecessary but undestructive, that of comfort, luxury, exuberance, etc.—they could perfectly well have central heating, subway trains, washing machines, and all kinds of marvelous devices not yet invented here, floating light-sources, fuelless power, a cure for the common cold. Or they could have none of that; it doesn't matter. As you like it. I incline to think that people from towns up and down the coast have been coming to Omelas during the last days before the Festival on very fast little trains and double-decked trams, and that the train station of Omelas is actually the handsomest building in town, though plainer than the magnificent Farmers' Market. But even granted trains, I fear that Omelas so far strikes some of you as goody-goody. Smiles, bells, parades, horses, bleh. If so, please add an orgy. If an orgy would help, don't hesitate. Let us not, however, have temples from which issue beautiful nude priests and priestesses already half in ecstasy and ready to copulate with any man or woman, lover or stranger, who desires union with the deep godhead of the blood, although that was my first idea. But really it would be better not to have any temples in Omelas—at least, not manned temples. Religion yes, clergy no. Surely the beautiful nudes can just wander about, offering themselves like divine soufflés to the hunger of the needy and the rapture of the flesh. Let them join the processions. Let tambourines be struck above the copulations, and the glory of desire be proclaimed upon the gongs, and (a not unimportant point) let the offspring of these delightful rituals be beloved and looked after by all. One thing I know there is none of in Omelas is guilt. But what else should there be? I thought at first there were no drugs, but that is puritanical. For those who like it, the faint insistent sweetness of *drooz* may perfume the ways of the city, *drooz* which first brings a great lightness and brilliance to the mind and limbs, and then after some hours a dreamy languor, and wonderful visions at last of the very arcana and inmost secrets of the Universe, as well as exciting the pleasure of sex beyond belief; and it is not habit-forming. For more modest tastes I think there ought to be beer. What else, what else belongs in the joyous city? The sense of victory, surely, the celebration of courage. But as we did without clergy, let us do without soldiers. The joy built upon successful slaughter is not the right kind of joy; it will not do; it is fearful and it is trivial. A boundless and generous contentment, a magnanimous triumph felt not against some outer enemy but in communion with the finest and fairest in the souls of all men everywhere and the splendor of the world's summer: this is what swells the hearts of the people of Omelas, and the victory they celebrate is that of life. I really don't think many of them need to take *drooz*.

Most of the processions have reached the Green Fields by now. A marvelous smell of cooking goes forth from the red and blue tents of the provisioners. The faces of small children are amiably sticky; in the benign gray beard of a man a couple of crumbs of rich pastry are entangled. The youths and girls have mounted their horses and are beginning to group around the starting line of the course. An old woman, small, fat, and laughing, is passing out flowers from a basket, and tall young men wear her flowers in their shining hair. A child of nine or ten sits at the edge of the crowd, alone, playing on a wooden flute. People pause to listen, and they smile, but they do not speak to him, for he never ceases playing and never sees them, his dark eyes wholly rapt in the sweet, thin magic of the tune.

He finishes, and slowly lowers his hands holding the wooden flute.

As if that little private silence were the signal, all at once a trumpet sounds from the pavilion near the starting line: imperious, melancholy, piercing. The horses rear on their slender legs, and some of them neigh in answer. Sober-faced, the young riders stroke the horses' necks and soothe them, whispering, "Quiet, quiet, there my beauty, my hope . . . ." They begin to form in rank along the starting line. The crowds along the race-course are like a field of grass and flowers in the wind. The Festival of Summer has begun.

Do you believe? Do you accept the festival, the city, the joy? No? Then let me describe one more thing.

In a basement under one of the beautiful public buildings of Omelas, or perhaps in the cellar of one of its spacious private homes, there is a room. It has one locked door, and no window. A little light seeps in dustily between cracks in the boards, secondhand from a cobwebbed window somewhere across the cellar. In one corner of the little room a couple of mops, with stiff, clotted, foul-smelling heads, stand near a rusty bucket. The floor is dirt, a little damp to the touch, as cellar dirt usually is. The room is about three paces long and two wide: a mere broom closet or dis-used tool room. In the room a child is sitting. It could be a boy or a girl. It looks about six, but actually is nearly ten. It is feeble-minded. Perhaps it was born defective, or perhaps it has become imbecile through fear, malnutrition, and neglect. It picks its nose and occasionally fumbles vaguely with its toes or genitals, as it sits hunched in the corner farthest from the bucket and the two mops. It is afraid of the mops. It find them horrible. It shuts its eyes, but it knows the mops are still standing there; and the door is locked; and nobody will come. The door is always locked; and nobody ever comes, except that sometimes—the child has no under-standing of time or interval—sometimes the door rattles terribly and opens, and a person, or several people, are there. One of them may come in and kick the child to make it stand up. The others never come close, but peer in at it with frightened, disgusted eyes. The food bowl and the water jug are hastily filled, the door is locked, the eyes disappear. The people at the door never say anything, but the child, who has not always lived in the tool room, and can remember sunlight and its mother's voice, sometimes speaks. "I will be good," it says. "Please let me out. I will be good!" They never answer. The child used to scream for help at night, and cry a good deal, but now it only makes a kind of whining "eh-haa, eh-haa" and it speaks less and less often. It is so thin there are no calves to its legs; its belly protrudes; it lives on a half-bowl of corn meal and grease a day. It is naked. Its buttocks and thighs are a mass of festered sores, as it sits in its own excrement continually.

They all know it is there, all the people of Omelas. Some of them have come to see it, others are content merely to know it is there. They all know that it has to be there. Some of them understand why, and some do not, but they all understand that their happiness, the beauty of their city, the tenderness of their friendships, the health of their children, the wisdom of their scholars, the skill of their makers, even the abundance of their harvest and the kindly weathers of their skies, depend wholly on this child's abominable misery.

This is usually explained to children when they are between eight and twelve, whenever they seem capable of understanding; and most of those who come to see the child are young people, though often enough an adult comes, or comes back, to see the child. No matter how well the matter has been explained to them, these young spectators are always shocked and sickened at the sight. They feel disgust, which they had thought themselves superior to. They feel anger, outrage, impotence, despite all the explanations. They would like to do something for the child. But there is nothing they can do. If the child were brought up into the sunlight out of that vile place, if it were cleaned and fed and comforted, that would be a good thing, indeed; but if it were done, in that day and hour all the prosperity and beauty and delight of Omelas would wither and be destroyed. Those are the terms. To exchange all the goodness and grace of every life in Omelas for that single, small improvement: to throw away the happiness of thousands for the chance of the happiness of one: that would be to let guilt within the walls indeed.

The terms are strict and absolute; there may not even be a kind word spoken to the child.

Often the young people go home in tears, or in a tearless rage, when they have seen the child and faced this terrible paradox. They may brood over it for weeks or years. But as time goes on they begin to realize that even if the child could be released, it would not get much good of its freedom: a little vague pleasure of warmth and food, no doubt, but little more. It is too degraded and imbecile to know any real joy. It has been afraid too long ever to be free of fear. Its habits are too uncouth for it to respond to humane treatment. Indeed, after so long it would probably be wretched without walls about it to protect it, and darkness for its eyes, and its own excrement to sit in. Their tears at the bitter injustice dry when they begin to perceive the terrible justice of reality, and to accept it. Yet it is their tears and anger, the trying of their generosity and the acceptance of their helplessness, which are perhaps the true source of the splendor of their lives. Theirs is no vapid, irresponsible happiness. They know that they, like the child, are not free. They know compassion. It is the existence of the child, and their knowledge of its existence, that makes possible the nobility of their architecture, the poignancy of their music, the profundity of their science. It is because of the child that they are so gentle with children. They know that if the wretched one were not there snivelling in the dark, the other one, the flute-player, could make no joyful music as the young riders line up in their beauty for the race in the sunlight of the first morning of summer.

Now do you believe in them? Are they not more credible? But there is one more thing to tell, and this is quite incredible.

At times one of the adolescent girls or boys who go to see the child does not go home to weep or rage, does not, in fact, go home at all. Sometimes also a man or woman much older falls silent for a day or two, and then leaves home. These people go out into the street, and walk down the street alone. They keep walking, and walk straight out of the city of Omelas, through the beautiful gates. They keep walking across the farmlands of Omelas. Each one goes alone, youth or girl, man or woman. Night falls; the traveler must pass down village streets, between the houses with yellow-lit windows, and on out into the darkness of the fields. Each alone, they go west or north, towards the mountains. They go on. They leave Omelas, they walk ahead into the darkness, and they do not come back. The place they go towards is a place even less imaginable to most of us than the city of happiness. I cannot describe it at all. It is possible that it does not exist. But they seem to know where they are going, the ones who walk away from Omelas.

Marilyn Bennett, an assistant professor of philosophy at the College of St. Catherine, holds a Ph.D. in philosophy from the University of Minnesota. Her areas of specialty are ethical theory, biomedical ethics, and social and political philosophy. She also has strong interests in environmental philosophy and philosophy of science and works with various groups in the community on ethical concerns in these fields.

Glossary/Some Philosophical Theories of Justice

Marilyn Bennett, Ph.D.

GSJ Glossary

absolutism: as an ethical position, absolutism holds that there are certain kinds of universal truths or universally valid moral principles (contrast with **relativism**).

anarchism: a political movement advocating abolition of the state and replacement of all forms of government authority by free association and voluntary cooperation of individuals and groups. An early English anarchist, William Godwin (d. 1836), was hostile to private property, but contemporary libertarians stress the right to own private property. Modern individualist American anarchists include Murray Rothbard and Robert Nozick.

capitalism: also known as the "market system" or "free enterprise system," capitalism is characterized by a continual effort to expand wealth, an economy coordinated by a network of markets rather than a personal authority such as a monarch, and a dual system of power (a private sector dominated by business enterprise and consumer judgment and a public sector in which the government exercises traditional powers and a limited regulatory influence over private business).

care ethics: a branch of feminist ethics which stresses personal relationships and the value of human connection. As an approach to ethics, this may be a corrective addition to more traditional theories or may be a radical rejection of other theories.

civil disobedience: a strategy of securing political goals by non-violent refusal to cooperate with the agents of government. A famous example is the strategy Gandhi had the Indian National Congress adopt in 1930: a mass ceremonial performance of illegal actions aimed at overloading the police and courts and impairing the credibility of the government. Other examples include the American civil rights movement and Vietnam war protests.

communism: a system of social organization in which property (particularly land and the means of production) is held in common. The modern Communist Movement aims to overthrow capitalism by revolutionary means and establish a classless society in which all goods are socially owned. (In contrast, **socialism** seeks similar goals through evolution rather than revolution). The idea of communism originated in ancient Greece (see Plato's *Republic*) and was seen among some early Christian communities and again in the manorial system of the Middle Ages. After the French Revolution, some small communist settlements were started in the U.S. Since 1900, communist parties have been active in Russia, China, and the U.S.

communitarian: a perspective on ethics and political philosophy which emphasizes the importance of belonging to a community and stresses the community context in justifying moral claims. This perspective contrasts particularly with classical **liberalism**. Communitarian elements are found in the Old and New Testaments, Catholic social teachings, and socialist doctrine. American examples in the 1980s include Charles Taylor, Michael Sandel, and Michael Walzer.

commutative justice: justice in exchange, as when goods are exchanged for money in a market system.

descriptive: a descriptive statement or theory discusses what is observed or found to be true in fact. Contrast with **normative**.

distributive justice: justice in arranging the benefits and burdens of membership in a social group other than punishments (e.g., fairness in taxation and demands for military service, fairness in giving out benefits such as emergency aid or clean air and water).

dualism: a dualistic theory holds that there is an ultimate, irreducible difference of nature between two different kinds of things. For example, as a theory of what exists in the universe, Descartes' mind-body dualism holds that both matter and mind have real existence and neither can be explained in terms of the other. Contrast with monistic theories such as materialism or idealism as theories of existence.

egalitarianism: an egalitarian system treats its members as equals in some respect (e.g., provides equal political freedoms to all, or equal material well-being). During the French Revolution, belief in the high value of equality and desire to remove inequalities led many to argue for a universally equal income. Marx later stressed the need for equality of classes rather than individuals. Note that removing one kind of inequality may create or increase other differences.

epistemology: a branch of philosophy which studies the nature of knowledge and the justification of knowledge claims.

equity: modifications in the application of stated laws which are made to secure justice in light of relevant circumstances in particular cases. Equity seeks to correct defects in stated law in order to preserve justice in the actual situation.

exploitation: in political theory, a situation in which one class abuses the labor of others; more generally, failure to respect rights and dignity, "using" someone to achieve one's own purposes. In Marx's theory, the laborer is exploited by owners who pay less than the value of the product.

idealism: as a theory of what exists in the universe, idealism holds that all that exists is ultimately contained in a mind (human, divine, or both). Things that appear to us to be material, such as ordinary physical objects, are explained as perceptions of some observer.

ideology: a set of ideas, beliefs, and attitudes which reflects or shapes someone's understandings of the social and political world. Often the term is used pejoratively to claim that someone's thinking has been distorted by historical circumstances.

inherent (intrinsic) value: something (or someone) with intrinsic value holds that value in virtue of its (or his/her) own nature, as opposed to being useful toward another goal. Contrast with **instrumental value.**

instrumental value: something with instrumental value has that value because it can be used as a means to something else. Contrast with **inherent value**.

liberalism: as an approach to political philosophy, liberalism is a tradition founded on freedom, toleration, individual rights, constitutional democracy, and the rule of law. In a liberal system, a framework of rules allows individuals to pursue their own goals in harmony with others who are allowed to do the same. Originating during the Renaissance and Reformation, liberalism has strongly influenced democratic societies and capitalist economic systems.

liberation theology: based on the belief that the Christian Gospel demands "a preferential option for the poor" and that the church should be involved in the struggle for economic and political justice, particularly where oppressions have been severe. The movement originated in Latin America during the 1960s. Its aims are to bring poor people together in Christian-based communities and to encourage them to study the Bible and fight for social justice. Liberation theologians interpret Christian tradition from the specific perspective of the poor and marginalized.

materialism: as a theory of what exists in the universe, materialism holds that all that exists is ultimately made of matter. What appears to us not to be material (e.g., minds, spirits) is explained as manifestations of matter in motion.

meritocracy: a system in which advancement is based on ability and achievement. The word was coined in 1958 by Michael Young, who described a government run by those who possess merit (meaning intelligence plus effort). **Egalitarians** apply this term to any elitist system of education or government.

metaethical: in philosophy, a metaethical claim concerns the status of ethical claims (for example, their sources or justification).

metaphysics: a branch of philosophy which studies ultimate being and existence, including "first principles" (e.g., "nothing comes from nothing"). Modern metaphysics tends to investigate the world (what really exists) by means of rational argument rather than mystical or direct intuition.

normative: a normative statement or theory holds that certain things ought to be done or ought to be the case. Rules, recommendations, and proposals are normative (they may also be described as "evaluative" or "prescriptive"). Contrast with **descriptive**.

Rastafarianism: a religious and cultural movement started in Jamaica during the 1930s. Its followers believe that Hailie Selassie I, Emperor of Ethiopia (d. 1975), is the messiah. The movement's beliefs were first articulated by Marcus Garvey and later become prominent as a means of expression of black identity in white societies such as 1970s Britain.

relativism: ethical relativism holds that the truth of a moral judgment depends on whether it is held to be true within a particular culture. **Epistemological relativism** holds that the truth of a factual claim depends on whether it is held to be true within a particular culture. Contrast with **absolutism**.

restorative justice: justice in making restitution for wrong actions (e.g., having a thief return what was stolen or repair what was damaged).

retributive justice: justice in punishing wrong actions (e.g., imposing a jail sentence or fine).

revitalization movements: political and religious movements promising deliverance from deprivation, elimination of foreign domination, and new interpretations of the human condition based on traditional cultural values. The movements are common in societies undergoing serious stress associated with colonial conquest and race or class exploitation. For example, Native Americans perform the Ghost Dance in the belief that the ritual will cause their ancestors and bison herds to return and white people to leave. (In 1890, more than 200 Sioux people were killed by the U.S. Army at Wounded Knee, S.D. because of their protest using the Ghost Dance.)

right: rights are strong moral claims that are socially established; usually a right is correlated with a duty to respect it (e.g., one person's right to life is correlated with a duty on the part of others not to take her life). A **liberty right** is a right to be left free to do something if you choose to; a **claim right** is a right to be provided with something.

satyagraha: Gandhi's approach of non-violent resistance to evil. It involved fasting, economic boycotts, and weaving and spinning by hand.

socialism: a general term describing political and economic theories that advocate a system of collective or government ownership and management of the means of production and distribution of goods. Socialism calls for cooperation and social service rather than competition and profit (contrast with **capitalism**). Early socialist movements developed in Europe during the late 18th and early 19th centuries as reactions to the industrial revolution. Democratic socialism arose in European politics after World War I, with parties active in government in Britain, Germany, Sweden, Belgium, and Holland. It has been a force in Latin America, Africa, and Asia, particularly since World War II.

syncretism: the process of mingling different philosophies, religions, or traditions of belief into hybrid forms. An example is Sikhism, which blends beliefs from Hinduism and Islam.

totalitarianism: a form of government in which a central political authority controls all aspects of life and suppresses expression of opposition. Examples are Nazism, Fascism, and the former Soviet Communism. These political systems were dominated by a single party and ideology, with dissidence suppressed and the flow of information monopolized.

utilitarianism: an ethical theory that holds that an action is right if it maximizes utility (this may be pleasure, happiness, ideals, or interests). Well-known examples of Utilitarian philosophers are Jeremy Bentham and John Stuart Mill.

Some Philosophical Theories of Justice

About the basic concept:

Plato and Aristotle both present justice as a virtue of special importance and as a rich and complex concept. It is not the only virtue, and it is distinguished from charity, generosity, and efficiency. Justice may be displayed at individual, group, state, and world levels. Aristotle is known for his "formal" definition of justice: it means treating equals equally and unequals in proportion with their relevant characteristics. This entails not discriminating among people without good, relevant reason. So, justice questions arise when there is occasion for discriminating treatment, and justice requires treating individuals impartially and according to principles.

Hume described justice as the "cautious, jealous" virtue, one that we could display in situations of "relative scarcity." When desired goods are so abundant that everyone can have all they want or so scarce that everyone is desperate, justice recedes. Justice questions become prominent when goods are available but moderately limited and we must make decisions about the right way to distribute them. How do we decide what constitutes a relevant basis for decisions about distribution of goods? Our ideas vary with the type of good in question: money, honors and awards, help, grades, respect are justly given out according to. . . ? Modern writers refer to "standard conceptions" of justice, most of which are mentioned by Aristotle. Traditional standard conceptions include merit (deservingness), social contributions such as work or money someone has offered or will provide in the future, ability to pay for goods, and need.

Note that justice is a moral concept or value, not a factually descriptive one. Deciding whether an action or situation is just requires us to evaluate facts according to concepts or principles we hold about justice. We cannot simply observe justice and injustice the way we can simply count objects, measure weight, or observe colors. When people disagree about whether something is just, it does not follow that anyone is in error.

Representative Political Theories (embodying various competing conceptions of justice):

1. Libertarian: liberty is the primary good to be protected and distributed by society (Locke, Nozick, Hayek).

Justice requires insuring equal maximum liberty to each citizen. People may, through contracts and agreements, voluntarily consent to give up some liberty in pursuing their own projects (as we do when we agree to work during certain hours in return for money), but only minimal restrictions may be placed on people without their explicit agreement. All are restricted from harming others, stealing their property, or violating their liberty rights since this set of restrictions is necessary if all are to have equal maximum liberty. We can also justly be required to contribute what is needed for protection of everyone's liberties (e.g., we can be taxed for police and court services) but nothing beyond this can justly be taken from us ("taxation is theft": when some portion of our work product is taken without our consent we are in essence slaves). We cannot be required by the government to provide for others' well-being or contribute to group projects we don't want to participate in. We are all free to give charity if we choose and to enter into social and economic arrangements as we decide to.

2. Socialist ("social welfarist"): the primary goods of social organization are material well-being and freedom from oppression, which should be distributed equally (Marx, Engels, Nielson).

Both nature and the history of economic structures fail to produce justice in that not everyone is equally able to get his needs met. The aim of government should be to correct these natural inequalities and historically-based oppressions. We are born with some set of traits and abilities which may or may not be valued or adaptive in the society into which we are born. Having or lacking the qualities required for economic success is more the result of circumstances than of anything we could be praised or blamed for. Oppression arises when the luckier and more powerful are in a position to control and exploit the less fortunate. So, justice requires distributing goods to make all equally well off and as well off as possible. "From each according to her ability, to each according to his need." Often, communal ownership of the "means of production" and other central goods, as well as minimal private property, are called for.

3. Contract liberal: neutrality toward various "conceptions of the good" and equality of basic rights and opportunities are primary (Kant, Rawls ["Justice as Fairness"], Dworkin).

These theories combine the goals of preserving maximum liberty and free choice with concern for equalizing material well-being and power to avoid oppressions. Often the device of the "hypothetical contract behind the veil of ignorance" is used: if rational people had no idea what values they might hold (for example, you don't know your religion or cultural values) or what their economic and social strengths and weaknesses would be (you don't know your health, intelligence, physical abilities, age, etc.), what rules and social arrangements would they be most likely to agree to in advance? Rawls says that your choices under these conditions will reflect your ideas about fairness and that the "veiling" (not letting you know in advance what your values and abilities are) will keep you impartial. He claims the rational people behind the veil would choose a first principle guaranteeing equal maximum basic liberties to all and a second principle (to be fulfilled only after the first is secured) of providing equal levels of material well-being unless some inequality will result in everyone, particularly the least fortunate, being made better off.

4. Utilitarian, communitarian: the well-being of all or interests of the community as a whole are primary (Plato in *The Republic*, Bentham and J. S. Mill [they're also "classical liberals"], Etzioni).

The utilitarian moral theory holds that a person's action is morally right if she could have done no other action that would have produced greater happiness for everyone affected. Utilitarian political theory broadens the scope from personal morality to social justice, holding that justice in a social order is achieved when no other social arrangement would produce greater happiness for the society as a whole.

a) In Plato's *Republic*, a Noble Lie is told to everyone so that all will be happy with their places in society and will perform their assigned functions well. A noble and pure Guardian class determines what functions are needed and which individuals should fulfill them; inequalities of wealth, education, information, and so on are accepted when they contribute to stability, harmony, and prosperity of the whole.

b) Utilitarians Bentham and Mill held that equality (meaning impartiality and equal consideration of interests of each person) was an important component of happiness and a component of our conception of justice, though this did not mean that the interests of some should never be sacrificed for group well-being. Mill argued that, since anything we would feel to be an injustice would cause us to be unhappy (he assumes open information and honesty in the society), there was little practical danger of conflict between utility and our considered ideas about justice.

5. Feminist: elimination of oppression, particularly that based on gender, is primary (Okin, Jaggar, Richards, Mill, Held).

Feminist theories of justice appear in every variety above as well as some more radical versions, but their common element is their attention to the role of gender in creating injustices. Feminists have criticized traditional theories of justice for ignoring the situations of citizens who are not adult or whose gender-based roles create obstacles to their full use of liberty and opportunities. Some recommend special compensation for certain disadvantages and elimination of others through education and transformation of social attitudes. Others propose radically restructuring society (sometimes through use of reproductive technologies) to create options of androgyny. Technology would be developed so that men and women would have equal reproductive options and be free of dependence on each other in this area. Character traits would come to be seen as virtues and vices of humans rather than of men and women (nurturing and artistic qualities, intelligence and practical competence, grace, energy, and independence would be good human traits without regard to whether the human was female or male).

Bishop Raymond A. Lucker (1927–2001) was head of the Diocese of New Ulm (Minnesota) from 1975 until 2000, when he retired due to illness. Bishop Lucker held a Ph.D. in sacred theology from the University of St. Thomas, Rome, and a Ph.D. in education from the University of Minnesota. In 1993, he received an honorary doctor of humane letters, honoris causa *from the College of St. Catherine for his efforts in promoting women in the church and society. The author of five books, he was also a well-known social justice advocate.*

Justice in the Church

The Church as Example

Bishop Raymond A. Lucker

"Anyone who ventures to speak to people about justice must first be just in their eyes." These words of the Synod of Bishops held in Rome in the fall of 1971 provide the context for my remarks concerning justice in the church. I speak from almost forty years of pastoral experience as religious educator, seminary professor, education administrator, parish pastor, and bishop of a small, rural diocese in Minnesota.

I attended minor and major seminaries in the 1940s when the social justice teaching of the church had an important place in the curriculum. We studied the "great encyclicals," especially those of Pope Leo XIII, Pope Pius XI, and Pope Pius XII. We learned of the dignity of the human person, and especially the dignity of workers and their right to organize and to bargain collectively. We were taught the concept of the common good and the call of the church to work for the transformation of society.

As a seminarian I eagerly read the *Catholic Worker* and studied the teachings of Canon Joseph Cardijn on the Young Christian Worker movement. I was excited about the priest worker movement in France. I read books by Cardinals Suhard and Saliege and Abbe Godin. Together with other seminarians I visited apostolic centers such as Friendship House, the Peter Maurin House, Catholic Worker Houses in Chicago, St. Paul, and Milwaukee. I was inspired by Dorothy Day, Catherine de Hueck, and Father Virgil Michel. I participated in special summer courses on Catholic action and on the social justice teachings of the church. I was a member of a small study group of seminarians who met each week to learn about and to apply the gospel message to social issues and to our own lives. Often, the great cry was for the active participation of priests as chaplains or spiritual directors in lay apostolic movements.

I was influenced by "labor priests" like Monsignor Francis Gilligan, who actively supported the labor union movement and who taught leadership and organizational skills in labor schools. (Later on, I was especially touched by Monsignor George Higgins, a colleague and friend, who epitomized clerical leadership in this field.)

At the same time, I grew up during a period when we thought of the church as the "perfect society," meaning that the church has within itself all of the means to reach its end. Nevertheless, we thought of it as a society which had all the answers and knew all the questions and, in general, could do no wrong. We never thought that the social justice teaching of the church had to be applied to the church itself. Such teaching was directed to society, to the world, and to conditions of injustice "out there."

Church leaders blessed the troops and the fleet as they went off to World War II to protect the world for democracy and freedom. In so many parts of the world the church was clearly allied with the political powers of the state. Only a few voices reminded us that the bombing of cities and the indiscriminate destruction of population centers was evil.

Pope John XXIII and Pope Paul VI advanced the church's social teaching and the documents of the Second Vatican Council laid the groundwork for calling every member of the church, especially the laity, to work for the transformation of society. The poor of the world were to be given special concern. We were becoming truly a world church, and we were beginning to see that all people and all of creation were related throughout this small planet.

There was only a gradual awareness on my part, and I suspect many in the church, that work for justice was a duty of everyone in the church, including me. As a young priest I looked at social justice concerns as something that merited the interest of church people, but such interest was a free choice. Some people could address social concerns and others could just as well be interested in some other aspect of the work of the church. My special work in the church was to promote religious education. Others, I felt, were called to social action.

Since the Vatican Council we have come to see more clearly that action on behalf of justice is indeed constitutive of preaching the gospel and essential to the ministry of the church in the redemption of humanity. The task of evangelization is intimately connected with working for justice. The Second Vatican Council called us to look at the joys and hopes, the griefs and anxieties of the whole world as the joys and anxieties of the whole church.

The Poor of Central America

A strong influence on my growing awareness of the call to justice has been the relationship of the Diocese of New Ulm to the church in Central America. The Bishops of Latin America, meeting in Medellin, Colombia, in 1968 and in Puebla, Mexico, in 1979, gave a new meaning and vision to the concept of a preferential option for the poor.

In the early 1960s Pope John XXIII urged all of the dioceses in North America to send missionaries to Central and South America. It was a call for a more just distribution of the personnel and resources of the church. The Diocese of New Ulm accepted an invitation to staff and support the parish of San Lucas Toliman in Guatemala.

The blessings that have returned to the Diocese of New Ulm through this over twenty-five-year commitment have been enormous. One of the most important is that the people of the Diocese of New Ulm have learned so much about poverty, injustice, hunger, oppression, torture, and killing. We have learned about the value of the widespread distribution of the land and the human rights of every individual. We have come to know of a church, which had aligned itself with the rich and the powerful, now having turned to the poor and oppressed, becoming a church of martyrs.

The church in Guatemala became for us a "church as example," calling us to look at our lifestyle, to work for justice and peace, to commit ourselves to nonviolence, to value human life and human rights.

In all of this we see the social justice teaching of the church as calling Christians to work for the transformation of the world. Only in recent years have we begun to look at the church itself as in need of reform. I was in Rome as a graduate student in theology during the Second Vatican Council. I remember how surprised I was when I learned that the church could, indeed had to, reform itself.

We came to realize more clearly that the church which speaks for the sacredness of all human life, for justice, for the poor, for peace must indeed be concerned about justice within its own life and institutions. We were being led by the Holy Spirit to reform and renewal within the church itself. The church must be an example of how members of society ought to live.

How are we as a church community to apply the message of the social encyclicals and the church's social teaching to our own institutions and practice? I write these pages as a few pastoral reflections drawing from my life and experience. I hope to shed a little light on this question by reviewing what is said in some recent church documents about justice in the church and by outlining the rights of church members as contained in council documents and in the Code of Canon Law. Further, I will offer some reflections on the nature of the church and consider a few examples of issues of justice within the church.

1971 Synod

The church must itself strive to be a just institution if it desires its social teaching to be taken seriously by others. I refer to the synodal document, *Justice in the World* (particularly the third section, "The Practice of Justice: The Church's Witness"), where the bishops call for an "examination of the modes of acting and of the possessions and lifestyle found within the church itself." The words with which I began this essay ring out: "Anyone who ventures to speak to people about justice must first be just in their eyes," say the synodal delegates from all over the world. Strong words indeed!

The document's words continue to prod us and perhaps make us uneasy. We are urged to promote and to secure the rights of persons within the church. We are reminded of our responsibility to give to those who work within the church a "sufficient livelihood." Lay employees are to be given "fair wages and a system for promotion." Lay people are to "exercise more important functions with regard to Church property" and "share in its administration."

Women are to "have their own share of responsibility and participation" in the life of the church. The church is to recognize "everyone's right to suitable freedom of expression and thought," including "the right of everyone to be heard in a spirit of dialogue." Church members have a right to proper and speedy judicial procedures. All church members have a right to "share in the drawing up of decisions," and such participation is to be fostered through "the setting up of councils at all levels."

With regard to "temporal possessions" and "positions of privilege," "it must never happen that the evangelical witness which the Church is required to give becomes ambiguous." "Our faith demands of us a certain sparingness in use, and the Church is obliged to live and administer its own goods in such a way that the gospel is proclaimed to the poor."

Finally, the lifestyle of all church members is to exemplify "that sparingness with regard to consumption which we preach to others as necessary in order that so many millions of hungry people throughout the world may be fed." While strides have been taken in some of these areas, we must admit that we have a long way to go.

Economic Pastoral

Fifteen years after the 1971 Synod, the United States bishops issued a pastoral letter on Catholic social teaching and the United States economy, *Economic Justice for All*. In paragraphs 347–58 of the pastoral, the bishops speak of "the Church as economic actor," and they reiterate the Synod's teaching that the church's own life and action must reflect the justice it preaches. The bishops recognize that "on the parish and diocesan level, through its agencies and institutions, the Church employs many people . . . has investments . . . extensive properties for worship and mission."

The bishops stress that "all the moral principles that govern the just operation of any economic endeavor apply to the Church and its agencies and institutions; indeed the Church should be exemplary." The notion of the church as example runs through this part of the pastoral letter. The church in all its institutions from the Holy See to small, rural parishes, from dioceses to families, from schools and universities to hospitals and nursing homes must teach justice, practice justice, and exemplify justice.

The institutional church is challenged to give just salaries and benefits to its employees, and church members are reminded of their responsibility to donate a just share of their time, talent, and treasure toward the church's support. Obviously the institutional church cannot meet its obligations in justice if its members do not meet theirs. Church institutions are urged to "fully recognize the rights of employees to organize and bargain collectively," and "to adopt new fruitful modes of cooperation."

Attention is called to the "continuing discrimination against women throughout the Church and society, especially reflected in both the inequities of salaries between women and men and in the concentration of women in jobs at the lower end of the wage scale." The church is also reminded of its responsibility to be a just steward of its properties and investments, of its "special call to be a servant of the poor, the sick, and the marginalized," and of its obligation "through all its members individually and through its agencies . . . to alleviate injustices that prevent some from participating fully in economic life" (the Campaign for Human Development is an example of the church's action in this area).

So, the church is called "to become a model of collaboration and participation," a model of justice. Church teaching regarding justice should reflect that the church is aware of its vocation to practice the justice it preaches. Sometimes, this is not the case.

The Congregation for Catholic Education, for example, issued a set of guidelines in 1988 for the study and teaching of the church's social doctrine in the formation of priests. It is an excellent summary of Catholic church teaching on social justice and social action. But, the ninety-one-page document does not mention the issue of justice in the church.

Rights in the Church

A centerpiece of the social justice teaching of the church is its concern for the rights of all persons. The revised Code of Canon Law issued in 1983 has a section that outlines the obligations and rights of all of the faithful, clergy and lay, and the obligations and rights of the lay Christian faithful.

This list of the rights of the Christian faithful flows from the Second Vatican Council's understanding of the church as the people of God. Every member of the church is called to participate actively in the life and mission of the church, and this call stems from baptism and confirmation. This foundational teaching of the Council is found in several places in the Council documents (*Lumen Gentium*, 33; *Apostolicam AActuositatem*, 3, 1522, 24; *Presbyterorum Ordinis*, 9).

The basis of all rights in the church is baptism. "As members, they share a common dignity from their rebirth in Christ." They are given the same grace and are called to the same life of holiness. "They possess in common one salvation, one hope and one undivided charity. Hence, there is in Christ and in the Church no inequality on the basis of race or nationality, social condition or sex" (*Lumen Gentium*, 32).

All Christians are equal, as the Second Vatican Council stated. The Second Vatican Council document on the church stated that "every type of discrimination, whether social or cultural, whether based on sex, race, color, social condition, language or religion, is to be overcome and eradicated as contrary to God's interest" (*Gaudium et Spes*, 29).

Throughout the Council documents there are other references to rights in the church and this led, after the Council, to the development of lists of rights in the church. In the project of revising and bringing up to date the Code of Canon Law, there was a proposal to add to the code a "fundamental law" of the church, which would list among other things the rights of members of the church.

Code of Canon Law

There is a list of rights contained in the Code of Canon Law in the section on the people of God. The Christian faithful are all called to holiness (c. 210) to proclaim the message of God and to spread the gospel (c. 211). Every member of the church has a right to receive the word of God and the sacraments and has a right to worship (c. 213, 214). Members have a right to establish and to participate in associations (c. 215).

All the Christian faithful "in accord with the knowledge, competence and preeminence which they possess . . . have the right and even at times a duty to manifest to the sacred pastors their opinion on matters which pertain to the good of the Church, and they have a right to make their opinion known to the other Christian faithful, with due regard for the integrity of faith and morals and reverence toward their pastors, and with consideration for the common good and dignity of persons" (c. 212). Every member has a right to participate in the mission of the church (c. 216).

All of the Christian faithful have a right to their good name and to protect their own privacy and to vindicate and defend their rights in the church before a competent ecclesiastical court (c. 220, 221).

In addition to these rights, which all Christians enjoy, lay people in the church have additional rights. They have a special duty to perfect the order of temporal affairs with the spirit of the gospel, the right to educate their children, to be installed in certain ministries. If they are church employees, they have the right to decent remuneration by which they are able to provide for their own needs and for those of their family. They likewise have a right to a pension, social security, and health benefits (c. 231). Other rights are acknowledged for members of the church throughout the Code of Canon Law.

Thus, there has been a growing awareness in the life of the church during these last one hundred years of human rights and the gradual recognition and application of those rights in the life of the church itself.

The Church: A Mystery, Human and Divine

Before considering specific issues of justice within the church, I want to reflect on some aspects of the nature of the church.

The church is a sacrament, a mystery. Jesus is the head of the church; the holy Spirit is the life of the church; and we are its members, with all of our weaknesses, sinfulness, ignorance, and mistakes. While the church is the body of Christ, it is poor, broken, human. Though called the Spotless Bride of Christ, the church can be unjust. Though marked by holiness, the church can be unholy. The members and leaders of the church are all human beings, born in original sin, prone to sin and mistakes, yet capable of growth and holiness.

It is hard for us to recognize our own sinfulness, sinfulness in the church. There can be a tendency to divinize the church. One effect of that is to minimize or even deny the way in which our doctrine, worship, and pastoral practice are historically conditioned and culturally limited. The principle of the incarnation has us take seriously the implications of human fallibility, vulnerability, change, growth, creativity, and flesh. All this within a community which Jesus promised to be with and to guide in all truth!

Karl Rahner often reminded us that the church needs to recognize its mistakes. It does grow; it always needs to reform. There have been many changes in noninfallible but authentic teachings in the church. This should not surprise us. We have changed in our teaching about women,

about race, about human liberty, about Galileo, about the Mosaic author-
ship of the Pentateuch, about torture, about who is a member of the
church, about abstaining from sexual relations before going to communion, about church and state.

According to *Mysterium Ecclesiae* (Congregation for the Doctrine of the
Faith, 1973), we are to recognize the historical, time-conditioned character of church pronouncements. Though the church can teach infallibly,
doctrinal definitions may be expressed at first incompletely, and may be
limited by the language and by changeable conceptions of a given time.
The gospel needs to be incarnated in every culture, in every time, in every
social and economic system.

The social teaching of the church continues to grow as well. In celebrating one hundred years of *Rerum Novarum*, we recognize that today it is an
inadequate document and superceded by the Second Vatican Council's
Constitution on the Church in the Modern World and the two social encyclicals of Pope John Paul II, *Laborem Exercens* (1981) and *Sollicitudo Rei
Socialis* (1987). Catholic social teaching must continually keep pace with
changes and needs in society.

Once we say as official church teaching that authentic but noninfallible
teaching can change (as we did in the Vatican II *Declaration on Religious
Liberty*), once we say all people are equal, all people have rights, then we
set ourselves on a course, a trajectory, that is not easily stopped or
changed. We are then willing to say that we have made mistakes and we
have grown in applying Catholic social teaching within the church. With
that in mind, I now want to focus on a number of particular issues.

Salaries and Benefits of Lay Employees

In recent years increasing numbers of lay persons are exercising ministerial roles traditionally carried out by priests, sisters, and brothers. People
give their talents, their gifts, their energies, their lives to promote the mission of the church. For this, they are supported by parishes, institutions,
dioceses, and religious congregations.

In 1986 the National Association of Church Policy Administrators published a position paper, "Just Treatment for Those Who Work for the
Church," calling on "Church-related institutions to model just treatment
for all persons working for them." Among the personnel practices recommended were clearly written personnel policies, involvement of
employees in decisions affecting them, just salaries and benefits, fair and
honest performance evaluations, grievance and termination procedures,
and the right to join employee associations.

The bishops' pastoral on economics identified salaries and benefits of lay
employees as a matter of special concern. They committed themselves to

the notion that all those who work for the church should receive sufficient livelihood and social benefits and called on all of the members of the church to recognize that this would call for increased contributions on their part.

In 1987 the National Conference of Diocesan Directors of Religious Education undertook a research project on just wages and benefits for lay and religious church employees. Fifteen other national Catholic organizations joined the project. The purpose of the study was to give guidance to church employers on decisions affecting salaries and benefits for those who work in the church. The study revealed that, depending upon what model of compensation was followed, church employees received anywhere from seventeen to forty percent below what was needed for a family to live in basic dignity or in comparison with people in similar positions.

Catholic schools throughout the country struggle to continue to provide quality education and at the same time bring pay scales to a more equitable level in relationship to professional scales in the public schools. Base starting salaries for teachers in Catholic schools are frequently sixty to seventy percent of what their counterparts in public schools make. After twenty or more years a Catholic school teacher is likely to be making fifty percent of a public school teacher's salary. The Catholic school teacher must be willing to work for less and be committed to this challenging and rewarding ministry. Still, justice demands that they receive "a sufficient livelihood," "fair wages," and "a system for promotion" (*Justice in the World*, 351).

Stipends and Retirement of Religious

Another issue of justice in the church concerns the retirement of members of religious congregations, especially women religious. In November of 1987 the bishops of the United States voted to have a national, annual collection to raise retirement funds for religious congregations.

I believe that all of us have a responsibility and should be given an opportunity to contribute to the support of retired religious men and women, who have given so much toward building up the church in our country.

We have been told by the Tri-Conference Retirement Project that religious communities were 2.9 billion dollars short in their retirement funds. In the past we simply did not provide for the retirement costs of religious women. Religious communities had set little aside for retirement. The stipend given to an active sister was hardly enough to provide even basic necessities much less put aside something for future retirement.

For ten or twelve years some dioceses, including the Diocese of New Ulm, had been regularly consulting with representatives of religious communities and stipends were instituted for sisters that took into account their needs, including the need to support elderly members of their communities. This has not been the practice throughout the country. The average stipend given to religious women in this country last year was something like $8,000. Religious women tell us that the minimum stipend needed is in the neighborhood of $15,000, not including housing, transportation, continuing education, and retirement needs. If the approximately fifty thousand active sisters received an average of $5,000 more per year, that would add 250 million dollars annually to the support of retired religious women. In ten years we would be closer to meeting the 2.9 billion dollar past service liability.

The Catholic people of the United States have been generous in supporting the national collection for the retirement needs of religious, and that effort needs continued support. We need to recognize, however, that the ten-year collection, even if it continues at a generous level, will never meet the needs or solve the longterm problem. It can only hope to generate ten percent of the support that is really needed.

A more just solution to the problem, in my opinion, calls for larger basic stipends or larger compensation packages based on some other system from parishes and institutions in which the sisters are employed throughout the country.

The sisters that I talk to are not asking for charity. They are asking for basic justice. The pastoral of the bishops of the United States on economics said, "It would be a breach of our obligations to these dedicated women and men who taught in our schools, worked in our hospitals, with very little remuneration, to let them, or their communities, face retirement without adequate funds."

Racism in the Church

While church teaching has developed with regard to racial justice, the church needs more effectively to practice such justice. When I attended the seminary in the 1940s and 1950s, it was almost impossible for a young black man or woman to attend a seminary or join a religious community. I was proud, I remember, that the St. Paul Seminary admitted black students, but this was an exception. They could join a few religious communities; some of them were set up especially for black candidates.

The official church at every level has condemned racism and the actions of racists. For example, the Pontifical Peace and Justice Commission declared, "Racism and racist acts must be condemned. The Church wants first and foremost to change racist attitudes including those within her own communities" (November 3, 1988, *Origins*, February 23, 1989). Pope

John Paul II has led the way in clear, unambiguous teaching on racism and discrimination.

Yet we have been told over and over again by African Americans, Hispanics, Native Peoples, and others that racism is found within the Catholic church in the United States. The same racism that exists in society can be found in the church. Some efforts have been made in recent years to overcome racism and to change the attitudes of Catholic people.

In their pastoral letter, "What We Have Seen and Heard," the African-American bishops forcefully remind us, "Blacks and other minorities still remain absent from many aspects of Catholic life and are only meagerly represented on the decision-making level. . . . This racism, at once subtle and masked, still festers within our Church as within our society. This stain of racism on the American Church continues to be a source of pain and disappointment to all, both Black and White, who love her and desire her to be the Bride of Christ" (p. 20).

Sexism in the Church

In 1981 I joined Bishop Victor Balke in issuing a pastoral letter to raise awareness among our people of Christian feminism and the sin of sexism. We also hoped that our pastoral letter would lead to a greater and fully just participation on the part of women in the life of the church.

We defined sexism as "the erroneous belief or conviction or attitude that one sex, male or female, is superior to the other in the very order of creation or by the very nature of things." We identified sexism as immoral and a social evil contrary to gospel teaching. "Sexism is a lie," we said. "It is a grievous sin diminished in its gravity only by indeliberate ignorance or by pathological fear." We were led to issue this pastoral letter by the growing awareness of a pervasive attitude of sexism in society and in the church.

In 1975 Pope Paul VI, speaking of the United Nations International Women's Year, noted that one of the aims of the year was "winning equal rights for women," and declared that "there are still millions of women who do not enjoy basic rights." He called for an examination of conscience. He said, "The examination has to do with the manner in which rights and duties of both men and women are respected and fostered and also with the participation of women in the life of society on one hand and in the life and mission of the Church on the other."

The very cornerstone of Catholic social teaching is that every human being is created equal and every person has human rights. Jesus demonstrated this to us by his life and teaching. Women accompanied him in his ministry. Jesus taught Mary, the sister of Martha, as a rabbi instructed a disciple. Jesus revealed himself as Messiah to the Samaritan woman, and she became one of the first evangelizers. He touched women, healed them, forgave them. Women were among the first to whom Jesus revealed his resurrection. Women took an active part in the early life of the church. "For all of you who were baptized into Christ have clothed yourselves with Christ," Paul wrote to the Galatians. "There is neither Jew nor Greek, there is neither slave nor free person, there is not male and female; for you are all one in Christ Jesus" (Gal 3: 27–28).

Through a whole series of historical and cultural circumstances society continued to regard women as unequal, as property, as unclean, as tempters of men. Such sinful attitudes entered into the very fabric of church life. Only in recent years has our awareness of sexism been raised, mostly through the development of the feminist movement and the many Christian feminists and women theologians who have examined their experience in the light of the gospel message. We, as a church, need to listen to their voices, examine our conscience as Pope Paul VI asked us, and apply the social justice teaching of the church in this very important area to our lives, to our institutions and through our daily practice.

In the consultation leading to the development of the Bishops' Pastoral Response to Women's Concerns, women from around the country told us that sexism is found at every level of the church. The church is a patriarchy; that is, an institution under the rule of men. It is a male-led and male-dominated church, rather than a discipleship of equals.

The second draft of the pastoral response concludes by saying, "Equality is not a privilege to be earned by women, but a right which belongs to them by virtue of their creation in the image of God." Equality leads to acceptance, respect, sharing, mutuality, appreciation, friendship and partnership; inequality to domination, superiority, disrespect, lack of appreciation, devaluing and stereotyping—in a word, to sexism. The bishops pledge themselves to work for the elimination of every trace of sexism or unequal treatment. They promise to "oppose the destructive power of sexism" by working to change structures, attitudes, and misconceptions that perpetuate this evil.

Some efforts have been made to mitigate this injustice, especially now that awareness has been raised on the issue. Still, women are not allowed certain positions of power and leadership in the church, and sexist language continues to pervade church hymns, documents, and pronouncements. The denial of women to serve at the liturgy continues to convey second-class status, even though they can participate as song leaders, cantors, lectors, and extraordinary ministers of the Holy Eucharist. Pressure will continue to be made on church leadership and on church members in general to work toward the full equality of men and women in church and society.

Due Process

It is one thing to have church statements and canon law speaking about rights of people in the church. It is another to set up procedures that will protect individuals who have been treated unjustly by either another member of the church or by one of its institutions.

Due process in the church provides the means to guarantee fundamental rights and freedom. It is a method of resolving disputes by setting forth and protecting the rights of persons involved in a conflict with church personnel, institutions, or those who have been wronged by administrative decisions. It is a protection against arbitrary exercise of power.

Certain rights are protected by due process: the right to fair employment practices, the right to be informed of proposed actions which affect individuals, the right of a person to be heard in defense of their rights, the right in the face of accusation to confront one's accusers, and the right not to be judged by one's accusers.

Due process procedures have been set up in over half of the dioceses in the United States. It is an in-house and in-family process. Where a due process system has been established in a diocese, usually two services are available: conciliation and arbitration. Most disputes can be resolved through conciliation. The two parties of the dispute come together with a third party, a conciliator, to resolve a problem. The process for arbitration is more formal and difficult and adds an important dimension that the two parties are willing to abide by the decision of the arbitrator.

Experience has shown that most of the conflicts presented to the diocesan due process boards have been conflicts around the hiring and firing of teachers and other church personnel and accusations about the arbitrary exercise of authority by pastors. Actually, where due process procedures are in place, few cases have been initiated. The availability of due process in the church is not yet widely known, and the very existence of due process procedures makes people more aware of the importance of treating others fairly. A committee on arbitration has been established by the National Conference of Catholic Bishops to resolve conflicts where a bishop or one of the conference agencies is involved.

There are still many widespread complaints that such procedures are needed in the offices in Rome as well, especially in regard to the treatment of theologians and priests who are seeking laicization.

Ordination of Women

One of the most divisive and controversial issues facing the church as we enter the third millennium is the ordination of women. The declaration issued by the Congregation for the Doctrine of the Faith in 1976, "On the

Question of the Admission of Women to the Ministerial Priesthood," said that the church "in fidelity to the example of the Lord, does not consider herself authorized to admit women to priestly ordination" (5). The actions of Jesus and the practice of the apostles are seen as normative.

Karl Rahner believed that the practice of the church can be understood as a human tradition and not as divine revelation and, therefore, can be changed.

The Pontifical Biblical Commission in 1976 declared that the New Testament by itself does not permit us to settle whether women can be ordained priests. A report from the American Biblical Association came to a similar conclusion.

It is necessary that this issue be open to discussion. The very fact that we are not able to teach openly about it or even discuss it is a sign of injustice in the church. This is such a critical issue in the church that it deserves full and open study by the best minds in the church.

As we celebrate the one hundredth anniversary of modern Catholic social teaching, we can be proud of a rich heritage. Justice and human rights have been promoted—this we celebrate. We continue to be challenged by our own teaching. The words of Jesus still echo, "This is the time of fulfillment. The reign of God is at hand! Reform your lives and believe in the gospel!" (Mk 1: 15).

bell hooks (Gloria Watkins) (b. 1952), a social critic, educator, and writer, has written extensively on feminist politics, race issues, and contemporary culture. She received her Ph.D. from the University of California at Santa Cruz and is a distinguished professor of English at City College of New York.

Theory as Liberatory Practice

bell hooks

I came to theory because I was hurting—the pain within me was so intense that I could not go on living. I came to theory desperate, wanting to comprehend—to grasp what was happening around and within me. Most importantly, I wanted to make the hurt go away. I saw in theory then a location for healing.

I came to theory young, when I was still a child. In *The Significance of Theory* Terry Eagleton says:

> Children make the best theorists, since they have not yet been educated into accepting our routine social practices as "natural," and so insist on posing to those practices the most embarrassingly general and fundamental questions, regarding them with a wondering estrangement which we adults have long forgotten. Since they do not yet grasp our social practices as inevitable, they do not see why we might not do things differently.

Whenever I tried in childhood to compel folks around me to do things differently, to look at the world differently, using theory as intervention, as a way to challenge the status quo, I was punished. I remember trying to explain at a very young age to Mama why I thought it was highly inappropriate for Daddy, this man who hardly spoke to me, to have the right to discipline me, to punish me physically with whippings. Her response was to suggest I was losing my mind and in need of more frequent punishment.

Imagine if you will this young black couple struggling first and foremost to realize the patriarchal norm (that is of the woman staying home, taking care of the household and children while the man worked) even though such an arrangement meant that economically, they would always be living with less. Try to imagine what it must have been like for them, each of them working hard all day, struggling to maintain a family of seven children, then having to cope with one bright-eyed child relentlessly questioning, daring to challenge male authority, rebelling against the very patriarchal norm they were trying so hard to institutionalize.

It must have seemed to them that some monster had appeared in their midst in the shape and body of a child—a demonic little figure who threatened to subvert and undermine all that they were seeking to build. No wonder then that their response was to repress, contain, punish. No wonder that Mama would say to me, now and then, exasperated, frustrated, "I don't know where I got you from, but I sure wish I could give you back."

Imagine then if you will, my childhood pain. I did not feel truly connected to these strange people, to these familial folks who could not only fail to grasp my worldview but who just simply did not want to hear it. As a child, I didn't know where I had come from. And when I was not desperately seeking to belong to this family community that never seemed to accept or want me, I was desperately trying to discover the place of my belonging. I was desperately trying to find my way home. How I envied Dorothy her journey in *The Wizard of Oz*, that she could travel to her worst fears and nightmares only to find at the end that "there is no place like home." Living in childhood without a sense of home, I found a place of sanctuary in "theorizing," in making sense out of what was happening. I found a place where I could imagine possible futures, a place where life could be lived differently. This "lived" experience of critical thinking, of reflection and analysis, became a place where I worked at explaining the hurt and making it go away. Fundamentally, I learned from this experience that theory could be a healing place.

Psychoanalyst Alice Miller lets you know in her introduction to the book *Prisoners of Childhood* that it was her own personal struggle to recover from the wounds of childhood that led her to rethink and theorize anew prevailing social and critical thought about the meaning of childhood pain, of child abuse. In her adult life, through her practice, she experienced theory as a healing place. Significantly, she had to imagine herself in the space of childhood, to look again from that perspective, to remember "crucial information, answers to questions which had gone unanswered throughout [her] study of philosophy and psychoanalysis." When our lived experience of theorizing is fundamentally linked to processes of self-recovery, of collective liberation, no gap exists between theory and practice. Indeed, what such experience makes more evident is the bond between the two—that ultimately reciprocal process wherein one enables the other.

Theory is not inherently healing, liberatory, or revolutionary. It fulfills this function only when we ask that it do so and direct our theorizing towards this end. When I was a child, I certainly did not describe the processes of thought and critique I engaged in as "theorizing." Yet, as I suggested in *Feminist Theory: From Margin to Center*, the possession of a term does not bring a process or practice into being; concurrently one may practice theorizing without ever knowing/possessing the term, just as we can live and act in feminist resistance without ever using the word "feminism."

Often individuals who employ certain terms freely—terms like "theory" or "feminism"—are not necessarily practitioners whose habits of being and living most embody the action, the practice of theorizing or engaging in feminist struggle. Indeed, the privileged act of naming often affords those in power access to modes of communication and enables them to project an interpretation, a definition, a description of their work and actions, that may not be accurate, that may obscure what is really taking place. Katie King's essay "Producing Sex, Theory, and Culture: Gay/Straight Re-Mappings in Contemporary Feminism" (in *Conflicts in Feminism*) offers a very useful discussion of the way in which academic production of feminist theory formulated in hierarchical settings often enables women, particularly white women, with high status and visibility to draw upon the works of feminist scholars who may have less or no status, less or no visibility, without giving recognition to these sources. King discusses the way work is appropriated and the way readers will often attribute ideas to a well-known scholar/feminist thinker, even if that individual has cited in her work that she is building on ideas gleaned from less well-known sources. Focusing particularly on the work of Chicana theorist Chela Sandoval, King states, "Sandoval has been published only sporadically and eccentrically, yet her circulating unpublished manuscripts are much more cited and often appropriated, even while the range of her influence is rarely understood." Though King risks positioning herself in a caretaker role as she rhetorically assumes the posture of feminist authority, determining the range and scope of Sandoval's influence, the critical point she works to emphasize is that the production of feminist theory is complex, that it is an individual practice less often than we think and usually emerges from engagement with collective sources. Echoing feminist theorists, especially women of color who have worked consistently to resist the construction of restrictive critical boundaries within feminist thought, King encourages us to have an expansive perspective on the theorizing process.

Critical reflection on contemporary production of feminist theory makes it apparent that the shift from early conceptualizations of feminist theory (which insisted that it was most vital when it encouraged and enabled feminist practice) begins to occur or at least becomes most obvious with the segregation and institutionalization of the feminist theorizing process in the academy, with the privileging of written feminist thought/theory over oral narratives. Concurrently, the efforts of black women and women of color to challenge and deconstruct the category "woman"—the insistence on recognition that gender is not the sole factor determining constructions of femaleness—was a critical intervention, one which led to a profound revolution in feminist thought and truly interrogated and disrupted the hegemonic feminist theory produced primarily by academic women, most of whom were white.

In the wake of this disruption, the assault on white supremacy made manifest in alliances between white women academics and white male peers seems to have been formed and nurtured around common efforts to formulate and impose standards of critical evaluation that would be used to define what is theoretical and what is not. These standards often led to appropriation and/or devaluation of work that did not "fit," that was suddenly deemed not theoretical—or not theoretical enough. In some circles, there seems to be a direct connection between white feminist scholars turning towards critical work and theory by white men, and the turning away of white feminist scholars from fully respecting and valuing the critical insights and theoretical offerings of black women or women of color.

Work by women of color and marginalized groups of white women (for example, lesbians, sex radicals), especially if written in a manner that renders it accessible to a broad reading public, is often de-legitimized in academic settings, even if that work enables and promotes feminist practice. Though such work is often appropriated by the very individuals setting restrictive critical standards, it is this work that they most often claim is not really theory. Clearly, one of the uses these individuals make of theory is instrumental. They use it to set up unnecessary and competing hierarchies of thought which reinscribe the politics of domination by designating work as either inferior, superior, or more or less worthy of attention. King emphasizes that "theory finds different uses in different locations." It is evident that one of the many uses of theory in academic locations is in the production of an intellectual class hierarchy where the only work deemed truly theoretical is work that is highly abstract, jargonistic, difficult to read, and containing obscure references. In Childers and hooks's "A Conversation about Race and Class" (also in *Conflicts in Feminism*) literary critic Mary Childers declares that it is highly ironic that "a certain kind of theoretical performance which only a small cadre of people can possibly understand" has come to be seen as representative of any production of critical thought that will be given recognition within many academic circles as "theory." It is especially ironic when this is the case with feminist theory. And, it is easy to imagine different locations, spaces outside academic exchange, where such theory would not only be seen as useless, but as politically nonprogressive, a kind of narcissistic, self-indulgent practice that most seeks to create a gap between theory and practice so as to perpetuate class elitism. There are so many settings in this country where the written word has only slight visual meaning, where individuals who cannot read or write can find no use for a published theory however lucid or opaque. Hence, any theory that cannot be shared in everyday conversation cannot be used to educate the public.

Imagine what a change has come about within feminist movements when students, most of whom are female, come to Women's Studies classes and read what they are told is feminist theory only to feel that what they are reading has no meaning, cannot be understood, or when understood in no way connects to "lived" realities beyond the classroom. As feminist activists we might ask ourselves, of what use is feminist theory that assaults the fragile psyches of women struggling to throw off patriarchy's oppressive yoke? We might ask ourselves, of what use is feminist theory that literally beats them down, leaves them stumbling bleary-eyed from classroom settings feeling humiliated, feeling as though they could easily be standing in a living room or bedroom somewhere naked with someone who has seduced them or is going to, who also subjects them to a process of interaction that humiliates, that strips them of their sense of value? Clearly, a feminist theory that can do this may function to legitimize Women's Studies and feminist scholarship in the eyes of the ruling patriarchy, but it undermines and subverts feminist movements. Perhaps it is the existence of this most highly visible feminist theory that compels us to talk about the gap between theory and practice. For it is indeed the purpose of such theory to divide, separate, exclude, keep at a distance. And because this theory continues to be used to silence, censor, and devalue various feminist theoretical voices, we cannot simply ignore it. Yet, despite its uses as an instrument of domination, it may also contain important ideas, thoughts, visions, that could, if used differently, serve a healing, liberatory function. However, we cannot ignore the dangers it poses to feminist struggle which must be rooted in a theory that informs, shapes, and makes feminist practice possible.

Within feminist circles, many women have responded to hegemonic feminist theory that does not speak clearly to us by trashing theory, and, as a consequence, further promoting the false dichotomy between theory and practice. Hence, they collude with those whom they would oppose. By internalizing the false assumption that theory is not a social practice, they promote the formation within feminist circles of a potentially oppressive hierarchy where all concrete action is viewed as more important than any theory written or spoken. Recently, I went to a gathering of predominantly black women where we discussed whether or not black male leaders, such as Martin Luther King and Malcolm X, should be subjected to feminist critiques that pose hard questions about their stance on gender issues. The entire discussion was less than two hours. As it drew to a close, a black woman who had been particularly silent, said that she was not interested in all this theory and rhetoric, all this talk, that she was more interested in action, in doing something, that she was "tired" of all the talk.

This woman's response disturbed me: it is a familiar reaction. Perhaps in her daily life she inhabits a world different from mine. In the world I live in daily, there are few occasions when black women or women-of-color thinkers come together to debate rigorously issues of race, gender, class, and sexuality. Therefore, I did not know where she was coming from when she suggested that the discussion we were having was common, so common as to be something we could dispense with or do without. I felt that we were engaged in a process of critical dialogue and theorizing that has long been taboo. Hence, from my perspective we were charting new journeys, claiming for ourselves as black women an intellectual terrain where we could begin the collective construction of feminist theory.

In many black settings, I have witnessed the dismissal of intellectuals, the putting down of theory, and remained silent. I have come to see that silence is an act of complicity, one that helps perpetuate the idea that we can engage in revolutionary black liberation and feminist struggle without theory. Like many insurgent black intellectuals, whose intellectual work and teaching is often done in predominantly white settings, I am often so pleased to be engaged with a collective group of black folks that I do not want to make waves, or make myself an outsider by disagreeing with the group. In such settings, when the work of intellectuals is devalued, I have in the past rarely contested prevailing assumptions, or have spoken affirmatively or ecstatically about intellectual process. I was afraid that if I took a stance that insisted on the importance of intellectual work, particularly theorizing, or if I just simply stated that I thought it was important to read widely, I would risk being seen as uppity, or as lording it over. I have often remained silent.

These risks to one's sense of self now seem trite when considered in relation to the crises we are facing as African Americans, to our desperate need to rekindle and sustain the flame of black liberation struggle. At the gathering I mentioned, I dared to speak, saying in response to the suggestion that we were just wasting our time talking, that I saw our words as an action, that our collective struggle to discuss issues of gender and blackness without censorship was subversive practice. Many of the issues that we continue to confront as black people—low self-esteem, intensified nihilism and despair, repressed rage and violence that destroys our physical and psychological well-being—cannot be addressed by survival strategies that have worked in the past. I insisted that we needed new theories rooted in an attempt to understand both the nature of our contemporary predicament and the means by which we might collectively engage in resistance that would transform our current reality. I was, however, not as rigorous and relentless as I would have been in a different setting in my efforts to emphasize the importance of intellectual work, the production of theory as a social practice that can be liberatory. Though not afraid to speak, I did not want to be seen as the one who "spoiled" the good time, the collective sense of sweet solidarity in blackness. This fear reminded me of what it was like more than ten years ago to be in feminist settings, posing questions about theory and practice, particularly about issues of race and racism that were seen as potentially disruptive of sisterhood and solidarity.

It seemed ironic that at a gathering called to honor Martin Luther King, Jr., who had often dared to speak and act in resistance to the status quo, black women were still negating our right to engage in oppositional political dialogue and debate, especially since this is not a common occurrence in black communities. Why did the black women there feel the need to police one another to deny one another a space within blackness where we could talk theory without being self-conscious? Why, when we could celebrate together the power of a black male critical thinker who dared to stand apart, was there this eagerness to repress any viewpoint that would suggest we might collectively learn from the ideas and visions of insurgent black female intellectuals/theorists, who by the nature of the work they do are necessarily breaking with the stereotype that would have us believe the "real" black woman is always the one who speaks from the gut, who righteously praises the concrete over the abstract, the material over the theoretical?

Again and again, black women find our efforts to speak, to break silence and engage in radical progressive political debates, opposed. There is a link between the silencing we experience, the censoring, the anti-intellectualism in predominantly black settings that are supposedly supportive (like all-black woman space), and that silencing that takes place in institutions wherein black women and women of color are told that we cannot be fully heard or listened to because our work is not theoretical enough. In "Travelling Theory: Cultural Politics of Race and Representation," cultural critic Kobena Mercer reminds us that blackness is complex and multifaceted and that black people can be interpolated into reactionary and antidemocratic politics. Just as some elite academics who construct theories of "blackness" in ways that make it a critical terrain which only the chosen few can enter—using theoretical work on race to assert their authority over black experience, denying democratic access to the process of theory making—threaten collective black liberation struggle, so do those among us who react to this by promoting anti-intellectualism by declaring all theory as worthless. By reinforcing the idea that there is a split between theory and practice or by creating such a split, both groups deny the power of liberatory education for critical consciousness, thereby perpetuating conditions that reinforce our collective exploitation and repression.

I was reminded recently of this dangerous anti-intellectualism when I agreed to appear on a radio show with a group of black women and men to discuss Shahrazad Ali's *The Blackman's Guide to Understanding the Black-woman*. I listened to speaker after speaker express contempt for intellectual work, and speak against any call for the production of theory. One black woman was vehement in her insistence that "we don't need no theory." Ali's book, though written in plain language, in a style that makes use of engaging black vernacular, has a theoretical foundation. It is rooted in theories of patriarchy (for example, the sexist, essentialist belief that male domination of females is "natural"), that misogyny is the only possible response black men can have to any attempt by women to be fully self-actualized. Many black nationalists will eagerly embrace critical theory and thought as a necessary weapon in the struggle against white supremacy, but suddenly lose the insight that theory is important when it comes to questions of gender, of analyzing sexism and sexist oppression in the particular and specific ways it is manifest in black experience. The discussion of Ali's book is one of many possible examples illustrating the way contempt and disregard for theory undermines collective struggle to resist oppression and exploitation.

Within revolutionary feminist movements, within revolutionary black liberation struggles, we must continually claim theory as necessary practice within a holistic framework of liberatory activism. We must do more than call attention to ways theory is misused. We must do more than critique the conservative and at times reactionary uses some academic women make of feminist theory. We must actively work to call attention to the importance of creating a theory that can advance renewed feminist movements, particularly highlighting that theory which seeks to further feminist opposition to sexism, and sexist oppression. Doing this, we necessarily celebrate and value theory that can be and is shared in oral as well as written narrative.

• • •

I am grateful to the many women and men who dare to create theory from the location of pain and struggle, who courageously expose wounds to give us their experience to teach and guide, as a means to chart new theoretical journeys. Their work is liberatory. It not only enables us to remember and recover ourselves, it charges and challenges us to renew our commitment to an active, inclusive feminist struggle. We have still to collectively make feminist revolution. I am grateful that we are collectively searching as feminist thinkers/theorists for ways to make this movement happen. Our search leads us back to where it all began, to that moment when an individual woman or child, who may have thought she was all alone, began a feminist uprising, began to name her practice, indeed began to formulate theory from lived experience. Let us imagine that this woman or child was suffering the pain of sexism and sexist oppression, that she wanted to make the hurt go away. I am grateful that I can be a witness, testifying that we can create a feminist theory, a feminist practice, a revolutionary feminist movement that can speak directly to the pain that is within folks, and offer them healing words, healing strategies, healing theory. There is no one among us who has not felt the pain of sexism and sexist oppression, the anguish that male domination can create in daily life, the profound and unrelenting misery and sorrow.

Mari Matsuda has told us that "we are fed a lie that there is no pain in war," and that patriarchy makes this pain possible. Catharine MacKinnon reminds us that "we know things with our lives and we live that knowledge, beyond what any theory has yet theorized." Making this theory is the challenge before us. For in its production lies the hope of our liberation, in its production lies the possibility of naming all our pain—of making all our hurt go away. If we create feminist theory, feminist movements that address this pain, we will have no difficulty building a mass-based feminist resistance struggle. There will be no gap between feminist theory and feminist practice.

Vandana Shiva, born in the Bronx of Indian parents, is an environmental activist with a master's degree in particle physics and a Ph.D. in the philosophy of science. She founded the Research Foundation for Science, Technology, and Ecology in Dehra Dun, Uttar Pradesh (India) in 1982, and has authored several books. Her activism efforts focus on biodiversity and sustainable agriculture.

Science, Nature, and Gender

Vandana Shiva

Let them come and see men and women and children who know how to live, whose joy of life has not yet been killed by those who claimed to teach other nations how to live.

—Chinua Achebe[1]

The Age of Enlightenment, and the theory of progress to which it gave rise, was centered on the sacredness of two categories: modern scientific knowledge and economic development. Somewhere along the way, the unbridled pursuit of progress, guided by science and development, began to destroy life without any assessment of how fast and how much of the diversity of life on this planet is disappearing. The act of living and of celebrating and conserving life in all its diversity—in people and in nature—seems to have been sacrificed to progress, and the sanctity of life been substituted by the sanctity of science and development.

Throughout the world, a new questioning is growing, rooted in the experience of those for whom the spread of what was called "enlightenment" has been the spread of darkness, of the extinction of life and life-enhancing processes. A new awareness is growing that is questioning the sanctity of science and development and revealing that these are not universal categories of progress, but the special projects of modern western patriarchy. This book has grown out of my involvement with women's struggles for survival in India over the last decade. It is informed both by the suffering and insights of those who struggle to sustain and conserve life, and whose struggles question the meaning of a progress, a science, a development which destroys life and threatens survival.

The death of nature is central to this threat to survival. The earth is rapidly dying: her forests are dying, her soils are dying, her waters are dying, her air is dying. Tropical forests, the creators of the world's climate, the cradle of the world's vegetational wealth, are being bull-dozed, burnt, ruined or submerged. In 1950, just over 100 million hectares of forests had been cleared—by 1975, this figure had more than doubled. During 1950–75, at least 120 million hectares of tropical forests were destroyed in South and Southeast Asia alone; by the end of the century, another 270 million could be eliminated. In Central America and Amazonia, cattle ranching for beef production is claiming at least 2.5 million hectares of forests each year; in India 1.3 million hectares of forests are lost every year to commercial plantation crops, river valley projects, mining projects and so on. Each year, 12 million hectares of forests are being eliminated from the face of the earth. At current rates of destruction, by the year 2050 all tropical forests will have disappeared, and with tropical forests, will disappear the diversity of life they support.

Up to 50 percent of all living things—at least five million species—are estimated to live in tropical forests. A typical four square-mile patch of rainforest contains up to 1,500 species of flowering plants, 750 species of trees, 125 of mammals, 400 of birds, 100 of reptiles, 60 of amphibians and 150 of butterflies. The unparalleled diversity of species within tropical forests means relatively few individuals of each; any forest clearance thus disrupts their life cycles and threatens them with rapid extinction. Current estimates suggest that we are losing one species of life a day from the 5–10 million species believed to exist. If present trends continue, we can expect an annual rate of loss as high as 50,000 species by the year 2000. In India alone, there exist 7,000 species of plant life not found anywhere else in the world; the destruction of her natural forests implies the disappearance of this rich diversity of animal and plant life.

Forests are the matrix of rivers and water sources, and their destruction in tropical regions amounts to the dessication and desertification of land. Every year 12 million hectares of land deteriorate into deserts and are unable to support vegetation or produce food. Sometimes land is laid waste through desertification, at other times through ill-conceived land use which destroys the fertility of fragile tropical soils. Desertification in the Sahel in Africa has already killed millions of people and animals. Globally, some 456 million people today are starving or malnourished because of the desertification of croplands. Most agricultural lands cropped intensively with green revolution techniques are either waterlogged or dessicated deserts. Nearly seven million hectares of land in India brought under irrigation have already gone out of production due to severe salinity, and an additional six million hectares have been seriously affected by water-logging. Green revolution agriculture has decreased genetic diversity and increased the vulnerability of crops to failure through lowering resistance to drought and pests.

With the destruction of forests, water and land, we are losing our life-support systems. This destruction is taking place in the name of "development" and progress, but there must be something seriously wrong with a concept of progress that threatens survival itself. The violence to nature, which seems intrinsic to the dominant development model, is also associated with violence to women who depend on nature for drawing sustenance for themselves, their families, their societies. This violence against nature and women is built into the very mode of perceiving both, and forms the basis of the current development paradigm. This book is an attempt to articulate how rural Indian women, who are still embedded in nature, experience and perceive ecological destruction and its causes, and how they have conceived and initiated processes to arrest the destruction of nature and begin its regeneration. From the diverse and specific grounds of the experience of ecological destruction arises a common identification of its causes in the developmental process and the view of nature with which it is legitimized. This book focuses on science and development as patriarchal projects not as a denial of other sources of patriarchy, such as religion, but because they are thought to be class, culture and gender neutral.

Seen from the experiences of Third World women, the modes of thinking and action that pass for science and development, respectively, are not universal and humanly inclusive, as they are made out to be; modern science and development are projects of male, western origin, both historically and ideologically. They are the latest and most brutal expression of a patriarchal ideology which is threatening to annihilate nature and the entire human species. The rise of a patriarchal science of nature took place in Europe during the fifteenth and seventeenth centuries as the scientific revolution. During the same period, the closely related industrial revolution laid the foundations of a patriarchal mode of economic development in industrial capitalism. Contemporary science and development conserve the ideological roots and biases of the scientific and industrial revolutions even as they unfold into new areas of activity and new domains of subjugation.

The scientific revolution in Europe transformed nature from *terra mater* into a machine and a source of raw material; with this transformation it removed all ethical and cognitive constraints against its violation and exploitation. The industrial revolution converted economics from the prudent management of resources for sustenance and basic needs satisfaction into a process of commodity production for profit maximisation. Industrialism created a limitless appetite for resource exploitation, and modern science provided the ethical and cognitive license to make such exploitation possible, acceptable—and desirable. The new relationship of man's domination and mastery over nature was thus also associated with new patterns of domination and mastery over women, and their exclusion from participation *as partners* in both science and development.

Contemporary development activity in the Third World superimposes the scientific and economic paradigms created by western, gender-based ideology on communities in other cultures. Ecological destruction and the marginalization of women, we know now, have been the inevitable results of most development programmes and projects based on such paradigms; they violate the integrity of one and destroy the productivity of the other. Women, as victims of the violence of patriarchal forms of development, have risen against it to protect nature and preserve their survival and sustenance. Indian women have been in the forefront of ecological struggles to conserve forests, land and water. They have challenged the western concept of nature as an object of exploitation and have protected her as *Prakriti*, the living force that supports life. They have challenged the western concept of economics as production of profits and capital accumulation with their own concept of economics as production of sustenance and needs satisfaction. A science that does not respect nature's needs and a development that does not respect people's needs inevitably threaten survival. In their fight to survive the onslaughts of both, women have begun a struggle that challenges the most fundamental categories of western patriarchy—its concepts of nature and women, and of science and development. Their ecological struggle in India is aimed simultaneously at liberating nature from ceaseless exploitation and themselves from limitless marginalisation. They are creating a feminist ideology that transcends gender, and a political practice that is humanly inclusive; they are challenging patriarchy's ideological claim to universalism not with another universalizing tendency, but with diversity; and they are challenging the dominant concept of power as violence with the alternative concept of nonviolence as power.

The everyday struggles of women for the protection of nature take place in the cognitive and ethical context of the categories of the ancient Indian worldview in which nature is *Prakriti*, a living and creative process, the feminine principle from which all life arises. Women's ecology movements, as the preservation and recovery of the feminine principle, arise from a nongender based ideology of liberation, different both from the gender-based ideology of patriarchy which underlies the process of ecological destruction and women's subjugation, and the gender-based responses which have, until recently, been characteristic of the west.

• • •

The recovery of the feminine principle is an intellectual and political challenge to maldevelopment as a patriarchal project of domination and destruction, of violence and subjugation, of dispossession and the dispensability of both women and nature. The politics of life centered on the feminine principle challenges fundamental assumptions not just in political economy, but also in the science of life-threatening processes.

Maldevelopment is intellectually based on, and justified through, reductionist categories of scientific thought and action. Politically and economically each project which has fragmented nature and displaced women from productive work has been legitimized as "scientific" by operationalizing reductionist concepts to realize uniformity, centralization and control. Development is thus the introduction of "scientific agriculture," "scientific animal husbandry," "scientific water management" and so on. The reductionist and universalizing tendencies of such "science" become inherently violent and destructive in a world which is inherently interrelated and diverse. The feminine principle becomes an oppositional category of nonviolent ways of conceiving the world, and of acting in it to sustain all life by maintaining the interconnectedness and diversity of nature. It allows an ecological transition from violence to nonviolence, from destruction to creativity, from anti-life to life-giving processes, from uniformity to diversity and from fragmentation and reductionism to holism and complexity.

It is thus not just "development" which is a source of violence to women and nature. At a deeper level, scientific knowledge, on which the development process is based, is itself a source of violence. Modern reductionist science, like development, turns out to be a patriarchal project, which has excluded women as experts, and has simultaneously excluded ecological and holistic ways of knowing which understand and respect nature's processes and interconnectedness *as science*.

Modern Science as Patriarchy's Project

Modern science is projected as a universal, value-free system of knowledge, which has displaced all other belief and knowledge systems by its universality and value neutrality, and by the logic of its method to arrive at objective claims about nature. Yet the dominant stream of modern science, the reductionist or mechanical paradigm, is a particular response of a particular group of people. It is a specific project of western man which came into being during the fifteenth and seventeenth centuries as the much-acclaimed Scientific Revolution. During the last few years feminist scholarship has begun to recognize that the dominant science system emerged as a liberating force not for humanity as a whole (though it legitimized itself in terms of universal betterment of the species), but as a masculine and patriarchal project which necessarily entailed the subjugation of both nature and women. Harding has called it a "western, bourgeois, masculine project,"[2] and according to Keller,

> Science has been produced by a particular sub-set of the human race, that is, almost entirely by white, middle class males. For the founding fathers of modern science, the reliance on the language of gender was explicit; they sought a philosophy that deserved to be called "masculine," that could be

distinguished from its ineffective predecessors by its "virile" powers, its capacity to bind Nature to man's service and make her his slave.[3]

Bacon (1561–1626) was the father of modern science, the originator of the concept of the modern research institute and industrial science, and the inspiration behind the Royal Society. His contribution to modern science and its organisation is critical. From the point of view of nature, women and marginal groups, however, Bacon's programme was not humanly inclusive. It was a special programme benefitting the middle class, European, male entrepreneur through the conjunction of human knowledge and power in science.

In Bacon's experimental method, which was central to this masculine project, there was a dichotomizing between male and female, mind and matter, objective and subjective, rational and emotional, and a conjunction of masculine and scientific dominating over nature, women and the nonwest. His was not a "neutral," "objective," "scientific" method—it was a masculine mode of aggression against nature and domination over women. The severe testing of hypotheses through controlled manipulations of nature, and the necessity of such manipulations if experiments are to be repeatable, are here formulated in clearly sexist metaphors. Both nature and inquiry appear conceptualized in ways modelled on rape and torture—on man's most violent and misogynous relationships with women—and this modelling is advanced as a reason to value science. According to Bacon "the nature of things betrays itself more readily under the vexations of art than in its natural freedom."[4] The discipline of scientific knowledge and the mechanical inventions it leads to, do not "merely exert a gentle guidance over nature's course; they have the power to conquer and subdue her, to shake her to her foundations."[5]

In *Tempores Partus Masculus* or *The Masculine Birth of Time*, translated by Farrington in 1951, Bacon promised to create "a blessed race of heroes and supermen" who would dominate both nature and society.[6] The title is interpreted by Farrington as suggesting a shift from the older science, represented as female—passive and weak—to a new masculine science of the scientific revolution which Bacon saw himself as heralding. In *New Atlantis*, Bacon's Bensalem was administered from Solomon's House, a scientific research institute, from which male scientists ruled over and made decisions for society, and decided which secrets should be revealed and which remain the private property of the institute.

Science-dominated society has evolved very much in the pattern of Bacon's Bensalem, with nature being transformed and mutilated in modern Solomon's Houses—corporate labs and the university programmes they sponsor. With the new biotechnologies, Bacon's vision of controlling reproduction for the sake of production is being realised, while the green revolution and the bio-revolution have realised what in *New Atlantis* was only a utopia.

"We make by act trees and flowers to come earlier or later than their seasons, and to come up and bear more speedily than by their natural course they do. We make them by act greater, much more than their nature, and their fruit greater and sweeter and of differing taste, smell, colour and figure from their nature."[7] For Bacon, nature was no longer Mother Nature, but a female nature, conquered by an aggressive masculine mind. As Carolyn Merchant points out, this transformation of nature from a living, nurturing mother to inert, dead and manipulable matter was eminently suited to the exploitation imperative of growing capitalism. The nurturing earth image acted as a cultural constraint on exploitation of nature. "One does not readily slay a mother, dig her entrails or mutilate her body." But the mastery and domination images created by the Baconian programme and the scientific revolution removed all restraint and functioned as cultural sanctions for the denudation of nature.

> The removal of animistic, organic assumptions about the cosmos constituted the death of nature—the most far-reaching effect of the scientific revolution. Because nature was now viewed as a system of dead, inert particles moved by external, rather than inherent forces, the mechanical framework itself could legitimate the manipulation of nature. Moreover, as a conceptual framework, the mechanical order had associated with it a framework of values based on power, fully compatible with the directions taken by commercial capitalism.[8]

Modern science was a consciously gendered, patriarchal activity. As nature came to be seen more like a woman to be raped, gender too was recreated. Science as a male venture, based on the subjugation of female nature and female sex provided support for the polarisation of gender. Patriarchy as the new scientific and technological power was a political need of emerging industrial capitalism.

While on the one hand the ideology of science sanctioned the denudation of nature, on the other it legitimized the dependency of women and the authority of men. Science and masculinity were associated in domination over nature and femininity, and the ideologies of science and gender reinforced each other. The witch-hunting hysteria which was aimed at annihilating women in Europe as knowers and experts was contemporous with two centuries of scientific revolution. It reached its peak with Galileo's *Dialogue* concerning the Two Chief World Systems and died with the emergence of the Royal Society of London and the Paris Academy of Sciences.[9]

> The interrogation of witches as a symbol for the interrogation of nature, the courtroom as model for its inquisition, and torture through mechanical

devices as a tool for the subjugation of disorder were fundamental to the scientific method as power. For Bacon, as for Harvey, sexual politics helped to structure the nature of the empirical method that would produce a new form of knowledge and a new ideology of objectivity seemingly devoid of cultural and political assumptions.[10]

The Royal Society, inspired by Bacon's philosophy, was clearly seen by its organizers as a masculine project. In 1664, Henry Oldenberg, Secretary of the Royal Society announced that the intention of the society was to "raise a *masculine philosophy* . . . whereby the Mind of Man may be ennobled with the knowledge of solid Truths."[11] And for Glanvill, the masculine aim of science was to know "the ways of captivating Nature, and making her subserve our purposes, thereby achieving the Empire of Man Over Nature."[12] Glanvill advocated chemistry as one of the most useful arts for "by the *violence* of its artful fires it is made to confess those latent parts, which upon less provocation it would not disclose."[13] The "de-mothering" of nature through modern science and the marriage of knowledge with power was simultaneously a source of subjugating women as well as non-European peoples. Robert Boyle, the famous scientist who was also the Governor of the New England Company, saw the rise of mechanical philosophy as an instrument of power not just over nature but also over the original inhabitants of America. He explicitly declared his intention of ridding the New England Indians of their ridiculous notions about the workings of nature. He attacked their perception of nature, "as a kind of goddess," and argued that "the veneration, wherewith men are imbued for what they call nature, has been a discouraging impediment to the empire of man over the inferior creatures of God."[14]

Today, with new ecological awareness, ecologists the world over turn to the beliefs of Native American and other indigenous peoples as a special source of learning how to live in harmony with nature. There are many today from the ecology and women's movements who see irrationality in Boyle's impulse for the empire of white man over nature and other peoples, and who see rationality in the words of Indian Chief Smohalla when he cried out: "You ask me to plough the ground: shall I take a knife and tear my mother's bosom? You ask me to cut grass and make hay and sell it and be rich like white men; but how dare I cut off my mother's hair?"[15]

Chief Seattle's letter, which has become a major inspiration for the ecology movement states, "This we know—the earth does not belong to man, man belongs to the earth. All things are connected like the blood which unites one family. Whatever befalls the earth befalls the sons of the earth. Man did not weave the web of life; he is merely a strand in it. Whatever he does to the web, he does to himself."

The ecological and feminist alternatives to reductionist science are clearly not the first attempts to create a science of nature that is not gendered and disruptive. The period of the scientific revolution itself was full of alternatives to the masculine project of mechanistic, reductionist science, and it was also full of struggles between gendered and nongendered science. Bacon and Paracelsus are the leading exponents of the two competing trends of modern science in seventeenth century Europe.[16] The Paracelsians belonged to the hermetic tradition which did not dichotomize between mind and matter, male and female. The mechanical school represented by Bacon created dichotomies between culture and nature, mind and matter and male and female, and devised a conceptual strategy for the former to dominate over the latter. The two visions of science were also two visions of nature, power and gender relations. For Paracelsus the male did not dominate over the female, the two complemented each other, and knowledge and power did not arise from dominating over nature but from "co-habiting with the elements,"[17] which were themselves interconnected to form a living organism. For the Paracelsian, "The whole world is knit and bound within itself: for the world is a living creature, everywhere both female and male," and knowledge of nature is derived through participating in these interconnections.[18]

With the formation of the Royal Society and in the context of emerging industrial capitalism, the contest between the mechanical and hermetic traditions was won by the masculine project which was the project of a particular class. Paracelsus and Bacon did not merely differ in their ideology of gender and science; they were also differently rooted in the politics of class, with Bacon committed to middle class values (finally becoming Lord Chancellor and Bacon Verulam in 1618 in the reign of James I) and identifying with capitalists, merchants and the State in his scientific project, and Paracelsus, on the side of the peasants in their uprising in the Tyrol.[19] Reductionist science became a major agent of economic and political change in the centuries to follow, dichotomizing gender and class relations and man's relationship with nature. "Given the success of modern science, defined in opposition to everything female, fears of both Nature and Woman could subside. With the one reduced to its mechanical sub-strata, and the other to her sexual virtue, the essence of *Mater* could be both tamed and conquered."[20]

For more than three centuries, reductionism has ruled as the only valid scientific method and system, distorting the history of the west as well as the nonwest. It has hidden its ideology behind projected objectivism, neutrality and progress. The ideology that hides ideology has transformed complex pluralistic traditions of knowledge into a monolith of gender-based, class-based thought and transformed this particular tradition into a superior and universal tradition to then be superimposed on all classes, genders and cultures which it helps in controlling and subjugating. This ideological projection has kept modern reductionist science inaccessible to criticism. The parochial roots of science in patriarchy and in a particular class and culture have been concealed behind a claim to universality, and can be seen only through other traditions—of women and nonwestern peoples. It is these subjugated traditions that are revealing how modern science is gendered, how it is specific to the needs and impulses of the dominant western culture and how ecological destruction and nature's exploitation are inherent to its logic. It is becoming increasingly clear that scientific neutrality has been a reflection of ideology, not history, and science is similar to all other socially constructed categories. This view of science as a social and political project of modern western man is emerging from the responses of those who were defined into nature and made passive and powerless: Mother Earth, women and colonized cultures. It is from these fringes that we are beginning to discern the economic, political and cultural mechanisms that have allowed a parochial science to dominate and how mechanisms of power and violence can be eliminated for a degendered, humanly inclusive knowledge.

The Violence of Reductionism

The myth that the "scientific revolution" was a universal process of intellectual progress is being steadily undermined by feminist scholarship and the histories of science of nonwestern cultures. These are relating the rise of the reductionist paradigm with the subjugation and destruction of women's knowledge in the west, and the knowledge of nonwestern cultures. The witch-hunts of Europe were largely a process of delegitimizing and destroying the expertise of European women. In 1511, England had an Act of Parliament directed against "common artificers, as smythes, weavers and women who attempted great cures and things of great difficulties: in the witch they partly use sorcerye and witch-craft."[21] By the sixteenth century women in Europe were totally excluded from the practice of medicine and healing because "wise women" ran the risk of being declared witches. A deeper, more violent form of exclusion of women's knowledge and expertise, and of the knowledge of tribal and peasant cultures is now under way with the spread of the masculinist paradigm of science through "development."

I characterise modern western patriarchy's special epistemological tradition of the "scientific revolution" as "reductionist" because it reduced the capacity of humans to know nature both by excluding other knowers and other ways of knowing, and it reduced the capacity of nature to creatively regenerate and renew itself by manipulating it as inert and fragmented matter. Reductionism has a set of distinctive characteristics which demarcates it from all other nonreductionist knowledge systems which it has subjugated and replaced. The basic ontological and epistemological assumptions of reductionism are based on homogeneity. It sees all systems as made up of the same basic constituents, discrete, unrelated and atomistic, and it assumes that all basic processes are mechanical. The mechanistic metaphors of reductionism have socially reconstituted nature and society. In contrast to the organic metaphors, in which concepts of order and power were based on interconnectedness and reciprocity, the metaphor of nature as a machine was based on the assumption of separability and manipulability. As Carolyn Merchant has remarked: "In investigating the roots of our current environmental dilemma and its connections to science, technology and the economy, we must re-examine the formation of a world-view and a science that, by reconceptualizing reality as a machine, rather than a living organism, sanctioned the domination of both nature and women."[22] This domination is inherently violent, understood here as the violation of integrity. Reductionist science is a source of violence against nature and women because it subjugates and dispossesses them of their full productivity, power and potential. The epistemological assumptions of reductionism are related to its ontological assumptions: uniformity allows the knowledge of parts of a system to be taken as knowledge of the whole. Separability allows context-free abstraction of knowledge and creates criteria of validity based on alienation and nonparticipation, then projected as "objectivity." "Experts" and "specialists" are thus projected as the only legitimate knowledge seekers and justifiers.

Profits, Reductionism, and Violence

The close nexus between reductionist science, patriarchy, violence and profits is explicit in 80 percent of scientific research that is devoted to the war industry, and is frankly aimed directly at lethal violence—violence, in modern times, not only against the enemy fighting force but also against the much larger civilian population. In this book I argue that modern science is related to violence and profits even in peaceful domain such as, for example, forestry and agriculture, where the professed objective of scientific research is human welfare. The relationship between reductionism, violence and profits is built into the genesis of masculinist science, for its reductionist nature is an epistemic response to an economic organization based on uncontrolled exploitation of nature for maximization of profits and capital accumulation.

Reductionism, far from being an epistemological accident, is a response to the needs of a particular form of economic and political organization.[23] The reductionist world-view, the industrial revolution and the capitalist economy were the philosophical, technological and economic components of the same process. Individual firms and the fragmented sector of the economy, whether privately owned or state owned, have only their own efficiency and profits in mind; and every firm and sector measures its efficiency by the extent to which it maximizes its gains, regardless of the maximization of social and ecological costs. The logic of this internal efficiency has been provided by reductionism. Only those properties of a resource system are taken into account which generate profits through exploitation and extraction; properties which stabilize ecological processes but are commercially nonexploitative are ignored and eventually destroyed.

Commercial capitalism is based on specialized commodity production. Uniformity in production, and the uni-functional use of natural resources is therefore required. Reductionism thus reduces complex ecosystems to a single component, and a single component to a single function. It further allows the manipulation of the ecosystem in a manner that maximizes the single-function, single-component exploitation. In the reductionist paradigm, a forest is reduced to commercial wood, and wood is reduced to cellulose fibre for the pulp and paper industry. Forests, land and genetic resources are then manipulated to increase the production of pulpwood, and this distortion is legitimized scientifically as overall productivity increase, even though it might decrease the output of water from the forest, or reduce the diversity of life forms that constitute a forest community. The living and diverse ecosystem is thus violated and destroyed by "scientific" forestry and forestry "development." In this way, reductionist science is at the root of the growing ecological crisis, because it entails a transformation of nature such that its organic processes and regularities and regenerative capacities are destroyed.

Women in sustenance economies, producing and reproducing wealth in partnership with nature, have been experts in their own right of a holistic and ecological knowledge of nature's processes. But these alternative modes of knowing, which are oriented to social benefits and sustenance needs, are not recognized by the reductionist paradigm, because it fails to perceive the interconnectedness of nature, or the connection of women's lives, work and knowledge with the creation of wealth.

The rationality and efficacy of reductionist and nonreductionist knowledge systems are never *evaluated* cognitively. The rationality of reductionist science is, a priori, declared superior. If reductionist science has displaced nonreductionist modes of knowing, it has done so not through cognitive competition, but through political support from the state: development policies and programmes provide the financial and material subsidies *as well as* the ideological support for the appropriation of nature of profits. Since the twin myths of progress (material prosperity) and superior rationality lost their sheen in the working out of development patterns and paradigms, and were visibly exploded by widespread ecological crises, the state stepped in to transform the myths into an ideology. When an individual firm or sector directly confronts the larger society in its appropriation of nature on grounds of progress and rationality, people can assess social costs and private benefits for themselves; they can differentiate between progress and regression, rationality and irrationality. But with the mediation of the state, subjects and citizens become objects of change rather than its determinants, and consequently lose both the capability and the right to assess progress. If they have to bear the costs instead of reaping the benefits of "development," this is justified as a minor sacrifice for the "national interest."

The nexus between the state, the dominant elite and the creation of surplus value provides the power with which reductionism establishes its supremacy. Institutions of learning in agriculture, medicine and forestry, selectively train people in the reductionist paradigms, in the name of "scientific" agriculture, medicine and forestry to establish the superiority of reductionist science. Stripped of the power the state invests it with, reductionism can be seen to be cognitively weak and ineffective in responding to problems posed by nature. Reductionist forestry has destroyed tropical forests, and reductionist agriculture is destroying tropical farming. As a system of knowledge about nature or life reductionist science is weak and inadequate; as a system of knowledge for the market, it is powerful and profitable. Modern science, as we have noted earlier, has a world-view that both supports and is supported by the socio-political-economic system of western capitalist patriarchy which dominates and exploits nature, women and the poor.

The ultimate reductionism is achieved when nature is linked with a view of economic activity in which money is the only gauge of value and wealth. Life disappears as an organizing principle of economic affairs. But the problem with money is that it has an asymmetric relationship to life and living processes. Exploitation, manipulation and destruction of the life in nature can be a source of money and profits but neither can ever become a source of nature's life and its life-supporting capacity. It is this assymmetry that accounts for a deepening of the ecological crises as a decrease in nature's life-producing potential, along with an increase of capital accumulation and the expansion of "development" as a process of replacing the currency of life and sustenance with the currency of cash and profits. The "development" of Africa by eastern experts is the primary cause for the destruction of Africa; the "development" of Brazil by transnational banks and corporations is the primary cause for the destruction of the richness of Amazonian rainforests, the highest expression of life. Natives of Africa and Amazonia had survived over centuries with their ecologically evolved, indigenous knowledge systems. What local people had conserved through history, western experts and knowledge destroyed in a few decades, a few years even.

It is this destruction of ecologies and knowledge systems that I characterize as the violence of reductionism which results in: *a) Violence against women:* women, tribals, peasants as the knowing subject are violated socially through the expert/nonexpert divide which converts them into nonknowers even in those areas of living in which through daily participation, they are the real experts—and in which responsibility of practice and action rests with them, such as in forestry, food and water systems. *b) Violence against nature:* nature as the object of knowledge is violated when modern science destroys its integrity of nature, both in the process of perception as well as manipulation. *c) Violence against the beneficiaries of knowledge:* contrary to the claim of modern science that people in general are ultimately the beneficiaries of scientific knowledge, they—particularly the poor and women—are its worst victims, deprived of their productive potential, livelihoods and life-support systems. Violence against nature recoils on man, the supposed beneficiary. *d) Violence against knowledge:* in order to assume the status of being the only legitimate mode of knowledge, rationally superior to alternative modes of knowing, reductionist science resorts *to the suppression and falsification of facts* and thus commits violence against science itself. It declares organic systems of knowledge irrational, and rejects the belief systems of others without full rational evaluation. At the time it protects itself from the exposure and investigation of the myths it has created by assigning itself a new sacredness that forbids any questioning of the claims of science.

Two Kinds of Facts

The conventional model of science, technology and society locates sources of violence in politics and ethics, in the *application* of science and technology, not in scientific knowledge itself. The assumed dichotomy between values and facts underlying this model implies a dichotomy between the world of values and the world of facts. In this view, sources of violence are located in the world of values while scientific knowledge inhabits the world of facts.

The fact-value dichotomy is a creation of modern reductionist science which, while being an epistemic response to a particular set of values, posits itself as independent of values. By splitting the world into facts vs. values, it conceals the real difference between two kinds of value-laden facts. Modern reductionist science is characterized in the received view as the discovery of the properties and laws of nature in accordance with a "scientific" method which generates claims of being "objective," "neutral" and "universal." This view of reductionist science as being a description of reality *as it is*, unprejudiced by value, is being rejected increasingly on historical and philosophical grounds. It has been historically established that all knowledge, including modern scientific knowledge, is built on the use of plurality of methodologies, and reductionism itself is only one of the scientific options available.

> There is no "scientific method"; there is no single procedure, or set of rules that underlies every piece of research and guarantees that it is scientific and, therefore, trustworthy. The idea of a universal and stable method that is an unchanging measure of adequacy and even the idea of a universal and stable rationality is as unrealistic as the idea of a universal and stable measuring instrument that measures any magnitude, no matter what the circumstances. Scientists revise their standards, their procedures, their criteria of rationality as they move along and enter new domains of research just as they revise and perhaps entirely replace their theories and their instruments as they move along and enter new domains of research.[24]

The assumption that science deals purely with facts has no support from the practise of science itself. The "facts" of reductionist science are socially constructed categories which have the cultural markings of the western bourgeois, patriarchal system which is their context of discovery and justification. Carolyn Merchant has shown how, until the sixteenth century in the west, organic metaphors were considered scientific and sane. "An organically oriented mentality in which female principles played an important role was undermined and replaced by a mechanically oriented mentality that either eliminated or used female principles in an exploitative manner. As western culture became increasingly mechanized in the 1600s, the female earth and virgin earth spirit were subdued by the machine."[25] The subjugation of other traditions of knowledge is similarly a displacement of one set of culturally constituted facts of nature by another, not the substitution of "superstition" by "fact." The cultural categories of scientific knowledge are not merely cognitive, they are also ethical.

Whereas the nurturing earth image can be viewed as a cultural constraint restricting the types of socially and morally sanctioned human actions allowable with respect to the earth, the new images of mastery and domination functioned as cultural sanctions for the denudation of nature. Controlling images which construct facts also operate as ethical restraints or sanctions as subtle "oughts" and "ought-nots."

In the Third World, the conflict between reductionist and ecological perceptions of the world are a contemporary and everyday reality, in which western trained male scientists and experts epitomize reductionist knowledge. The political struggle for the feminist and ecology movements involves an epistemological shift in the criteria of assessment of the rationality of knowledge. The worth and validity of reductionist claims and beliefs need to be measured against ecological criteria when the crisis of sustainability and survival is the primary intellectual challenge. The view of reductionist scientific knowledge as a purely factual description of nature, superior to competing alternatives, is found to be ecologically unfounded. Ecology perceives relationships between different elements of an ecosystem: what properties will be selected for a particular resource element will depend on what relationships are taken as the context defining the properties. The context is fixed by priorities and values guiding the perception of nature. Selection of the context is a value determined process and the selection in turn determines what properties are seen. There is nothing like a neutral fact about nature *independent of the value determined by human cognitive and economic activity*. Properties perceived in nature will depend on how one looks and how one looks depends on the economic interest one has in the resources of nature. The value of profit maximization is thus linked to reductionist systems, while the value of life and the maintenance of life is linked to holistic and ecological systems.

Two Kinds of Rationality

The ontological and epistemological components of the reductionist world-view provide the framework for a particular practice of science. According to Descartes, "Method consists entirely in the order as a disposition of the objects towards which our mental vision must be directed if we would find out any truth. We shall comply with it exactly if we *reduce* involved and obscure propositions step by step to those that are simpler, and then starting with the intuitive apprehension of all those that are absolutely simple, attempt to ascend to the knowledge of all others by precisely similar steps."[26] This method was, in Descartes' view, the method to "render ourselves the masters and possessors of nature." Yet it singularly fails to lead to a perception of reality (truth) in the case of living organisms such as nature (including man), in which the whole is not merely the sum of parts, because parts are so cohesively inter-related that isolating any one distorts the whole.

Kuhn, Feyerband, Polanyi and others have convincingly argued that modern science is not practiced according to a well defined and stable scientific method; all that can be granted it is that it is a single mode of thought, among many.

The controlled experiment and the laboratory are a central element of the methodology of reductionist science. The object of study is arbitrarily isolated from its natural surroundings, from its relationship with other objects and the observer(s). The context (the value framework) so provided determines what properties are perceived, and leads to a particular set of beliefs. The Baconian programme of domination over nature was centrally based on the controlled experiment which was formulated and conceived in the language and metaphor of rape, torture and the inquisition. The "controlled" experiment was therefore a political choice, aimed at control of nature and exclusion of other ways of knowing. It was assumed that the truth of nature was more accessible through violence, and it was recognised that this truth is a basis of power. In this way, "human knowledge and human power meet as one."[27] Sandra Harding has characterized this as the contemporary "alliance of perverse knowledge claims with the perversity of dominating power."

The knowledge and power nexus is inherent to the reductionist system because the mechanistic order, as a conceptual framework, was associated with a set of values based on power which were compatible with the needs of commercial capitalism. It generates inequalities and domination by the way knowledge is generated and structured, the way it is legitimized, and by the way in which such knowledge transforms nature and society. The domination of the South by the North, of women by men, of nature by westernized man are now being identified as being rooted in the domination inherent to the world-view created by western man over the last three centuries through which he could subjugate or exclude the rest of humanity on grounds of humanity. As Harding observes,

> We can now discern the effects of these cultural markings in the discrepancies between the methods of knowing and the interpretations of the world provided by the creators of modern western culture and those characteristic of the rest of us. Western culture's favoured beliefs mirror in sometimes clear and sometimes distorting ways not the world as it is or as we might want it to be, but the social projects of their historically identifiable creators.[28]

Exclusion of other traditions of knowledge by reductionist science is threefold: (i) ontological, in that other properties are just not taken note of, (ii) epistemological, in that other ways of perceiving and knowing are not recognized; and (iii) sociological, in that the nonspecialist and nonexpert is deprived of the right both to access to knowledge and to judging claims made on its behalf. All this is the stuff of politics, not science. Picking one group of people (the specialists), who adopt one way of knowing the physical world (the reductionist), to find one set of properties in nature (the mechanistic) is a political, not a scientific mode. Knowledge so obtained is presented as "the laws of nature," wholly "objective" and altogether universal. Feyerband is therefore right in saying: "The appearance of objectivity that is attached to some value judgments comes from the fact that a particular tradition is used but not recognized. Absence of the impression of subjectivity is not proof of objectivity, but an oversight." The "controlled" experiment which was assumed to be a mode for "neutral" observation was, in effect, a political tool for exclusion such that people's experimentation in their daily lives was denied access to the status of the scientific.

It is argued in defence of modern science that it is not science itself but the political misuse and unethical technological application of it that lead to violence. The speciousness of this argument was always clear, but it is totally untenable today, when science and technology have become cognitively inseparable and the amalgam has been incorporated into the scientific-military-industrial complex of capitalist patriarchy. The fragmentation of science into a variety of specializations and sub-specializations is used as a smoke-screen to blur the perception of this linkage between science and a particular model of social organisation, that is, a particular ideology. Science claims that since scientific truths are verifiable and neutral, they are justified beliefs and therefore universal, regardless of the social context. Yet from the perspective of subjugated traditions, the "truths" of reductionism are falsehoods for the subjugated. Why should we regard the emergence of modern science as a great advance for humanity when it was achieved only at the cost of a deterioration in social status for most of humanity including women and non-western cultures? Sandra Harding, locating the culture of destruction and domination in science-as-usual, not in bad science, asks,

> Could the uses of science to create ecological disaster, support militarism, turn human labour into physically and mentally mutilating work, develop ways of controlling "others"—the colonized, the women, the poor—be just misuses of applied science? Or does this kind of conceptualization of the character and purposes of experimental method ensure that what is called bad science or misused science will be a distinctively masculinist science as usual?[29]

• • •

Nature as the Feminine Principle

Women in India are an intimate part of nature, both in imagination and in practise. At one level nature is symbolised as the embodiment of the feminine principle, and at another, she is nurtured by the feminine to produce life and provide sustenance.

From the point of view of Indian cosmology, in both the exoteric and esoteric traditions, the world is produced and renewed by the dialectical play of creation and destruction, cohesion and disintegration. The tension between the opposites from which motion and movement arises is depicted as the first appearance of dynamic energy (Shakti). All existence arises from this primordial energy which is the substance of everything, pervading everything. The manifestation of this power, this energy, is called nature

(*Prakriti*).[30] Nature, both animate and inanimate, is thus an expression of Shakti, the feminine and creative principle of the cosmos; in conjunction with the masculine principle (Purusha), *Prakriti* creates the world.

Nature as *Prakriti* is inherently active, a powerful, productive force in the dialectic of the creation, renewal and sustenance of *all* life. In *Kulacud-amim Nigama, Prakriti* says:

> There is none but Myself
>
> Who is the Mother to create.[31]

Without Shakti, Shiva, the symbol for the force of creation and destruction, is as powerless as a corpse. "The quiescent aspect of Shiva is, by definition, inert . . . Activity is the nature of Nature *(Prakriti)*."[32]

Prakriti is worshipped as Aditi, the primordial vastness, the inexhaustible, the source of abundance. She is worshipped as Adi Shakti, the primordial power. All the forms of nature and life in nature are the forms, the children, of the Mother of Nature who is nature itself born of the creative play of her thought.[33] Hence *Prakriti* is also called Lalitha,[34] the Player because *lila* or play, as free spontaneous activity, is her nature. The will-to-become many (Bahu-Syam-Prajayera) is her creative impulse and through this impulse, she creates the diversity of living forms in nature. The common yet multiple life of mountains, trees, rivers, animals is an expression of the diversity that *Prakriti* gives rise to. The creative force and the created world are not separate and distinct, nor is the created world uniform, static and fragmented. It is diverse, dynamic and interrelated.

The nature of Nature as *Prakriti* is activity *and* diversity. Nature symbols from every realm of nature are in a sense signed with the image of Nature. *Prakriti* lives in stone or tree, pool, fruit or animal, and is identified with them. According to the *Kalika Purana*:

> Rivers and mountains have a dual nature. A river is but a form of water, yet it has a distinct body. Mountains appear a motionless mass, yet their true form is not such. We cannot know, when looking at a lifeless shell, that it contains a living being. Similarly, within the apparently inanimate rivers and mountains there dwells a hidden consciousness. Rivers and mountains take the forms they wish.[35]

The living, nurturing relationship between man and nature here differs dramatically from the notion of man as separate from and dominating over nature. A good illustration of this difference is the daily worship of the sacred tulsi within Indian culture and outside it. Tulsi (*Ocimum sanctum*) is a little herb planted in every home, and worshipped daily. It has been used in Ayurveda for more than 3000 years, and is now also being legitimized as a source of diverse healing powers by western medicine. However, all this is incidental to its worship. The tulsi is sacred not merely as a plant with beneficial properties but as Brindavan, the symbol of the cosmos. In their daily watering and worship women renew the relationship of the home with the cosmos and with the world process. Nature as a creative expression of the feminine principle is both in ontological continuity with humans as well as above them. Ontologically, there is no divide between man and nature, or between man and woman, because life in all its forms arises from the feminine principle.

Contemporary western views of nature are fraught with the dichotomy or duality between man and woman, and person and nature. In Indian cosmology, by contrast, person and nature (Purusha-*Prakriti*) are a duality in unity. They are inseparable complements of one another in nature, in woman, in man. Every form of creation bears the sign of this dialectical unity, of diversity within a unifying principle, and this dialectical harmony between the male and female principles and between nature and man, becomes the basis of ecological thought and action in India. Since, ontologically, there is no dualism between man and nature and because nature as *Prakriti* sustains life, nature has been treated as integral and inviolable. *Prakriti*, far from being an esoteric abstraction, is an everyday concept which organizes daily life. There is no separation here between the popular and elite imagery or between the sacred and secular traditions. As an embodiment and manifestation of the feminine principle it is characterized by (a) creativity, activity, productivity; (b) diversity in form and aspect; (c) connectedness and inter-relationship of all beings, including man; (d) continuity between the human and natural; and (e) sanctity of life in nature.

Conceptually, this differs radically from the Cartesian concept of nature as "environment" or a "resource." In it, the environment is seen as separate from man: it is his surrounding, not his substance. The dualism between man and nature has allowed the subjugation of the latter by man and given rise to a new world-view in which nature is (a) inert and passive; (b) uniform and mechanistic; (c) separable and fragmented within itself; (d) separate from man; and (e) inferior, to be dominated and exploited by man.

The rupture within nature and between man and nature, and its associated transformation from a life-force that sustains to an exploitable resource characterizes the Cartesian view which has displaced more ecological worldviews and created a development paradigm which cripples nature and woman simultaneously.

The ontological shift for an ecologically sustainable future has much to gain from the world-views of ancient civilizations and diverse cultures which survived sustainably over centuries. These were based on an ontology of the feminine as the living principle, and on an ontological continuity between society and nature—the humanization of nature and the naturalization of society. Not merely did this result in an ethical context which excluded possibilities of exploitation and domination, it allowed the creation of an earth family.

The dichotomized ontology of man dominating woman and nature generates maldevelopment because it makes the colonizing male the agent and model of "development." Women, the Third World and nature become underdeveloped, first by definition, and then, through the process of colonisation, in reality.

The ontology of dichotomization generates an ontology of domination, over nature and people. Epistemologically, it leads to reductionism and fragmentation, thus violating women as subjects and nature as an object of knowledge. This violation becomes a source of epistemic and real violence—I would like to interpret ecological crises at both levels—as a disruption of ecological perceptions of nature.

Ecological ways of knowing nature are necessarily participatory. Nature herself is the experiment and women, as sylviculturalists, agriculturists and water resource managers, the traditional natural scientists. Their knowledge is ecological and plural, reflecting both the diversity of natural ecosystems and the diversity in cultures that nature-based living gives rise to. Throughout the world, the colonization of diverse peoples was, at its root, a forced subjugation of ecological concepts of nature and of the Earth as the repository of all forms, latencies and powers of creation, the ground and cause of the world. The symbolism of Terra Mater, the earth in the form of the Great Mother, creative and protective, has been a shared but diverse symbol across space and time, and ecology movements in the West today are inspired in large part by the recovery of the concept of Gaia, the earth goddess.[36]

The shift from *Prakriti* to "natural resources," from Mater to "matter" was considered (and in many quarters is still considered) a progressive shift from superstition to rationality. Yet, viewed from the perspective of nature, or women embedded in nature, in the production and preservation of sustenance, the shift is regressive and violent. It entails the disruption of nature's processes and cycles, and her inter-connectedness. For women, whose productivity in the sustaining of life is based on nature's productivity, the death of *Prakriti* is simultaneously a beginning of their marginalization, devaluation, displacement and ultimate dispensability. The ecological crisis is, at its root, the death of the feminine principle, symbolically as well as in contexts such as rural India, not merely in form and symbol, but also in the everyday processes of survival and sustenance.

Notes

1 Chinua Achebe, *No Longer at Ease*, London: Heinemann, 1960, p. 45.

2 Sandra Harding, *The Science Question in Feminism*, Ithaca: Cornell University Press, 1986, p. 8.

3 Evelyn F. Keller, *Reflections on Gender and Science*, New Haven: Yale University Press, 1985, p. 7.

4 F. H. Anderson, (ed.), *Francis Bacon: The New Organon and Related Writings*, Indianapolis: Bobbs-Merrill, 1960, p. 25.

5 J. Spedding, et al. (eds.) *The Works of Francis Bacon* (Reprinted), Stuttgart: F.F. Verlag, 1963, Vol. V, p. 506.

6 Quoted in Keller, op. cit., pp. 38–39.

7 Carolyn Merchant, *The Death of Nature: Women, Ecology and the Scientific Revolution*, New York: Harper & Row, 1980, p. 182.

8 Merchant, op. cit., p. 193.

9 Brian Easlea, *Science and Sexual Oppression: Patriarchy's Confrontation with Woman and Nature*, London: Weidenfeld and Nicholson, 1981, p. 64.

10 Merchant, op. cit., p. 172.

11 Easlea, op. cit., p. 70.

12 Easlea, op. cit., p. 70.

13 Merchant, op. cit., p. 189.

14 Easlea, op. cit., p. 73.

15 Easlea, op. cit., p. 73.

16 J. P. S. Oberoi, *The Other Mind of Europe: Goethe as a Scientist*, Delhi: Oxford University Press, 1984.

17 Keller, op. cit., 48.

18 Merchant, op. cit., p. 104.

19 Oberoi, op. cit., p. 21.

20 Keller, op. cit., p. 60.

21 Quoted in Muriel J. Hughes, *Women Healers in Medieval Life and Literature*, New York: Libraries Press, 1968, p. 86.

22 Merchant, op. cit., p. xvii.

23 J. Bandyopadhyay & V. Shiva, "Ecological Sciences: A Response to Ecological Crises" in J. Bandyopadhyay, et al., *India's Environment*, Dehradun: Natraj, 1985, p. 196; and J. Bandyopadhyay & V. Shiva, "Environmental Conflicts and Public Interest Science," in *Economic and Political Weekly*, Vol. XXI, No. 2, Jan. 11, 1986, pp. 84–90.

24 Paul Feyerband, *Science in a Free Society*. New Left Books, 1978, p. 10.

25 Merchant, op. cit., p. 2.

26 Descartes, *A Discourse on Method*, London: Everymans, 1981, p. xv.

27 Quoted in Merchant, op. cit., p. 171.

[28] Harding, op. cit., p. 15.

[29] Harding, op. cit., p. 102.

[30] *"Prakriti"* is a popular category, and one through which ordinary women in rural India relate to nature. It is also a highly evolved philosophical category in Indian cosmology. Even those philosophical streams of Indian thought which were patriarchal and did not give the supreme place to divinity as a woman, a mother, were permeated by the prehistoric cults and the living "little" traditions of nature as the primordial mother goddess.

[31] For an elaboration of the concept of the feminine principle in Indian thought see Alain Danielon, *The Gods of India*, New York: Inner Traditions International Ltd., 1985; Sir John Woodroffe, *The Serpent Power*, Madras: Ganesh and Co., 1931; and Sir John Woodroffe, *Shakti and Shakta*, Luzaz and Co., 1929.

[32] Woodroffe, op. cit., (1931), p 27.

[33] W. C. Beane, *Myth, Cult and Symbols in Sakta Hinduism: A Study of the Indian Mother Goddess*, Leiden: E. J. Brill, 1977.

[34] *Lalitha Sahasranama*, (Reprint), Delhi: Giani Publishing House, 1986.

[35] *Kalika Purana*, 22.10–13, Bombay: Venkateshwara Press, 1927.

[36] Erich Neumann, *The Great Mother*, New York: Pantheon Books, 1955.

Charles M. Payne, professor of history at Duke University, is the author of I've Got the Light of Freedom: The Organizing Tradition and the Mississippi Freedom Struggle *(1995), and* Getting What We Ask For: The Ambiguity of Success and Failure in Urban Education *(1984). His academic work focuses on social change, urban education, and the civil rights movement.*

Ella Baker and Models of Social Change

Charles Payne

Ella Jo Baker died in 1986. Her entire adult life was devoted to building organizations that worked for social change by encouraging individual growth and individual empowerment. Nonetheless even among those generally knowledgeable about the modern history of the Afro-American struggle, neither her name nor her sense of how we make change are widely known. She worked during a time when few Americans were capable of taking a Black woman seriously as a political figure. Yet, Ella Baker was a central figure in Afro-American activism as an organizer and as an advocate of developing the extraordinary potential of ordinary people. Few activists can claim a depth and breadth of political experience comparable to Ella Baker's half-century of struggle. She was associated with whatever organization in the Black community was on the cutting edge of the era—the NAACP (National Association for the Advancement of Colored People) in the forties, the Southern Christian Leadership Conference (SCLC) in the fifties, and the Student Nonviolent Coordinating Committee (SNCC) in the sixties.

Miss Baker's activism—and she was always pointedly Miss Baker to the people she worked with, a mark of respect[1]—was strongly influenced by her family and childhood community. Born in 1903, she grew up primarily in rural North Carolina. She took pride in being from a family with a tradition of social consciousness. Her grandparents bought part of the land they had worked as slaves. She grew up hearing stories of slave revolts from her grandmother, who as a slave had been whipped for refusing to marry the man selected for her by her master. She described her grandfather as a Reconstruction-era activist, a man who tried to create a model Black community and who mortgaged his farm after a flood so that he could buy food for other families. Similarly, her mother and grandmother were independent women, central to the lives of their communities, the people to whom others turned in time of need.[2] Her mother was a talented public speaker and an ardent church worker active in local missionary societies. Ella later said, "I became active in things largely because my mother was active in the field of religion."[3] Before she was out of grade school Ella had acquired a local reputation herself as an effective public speaker.

She remembered the world of her childhood as a kind of "family social-ism," a world in which food and tools and homes were shared, where informal adoption of children was taken for granted, a world with a min-imal sense of social hierarchy "in terms of those who have, having the right to look down upon, or to evaluate as a lesser breed, those who did-n't have. Your relationship to human beings was far more important than your relationship to the amount of money that you made."[4] As an activist she self-consciously saw herself as a bridge across the sharpening social class divisions in the Black community.[5] By her own interpretation, hav-ing been raised where there was a pervasive sense of community among Blacks "helped to strengthen my concept about the need for people to have a sense of their own value and *their* strengths and it became accen-tuated when I began to travel in the forties for the National Association for the Advancement of Colored People. . . . As people moved to towns and cities, the sense of community diminished."[6] Looking for ways to reestablish among Blacks and other dispossessed groups the self-suffi-ciency and community of her youth was to be an important element in her thinking all of her life.

She was valedictorian of her class at Shaw University in 1922, and the administration was probably glad to see her leave; she had been protest-ing the school's restrictive dress code for students and its policy of hav-ing students sing Negro spirituals for visitors. She wanted to go to graduate school to study sociology or to become a medical missionary, but the family's financial situation would allow neither. Instead, she moved to New York where she could find only factory or domestic work. She refused to go into teaching since that was just what a Black woman with a degree was expected to do. Exactly how she first became involved in organizing is not clear—she says she left college with conventional notions of personal success[7]—but it is clear that the smorgasbord politi-cal environment of New York intrigued her. "And so wherever there was a discussion, I'd go. It didn't matter if it was all men. . . . You see, New York was the hotbed of—let's call it radical thinking. . . Boy, it was *good*, stimulating." Subsequently, the economic dislocations of the Depression played an important part in her rejection of "the American illusion that anyone who is determined and persistent can get ahead."[9]

Between 1929 and 1932, she was on the editorial staffs of at least two newspapers, the *American West Indian News* and *Negro National News*. During the Depression, she became national director of the Young Negros' Cooperative League, which established stores, buying clubs that encouraged poor people to pool their purchasing power, and other cooperative economic ventures in Black neighborhoods. During the same period, she worked with a variety of labor organizations in Harlem, including the Women's Day Workers and Industrial League, which focused on the problems of domestic workers. In 1935 Miss Baker herself pretended to be a domestic worker in order to investigate the employment conditions of Black domestics.[10]

Her organizing work in Harlem brought her to the attention of some people active in NAACP circles, and in 1941 she applied to the NAACP for a job as an assistant field secretary. The job involved extensive travel throughout her native South, raising funds, memberships, and consciousness, trying to get people to see the relevance of the organization to their lives and trying to help them work through their very real fears about being associated with the NAACP. She spent about half of each year organizing membership drives and new chapters in the South—Florida, Alabama, Georgia, and Virginia—thus becoming exposed to a wide variety of leadership styles and organizational structures while making innumerable contacts with grassroots leadership, contacts that would become important in her work with the SCLC and SNCC.

In 1943 she became the NAACP's National Director of Branches. In what seems to be the pattern of her life, she was more in the organization than of it. She was a critic—not always a gentle one—of that organization's style of work. By 1941, she was calling the program "stale and uninteresting."[11] She thought the leadership was overly concerned with recognition from whites, overly oriented to a middle-class agenda, unaware of the value of mass-based, confrontational politics, not nearly aggressive enough on economic issues, and too much in the hands of the New York office.[12] She was particularly critical of the organization's tendency to stress membership size without attempting to involve those members more meaningfully in its program. She saw the organization as the victim of its own success. It was successful enough with its program of attacking the legal bases of racial oppression that its very success blinded the organization to its shortcomings. The legal emphasis meant that the huge mass base of the NAACP—400,000 by 1944—could not play a meaningful role in the development of policy and strategy.

She urged the organization to recruit more low-income members by, for example, sending organizers into pool rooms and taverns; her experience had been that some people would join up out of sheer surprise.[13] The branches, she argued, not the national office, should be the focal point of struggle. "Any branch which says it has nothing around which it can build a program," she wrote, "is simply too lazy to concern itself with things on its own doorstep."[14] While many of her recommendations were ignored, she was able in 1944 to initiate a series of regional leadership conferences. The conferences, one of which was attended by Rosa Parks, were intended to help local leaders search for more effective ways to attack local problems and at the same time see how local issues were, inevitably, expressions of broader social issues.[15]

She left the national office in 1946, partly as a result of having accepted responsibility for raising a niece and partly as a result of her conflicts with the organization's viewpoint.[16] She worked for a while as a fund-raiser for the National Urban League and continued to work with the NAACP at the local level, becoming president of the New York City branch which, in her phrase, she tried to "bring back to the people" by moving the office to a location where it would be more visible to the Harlem community and by developing a program in which Black and Hispanic parents actively worked on issues involving school desegrega-tion and the quality of education. For her, the point was that the parents work on the issues themselves rather than having civil rights profession-als work on their behalf.[17]

In the mid-1950s, with Bayard Rustin and Stanley Levison, she helped organize In Friendship, an organization that offered economic support for Blacks suffering reprisals for political activism in the South. This same group helped develop the idea of a mass-based organization to continue the momentum that came out of the Montgomery bus boycott. From that idea, developed by several groups almost simultaneously, grew the Southern Christian Leadership Conference. The initial meeting of the embryonic SCLC was called by the Reverend C. K. Steele, one of the con-tacts Baker had made in the South, and it was the In Friendship group that encouraged Steele to call the meeting.

Levison and Rustin felt that the fledgling SCLC needed an experienced organizer and were able to talk a reluctant Ella Baker into taking the job. In 1957, she went south, intending to stay only a few weeks. She wound up staying two and a half years, becoming the first full-time executive director. At the beginning, she used to joke, SCLC's "office" was her purse and the nearest phone booth. She was responsible for organizing the voter registration and citizenship training drives that constituted the SCLC program during this period. She did this largely by exploiting the network of personal contacts she had developed while with the NAACP.[18]

As with the NAACP, she had trouble getting her own thinking reflected in the programs of the SCLC. She tried to get the leadership to go into some of the rural counties where Blacks were not voting at all. Propheti-cally, she tried, also without success, to get the organization to place more emphasis on women and young people, the constituencies that would soon carry much of the movement. Miss Baker's emphasis on women reflected her sense of how southern Black organizations worked. "All of the churches depended, in terms of things taking place, on women, not men. Men didn't do the things that had to be done and you had a large number of women who were involved in the bus boycott. They were the people who kept the spirit going [the women] and the young people."[19] Being ignored was hardly a surprise to her: "I had known . . . that there would never be any role for me in a leadership capacity with SCLC. Why? First, I'm a woman. Also, I'm not a minister. . . . The basic attitude of men and especially ministers, as to . . . the role of women in their church setups is that of taking orders, not providing leadership."[20]

Despite the difficulties, her association with SCLC put her in a position to help create and shape one of the most significant organizations of the sixties, the Student Nonviolent Coordinating Committee (SNCC). When the sit-in movement among Black college students first began, Ella Baker, like several other adult activists, used her extensive contact list to help it spread.[21] The sit-in phenomenon at the time was essentially a series of disconnected local actions. Feeling that the movement might be more effective with some coordination, Ella talked SCLC into sponsoring a meeting of activist students on the campus of her alma mater, Shaw University. From that meeting, held Easter weekend, 1960, evolved SNCC.

Adult civil rights organizations sent representatives to the organizing meeting with hopes of co-opting all that youthful energy. Three organizations—SCLC, the NAACP, and the Congress of Racial Equality (CORE)—wanted in on the action. The SCLC felt it had the inside track, since many SCLC leaders had worked with the student leaders and, after all, one of the SCLC staff members was in charge of the organizing meeting.[22] They should have consulted with the staff member.

Miss Baker preferred that the students remain independent. Indeed, at one point she walked out of a staff meeting where strategies to bring the students into the SCLC were discussed.[23] In Raleigh, she reinforced the feelings of those students who saw traditional adult leadership as too accommodating and unimaginative; and SNCC remained independent.

By this time, Miss Baker had been working in the South on and off for almost twenty years. In its early years SNCC, like SCLC previously, had her contact network at its disposal. Thus, when SNCC's Bob Moses first ventured into Mississippi she was able to send him to Amzie Moore, a courageous older activist whom Baker had met years before, probably through In Friendship. Much of what would happen in that state for the next four years was predicated on the relationship between these two strangers whom she brought together.

By 1961 SNCC had become the kind of organization that Ella Baker had been trying to create for some years. It went into the rural areas that other groups were reluctant to enter, it was far more open to the participation of women and young people than the established civil rights groups, and it disdained centralization and bureaucracy and insisted that leadership had to be discovered and developed at the local level. Clay Carson notes that "Baker's notion of 'group-centered leadership' had taken hold among student activists, and they strongly opposed any hierarchy of authority such as existed in other civil rights organizations."[24]

Baker was key in preventing all internal dispute from splintering the organization. By 1961 a split had developed between those who wanted the organization involved in voter registration work and those who wanted it to continue in the direct-action tradition in which it had been born. Ella Baker's advice was ordinarily couched in questions, but this time she interceded more directly, suggesting that the students compromise by developing programs in both areas.[25]

Thus, she played a crucial role in creating and shaping a movement organization that set much of the direction and pace of struggle in the early sixties. Bernice Reagon notes that the struggle for civil rights was the "borning" struggle of the decade, the struggle that helped generate and give form to many of the era's battles for social justice.[26] In the same sense SNCC, even more directly than the other civil rights organizations, may be regarded as the "borning" organization, and it is difficult to see how SNCC as we knew it could have come into existence without Ella Baker.

Miss Baker continued to work with a variety of groups through the sixties and well into the seventies. With SNCC, she helped organize the Mississippi Freedom Democratic Party (FDP), a vehicle to give the poor of that state some political voice. She also helped organize the challenge FDP made at the 1964 Democratic National Convention. She had a significant influence on the early leaders of SDS (Students for a Democratic Society), which in its early years adopted a style of work that duplicated the style she encouraged SNCC to adopt. Aldon Morris says she was the "mother" of the activist phase of both organizations.[27] She also influenced the political development of some young women, including Mary King and Casey Hayden, who were later influential in shaping the growth of the contemporary feminist movement.[28] She was involved with attempts to reform urban schools, with South African support groups, with Third World women's organizations, and attempts to organize poor whites in the South.[29] Hers was a wonderfully eclectic style. Whatever the form of the injustice, she was willing to oppose it.

The ideas which undergirded her long activist career do not seem to have changed substantially since the 1930s. If there is one idea that seems central to her approach, it may be the idea of group-centered leadership rather than leader-centered groups. "I have always thought what is needed is the development of people who are interested not in being leaders as much as in developing leadership among other people."[30] In contrast to the more traditional conception of leadership as moving people and directing events, hers was a conception of leadership as teaching, a conception that changes the nature of what it means to be successful. How many people show up for a rally may matter less than how much the people who organize the rally learn from doing so. If the attempt to organize the rally taught them anything about the mechanics of organizing, if the mere act of trying caused them to grow in self-confidence, if the organizers developed stronger bonds among themselves from striving together, then the rally may have been a success even if no one showed up for it. As she said, "You're organizing people to be self-sufficient rather than to be dependent upon the charismatic leader."[31] If growth toward self-sufficiency is the point, then there may be times when people will have to be allowed to make "wrong" decisions, since making decisions and learning from the consequences are necessary to such growth. That was why Ella Baker tried to avoid exerting too much influence on the decision making in SNCC, for example. "Most of the youngsters had been trained to believe in or to follow adults. . . . I felt they ought to have a chance to learn to think things through and to make the decisions."[32]

It follows that she had a poor opinion of centralized leadership, even if skillful and well intentioned.

> I have always felt it was a handicap for oppressed people to depend so largely on a leader, because unfortunately in our culture, the charismatic leader usually becomes a leader because he has found a spot in the public limelight. It usually means that the media made him, and the media may undo him. There is also the danger in our culture that, because a person is called upon to give public statements and is acclaimed by the establishment, such a person gets to the point of believing that he *is* the movement. Such people get so involved with playing the game of being important that they exhaust themselves and their time and they don't do the work of actually organizing people.[33]

From her perspective, the very idea of leading people to freedom is a contradiction in terms. Freedom requires that people be able to analyze their own social position and understand their collective ability to do something about it without relying on leaders. "Strong people," she said in one interview, "don't need strong leaders."[34] "My basic sense of it has always been to understand that in the long run they themselves are the only protection they have against violence or injustice. . . . People have to be made to understand that they cannot look for salvation anywhere but to themselves."[35]

Whether people develop a sense of their own strength depends partly on the organizational context in which they are working. Ella Baker had misgivings about the common assumption that the bigger the political organization, the better, as well as the parallel assumption that rapid growth is always a sign of organizational vitality.[36] Large organizations more easily become antidemocratic, are not as likely to offer the kind of nurturing of individual growth that smaller ones can provide, and may be especially off-putting to members of low-income communities, where the predominant style of relating to individuals is still prebureaucratic. It is easy to forget that during most of the time when SNCC was at the forefront of the southern movement, the organization had only a few hundred very dedicated members. Part of what made that dedication possible, no doubt, was the organization's ability to generate a strong sense of community among its members in the early years. Its scale helped make that community possible, just as it helped each member of the organization to feel that his or her contribution mattered. It also seems that the decline of the organization was related to the sudden growth in the size of its membership after 1964. According to SNCC members like Cleveland Sellers and Mary King, the rapid growth led to the development of political factions and a general deterioration in the quality of relationships within the organization.[37]

Mary King writes about how Ella Baker encouraged her political growth: "Periodically, Miss Baker would stop whatever Bobbi or I was doing and probe with a series of questions. With Socratic persistence, in her resonant and commanding voice, she would query, 'Now let me ask this again, what is our purpose here? What are we trying to accomplish?' Again and again, she would force us to articulate our assumptions. Sometimes I felt intimidated by her scrutiny."[38]

Baker could be very intimidating indeed when she chose to be. That her persistent questioning could have such positive impact on so many young people is probably partly a reflection of her ability to appear nonjudgmental.[39] Though it is not impossible for such detailed attention to the intellectual growth of the individual to take place in large organizations, their scale certainly militates against it. On the other hand, if part of progressive politics is helping other people grow, no organization can be too small for that.

Ella Baker was much impressed by cell structures, including that of the Communist party. "I don't think we had any more effective demonstration of organizing people for whatever purpose."[40] She thought that one of the most sensible structures for change-oriented organizations would have small groups of people maintaining effective working relationships among themselves but also retaining contact in some form with other such cells, so that coordinated action would be possible whenever large numbers really were necessary.

Her awareness of the value of small organizations is part of a larger theme, a consistent concern for the well-being of particular individuals—not just the "community," or "Black people," or some other abstraction. Before a meeting she habitually tried to find out if anyone had a personal problem that needed attention.[41] Her sensitivity to this kind of question may be partly a reflection of the fact that she was a woman, and quite self-consciously so, or a reflection of her rootedness in the highly personal culture of the South.

Her concern extended to the quality of relationships among activists themselves. Conflicts over the direction of the movement as well as purely personal conflicts were ongoing, of course, but Ella Baker was concerned that some of them were more destructive than they had to be. One of the reasons for this, she suggested more than once, was "the old business of groups that are better prepared to advocate their position sometimes engendering a defensiveness on the part of those who are less prepared."[42] The real issues involved are then submerged under the resentment, and the losing side may withdraw or bide its time for revenge.

While not committed to nonviolence herself, she seems to have appreciated its value as a force for regulating behavior within the movement. Referring to the young people of early SNCC, she spoke approvingly of the fact that "they were so keen about the concept of nonviolence that they were trying to exercise a degree of consciousness and care about not being violent in their manner of judgment of others."[43]

How shall we deal with the differences and disagreements among ourselves, real or imagined, without alienating one another? That question crops up repeatedly in Ella Baker's thinking, but it has received far too little attention from those concerned with social change, with the exception of some feminists. Products of the society we wish to change, we carry within ourselves some of its worst tendencies, including tendencies that will lead to self-aggrandizing and exploitative relationships. Once, in the context or an argument within SNCC over who had the right to participate in the movement, Baker said, "We need to penetrate the mystery of life and perfect the mastery of life and the latter requires understanding that human beings are human beings."[44] Unless we do a better job of responding to the human contradictions and weaknesses of the people we work with, we are likely to continue to create politics that are progressive in the ideas expressed but disempowering in the way individuals expressing those ideas relate to one another.

Group-centered leadership is leadership in which the ego needs of leaders are placed beneath the developmental needs of the group. It requires leaders who can deal nondestructively with their own need for recognition. Ella Baker held a special fear of the need of leaders for some sort of recognition from the larger society, seeing it as part of the pattern by which initially progressive American movements have traditionally been routinized.[45]

Among Blacks she saw it as a distorting factor across several generations of leadership and across various ideological lines. Black radicals as well as Black moderates have allowed the desire to be recognized to blunt the thrust of their activism. Thus, in the NAACP of the forties and fifties, Ella Baker thought the thirst for recognition was one of the factors leading to accommodationist politics at a time when many of the members were ready for a more militant program. The thirst for recognition was also a problem for the radicals of the late 1960s, some of whom became so enamored of the coverage they were receiving from the press that they began performing for the press. As she saw it: "I think they got caught up in their own rhetoric. . . . To me, it is a part of our system which says that success is registered in terms of, if not money, then how much prestige and how much recognition you have. . . . So these youngsters with their own need for recognition began to respond to the press."[46] It is not difficult to imagine what media recognition must have done to the egos of the leaders involved or how it must have poisoned their relationships with other, less-recognized activists who were working just as hard, risking just as much, as the handful of media celebrities.

The distorting potential of media recognition underscores again the case for groups not being too dependent upon leaders. Part of the reason Ella Baker is not a household name is her conviction that political organizers lose a certain kind of effectiveness when they allow themselves to become media stars. Typically, at the conference at which SNCC was organized, she was at pains to put some distance between the students and the press, and in its early years none of SNCC's leading figures became media celebrities. We do not know whether that pattern was due in any measure to the influence of Ella Baker, but it is certainly consistent with what she advocated.

Miss Baker seems to have viewed the press as more useful in the process of mobilizing than in the process of organizing. The distinction between mobilizing and organizing was crucial for her. Organizing, according to Ella Baker, involves creating ongoing groups that are mass-based in the sense that the people a group purports to represent have real impact on the group's direction. Mobilizing is more sporadic, involving large numbers of people for relatively short periods of time and probably for relatively dramatic activities. What SNCC did in rural Mississippi, Alabama, and Georgia was organizing. Activists went into a community committed to staying there for a period of time, trying to identify local leadership, strengthen it, and help it find ways to create organizations and programs that would help local people reach a point of development where they would no longer need to rely on SNCC or anything similar. The intention was to leave behind enduring organizations led by the people in whose name they were created, organizations like the Freedom Democratic Party in Mississippi and the Lowndes County Freedom Organization in Alabama. At least, organizing under this conception involves the creation of stable, ongoing relationships and of ongoing attempts at political education.

By way of contrast, what the SCLC did in Birmingham and Albany and elsewhere was mobilizing—going in for a matter of weeks or months, leading massive demonstrations aimed at bettering the conditions under which people lived, and then moving on. By its nature, mobilizing is more likely to be public and to be dependent upon generating appropriate publicity. The point is not that one or the other is more important historically—both are clearly necessary—but that they are two different political activities.

The distinction between organizing and mobilizing has become increasingly muddled. Young people looking back at the movement tend to see the mobilizing but not the organizing. They see the great demonstrations and the rallies and take that to be the movement. They do not see the organizing effort, often years of such effort, that made the grand moments possible. They do not see organizers going door to door for months on end trying to win trust, overcome fear, and educate people to the ways the movement might connect with their lives. Cordell Reagon, one of the young SNCC organizers in the Albany, Georgia, movement remembers the early phase of organizing in that city as largely hanging around the student union talking to students, hanging around playgrounds, visiting people in their homes.[47] In general, Deep South organizing was a process of trying to become a part of the lives of the people one was trying to work with, and there was frequently nothing very dramatic about it.

Ella Baker understood the failure of the radical thrust of the late sixties as being partly a failure to continue the undramatic work of organizing. She thought that much of what Stokely Carmichael, for instance, was saying around 1968 was thoughtful and grounded in his many years of working to change the system. Then his ideas became a slogan for people who were less thoughtful and had done less work. The rhetoric, as Ella Baker said, got far ahead of the organization.[48] At least a part of what was missing was "a greater degree of real concentration on organizing people. I keep bringing this up. I'm sorry, but it's part of me. I just don't see any-thing to be substituted for having people understand their position and understand their potential power and how to use it. This can only be done, as I see it, through the long route, almost of actually organizing people in small groups and parlaying those into larger groups."[49] She was always dubious about the real value of demonstrations. Lobbying and demonstrations may produce some gains from the powers that be rela-tively quickly, but the same powers may retract those gains as soon as the political winds shift. What Miss Baker called "real organizing" might mean that results would take longer to achieve, but it might also mean these results would be better protected.

My purpose in writing this essay was to introduce the Grand Lady, as her grandfather used to call her, to people who may not have heard much about her way of working and thinking. That Ella Baker could have lived the life she did and remain so little known even among the politically knowledgeable is important in itself. It reminds us once more of how much our collective past has been distorted—and distorted in disem-powering ways. What I know of Ella Baker's thinking does not strike me, and never struck her, as offering any complete set of answers, but I think it does offer a more promising way to begin framing questions about where we are and how we get to the next stage than the ideas of many activists who did become media figures.

One has to wonder how she sustained her involvement for so long. It is not difficult to imagine how much frustration was built into the work she chose for herself. Nowadays we tend to think that anyone who works for social change for a year or two has made an enormous sacrifice. In the few places I know of where she comments on this, there is a suggestion that she was sustained by the faith that her work was a part of something on-going:

> Every time I see a young person who has come through the system to a stage where he could profit from the system and identify with it, but who identi-fies more with the struggle of black people who have not had his chance, every time I find such a person I take new hope. I feel new life as a result.[50]

> It isn't impossible that what those who came along with me went through, might stimulate others to continue to fight for a society that does not have those kinds of problems. Somewhere down the line the numbers increase, the tribe increases. So how do you keep on? I can't help it. I don't claim to have any corner on an answer, but I believe that the struggle is eternal. Somebody else carries on.[51]

Notes

1 Mary King, Freedom Song (New York: William Morrow, 1987), 43.

2 John Britton, "Interview with Ella Baker: June 19, 1968," Moorland-Spingarn Collection, Howard University, 4; Ellen Cantarow with Susan O'Malley, Moving the Mountain: Women Working for Social Change (Old Westbury, NY: Feminist Press, 1980), 56–60; Howard Zinn, SNCC: The New Abolitionists (Boston: Beacon, 1965), 32–34.

3 Lenore Hagan, "Ella Baker Interview, March 4, 1978," Archives, Highlander Research and Education Center, New Market, Tennessee, 15.

4 Ibid., 79.

5 Cantarow and O'Malley, 68, 70.

6 Ibid., 61.

7 Britton, 1.

8 Cantarow and O'Malley, 64.

9 Ella Baker with Marvel Cooke, "The Bronx Slave Market," Crisis, no. 42 (November 1935), 340.

10 Cantarow and O'Malley, 63–64; Baker with Cooke.

11 Ella Baker, "Report of Branch Coordinator," Papers of the NAACP University Publications (Frederick, Md., 1982), microfilm reel 5, frame 0547.

12 Britton (n. 2 above), 11–12, 76–82; Harper, 21.

13 Untitled memo, NAACP papers, reel 6, frame 0654.

14 Ella Baker, "Conducting Membership Drives" (1942), NAACP papers, reel 11, frame 199.

15 Hagan (n. 3 above), 21; Susan Thrasher and Casey Hayden, "Ella Baker Interview, April 19, 1977," Southern Oral History Collection, University of North Carolina at Chapel Hill, 49.

16 Thrasher and Hayden, 51; Cantarow and O'Malley, 74, 156.

17 Ella Baker, "Developing Community Leadership," in Black Women in White America, ed. Gerda Lerner (New York: Vintage, 1973).

18 Britton, 33–34; Hagan, 63.

19 Eugene Walker, "Interview with Ella Baker, September 4, 1974," Southern Oral History Collection, University of North Carolina at Chapel Hill, 21.

20 Britton, 34–35.

21 Aldon Morris, Origins of the Civil Rights Movement (New York; Free Press, 1984), 201

22 Ibid., 216.

23 Cantarow and O'Malley, 84.

24 Claybourne Carson, In Struggle: SNCC and the Black Awakening of the 1960s (Cambridge, Mass.: Harvard University Press, 1981), 30.

25 Ibid., 41–42.

[26] Bernice Reagon, "The Borning Struggle," in They Should Have Served That Cup of Coffee—ed. Dick Cluster (Boston: South End Fress, 1979), 38.

[27] Morris, 223.

[28] King (n. 1 above), 42–48, 59–62; Sara Evans, Personal Politics (New York: Random House, 1979), 52–54.

[29] Cantarow and O'Malley, 54–56.

[30] Baker, "Developing Community Leadership" (n. 17 above), 352.

[31] Britton (n. 2 above), 37.

[32] Cantarow and O'Malley, 87.

[33] Baker, "Developing Community Leadership," 351.

[34] Canterow and O'Malley, 53.

[35] Baker, "Developing Community Leadership," 347.

[36] Britton, 79.

[37] Cleveland Sellers, River of No Return (New York: Morrow, 1973), 130–31; King (n. 1 above), 520.

[38] King, 60.

[39] See Jeanne Grant, "Fundi. The Story of Ella Baker" (New York: First Run Films, 1981), videocassette, for a sense of the numbers of young activists influenced by Baker.

[40] Britton, 81.

[41] See "Fundi."

[42] Britton, 57.

[43] Ibid., 94.

[44] Zinn (n. 2 above), 186.

[45] Britton, 11, 69.

[46] Ibid., 66.

[47] Morris, 240.

[48] Britton, 67.

[49] Ibid., 79

[50] Baker, "Developing Community Leadership" (n. 17 above), 352.

[51] Cantarow and O'Malley (n. 2 above), 93.

The Reflective Woman
Bridge Readings

Peggy McIntosh, Ph.D., is the associate director of the Wellesley College Center for Research on Women, and is founder and co-director of the national S.E.E.D. (Seeking Educational Equity and Diversity) Project on Inclusive Curriculum. She has lectured worldwide and is considered an authority on multicultural and gender-fair curricula in higher education. Her many articles have examined aspects of race and the integration of feminist theories into traditional curricula.

White Privilege and Male Privilege

A Personal Account of Coming to See Correspondences Through Work in Women's Studies (1988)

Peggy McIntosh

Through work to bring materials and perspectives from Women's Studies into the rest of the curriculum, I have often noticed men's unwillingness to grant that they are overprivileged in the curriculum, even though they may grant that women are disadvantaged. Denials that amount to taboos surround the subject of advantages that men gain from women's disadvantages. These denials protect male privilege from being fully recognized, acknowledged, lessened, or ended.

Thinking through unacknowledged male privilege as a phenomenon with a life of its own, I realized that since hierarchies in our society are interlocking, there was most likely a phenomenon of white privilege that was similarly denied and protected, but alive and real in its effects. As a white person, I realized I had been taught about racism as something that puts others at a disadvantage, but had been taught not to see one of its corollary aspects, white privilege, which puts me at an advantage.

I think whites are carefully taught not to recognize white privilege, as males are taught not to recognize male privilege. So I have begun in an untutored way to ask what it is like to have white privilege. This paper is a partial record of my personal observations and not a scholarly analysis. It is based on my daily experiences within my particular circumstances.

I have come to see white privilege as an invisible package of unearned assets that I can count on cashing in each day, but about which I was "meant" to remain oblivious. White privilege is like an invisible weightless knapsack of special provisions, assurances, tools, maps, guides, codebooks, passports, visas, clothes, compass, emergency gear, and blank checks.

Since I have had trouble facing white privilege, and describing its results in my life, I saw parallels here with men's reluctance to acknowledge male privilege. Only rarely will a man go beyond acknowledging that women are disadvantaged to acknowledging that men have unearned advantage, or that unearned privilege has not been good for men's development as human beings, or for society's development, or that privilege systems might ever be challenged and *changed*.

I will review here several types or layers of denial that I see at work protecting, and preventing awareness about, entrenched male privilege. Then I will draw parallels, from my own experience, with the denials that veil the facts of white privilege. Finally, I will list forty-six ordinary and daily ways in which I experience having white privilege, by contrast with my African American colleagues in the same building. This list is not intended to be generalizable. Others can make their own lists from within their own life circumstances.

Writing this paper has been difficult, despite warm receptions for the talks on which it is based.[1] For describing white privilege makes one newly accountable. As we in Women's Studies work reveal male privilege and ask men to give up some of their power, so one who writes about having white privilege must ask, "Having described it, what will I do to lessen or end it?"

The denial of men's overprivileged state takes many forms in discussions of curriculum change work. Some claim that men must be central in the curriculum because they have done most of what is important or distinctive in life or in civilization. Some recognize sexism in the curriculum but deny that it makes male students seem unduly important in life. Others agree that certain *individual* thinkers are male oriented but deny that there is any *systemic* tendency in disciplinary frameworks or epistemology to overempower men as a group. Those men who do grant that male privilege takes institutionalized and embedded forms are still likely to deny that male hegemony has opened doors for them personally. Virtually all men deny that male overreward alone can explain men's centrality in all the inner sanctums of our most powerful institutions. Moreover, those few who will acknowledge that male privilege systems have overempowered them usually end up doubting that we could dismantle these privilege systems. They may say they will work to improve women's status, in the society or in the university, but they can't or won't support the idea of lessening men's. In curricular terms, this is the point at which they say that they regret they cannot use any of the interesting new scholarship on women because the syllabus is full. When the talk turns to giving men less cultural room, even the most thoughtful and fair-minded of the men I know will tend to reflect, or fall back on, conservative assumptions about the inevitability of present gender relations and distributions of power, calling on precedent or sociobiology and psychobiology to demonstrate that male domination is natural and follows inevitably from evolutionary pressures. Others resort to arguments from "experience" or religion or social responsibility or wishing and dreaming.

After I realized, through faculty development work in Women's Studies, the extent to which men work from a base of unacknowledged privilege, I understood that much of their oppressiveness was unconscious. Then I remembered the frequent charges from women of color that white women whom they encounter are oppressive. I began to understand why we are justly seen as oppressive, even when we don't see ourselves that way. At the very least, obliviousness of one's privileged state can make a person or group irritating to be with. I began to count the ways in which I enjoy unearned skin privilege and have been conditioned into oblivion about its existence, unable to see that it put me "ahead" in any way, or put my people ahead, overrewarding us and yet also paradoxically damaging us, or that it could or should be changed.

My schooling gave me no training in seeing myself as an oppressor, as an unfairly advantaged person, or as a participant in a damaged culture. I was taught to see myself as an individual whose moral state depended on her individual moral will. At school, we were not taught about slavery in any depth; we were not taught to see slaveholders as damaged people. Slaves were seen as the only group at risk of being dehumanized. My schooling followed the pattern which Elizabeth Minnich has pointed out: whites are taught to think of their lives as morally neutral, normative, and average, and also ideal, so that when we work to benefit others, this is seen as work that will allow "them" to be more like "us." I think many of us know how obnoxious this attitude can be in men.

After frustration with men who would not recognize male privilege, I decided to try to work on myself at least by identifying some of the daily effects of white privilege in my life. It is crude work, at this stage, but I will give here a list of special circumstances and conditions I experience that I did not earn but that I have been made to feel are mine by birth, by citizenship, and by virtue of being a conscientious law-abiding "normal" person of goodwill. I have chosen those conditions that I think in my case *attach somewhat more to skin-color privilege* than to class, religion, ethnic status, or geographical location, though these other privileging factors are intricately intertwined. As far as I can see, my Afro-American co-workers, friends, and acquaintances with whom I come into daily or frequent contact in this particular time, place, and line of work cannot count on most of these conditions.

1. I can, if I wish, arrange to be in the company of people of my race most of the time.

2. I can avoid spending time with people whom I was trained to mistrust and who have learned to mistrust my kind or me.

3. If I should need to move, I can be pretty sure of renting or purchasing housing in an area which I can afford and in which I would want to live.

4. I can be reasonably sure that my neighbors in such a location will be neutral or pleasant to me.

5. I can go shopping alone most of the time, fairly well assured that I will not be followed or harassed by store detectives.

6. I can turn on the television or open to the front page of the paper and see people of my race widely and positively represented.

7. When I am told about our national heritage or about "civilization," I am shown that people of my color made it what it is.

8. I can be sure that my children will be given curricular materials that testify to the existence of their race.

9. If I want to, I can be pretty sure of finding a publisher for this piece on white privilege.

10. I can be fairly sure of having my voice heard in a group in which I am the only member of my race.

11. I can be casual about whether or not to listen to another woman's voice in a group in which she is the only member of her race.

12. I can go into a book shop and count on finding the writing of my race represented, into a supermarket and find the staple foods that fit with my cultural traditions, into a hairdresser's shop and find someone who can deal with my hair.

13. Whether I use checks, credit cards, or cash, I can count on my skin color not to work against the appearance that I am financially reliable.

14. I could arrange to protect our young children most of the time from people who might not like them.

15. I did not have to educate our children to be aware of systemic racism for their own daily physical protection.

16. I can be pretty sure that my children's teachers and employers will tolerate them if they fit school and workplace norms; my chief worries about them do not concern others' attitudes toward their race.

17. I can talk with my mouth full and not have people put this down to my color.

18. I can swear, or dress in secondhand clothes, or not answer letters, without having people attribute these choices to the bad morals, the poverty, or the illiteracy of my race.

19. I can speak in public to a powerful male group without putting my race on trial.

20. I can do well in a challenging situation without being called a credit to my race.

21. I am never asked to speak for all the people of my racial group.

22. I can remain oblivious to the language and customs of persons of color who constitute the world's majority without feeling in my culture any penalty for such oblivion.

23. I can criticize our government and talk about how much I fear its policies and behavior without being seen as a cultural outsider.

24. I can be reasonably sure that if I ask to talk to "the person in charge," I will be facing a person of my race.

25. If a traffic cop pulls me over or if the IRS audits my tax return, I can be sure I haven't been singled out because of my race.

26. I can easily buy posters, postcards, picture books, greeting cards, dolls, toys, and children's magazines featuring people of my race.

27. I can go home from most meetings of organizations I belong to feeling somewhat tied in, rather than isolated, out of place, outnumbered, unheard, held at a distance, or feared.

28. I can be pretty sure that an argument with a colleague of another race is more likely to jeopardize her chances for advancement than to jeopardize mine.

29. I can be fairly sure that if I argue for the promotion of a person of another race, or a program centering on race, this is not likely to cost me heavily within my present setting, even if my colleagues disagree with me.

30. If I declare there is a racial issue at hand, or there isn't a racial issue at hand, my race will lend me more credibility for either position than a person of color will have.

31. I can choose to ignore developments in minority writing and minority activist programs, or disparage them, or learn from them, but in any case, I can find ways to be more or less protected from negative consequences of any of these choices.

32. My culture gives me little fear about ignoring the perspectives and powers of people of other races.

33. I am not made acutely aware that my shape, bearing, or body odor will be taken as a reflection on my race.

34. I can worry about racism without being seen as self-interested or self-seeking.

35. I can take a job with an affirmative action employer without having my co-workers on the job suspect that I got it because of my race.

36. If my day, week, or year is going badly, I need not ask of each negative episode or situation whether it has racial overtones.

37. I can be pretty sure of finding people who would be willing to talk with me and advise me about my next steps, professionally.

38. I can think over many options, social, political, imaginative, or professional, without asking whether a person of my race would be accepted or allowed to do what I want to do.

39. I can be late to a meeting without having the lateness reflect on my race.

40. I can choose public accommodation without fearing that people of my race cannot get in or will be mistreated in the places I have chosen.

41. I can be sure that if I need legal or medical help, my race will not work against me.

42. I can arrange my activities so that I will never have to experience feelings of rejection owing to my race.

43. If I have low credibility as a leader, I can be sure that my race is not the problem.

44. I can easily find academic courses and institutions that give attention only to people of my race.

45. I can expect figurative language and imagery in all of the arts to testify to experiences of my race.

46. I can choose blemish cover or bandages in "flesh" color and have them more or less match my skin.

I repeatedly forgot each of the realizations on this list until I wrote it down. For me, white privilege has turned out to be an elusive and fugitive subject. The pressure to avoid it is great, for in facing it I must give up the myth of meritocracy. If these things are true, this is not such a free country; one's life is not what one makes it; many doors open for certain people through no virtues of their own. These perceptions mean also that my moral condition is not what I had been led to believe. The appearance of being a good citizen rather than a troublemaker comes in large part from having all sorts of doors open automatically because of my color.

A further paralysis of nerve comes from literary silence protecting privilege. My clearest memories of finding such analysis are in Lillian Smith's unparalleled *Killers of the Dream* and Margaret Andersen's review of Karen and Mamie Fields' *Lemon Swamp*. Smith, for example, wrote about walking toward black children on the street and knowing they would step into the gutter; Andersen contrasted the pleasure that she, as a white child, took on summer driving trips to the south with Karen Fields' memories of driving in a closed car stocked with all necessities lest, in stopping, her black family should suffer "insult, or worse." Adrienne Rich also recognizes and writes about daily experiences of privilege, but in my observation, white women's writing in this area is far more often on systemic racism than on our daily lives as light-skinned women.[2]

In unpacking this invisible knapsack of white privilege, I have listed conditions of daily experience that I once took for granted, as neutral, normal, and universally available to everybody, just as I once thought of a male-focused curriculum as the neutral or accurate account that can speak for all. Nor did I think of any of these perquisites as bad for the holder. I now think that we need a more finely differentiated taxonomy of privilege, for some of these varieties are only what one would want for everyone in a just society, and others give license to be ignorant, oblivious, arrogant, and destructive. Before proposing some more finely tuned categorization, I will make some observations about the general effects of these conditions on my life and expectations.

In this potpourri of examples, some privileges make me feel at home in the world. Others allow me to escape penalties or dangers that others suffer. Through some, I escape fear, anxiety, insult, injury, or a sense of not being welcome, not being real. Some keep me from having to hide, to be in disguise, to feel sick or crazy, to negotiate each transaction from the position of being an outsider or, within my group, a person who is suspected of having too close links with a dominant culture. Most keep me from having to be angry.

I see a pattern running through the matrix of white privilege, a pattern of assumptions that were passed on to me as a white person. There was one main piece of cultural turf; it was my own turf, and I was among those who could control the turf. I could measure up to the cultural standards and take advantage of the many options I saw around me to make what the culture would call a success of my life. *My skin color was an asset for any move I was educated to want to make.* I could think of myself as "belonging" in major ways and of making social systems work for me. I could freely disparage, fear, neglect, or be oblivious to anything outside of the dominant cultural forms. Being of the main culture, I could also criticize it fairly freely. My life was reflected back to me frequently enough so that I felt, with regard to my race, if not to my sex, like one of the real people.

 Whether through the curriculum or in the newspaper, the television, the economic system, or the general look of people in the streets, I received daily signals and indications that my people counted and that others *either didn't exist or must be trying, not very successfully, to be like people of my race.* I was given cultural permission not to hear voices of people of other races or a tepid cultural tolerance for hearing or acting on such voices. I was also raised not to suffer seriously from anything that darker-skinned people might say about my group, "protected," though perhaps I should more accurately say *prohibited*, through the habits of my economic class and social group, from living in racially mixed groups or being reflective about interactions between people of differing races.

In proportion as my racial group was being made confident, comfortable, and oblivious, other groups were likely being made unconfident, uncomfortable, and alienated. Whiteness protected me from many kinds of hostility, distress, and violence, which I was being subtly trained to visit in turn upon people of color.

For this reason, the word "privilege" now seems to me misleading. Its connotations are too positive to fit the conditions and behaviors which "privilege systems" produce. We usually think of privilege as being a favored state, whether earned, or conferred by birth or luck. School graduates are reminded they are privileged and urged to use their (enviable) assets well. The word "privilege" carries the connotation of being something everyone must want. Yet some of the conditions I have described here work to systemically overempower certain groups. Such privilege simply *confers dominance*, gives permission to control, because of one's race or sex. The kind of privilege that gives license to some people to be, at best, thoughtless and, at worst, murderous should not continue to be referred to as a desirable attribute. Such "privilege" may be widely desired without being in any way beneficial to the whole society.

Moreover, though "privilege" may confer power, it does not confer moral strength. Those who do not depend on conferred dominance have traits and qualities that may never develop in those who do. Just as Women's Studies courses indicate that women survive their political circumstances to lead lives that hold the human race together, so "underprivileged" people of color who are the world's majority have survived their oppression and lived survivors' lives from which the white global minority can and must learn. In some groups, those dominated have actually become strong through *not* having all of these unearned advantages, and this gives them a great deal to teach the others. Members of so-called privileged groups can seem foolish, ridiculous, infantile, or dangerous by contrast.

I want, then, to distinguish between earned strength and unearned power conferred systemically. Power from unearned privilege can look like strength when it is, in fact, permission to escape or to dominate. But not all of the privileges on my list are inevitably damaging. Some, like the expectation that neighbors will be decent to you, or that your race will not count against you in court, should be the norm in a just society and should be considered as the entitlement of everyone. Others, like the privilege not to listen to less powerful people, distort the humanity of the holders as well as the ignored groups. Still others, like finding one's staple foods everywhere, may be a function of being a member of a numerical majority in the population. Others have to do with not having to labor under pervasive negative stereotyping and mythology.

We might at least start by distinguishing between positive advantages that we can work to spread, to the point where they are not advantages at all but simply part of the normal civic and social fabric, and negative types of advantage that unless rejected will always reinforce our present hierarchies. For example, the positive "privilege" of belonging, the feeling that one belongs within the human circle, as Native Americans say, fosters development and should not be seen as privilege for a few. It is, let us say, an entitlement that none of us should have to earn; ideally it is an *unearned entitlement*. At present, since only a few have it, it is an *unearned advantage* for them. The negative "privilege" that gave me cultural permission not to take darker-skinned Others seriously can be seen as arbitrarily conferred dominance and should not be desirable for anyone. This paper results from a process of coming to see that some of the power that I originally saw as attendant on being a human being in the United States consisted in *unearned advantage* and *conferred dominance*, as well as other kinds of special circumstance not universally taken for granted.

In writing this paper I have also realized that white identity and status (as well as class identity and status) give me considerable power to choose whether to broach this subject and its trouble. I can pretty well decide whether to disappear and avoid and not listen and escape the dislike I may engender in other people through this essay, or interrupt, answer, interpret, preach, correct, criticize, and control to some extent what goes on in reaction to it. Being white, I am given considerable power to escape many kinds of danger or penalty as well as to choose which risks I want to take.

There is an analogy here, once again, with Women's Studies. Our male colleagues do not have a great deal to lose in supporting Women's Studies, but they do not have a great deal to lose if they oppose it either. They simply have the power to decide whether to commit themselves to more equitable distributions of power. They will probably feel few penalties whatever choice they make; they do not seem, in any obvious short-term sense, the ones at risk, though they and we are all at risk because of the behaviors that have been rewarded in them.

Through Women's Studies work I have met very few men who are truly distressed about systemic, unearned male advantage and conferred dominance. And so one question for me and others like me is whether we will be like them, or whether we will get truly distressed, even outraged, about unearned race advantage and conferred dominance and if so, what we will do to lessen them. In any case, we need to do more work in identifying how they actually affect our daily lives. We need more down-to-earth writing by people about these taboo subjects. We need more understanding of the ways in which white "privilege" damages white people, for these are not the same ways in which it damages the victimized. Skewed white psyches are an inseparable part of the picture, though I do not want to confuse the kinds of damage done to the holders of special assets and to those who suffer the deficits. Many, perhaps most, of our white students in the United States think that racism doesn't affect them because they are not people of color; they do not see "whiteness" as a racial identity. Many men likewise think that Women's Studies does not bear on their own existences because they are not female; they do not see themselves as having gendered identities. Insisting on the universal "effects" of "privilege" systems, then, becomes one of our chief tasks, and being more explicit about the *particular* effects in particular contexts is another. Men need to join us in this work.

In addition, since race and sex are not the only advantaging systems at work, we need to similarly examine the daily experience of having age advantage, or ethnic advantage, or physical ability, or advantage related to nationality, religion, or sexual orientation. Professor Marnie Evans suggested to me that in many ways the list I made also applies directly to heterosexual privilege. This is a still more taboo subject than race privilege: the daily ways in which heterosexual privilege makes some persons comfortable or powerful, providing supports, assets, approvals, and rewards to those who live or expect to live in heterosexual pairs. Unpacking that content is still more difficult, owing to the deeper imbeddedness of heterosexual advantage and dominance and stricter taboos surrounding these.

But to start such an analysis I would put this observation from my own experience: the fact that I live under the same roof with a man triggers all kinds of societal assumptions about my worth, politics, life, and values and triggers a host of unearned advantages and powers. After recasting many elements from the original list I would add further observations like these:

1. My children do not have to answer questions about why I live with my partner (my husband).

2. I have no difficulty finding neighborhoods where people approve of our household.

3. Our children are given texts and classes that implicitly support our kind of family unit and do not turn them against my choice of domestic partnership.

4. I can travel alone or with my husband without expecting embarrassment or hostility in those who deal with us.

5. Most people I meet will see my marital arrangements as an asset to my life or as a favorable comment on my likability, my competence, or my mental health.

6. I can talk about the social events of a weekend without fearing most listeners' reactions.

7. I will feel welcomed and "normal" in the usual walks of public life, institutional and social.

8. In many contexts, I am seen as "all right" in daily work on women because I do not live chiefly with women.

Difficulties and dangers surrounding the task of finding parallels are many. Since racism, sexism, and heterosexism are not the same, the advantages associated with them should not be seen as the same. In addition, it is hard to isolate aspects of unearned advantage that derive chiefly from social class, economic class, race, religion, region, sex, or ethnic identity. The oppressions are both distinct and interlocking, as the Combahee River Collective statement of 1977 continues to remind us eloquently.[3]

One factor seems clear about all of the interlocking oppressions. They take both active forms that we can see and embedded forms that members of the dominant group are taught not to see. In my class and place, I did not see myself as racist because I was taught to recognize racism only in individual acts of meanness by members of my group, never in invisible systems conferring racial dominance on my group from birth. Likewise, we are taught to think that sexism or heterosexism is carried on only through intentional, individual acts of discrimination, meanness, or cruelty, rather than in invisible systems conferring unsought dominance on certain groups. Disapproving of the systems won't be enough to change them. I was taught to think that racism could end if white individuals changed their attitudes; many men think sexism can be ended by individual changes in daily behavior toward women. But a man's sex provides advantage for him whether or not he approves of the way in which dominance has been conferred on his group. A "white" skin in the United States opens many doors for whites whether or not we approve of the way dominance has been conferred on us. Individual acts can palliate, but cannot end, these problems. To redesign social systems, we need first to acknowledge their colossal unseen dimensions. The silences and denials surrounding privilege are the key political tool here. They keep the thinking about equality or equity incomplete, protecting unearned advantage and conferred dominance by making these taboo subjects. Most talk by whites about equal opportunity seems to me now to be about equal opportunity to try to get into a position of dominance while denying that *systems* of dominance exist.

Obliviousness about white advantage, like obliviousness about male advantage, is kept strongly inculturated in the United States so as to maintain the myth of meritocracy, the myth that democratic choice is equally available to all. Keeping most people unaware that freedom of confident action is there for just a small number of people props up those in power and serves to keep power in the hands of the same groups that have most of it already. Though systemic change takes many decades, there are pressing questions for me and I imagine for some others like me if we raise our daily consciousness on the perquisites of being light-skinned. What will we do with such knowledge? As we know from watching men, it is an open question whether we will choose to use unearned advantage to weaken invisible privilege systems and whether we will use any of our arbitrarily awarded power to try to reconstruct power systems on a broader base.

Notes

[1] This paper was presented at the Virginia Women's Studies Association conference in Richmond in April, 1986, and the American Educational Research Association conference in Boston in October, 1986, and discussed with two groups of participants in the Dodge seminars for Secondary School Teachers in New York and Boston in the spring of 1987.

[2] Andersen, Margaret, "Race and the Social Science Curriculum: A Teaching and Learning Discussion." *Radical Teacher*, November, 1984, pp. 17–20. Smith, Lillian, *Killers of the Dream*, New York: W. W. Norton, 1949.

[3] "A Black Feminist Statement," The Combahee River Collective, pp. 13–22 in G. Hull, P. Scott, B. Smith, Eds., *All the Women Are White, All the Blacks Are Men, But Some of Us Are Brave: Black Women's Studies*, Old Westbury, NY: The Feminist Press, 1982.

Mohandas K. Gandhi (1869–1948) was called the Mahatma (Great Soul); he is known as a great national and spiritual leader of India, who helped free India from British rule through nonviolent resistance. He was assassinated in 1948.

from Principles of Nonviolence

Mohandas K. Gandhi

53

I see so much misapprehension about *satyagraha* amongst us, as well as amongst Englishmen that, though I have said and written much about it, I think it proper to say something even at the risk of repetition.

Satyagraha was a word coined in South Africa to name a certain movement. First, even the Gujarati word for the great movement that our countrymen in South Africa were carrying on was "passive resistance." Once I happened to address a meeting of Europeans in connection with the movement, and on that occasion the European president of the meeting said there was nothing active in the power of the Indians—who were voteless and unarmed—to offer passive resistance, which could only be a weapon of the weak. He was my friend. He expressed these views without meaning any insult to us, but I felt humiliated. I was conscious that the nature of the fight that the Indians were offering in South Africa was not the result of their weakness. They had purposely decided on that sort of agitation. I took the earliest opportunity to correct my friend's views and demonstrate to him that it was beyond the power of weak men to put up a fight of the nature the Indians in South Africa were doing. They were exhibiting greater courage than that required of a soldier.

Whilst I was in England, in connection with the same movement, I saw that the suffragist women were burning buildings and whipping officers and calling their agitation "passive resistance," and the people also called it so. In the agitation of the Indians in South Africa there was no room for these violent acts. I thus saw that to let our movement be known by the name of "passive resistance" was fraught with dangers. I could not find an English word that could correctly express our movement. In the meeting of Europeans above referred to I called our movement one of "soul force." But I did not dare to make the word current as expressive of our movement. Some capable Englishmen could see the imperfectness of the words "passive resistance," but they could not suggest a better phrase. I now see that "Civil Resistance" is the phrase which can correctly express our movement. Some time ago I somehow hit upon this phrase, and so I have now been using it in English. "Civil Resistance" expresses much more than is conveyed by the phrase "Civil Disobedience," though it expresses much less than *satyagraha*.

I also saw that in South Africa, truth and justice were our only weapons, that the force we were putting forth was not brute force but soul force, be it ever so little. This force is not found to be within the power of brutes, and as truth ever contains soul force, the South African agitation began to be known in our vernacular by the name of *satyagraha*.

That *satyagraha* is thus based on purity is no exaggeration. We can now understand that *satyagraha* is not merely Civil Disobedience. At times, it may be *satyagraha* not to offer Civil Disobedience. When it appears to us to be our duty to offer Civil Disobedience—when not to offer it seems to us derogatory to our manliness and to our soul—then only Civil Disobedience can be *satyagraha*.

This *satyagraha* can be offered not only against Government but against family and society. In short, *satyagraha* may be used as between husband and wife, [between] father and son, and between friends. We may use this weapon in any sphere of life and to get redress of any grievance. The weapon purifies the one who uses it as well as the one against whom it is used. A good use of the weapon can never be undesirable and it is ever infallible. If *satyagraha* is converted into *duragraha* and thus becomes fruitful of evil results, *satyagraha* cannot be blamed.

This sort of *satyagraha* consciously or unconsciously appears to be used mostly in families. That is to say, if a son finds that his father is unjust to him, he does not put up with the injustice, and he pays the penalty with pleasure. In the end he succeeds in winning over his callous father and in having justice from him. But a deadening inertia prevents us from carrying *satyagraha* beyond the family sphere. And I have therefore thought the use of *satyagraha* in the political and social sphere to be a new experiment. Tolstoy in one of his letters drew attention to the fact that this was a new experiment.

There are some who believe that *satyagraha* may be used only in the religious sphere. My wide experience points to a contrary conclusion. We may use it in other spheres and spiritualize them, and by so doing we hasten the victory and are saved many a false thing. I am firmly of the opinion that *satyagraha* contains the observance of the manifest laws of economics, and therefore I believe *satyagraha* to be a practical affair. *Satyagraha* being, as I have shown above, a new weapon, it may take time to be understood and accepted by the people—and things pregnant with results great and good do take time—but when it pervades the land, then political and social reforms, which today take very long to be achieved, will be obtained in comparatively less time, the gulf that separates rulers and the ruled will be bridged over, and trust and love will take the place of distrust and estrangement.

There is only one thing needful for a wide propagation of *satyagraha*. If the leaders understand it correctly and put it before the people, I am sure the people are ready to welcome it. To understand its true beauty one should have unflinching faith in Truth and nonviolence. Truth does not require to be explained. I do not mean to enter here into a minute explanation of nonviolence. It means, in brief, that we should not be actuated by spite against him from whom we seek to obtain justice, that we should never think of obtaining anything from him by any violence to his person, but by pure civility. If we can trust ourselves to be equal to only this much nonviolence, the required reforms can be easily achieved.

When the whole nation adopts *satyagraha* as an eternal weapon, all our movements will take a new form. We shall be spared much of the hubbub and stump oratory, much of the petition making and passing of resolutions, and much of our mean selfishness. I see nothing in which lies social, economic, and political advancement of the nation so much as in *satyagraha*.

Satyagraha differs from Passive Resistance as the North Pole from the South. The latter has been conceived as a weapon of the weak and does not exclude the use of physical force or violence for the purpose of gaining one's end. Whereas, the former has been conceived as a weapon of the strongest and excludes the use of violence in any shape or form. . . .

Satyagraha is utter self-effacement, greatest humiliation, greatest patience, and brightest faith. It is its own reward. . . .

54

Its [*satyagraha's*] root meaning is holding on to Truth, hence Truth force. I have called it Love force or Soul force. I discovered in the earliest stages that pursuit of Truth did not admit of violence being inflicted on one's opponent, but that he must be weaned from error by patience and sympathy. For, what appears to be Truth to the one may appear to be error to the other. And patience means self-suffering. So the doctrine came to mean vindication of Truth, not by infliction of suffering on the opponent, but on oneself.

When I refuse to do a thing that is repugnant to my conscience, I use soul force. For instance, the government of the day has passed a law which is applicable to me. I do not like it. If, by using violence, I force the government to repeal the law, I am employing what may be termed body force.

If I do not obey the law, and accept the penalty for its breach, I use soul force. It involves sacrifice of self.

Soul force begins when man recognizes that body force, be it ever so great, is nothing compared to the force of the soul within, which pervades not only him but all creation.

55

The fact that there are so many men still alive in the world shows that it is based not on the force of arms but on the force of truth or love. Therefore, the greatest and most unimpeachable evidence of the success of this force is to be found in the fact that, in spite of the wars of the world, it still lives on.

Thousands, indeed tens of thousands, depend for their existence on a very active working of this force. Little quarrels of millions of families in their daily lives disappear before the exercise of this force. Hundreds of nations live in peace. History does not and cannot take note of this fact.

56

History is really a record of every interruption of the even working of the force of love or of the soul. Two brothers quarrel, one of them repents and reawakens the love that was lying dormant in him, the two again begin to live in peace; nobody takes note of this. But if the two brothers, through the intervention of solicitors or for some other reason, take up arms or go to law—which is another form of the exhibition of brute force—their doings would be immediately noticed in the press, they would be the talk of their neighbors and would probably go down in history.

And what is true of families and communities is true of nations. There is no reason to believe that there is one law for families and another for nations. History, then, is a record of interruptions in the course of nature. Soul force, being natural, is not noted in history.

57

I have more than once dilated in my writings on the limits of *satyagraha*. *Satyagraha* presupposes self-discipline, self-control, self-purification, and a recognized social status in the person offering it. A *satyagrahi* must never forget the distinction between evil and the evil-doer. He must not harbor ill will or bitterness against the latter. He may not even employ needlessly offensive language against the evil person, however unrelieved his evil might be. For it should be an article of faith with every *satyagrahi* that there is no one so fallen in this world but can be converted by love. A *satyagrahi* will always try to overcome evil by good, anger by love, untruth by truth, *himsa* by *ahimsa*. *There is no other way of purging the world of evil.* Therefore, a person who claims to be a *satyagrahi* always tries by close and prayerful self-introspection and self-analysis to find out whether he is himself completely free from the taint of anger, ill will and such other human infirmities, whether he is not himself capable of those very evils against which he is out to lead a crusade. In self-purification and penance lies half the victory of a *satyagrahi*. A *satyagrahi* has faith that the silent and undemonstrative action of truth and love produces far more permanent and abiding results than speeches or such other showy performances. . . .

60

It is a fundamental principle of *satyagraha* that the tyrant whom the *satyagrahi* seeks to resist has power over his body and material possessions, but he can have no power over the soul. The soul can remain unconquered and unconquerable even when the body is imprisoned. The whole science of *satyagraha* was born from a knowledge of this fundamental truth.

61

Defeat has no place in the dictionary of nonviolence.

The path of a *satyagrahi* is beset with insurmountable difficulties. But in true *satyagraha* there is neither disappointment nor defeat. As truth is all-powerful, *satyagraha* can never be defeated.

There is no time limit for a *satyagrahi,* nor is there a limit to his capacity for suffering. Hence, there is no such thing as defeat in *satyagraha*. The so-called defeat may be the dawn of victory. It may be the agony of birth. . . .

64

The triumph of *satyagraha* consists in meeting death in the insistence on Truth.

65

From the standpoint of pure Truth, the body too is a possession. It has been truly said that desire for enjoyment creates bodies for the soul. When this desire vanishes, there remains no further need for the body, and man is free from the vicious cycle of births and deaths. The soul is omnipresent; why should she care to be confined within the cagelike body or do evil and even kill for the sake of that cage? We thus arrive at the ideal of total renunciation and learn to use the body for the purposes of service so long as it exists, so much so that service, and not bread, becomes with us the staff of life. We eat and drink, sleep and wake, for service alone. Such an attitude of mind brings us real happiness and the beatific vision in the fullness of time. . . .

70

The man who is saturated with the spirit of nonviolence has never any quarrel with a single individual. His opposition is directed to a system, to the evil in man, not against the man himself.

Letter from a Birmingham Jail

Martin Luther King, Jr.

Birmingham City Jail
April 16, 1963

Bishop C. C. J. Carpenter
Bishop Joseph A. Durick
Rabbi Milton L. Grafman
Bishop Paul Hardin
Bishop Nolan B. Harmon
The Reverend George M. Murray
The Reverend Edward V. Ramage
The Reverend Earl Stallings

My dear Fellow Clergymen,

While confined here in Birmingham City jail, I came across your recent statement calling our present activities "unwise and untimely." Seldom, if ever, do I pause to answer criticism of my work and ideas. If I sought to answer all of the criticisms that cross my desk, my secretaries would be engaged in little else in the course of the day and I would have no time for constructive work. But since I feel that you are men of genuine good will and your criticisms are sincerely set forth, I would like to answer your statement in what I hope will be patient and reasonable terms.

I think I should give the reason for my being in Birmingham, since you have been influenced by the argument of "outsiders coming in." I have the honor of serving as president of the Southern Christian Leadership Conference, an organization operating in every Southern state with head-quarters in Atlanta, Georgia. We have some eighty-five affiliate organizations all across the South—one being the Alabama Christian Movement for Human Rights. Whenever necessary and possible we share staff, educational, and financial resources with our affiliates. Several months ago our local affiliate here in Birmingham invited us to be on call to engage in a nonviolent direct action program if such were deemed necessary. We readily consented and when the hour came we lived up to our promises. So I am here, along with several members of my staff, because we were invited here. I am here because I have basic organizational ties here.

Beyond this, I am in Birmingham because injustice is here. Just as the eighth century prophets left their little villages and carried their "thus saith the Lord" far beyond the boundaries of their home town, and just as the Apostle Paul left his little village of Tarsus and carried the gospel of Jesus Christ to practically every hamlet and city of the Graeco-Roman world, I too am compelled to carry the gospel of freedom beyond my particular home town. Like Paul, I must constantly respond to the Macedonian call for aid.

Moreover, I am cognizant of the interrelatedness of all communities and states. I cannot sit idly by in Atlanta and not be concerned about what happens in Birmingham. Injustice anywhere is a threat to justice everywhere. We are caught in an inescapable network of mutuality tied in a single garment of destiny. Whatever affects one directly affects all indirectly. Never again can we afford to live with the narrow, provincial "outside agitator" idea. Anyone who lives inside the United States can never be considered an outsider anywhere in this country.

You deplore the demonstrations that are presently taking place in Birmingham. But I am sorry that your statement did not express a similar concern for the conditions that brought the demonstrations into being. I am sure that each of you would want to go beyond the superficial social analyst who looks merely at effects, and does not grapple with underlying causes. I would not hesitate to say that it is unfortunate that so-called demonstrations are taking place in Birmingham at this time, but I would say in more emphatic terms that it is even more unfortunate that the white power structure of this city left the Negro community with no other alternative.

In any nonviolent campaign there are four basic steps: (1) collection of the facts to determine whether injustices are alive; (2) negotiation; (3) self-purification; and (4) direct action. We have gone through all of these steps in Birmingham. There can be no gainsaying of the fact that racial injustice engulfs this community. Birmingham is probably the most thoroughly segregated city in the United States. Its ugly record of police brutality is known in every section of this country. Its unjust treatment of Negroes in the courts is a notorious reality. There have been more unsolved bombings of Negro homes and churches in Birmingham than any city in this nation. These are the hard, brutal, and unbelievable facts. On the basis of these conditions Negro leaders sought to negotiate with the city fathers. But the political leaders consistently refused to engage in good faith negotiation.

Then came the opportunity last September to talk with some of the leaders of the economic community. In these negotiating sessions certain promises were made by the merchants—such as the promise to remove the humiliating racial signs from the stores. On the basis of these promises Rev. Shuttlesworth and the leaders of the Alabama Christian Movement for Human Rights agreed to call a moratorium on any type of demonstrations. As the weeks and months unfolded we realized that we were the victims of a broken promise. The signs remained. As in so many experiences of the past we were confronted with blasted hopes, and the dark shadow of a deep disappointment settled upon us. So we had no alternative except that of preparing for direct action, whereby we would present our very bodies as a means of laying our case before the conscience of the local and national community. We were not unmindful of the difficulties involved. So we decided to go through a process of self-purification. We started having workshops on nonviolence and repeatedly asked ourselves the questions, "Are you able to accept blows without retaliating?" "Are you able to endure the ordeals of jail?"

We decided to set our direct action program around the Easter season, realizing that with the exception of Christmas, this was the largest shopping period of the year. Knowing that a strong economic withdrawal program would be the by-product of direct action, we felt that this was the best time to bring pressure on the merchants for the needed changes. Then it occurred to us that the March election was ahead, and so we speedily decided to postpone action until after election day. When we discovered that Mr. Connor was in the runoff, we decided again to postpone action so that the demonstrations could not be used to cloud the issues. At this time we agreed to begin our nonviolent witness the day after the runoff.

This reveals that we did not move irresponsibly into direct action. We too wanted to see Mr. Connor defeated; so we went through postponement after postponement to aid in this community need. After this we felt that direct action could be delayed no longer.

You may well ask, "Why direct action? Why sit-ins, marches, etc.? Isn't negotiation a better path?" You are exactly right in your call for negotiation. Indeed, this is the purpose of direct action. Nonviolent direct action seeks to create such a crisis and establish such creative tension that a community that has constantly refused to negotiate is forced to confront the issue. It seeks so to dramatize the issue that it can no longer be ignored. I just referred to the creation of tension as a part of the work of the nonviolent resister. This may sound rather shocking. But I must confess that I am not afraid of the word tension. I have earnestly worked and preached against violent tension, but there is a type of constructive nonviolent tension that is necessary for growth. Just as Socrates felt that it was necessary to create a tension in the mind so that individuals could rise from the bondage of myths and half-truths to the unfettered realm of creative analysis and objective appraisal, we must see the need of having nonviolent gadflies to create the kind of tension in society that will help men rise from the dark depths of prejudice and racism to the majestic heights of understanding and brotherhood. So the purpose of the direct action is to create a situation so crisis-packed that it will inevitably open the door to negotiation. We, therefore, concur with you in your call for negotiation. Too long has our beloved Southland been bogged down in the tragic attempt to live in monologue rather than dialogue.

One of the basic points in your statement is that our acts are untimely. Some have asked, "Why didn't you give the new administration time to act?" The only answer that I can give to this inquiry is that the new administration must be prodded about as much as the outgoing one before it acts. We will be sadly mistaken if we feel that the election of Mr. Boutwell will bring the millennium to Birmingham. While Mr. Boutwell is much more articulate and gentle than Mr. Connor, they are both segregationists dedicated to the task of maintaining the status quo. The hope I see in Mr. Boutwell is that he will be reasonable enough to see the futility of massive resistance to desegregation. But he will not see this without pressure from the devotees of civil rights. My friends, I must say to you that we have not made a single gain in civil rights without determined legal and nonviolent pressure. History is the long and tragic story of the fact that privileged groups seldom give up their privileges voluntarily. Individuals may see the moral light and voluntarily give up their unjust posture; but as Reinhold Niebuhr has reminded us, groups are more immoral than individuals.

We know through painful experience that freedom is never voluntarily given by the oppressor; it must be demanded by the oppressed. Frankly I have never yet engaged in a direct action movement that was "well timed," according to the timetable of those who have not suffered unduly from the disease of segregation. For years now I have heard the word "Wait!" It rings in the ear of every Negro with a piercing familiarity. This "wait" has almost always meant "never." It has been a tranquilizing thalidomide, relieving the emotional stress for a moment, only to give birth to an ill-formed infant of frustration. We must come to see with the distinguished jurist of yesterday that "justice too long delayed is justice denied." We have waited for more than three hundred and forty years for our constitutional and God-given rights. The nations of Asia and Africa are moving with jet-like speed toward the goal of political independence, and we still creep at horse and buggy pace toward the gaining of a cup of coffee at a lunch counter.

I guess it is easy for those who have never felt the stinging darts of segregation to say wait. But when you have seen vicious mobs lynch your mothers and fathers at will and drown your sisters and brothers at whim; when you have seen hate-filled policemen curse, kick, brutalize, and even kill your black brothers and sisters with impunity; when you see the vast majority of your twenty million Negro brothers smothering in an airtight cage of poverty in the midst of an affluent society; when you suddenly find your tongue twisted and your speech stammering as you seek to explain to your six-year-old daughter why she can't go to the public amusement park that has just been advertised on television, and see tears welling up in her little eyes when she is told that Funtown is closed to colored children, and see the depressing clouds of inferiority begin to form in her little mental sky, and see her begin to distort her little personality by unconsciously developing a bitterness toward white people; when you have to concoct an answer for a five-year-old son asking in agonizing pathos: "Daddy, why do white people treat colored people so mean?"; when you take a cross-country drive and find it necessary to sleep night after night in the uncomfortable corners of your automobile because no motel will accept you; when you are humiliated day in and day out by nagging signs reading "white" men and "colored"; when your first name becomes "nigger" and your middle name becomes "boy" (however old you are) and your last name becomes "John," and when your wife and mother are never given the respected title "Mrs."; when you are harried by day and haunted by night by the fact that you are a Negro, living constantly at tip-toe stance never quite knowing what to expect next, and plagued with inner fears and outer resentments; when you are forever fighting a degenerating sense of "nobodiness";—then you will understand why we find it very difficult to wait. There comes a time when the cup of our endurance runs over, and men are no longer willing to be plunged into an abyss of injustice where they experience the bleakness of a corroding despair. I hope, sirs, you can understand our legitimate and unavoidable impatience.

You express a great deal of anxiety over our willingness to break laws. This is certainly a legitimate concern. Since we so diligently urge people to obey the Supreme Court's decision of 1954 outlawing segregation in the public schools, it is rather strange and paradoxical to find us consciously breaking laws. One may well ask, "How can you advocate breaking some laws and obeying others?" The answer is found in the fact that there are two types of laws. There are *just* laws and there are *unjust* laws. I would be the first to advocate obeying just laws. One has not only a legal but moral responsibility to obey just laws. Conversely, one has a moral responsibility to disobey unjust laws. I would agree with Saint Augustine that "An unjust law is no law at all."

Now what is the difference between the two? How does one determine when a law is just or unjust? A just law is a man-made code that squares with the moral law or the law of God. An unjust law is a code that is out of harmony with the moral law. To put it in the terms of Saint Thomas Aquinas, an unjust law is a human law that is not rooted in eternal and natural law. Any law that uplifts human personality is just. Any law that degrades human personality is unjust. All segregation statutes are unjust because segregation distorts the soul and damages the personality. It gives the segregator a false sense of superiority and the segregated a false sense of inferiority. To use the words of Martin Buber, the great Jewish philosopher, segregation substitutes an "I-it" relationship for the "I-thou" relationship, and ends up relegating persons to the status of things. So segregation is not only politically, economically, and sociologically unsound, but it is morally wrong and sinful. Paul Tillich has said that sin is separation. Isn't segregation an existential expression of man's tragic separation, an expression of his awful estrangement, his terrible sinfulness? So I can urge men to obey the 1954 decision of the Supreme Court because it is morally right, and I can urge them to disobey segregation ordinances because they are morally wrong.

Let us turn to a more concrete example of just and unjust laws. An unjust law is a code that a majority inflicts on a minority that is not binding on itself. This is *difference* made legal. On the other hand a just law is a code that a majority compels a minority to follow that it is willing to follow itself. This is *sameness* made legal.

Let me give another explanation. An unjust law is a code inflicted upon a minority which that minority had no part in enacting or creating because they did not have the unhampered right to vote. Who can say the legislature of Alabama which set up the segregation laws was democratically elected? Throughout the State of Alabama all types of conniving methods are used to prevent Negroes from becoming registered voters and there are some counties without a single Negro registered to vote despite the fact that the Negro constitutes a majority of the population. Can any law set up in such a state be considered democratically structured?

These are just a few examples of unjust and just laws. There are some instances when a law is just on its face but unjust in its application. For instance, I was arrested Friday on a charge of parading without a permit. Now there is nothing wrong with an ordinance which requires a permit for a parade, but when the ordinance is used to preserve segregation and to deny citizens the First Amendment privilege of peaceful assembly and peaceful protest, then it becomes unjust.

I hope you can see the distinction I am trying to point out. In no sense do I advocate evading or defying the law as the rabid segregationist would do. This would lead to anarchy. One who breaks an unjust law must do it *openly, lovingly* (not hatefully as the white mothers did in New Orleans when they were seen on television screaming "nigger, nigger, nigger") and with a willingness to accept the penalty. I submit that an individual who breaks a law that conscience tells him is unjust, and willingly accepts the penalty by staying in jail to arouse the conscience of the community over its injustice, is in reality expressing the very highest respect for law.

Of course there is nothing new about this kind of civil disobedience. It was seen sublimely in the refusal of Shadrach, Meshach, and Abednego to obey the unjust laws of Nebuchadnezzar because a higher moral law was involved. It was practiced superbly by the early Christians who were willing to face hungry lions and the excruciating pain of chopping blocks, before submitting to certain very unjust laws of the Roman Empire. To a degree our academic freedom is a reality today because Socrates practiced civil disobedience.

We can never forget that everything Hitler did in Germany was "legal" and everything the Hungarian freedom fighters did in Hungary was "illegal." It was "illegal" to aid and comfort a Jew in Hitler's Germany. But I am sure that, if I had lived in Germany during that time, I would have aided and comforted my Jewish brothers even though it was illegal. If I lived in a communist country today where certain principles dear to the Christian faith are suppressed, I believe I would openly advocate disobeying these antireligious laws.

I must make two honest confessions to you, my Christian and Jewish brothers. First I must confess that over the last few years I have been gravely disappointed with the white moderate. I have almost reached the regrettable conclusion that the Negroes' great stumbling block in the stride toward freedom is not the White Citizens' "Councilor" or the Ku Klux Klanner, but the white moderate who is more devoted to "order" than to justice; who prefers a negative peace which is the absence of tension to a positive peace which is the presence of justice; who constantly says "I agree with you in the goal you seek, but I can't agree with your methods of direct action"; who paternalistically feels that he can set the timetable for another man's freedom; who lives by the myth of time and who constantly advises the Negro to wait until a "more convenient season." Shallow understanding from people of good will is more frustrating than absolute misunderstanding from people of ill will. Lukewarm acceptance is much more bewildering than outright rejection.

I had hoped that the white moderate would understand that law and order exist for the purpose of establishing justice, and that when they fail to do this they become the dangerously structured dams that block the flow of social progress. I had hoped that the white moderate would understand that the present tension in the South is merely a necessary phase of the transition from an obnoxious negative peace, where the Negro passively accepted his unjust plight, to a substance-filled positive peace, where all men will respect the dignity and worth of human personality. Actually, we who engage in nonviolent direct action are not the creators of tension. We merely bring to the surface the hidden tension that is already alive. We bring it out in the open where it can be seen and dealt with. Like a boil that can never be cured as long as it is covered up but must be opened with all its pus-flowing ugliness to the natural medicines of air and light, injustice must likewise be exposed, with all of the tension its exposing creates, to the light of human conscience and the air of national opinion before it can be cured.

In your statement you asserted that our actions, even though peaceful, must be condemned because they precipitate violence. But can this assertion be logically made? Isn't this like condemning the robbed man because his possession of money precipitated the evil act of robbery? Isn't this like condemning Socrates because his unswerving commitment to truth and his philosophical delvings precipitated the misguided popular mind to make him drink the hemlock? Isn't this like condemning Jesus because His unique God consciousness and never-ceasing devotion to His will precipitated the evil act of crucifixion? We must come to see, as federal courts have consistently affirmed, that it is immoral to urge an individual to withdraw his efforts to gain his basic constitutional rights because the quest precipitates violence. Society must protect the robbed and punish the robber.

I had also hoped that the white moderate would reject the myth of time. I received a letter this morning from a white brother in Texas which said: "All Christians know that the colored people will receive equal rights eventually, but is it possible that you are in too great of a religious hurry? It has taken Christianity almost 2000 years to accomplish what it has.The teachings of Christ take time to come to earth." All that is said here grows out of a tragic misconception of time. It is the strangely irrational notion that there is something in the very flow of time that will inevitably cure all ills. Actually time is neutral. It can be used either destructively or constructively. I am coming to feel that the people of ill will have used time much more effectively than the people of good will. We will have to repent in this generation not merely for the vitriolic words and actions of the bad people, but for the appalling silence of the good people. We must come to see that human progress never rolls in on wheels of inevitability. It comes through the tireless efforts and persistent work of men willing to be co-workers with God, and without this hard work time itself becomes an ally of the forces of social stagnation.

We must use time creatively, and forever realize that the time is always ripe to do right. Now is the time to make real the promise of democracy, and transform our pending national elegy into a creative psalm of brotherhood. Now is the time to lift our national policy from the quicksand of racial injustice to the solid rock of human dignity.

You spoke of our activity in Birmingham as extreme. At first I was rather disappointed that fellow clergymen would see my nonviolent efforts as those of the extremist. I started thinking about the fact that I stand in the middle of two opposing forces in the Negro community. One is a force of complacency made up of Negroes who, as a result of long years of oppression, have been so completely drained of self-respect and a sense of "somebodiness" that they have adjusted to segregation, and of a few Negroes in the middle class who, because of a degree of academic and economic security, and because at points they profit by segregation, have unconsciously become insensitive to the problems of the masses. The other force is one of bitterness and hatred and comes perilously close to advocating violence. It is expressed in the various black nationalist groups that are springing up over the nation, the largest and best known being Elijah Muhammad's Muslim movement. This movement is nourished by the contemporary frustration over the continued existence of racial discrimination. It is made up of people who have lost faith in America, who have absolutely repudiated Christianity, and who have concluded that the white man is an incurable "devil." I have tried to stand between these two forces saying that we need not follow the "do-nothingism" of the complacent or the hatred and despair of the black nationalist. There is the more excellent way of love and nonviolent protest. I'm grateful to God that, through the Negro church, the dimension of nonviolence entered our struggle. If this philosophy had not emerged I am convinced that by now many streets of the South would be flowing with floods of blood. And I am further convinced that if our white brothers dismiss us as "rabble rousers" and "outside agitators"—those of us who are working through the channels of nonviolent direct action—and refuse to support our nonviolent efforts, millions of Negroes, out of frustration and despair, will seek solace and security in black nationalist ideologies, a development that will lead inevitably to a frightening racial nightmare.

Oppressed people cannot remain oppressed forever. The urge for freedom will eventually come. This is what has happened to the American Negro. Something within has reminded him of his birthright of freedom; something without has reminded him that he can gain it. Consciously and unconsciously, he has been swept in by what the Germans call the *Zeitgeist*, and with his black brothers of Africa, and his brown and yellow brothers of Asia, South America, and the Caribbean, he is moving with a sense of cosmic urgency toward the promised land of racial justice. Recognizing this vital urge that has engulfed the Negro community, one should readily understand public demonstrations. The Negro has many pent-up resentments and latent frustrations. He has to get them out. So let him march sometime; let him have his prayer pilgrimages to the city hall; understand why he must have sit-ins and freedom rides. If his repressed emotions do not come out in these nonviolent ways, they will come out in ominous expressions of violence. This is not a threat; it is a fact of history. So I have not said to my people, "Get rid of your discontent." But I have tried to say that this normal and healthy discontent can be channeled through the creative outlet of nonviolent direct action. Now this approach is being dismissed as extremist. I must admit that I was initially disappointed in being so categorized.

But as I continued to think about the matter I gradually gained a bit of satisfaction from being considered an extremist. Was not Jesus an extremist in love? "Love your enemies, bless them that curse you, pray for them that despitefully use you." Was not Amos an extremist for justice—"Let justice roll down like waters and righteousness like a mighty stream." Was not Paul an extremist for the gospel of Jesus Christ—"I bear in my body the marks of the Lord Jesus." Was not Martin Luther an extremist— "Here I stand; I can do none other so help me God." Was not John Bunyan an extremist—"I will stay in jail to the end of my days before I make a butchery of my conscience." Was not Abraham Lincoln an extremist— "This nation cannot survive half slave and half free." Was not Thomas Jefferson an extremist—"We hold these truths to be self-evident that all men are created equal." So the question is not whether we will be extremist but what kind of extremist will we be. Will we be extremists for hate or will we be extremists for love? Will we be extremists for the preservation of injustice—or will we be extremists for the cause of justice? In that dramatic scene on Calvary's hill three men were crucified. We must never forget that all three were crucified for the same crime—the crime of extremism. Two were extremists for immorality, and thus fell below their environment. The other, Jesus Christ, was an extremist for love, truth, and goodness, and thereby rose above His environment. So, after all, maybe the South, the nation, and the world are in dire need of creative extremists.

I had hoped that the white moderate would see this. Maybe I was too optimistic. Maybe I expected too much. I guess I should have realized that few members of a race that has oppressed another race can understand or appreciate the deep groans and passionate yearnings of those that have been oppressed, and still fewer have the vision to see that injustice must be rooted out by strong, persistent, and determined action. I am thankful, however, that some of our white brothers have grasped the meaning of this social revolution and committed themselves to it. They are still all too small in quantity, but they are big in quality. Some like Ralph McGill, Lillian Smith, Harry Golden, and James Dabbs have written about our struggle in eloquent, prophetic, and understanding terms. Others have marched with us down nameless streets of the South. They have languished in filthy, roach-infested jails, suffering the abuse and brutality of angry policemen who look on them as "dirty nigger lovers." They, unlike so many of their moderate brothers and sisters, have recognized the urgency of the moment and sensed the need for powerful "action" antidotes to combat the disease of segregation.

Let me rush on to mention my other disappointment. I have been so greatly disappointed with the white Church and its leadership. Of course there are some notable exceptions. I am not unmindful of the fact that each of you has taken some significant stands on this issue. I commend you, Rev. Stallings, for your Christian stand on this past Sunday, in welcoming Negroes to your service on a non-segregated basis. I commend the Catholic leaders of this state for integrating Springhill College several years ago.

But despite these notable exceptions I must honestly reiterate that I have been disappointed with the Church. I do not say that as one of those negative critics who can always find something wrong with the Church. I say it as a minister of the gospel, who loves the Church; who was nurtured in its bosom; who has been sustained by its spiritual blessings and who will remain true to it as long as the cord of life shall lengthen.

I had the strange feeling when I was suddenly catapulted into the leadership of the bus protest in Montgomery several years ago that we would have the support of the white Church. I felt that the white ministers, priests, and rabbis of the South would be some of our strongest allies. Instead, some have been outright opponents, refusing to understand the freedom movement and misrepresenting its leaders; all too many others have been more cautious than courageous and have remained silent behind the anesthetizing security of stained glass windows.

In spite of my shattered dreams of the past, I came to Birmingham with the hope that the white religious leadership of this community would see the justice of our cause and, with deep moral concern, serve as the channel through which our just grievances could get to the power structure. I had hoped that each of you would understand. But again I have been disappointed.

I have heard numerous religious leaders of the South call upon their worshippers to comply with a desegregation decision because it is the law, but I have longed to hear white ministers say: "Follow this decree because integration is morally right and the Negro is your brother." In the midst of blatant injustices inflicted upon the Negro, I have watched white churches stand on the sideline and merely mouth pious irrelevancies and sanctimonious trivialities. In the midst of a mighty struggle to rid our nation of racial and economic injustice, I have heard so many ministers say, "Those are social issues with which the Gospel has no real concern." and I have watched so many churches commit themselves to a completely otherworldly religion which made a strange distinction between body and soul, the sacred and the secular.

So here we are moving toward the exit of the twentieth century with a religious community largely adjusted to the status quo, standing as a taillight behind other community agencies rather than a headlight leading men to higher levels of justice.

I have travelled the length and breadth of Alabama, Mississippi, and all the other Southern states. On sweltering summer days and crisp autumn mornings I have looked at her beautiful churches with their spires pointing heavenward. I have beheld the impressive outlay of her massive religious education buildings. Over and over again I have found myself asking: "Who worships here? Who is their God? Where were their voices when the lips of Governor Barnett dripped with words of interposition and nullification? Where were they when Governor Wallace gave the clarion call for defiance and hatred? Where were their voices of support when tired, bruised, and weary Negro men and women decided to rise from the dark dungeons of complacency to the bright hills of creative protest?"

Yes, these questions are still in my mind. In deep disappointment, I have wept over the laxity of the Church. But be assured that my tears have been tears of love. There can be no deep disappointment where there is not deep love. Yes, I love the Church; I love her sacred walls. How could I do otherwise? I am in the rather unique position of being the son, the grandson, and the great-grandson of preachers. Yes, I see the Church as the body of Christ. But, oh! How we have blemished and scarred that body through social neglect and fear of being nonconformist.

There was a time when the Church was very powerful. It was during that period when the early Christians rejoiced when they were deemed worthy to suffer for what they believed. In those days the Church was not merely a thermometer that recorded the ideas and principles of popular opinion; it was a thermostat that transformed the mores of society. Wherever the early Christians entered a town the power structure got disturbed and immediately sought to convict them for being "disturbers of the peace" and "outside agitators." But they went on with the conviction that they were a "colony of heaven" and had to obey God rather than man. They were small in number but big in commitment. They were too

God-intoxicated to be "astronomically intimidated." They brought an end to such ancient evils as infanticide and gladiatorial contest.

Things are different now. The contemporary Church is so often a weak, ineffectual voice with an uncertain sound. It is so often the arch-supporter of the status quo. Far from being disturbed by the presence of the Church, the power structure of the average community is consoled by the Church's silent and often vocal sanction of things as they are.

But the judgment of God is upon the Church as never before. If the Church of today does not recapture the sacrificial spirit of the early Church, it will lose its authentic ring, forfeit the loyalty of millions, and be dismissed as an irrelevant social club with no meaning for the twentieth century. I am meeting young people every day whose disappointment with the Church has risen to outright disgust.

Maybe again I have been too optimistic. Is organized religion too inextricably bound to the status quo to save our nation and the world? Maybe I must turn my faith to the inner spiritual Church, the church within the Church, as the true *eccelesia* and the hope of the world. But again I am thankful to God that some noble souls from the ranks of organized religion have broken loose from the paralyzing chains of conformity and joined us as active partners in the struggle for freedom. They have left their secure congregations and walked the streets of Albany, Georgia, with us. They have gone through the highways of the South on torturous rides for freedom. Yes, they have gone to jail with us. Some have been kicked out of their churches and lost the support of their bishops and fellow ministers. But they have gone with the faith that right defeated is stronger than evil triumphant. These men have been the leaven in the lump of the race. Their witness has been the spiritual salt that has preserved the true meaning of the Gospel in these troubled times. They have carved a tunnel of hope through the dark mountain of disappointment.

I hope the Church as a whole will meet the challenge of this decisive hour. But even if the Church does not come to the aid of justice, I have no despair about the future. I have no fear about the outcome of our struggle in Birmingham, even if our motives are presently misunderstood. We will reach the goal of freedom in Birmingham and all over the nation, because the goal of America is freedom. Abused and scorned though we may be, our destiny is tied up with the destiny of America. Before the pilgrims landed at Plymouth, we were here. Before the pen of Jefferson etched across the pages of history the majestic words of the Declaration of Independence, we were here. For more than two centuries our foreparents labored in this country without wages; they made cotton "king"; and they built the homes of their masters in the midst of brutal injustice and shameful humiliation—and yet out of a bottomless vitality they continued to thrive and develop. If the inexpressible cruelties of slavery could not stop us, the opposition we now face will surely fail. We will win our freedom because the sacred heritage of our nation and the eternal will of God are surely embodied in our echoing demands.

I must close now. But before closing I am impelled to mention one other point in your statement that troubled me profoundly. You warmly commended the Birmingham police force for keeping "order" and "preventing violence." I don't believe you would have so warmly commended the police force if you had seen its angry violent dogs literally biting six unarmed, nonviolent Negroes. I don't believe you would so quickly commend the policemen if you would observe their ugly and inhuman treatment of Negroes here in the city jail; if you would watch them push and curse old Negro women and young Negro girls; if you would see them slap and kick old Negro men and young Negro boys; if you will observe them, as they have done on two occasions, refuse to give us food because we wanted to sing our grace together. I'm sorry that I can't join you in your praise for the police department.

It is true that they have been rather disciplined in their public handling of the demonstrators. In this sense they have been rather publicly "nonviolent." But for what purpose? To preserve the evil system of segregation. Over the last few years I have consistently preached that nonviolence demands that the means we use must be as pure as the ends we seek. So I have tried to make it clear that it is wrong to use immoral means to attain moral ends. But now I must affirm that it is just as wrong, or even more so, to use moral means to preserve immoral ends. Maybe Mr. Connor and his policemen have been publicly nonviolent, as Chief Prichett was in Albany, Georgia, but they have used the moral means of nonviolence to maintain the immoral end of flagrant racial injustice. T. S. Eliot has said that there is no greater treason than to do the right deed for the wrong reason.

I wish you had commended the Negro sit-inners and demonstrators of Birmingham for their sublime courage, their willingness to suffer, and their amazing discipline in the midst of the most inhuman provocation. One day the South will recognize its real heroes. They will be the James Merediths, courageously and with a majestic sense of purpose, facing jeering and hostile mobs and the agonizing loneliness that characterizes the life of the pioneer. They will be old, oppressed, battered Negro women, symbolized in a seventy-two year old woman of Montgomery, Alabama, who rose up with a sense of dignity and with her people decided not to ride the segregated buses, and responded to one who inquired about her tiredness with ungrammatical profundity: "My feets is tired, but my soul is rested." They will be young high school and college students, young ministers of the gospel and a host of the elders, courageously and nonviolently sitting in at lunch counters and willingly going to jail for conscience sake. One day the South will know that when these disinherited children of God sat down at lunch counters they were in reality standing up for the best in the American dream and the most sacred values in our Judeo-Christian heritage, and thus carrying our whole nation back to great wells of democracy which were dug deep by the founding fathers in the formulation of the Constitution and the Declaration of Independence.

Never before have I written a letter this long (or should I say a book?). I'm afraid that it is much too long to take your precious time. I can assure you that it would have been much shorter if I had been writing from a comfortable desk, but what else is there to do when you are alone for days in the dull monotony of a narrow jail cell other than write long letters, think strange thoughts, and pray long prayers?

If I have said anything in this letter that is an overstatement of the truth and is indicative of an unreasonable impatience, I beg you to forgive me. If I have said anything in this letter that is an understatement of the truth and is indicative of my having a patience that makes me patient with anything less than brotherhood, I beg God to forgive me.

I hope this letter finds you strong in the faith. I also hope that circumstances will soon make it possible for me to meet each of you, not as an integrationist or a civil rights leader, but as a fellow clergyman and a Christian brother. Let us all hope that the dark clouds of racial prejudice will soon pass away and the deep fog of misunderstanding will be lifted from our fear-drenched communities and in some not too distant tomorrow the radiant stars of love and brotherhood will shine over our great nation with all of their scintillating beauty.

Yours for the cause of Peace and Brotherhood

Martin Luther King, Jr.

Pamela R. Fletcher is a writer, editor, critic, and educator. Currently, she is on the English faculty at the College of St. Catherine, where she teaches creative and expository writing and literature. Ms. Fletcher has taught at Carleton College; Hamline University, MFA Program; the Loft: A Place for Writing and Literature; and, the Creative and Professional Writing Program, Department of English, the Department of African/African American Studies and the Department of Women's Studies at the University of Minnesota.

A Dream Deferred[1]

Pamela Fletcher

Prancing on Seal Beach waves atop our slippery surfboards, we wiped out and choked on the foamy, pickled sea and giggled and pranced and wiped out and choked and giggled and pranced under a hot sun that browned B.K. like a chicken breast in a pan of sweet butter and blackened me like a filet of red snapper dusted with savory spices and fried over a high blue flame.

Occasionally B.K. and I took breaks to replenish our energy, eating sandwiches Mama Bindels made so lovingly with Wonder bread, margarine, and chocolate sprinkles. We also munched juicy black plums that Mama Bindels had picked from the plum tree in their backyard. To cool down, we drank enormous bottles of RC cola that I could barely swallow because the bubbly syrup stung my throat. B.K. and her older sisters glugged the liquid in large gulps and were instantly revived.

Mama and Papa Bindels waved at us with dark-shaded eyes and sun-lightened grins. Every now and then Papa Bindels swam quickly behind us, squealing and splashing and breaking our concentration when it appeared that we were about to ascend a giant wave. I adored him and his mischievous manner. He loved to tease and do pranks. Whenever I saw him, he gave me wholesome, warm hugs and tenderly patted my head. Most of the time I didn't completely understand his words when he talked to me because he spoke in a melodious Dutch accent that confused and delighted me. Yet I understood that he thought of me as his daughter and I felt quite special to have both him and my father care about me. I often wondered how it would feel to really be Mr. Bindels' daughter. He and my father were very different men, separated by age, color, and opportunity. I knew they were different, but at nine years old I had no idea just how different their lives were. I wonder now just what it's like to be the daughter of a man who is not routinely beaten with a thick switch broken from a branch of the lynching tree.

B.K., blonde, tall, and Canadian, and I, dark, tall, and American, loved each other more than we loved our own sisters. In the summer of 1965, as in the previous two years, this love kept me afloat in the hostile suburban community of La Puente, located approximately thirty miles east of Watts where rebellion would soon erupt. I had no knowledge of what racism and discrimination meant; I never had heard the words before. But I was familiar with the slur "nigger" that the white and Mexican children fired like poison gas in my face and in the faces of my siblings. I vaguely remember hearing that Malcolm X was shot to death that year on February 21, the day of my brother's eighth birthday, but I didn't know who Malcolm X was and didn't know that I should even care. I also didn't understand the significance of the civil rights march that King and some thirty-five thousand national supporters had recently accomplished in Alabama. As far as I knew, Watts and Alabama were strange lands with voting rights violations, unfair housing, segregated schools, separate public accommodations, and police brutality that had nothing, whatsoever, to do with my life. Living in La Puente at nine years old, I had no idea what those problems meant at all. Besides, Mama and Daddy never mentioned them nor commented on the news. They moved us to San Gabriel Valley so we wouldn't have to worry about such things.

The Fletchers and the Bindels were oblivious to what was happening outside our suburban cocoon. All I cared about was how often B.K. and I would play together and how soon we would make up after a fight. About once a month we underwent a power struggle about some petty thing, nothing memorable. We had it down to a science: we screamed at each other, stomped our feet, and cried; then she ran away and I nervously awaited her return (sometimes it took a day or two), and then we hugged, laughed, and began anew. Our families did not understand our combative interaction, but these theatrics simply became our ritual for emotional adventure.

B.K. ran wild and barefooted, her straight hair swinging every which way. I didn't like getting my feet dirty so I wore tennis shoes, and since it was not proper for a colored girl to let her hair go its own direction, I captured its unruly nature in a ponytail. Once, while we played house, Valerie, my baby sister, attempted to braid B.K.'s hair but the ends would not stay. "It just won't act right," Valerie sighed, trying to braid B.K.'s hair as tightly as possible. As the braid unraveled, B.K. hunched her shoulders and we giggled, and left it up to God. This difference between our hair and hers mystified us sometimes. It struck me that while Mama permed our hair to straighten it, B.K.'s big sister, Bianca, permed her hair to curl it. I began to realize that girls spent a lot of time worrying about their hair, especially as they grew older. Bianca and her friends regularly changed their hair color and hair styles. B.K., though, liked her hair plain and natural. Once in a while she wore a ponytail, but she never wore braids. We colored girls kept our hair in bondage. Braiding it seemed to be the easiest way to create a presentable colored appearance. I envied B.K.'s nonchalance about hair; she never worried about being presentable. This child of Dutch ancestry, named after Queen Beatrix of Holland, had such confidence and spunk. I envied her rebellious spirit. She had the audacity to defy everyone, including her parents, especially Papa Bindels, who grounded her at every turn. But he never forbade us to see each other; somehow he knew that it would be cruel and unusual punishment. When he banished her to her room, I just moved in, and we often spent hours planning or replanning our next beach trip and laughing about the silly things we did the last time we went surfing.

In 1968 our elementary school years came to an abrupt end. One day, when we weren't looking, our bodies abandoned us and moved to some foreign land while our minds had yet to venture beyond the fifth grade. Feeling awkward and insecure, we began to experience things that we could not or would not mention to each other. For instance, although we didn't tell each other when we began to menstruate, I could tell her time had come because she acted guilty just like I acted once I began menstruating. Suddenly we discovered a horrible secret we didn't want anyone else to know. We no longer laughed easily. We walked with constraint and held our bodies close. We stopped wrestling, climbing trees, and playing house. We began to see through wide eyes that there was a direct correlation between our new external selves and how the world reacted to us. "Keep your legs shut!" Daddy said. "Stop rolling around out there on that grass like you somebody wild," Mama said. Men leered at us when we walked around the shopping center.

Yet, initially, I didn't see everything so clearly. I didn't see how much the world's reaction to our friendship would change our lives forever—until one certain day. That day we walked home from school together, talking and laughing just like our old selves. Suddenly B.K. startled me with a tone of voice that I hadn't heard before. It wasn't her angry I-will-never-speak-to-you-again voice; it was a voice that no longer recognized me.

"Quick! Get behind me. Walk behind me."

"Huh?" I said. "What do you mean?"

"Walk behind me," she repeated. But then she rushed ahead of me and walked away fast as if we weren't walking together. As she walked ahead, a car slowed, approaching us.

"Hey, B.K.! What cha doing?" a blonde girl yelled out of the car window.

"Hey, Cathy! You coming over later?"

"My mom says she might drop me off while she goes shopping. I'll call ya."

"Okay. See you guys later," B.K. waved as the car gained speed.

She maintained a safe distance from me until the car turned the corner and then she stopped and waited for me to catch up. B.K. resumed the conversation as if nothing had happened and I forced myself to withhold my riotous and jealous rage, though I did not know why. I may have been afraid of what I would have done if I released my fury; after all, I was not supposed to be this angry, so angry I could have killed her. Unlike most colored people, I was living the integrated dream of the late Martin Luther King and it was supposed to be good and equal, but over time I began to realize that it wasn't what my parents had expected and what they had led me to believe it would be. As we walked along that wide street together, I found that it didn't matter that for years B.K. and I lived in the same neighborhood on the same side of the street, one house away from each other, that we ate and slept in each other's homes, that we shared silly secrets and protected each other, that we went to the same schools and shopped in the same stores. Together. The fact that we were different colors still separated us.

King's recent death had touched so many people, including my family, and I began to pay close attention to what was happening around the country and what was happening to me as I was growing into someone brand new. The world exploded with talk about race and violence and civil rights, and I ascertained that society was forcing me to choose between being a person and being a "black" person. When I looked at B.K. then, she was no longer B.K.; she was now a "white" girl, representative of all the whites who had rejected and oppressed me. Although she walked beside me now, I realized that she had just relegated me to that "place" where black people are meant to placate or perish. As she assumed her privileged position in the white world, we were torn asunder. My best friend whom I considered my sister died right in front of my very eyes. And a piece of me died right along with her. Yet, my rage gave birth to an awareness that Watts and Alabama were not so distant from La Puente after all. It occurred to me that no matter where we lived, black people still had so much to overcome. While B.K. talked, I nodded my head for fear that if I opened my mouth, I would flood her with murderous grief. When we reached Barrydale Street, instead of stopping at her corner house as usual, I said good-bye with averted, teary eyes and walked away.

That afternoon I buried B.K. along with my innocent belief that love is a protective shield that saves one from being devoured by a world that eats the hearts of those who dare to be human and who dare to accept the humanity of someone else. B.K. and I had never discussed our blatant difference so I naively thought that for once it didn't matter. After having suffered loneliness for so long in La Puente, I thought I finally had found a friend who loved me regardless of how I looked, who loved me for my "character." Forever. I had never imagined that once we reached Edgewood Junior High our emotional points would no longer intersect simply because I was black and she was white. Although I had willed myself to forget that day, deep in my heart I was afraid I would never recover; I was afraid that I would continue to mourn the loss of the dream.

Yet, like the living dead who didn't die a timely death or get a proper burial, the dream can't rest. It's as alive as my vivid memory of B.K. and me prancing on those waves. Together.

Note

[1] Taken from a line in Langston Hughes' poem, "Dream Boogie."

Audre Lorde (1934–1992), born in New York of West Indian parents, was a self-described "black feminist lesbian poet, mother of two and member of an interracial couple." A writer and activist, her poetry and essays have made a significant contribution to the contemporary feminist movement.

The Transformation of Silence into Language and Action

Audre Lorde

I have come to believe over and over again that what is most important to me must be spoken, made verbal and shared, even at the risk of having it bruised or misunderstood. That the speaking profits me, beyond any other effect. I am standing here as a Black lesbian poet, and the meaning of all that waits upon the fact that I am still alive, and might not have been. Less than two months ago I was told by two doctors, one female and one male, that I would have to have breast surgery, and that there was a 60 to 80 percent chance that the tumor was malignant. Between that telling and the actual surgery, there was a three-week period of the agony of an involuntary reorganization of my entire life. The surgery was completed, and the growth was benign.

But within those three weeks, I was forced to look upon myself and my living with a harsh and urgent clarity that has left me still shaken but much stronger. This is a situation faced by many women, by some of you here today. Some of what I experienced during that time has helped elucidate for me much of what I feel concerning the transformation of silence into language and action.

In becoming forcibly and essentially aware of my mortality and of what I wished and wanted for my life, however short it might be, priorities and omissions became strongly etched in a merciless light, and what I most regretted were my silences. Of what had I *ever* been afraid? To question or to speak as I believed could have meant pain, or death. But we all hurt in so many different ways, all the time, and pain will either change or end. Death, on the other hand, is the final silence. And that might be coming quickly, now, without regard for whether I had ever spoken what needed to be said, or had only betrayed myself into small silences, while I planned someday to speak, or waited for someone else's words. And I began to recognize a source of power within myself that comes from the knowledge that while it is most desirable not to be afraid, learning to put fear into a perspective gave me great strength.

I was going to die, if not sooner then later, whether or not I had ever spoken myself. My silences had not protected me. Your silence will not protect you. But for every real word spoken, for every attempt I had ever made to speak those truths for which I am still seeking, I had made contact with other women while we examined the words to fit a world in which we all believed, bridging our differences. And it was the concern and caring of all those women which gave me strength and enabled me to scrutinize the essentials of my living.

The women who sustained me through that period were Black and white, old and young, lesbian, bisexual, and heterosexual, and we all shared a war against the tyrannies of silence. They all gave me a strength and concern without which I could not have survived intact. Within those weeks of acute fear came the knowledge—within the war we are all waging with the forces of death, subtle and otherwise, conscious or not—I am not only a casualty, I am also a warrior.

What are the words you do not yet have? What do you need to say? What are the tyrannies you swallow day by day and attempt to make your own, until you will sicken and die of them, still in silence? Perhaps for some of you here today, I am the face of one of your fears. Because I am woman, because I am Black, because I am lesbian, because I am myself—a Black woman warrior poet doing my work—come to ask you, are you doing yours?

And of course I am afraid, because the transformation of silence into language and action is an act of self-revelation, and that always seems fraught with danger. But my daughter, when I told her of our topic and my difficulty with it, said, "Tell them about how you're never really a whole person if you remain silent, because there's always that one little piece inside you that wants to be spoken out, and if you keep ignoring it, it gets madder and madder and hotter and hotter, and if you don't speak it out one day it will just up and punch you in the mouth from the inside."

In the cause of silence, each of us draws the face of her own fear—fear of contempt, of censure, or some judgment, or recognition, of challenge, of annihilation. But most of all, I think, we fear the visibility without which we cannot truly live. Within this country where racial difference creates a constant, if unspoken, distortion of vision, Black women have on one hand always been highly visible, and so, on the other hand, have been rendered invisible through the depersonalization of racism. Even within the women's movement, we have had to fight, and still do, for that very visibility which also renders us most vulnerable, our Blackness. For to survive in the mouth of this dragon we call America, we have had to learn this first and most vital lesson—that we were never meant to survive. Not as human beings. And neither were most of you here today, Black or not. And that visibility which makes us most vulnerable is that which also is the source of our greatest strength. Because the machine will try to grind you into dust anyway, whether or not we speak. We can sit in our corners mute forever while our sisters and our selves are wasted, while our children are distorted and destroyed, while our earth is poisoned; we can sit in our safe corners mute as bottles, and we will still be no less afraid.

In my house this year we are celebrating the feast of Kwanza, the African-American festival of harvest which begins the day after Christmas and lasts for seven days. There are seven principles of Kwanza, one for each day. The first principle is Umoja, which means unity, the decision to strive for and maintain unity in self and community. The principle for yesterday, the second day, was Kujichagulia—self-determination—the decision to define ourselves, name ourselves, and speak for ourselves, instead of being defined and spoken for by others. Today is the third day of Kwanza, and the principle for today is Ujima—collective work and responsibility—the decision to build and maintain ourselves and our communities together and to recognize and solve our problems together.

Each of us is here now because in one way or another we share a commitment to language and to the power of language, and to the reclaiming of that language which has been made to work against us. In the transformation of silence into language and action, it is vitally necessary for each one of us to establish or examine her function in that transformation and to recognize her role as vital within that transformation.

For those of us who write, it is necessary to scrutinize not only the truth of what we speak, but the truth of that language by which we speak it. For others, it is to share and spread also those words that are meaningful to us. But primarily for us all, it is necessary to teach by living and speaking those truths which we believe and know beyond understanding. Because in this way alone we can survive, by taking part in a process of life that is creative and continuing, that is growth.

And it is never without fear—of visibility, of the harsh light of scrutiny and perhaps judgment, of pain, of death. But we have lived through all of those already, in silence, except death. And I remind myself all the time now that if I were to have been born mute, or had maintained an oath of silence my whole life long for safety, I would still have suffered, and I would still die. It is very good for establishing perspective.

And where the words of women are crying to be heard, we must each of us recognize our responsibility to seek those words out, to read them and share them and examine them in their pertinence to our lives. That we not hide behind the mockeries of separations that have been imposed upon us and which so often we accept as our own. For instance, "I can't possibly teach Black women's writing—their experience is so different from mine." Yet how many years have you spent teaching Plato and Shakespeare and Proust? Or another, "She's a white woman and what could she possibly have to say to me?" Or, "She's a lesbian, what would my husband say, or my chairman?" Or again, "This woman writes of her sons and I have no children." And all the other endless ways in which we rob ourselves of ourselves and each other.

We can learn to work and speak when we are afraid in the same way we have learned to work and speak when we are tired. For we have been socialized to respect fear more than our own needs for language and definition, and while we wait in silence for that final luxury of fearlessness, the weight of that silence will choke us.

The fact that we are here and that I speak these words is an attempt to break that silence and bridge some of those differences between us, for it is not difference which immobilizes us, but silence. And there are so many silences to be broken.

from The New Revised Standard Version of the Bible

The Good Samaritan

(Luke 10: 29–37)

But wanting to justify himself, he asked Jesus, "And who is my neighbor?" Jesus replied, "A man was going down from Jerusalem to Jericho and fell into the hands of robbers, who stripped him, beat him, and went away, leaving him half dead. Now by chance a priest was going down that road; and when he saw him, he passed by on the other side. So likewise a Levite, when he came to the place and saw him, passed by on the other side. But a Samaritan while traveling came near him; and when he saw him, he was moved to pity. He went to him and bandaged his wounds, having poured oil and wine on them. Then he put him on his own animal, brought him to an inn, and took care of him. The next day he took out two denarii, gave them to the innkeeper, and said, 'Take care of him; and when I come back, I will repay whatever you spend.' " "Which of these three, do you think, was a neighbor to the man who fell into the hands of robbers?" He said, "The one who showed him mercy." Jesus said to him, "Go and do likewise."

Paul's Teaching on Love

(I Cor. 13: 1–13)

If I speak in tongues of mortals and of angels, but do not have love, I am a noisy gong or a clanging cymbal. And if I have prophetic powers, and understand all mysteries and all knowledge, and if I have all faith, so as to remove mountains, but do not have love, I am nothing. If I give away all my possessions, and hand over my body so that I may boast, but do not have love, I gain nothing.

Love is patient; love is kind; love is not envious or boastful or arrogant or rude. It does not insist on its own way; it is not irritable or resentful; it does not rejoice in wrongdoing, but rejoices in truth. It bears all things, believes all things, hopes all things, endures all things.

Love never ends. But as for the prophecies, they will come to an end; as for tongues, they will cease; as for knowledge, it will come to an end. For we know only in part; and we prophesy only in part; but when the complete comes, the partial will come to an end. When I was a child, I spoke like a child, I thought like a child, I reasoned like a child; when I became an adult, I put an end to the childish ways. For now we see in a mirror, dimly, but then we will see face to face. Now I know only in part; then I will know fully, even as I have been fully known. And now faith, hope, and love abide, these three; and the greatest of these is love.

Sermon on the Mount

(Matthew 5: 1–16)

When Jesus saw the crowds he went up the mountain; and after he sat down, his disciples came to him. Then he began to speak, and taught them saying:

"Blessed are the poor in spirit, for theirs is the kingdom of heaven."

"Blessed are those who mourn, for they will be comforted."

"Blessed are the meek, for they will inherit the earth."

"Blessed are those who hunger and thirst for righteousness, for they will be filled."

"Blessed are the merciful, for they will receive mercy."

"Blessed are the pure in heart, for they will see God."

"Blessed are the peacemakers, for they will be called children of God."

"Blessed are you when people revile you and persecute you and utter all kinds of evil against you falsely on my account. Rejoice and be glad, for your reward is great in heaven, for in the same way they persecuted the prophets who were before you."

"You are the salt of the earth; but if salt has lost its taste, how can its saltiness be restored? It is no longer good for anything, but is thrown out and trampled under foot."

"You are the light of the world. A city built on a hill cannot be hid. No one after lighting a lamp puts it under a bushel basket, but on the lampstand, and it gives light to all in the house. In the same way, let your light shine before others, so that they may see your good works and give glory to your father in heaven."

Thomas H. West (b. 1942 in Minneapolis) entered the University of Minnesota in 1960 on an Evans Scholarship. He graduated in 1964 with a B.A. in humanities, then completed an M.A. in theology at Marquette University. After studying philosophy and theology in Germany from 1967–69, he began work on a Ph.D. in the philosophy of religion, a program offered jointly by the University of California, Berkeley, and the Graduate Theological Union. He received his Ph.D. in 1975, and, after teaching at Santa Clara University and the University of St. Thomas, took a position at the College of St. Catherine in 1979 where he is currently professor of Theology. Dr. West is author of Ultimate Hope Without God: The Atheistic Eschatology of Ernst Bloch *(Peter Lang, 1991) and* Jesus and the Quest for Meaning: Entering Theology *(Fortress, 2001).*

Love into Justice:
The Good Samaritan Revisited

Thomas H. West, Ph.D.

Most Christians would say that the foundation of social justice is love, especially love of neighbor, *agape*. But how do we get from agap to an active commitment to social justice? We do not answer this question well if we say simply that agapic love and social justice are the same thing. They are not. Yet I want to argue that work for social justice is a necessary expression of agapic love.

In the New Testament, the epitome of agapic love is the Good Samaritan. We do not ordinarily think of the Good Samaritan as practicing social justice. We see him as practicing compassion, performing an act of charity, carrying out a mission of mercy, not, surely, working for social justice. What the Good Samaritan did and what a social reformer like Martin Luther King Jr. did are clearly very different things.

But is social justice so sharply different from agapic love? In this chapter I shall argue that there is indeed a distinction between agapic love and social justice, but it is a distinction within a unity.

Luke's Parable of the Good Samaritan

Here is the parable of the Good Samaritan as told in Luke's gospel:

> Just then a lawyer stood up to test Jesus. "Teacher," he said, "what must I do to inherit eternal life?" He said to him, "What is written in the law? What do you read there?" He answered, "You shall love the Lord your God with all your heart, and with all your soul, and with all your strength, and with all your mind; and your neighbor as yourself." And he said to him, "You have given the right answer; do this, and you will live."

> But wanting to justify himself, he asked Jesus, "And who is my neighbor?" Jesus replied, A man was going down from Jerusalem to Jericho, and fell into the hands of robbers, who stripped him, beat him, and went away, leaving him half dead. Now by chance a priest was going down the road; and when he saw him, he passed by on the other side. So likewise a Levite, when he came to the place and saw him, passed by on the other side. But a Samaritan while traveling came near him; and when he saw him, he was moved with compassion. He went to him and bandaged his wounds, having poured oil and wine on them. Then he put him on his own animal, brought him to an inn, and took care of him. The next day he took out two denarii, gave them to the innkeeper, and said, "Take care of him; and when I come back, I will repay you whatever more you spend" (Luke 10:25–35).

Luke situates the parable of the Good Samaritan within the "travel narrative" (Luke 9: 51–19: 27) that follows Jesus' journey from Galilee to Jerusalem.[1]

During the journey Jesus frequently pauses to instruct his followers in the way of discipleship. One day he instructed them by telling the parable of the Good Samaritan.

The Good Samaritan parable is classified by Joachim Jeremias as a "parable of realized discipleship,"[2] though it is not a parable in the narrow or typical sense. Rather, it is an *example story*, not an extended metaphor or simile where the figures and events symbolize something else, as when the mustard seed symbolizes the reign of God (see Mt. 13: 31–32) or the generous vineyard owner (see Mt. 20: 1–16), God's unconditional love.[3] The Good Samaritan parable does not refer beyond itself in this way. Jesus is not saying that "God acts like the Good Samaritan," but rather, "You should act like the Good Samaritan."

The Good Samaritan story does, however, display other elements typical of a parable, most obviously the element of surprise. The surprise is not that the priest and the Levite (a Temple official subordinate to the priests) pass by an injured man. Out in the countryside, "anti-clericalism" was widespread among Jews. That Jesus would portray Temple officials as morally callous would evoke a knowing murmur from his Jewish audience. His audience would then expect Jesus to finish off his story by having an Israelite layperson like themselves stop and do the right thing.[4] Instead, the *Samaritan* stops, and, "moved with compassion," does the right thing. This is a major surprise to Jesus' Jewish audience. John Donahue reminds us: "Centuries of pious reflection have dulled our sensibilities to the hatred that existed between Jews and Samaritans." Jews regarded Samaritans not only as a mongrel people who had intermarried with pagan invaders, but as deserters of the Jewish religion.[5] That a Jew could love the Samaritan as a neighbor, and a Samaritan could love the Jew as a neighbor, well, it's a scandal, it's out of the question. When the lawyer asked Jesus, "Who is my neighbor?" he was being serious. There was genuine debate among Jews at this time about who was included under "neighbor." According to Jeremias, "It was generally agreed that the term connoted fellow countrymen, including full proselytes."[6] It did not include Samaritans. Jesus defines *neighbor* to include the hated Samaritan, depicting the Samaritan as one who is a neighbor precisely by treating the injured Jew as a neighbor. This is a surprise. This is a shock.

In the parable of the Good Samaritan, Jesus offers an example of agapic love in action. Such love imitates the love shown by Jesus, and Jesus' love is in turn an imitation of God's love. Such is the nature of Jesus' radical moral demand on those called to the mission of bringing people into the reign of God. In the parable, agapic love shows the following qualities:

- It is unconditional. The Samaritan does not demand that the person injured fulfill any conditions before the Samaritan is willing to give help.
- This love is universal. The Samaritan does not care to which gender, race, class, religion, or ethnic group the injured person belongs. A human being is hurt. This Samaritan would have reached out to any human being who was suffering.
- This love is unconcerned with merit or just deserts. The Samaritan does not say to himself, "This person in the ditch half dead does not deserve my help because he had it coming. He didn't take sufficient care to avoid the threat of robbery." The Samaritan does not say to himself, "There is probably some past sin in the victim's life. God through this violent assault and robbery is punishing him."
- It is love moved by compassion. The Samaritan is moved by feeling. Indeed, one can imagine him seized by feeling and impelled to the ditch beside the road.
- It is a love that is spontaneous and uncalculating. The Samaritan is moved to act, quickly. He is not shown pondering the pros and cons. He is not shown engaging in subtle calculations about precisely what he should do. He spends no time in rational analysis.
- It is a love that goes beyond the minimum one would expect of even the most decent person. That is, it is supererogatory; it goes beyond what is asked. He doesn't just bandage the injured man's wounds and get him to the next town, but stays with him, takes care of him, pays his lodging, and then—and here is the special touch—says to the innkeeper: "If it comes to more than this, I'll pay the difference on my way back." Here the Samaritan shows himself to be a virtuoso of the supererogatory.[7]

These qualities constitute agapic, that is, Christian, love in action, in the public sphere, among strangers, who through love become neighbors and friends.

Now if the Christian moral life were simply a matter of letting oneself be moved to uncalculating love towards any human being in special need, we would have no need for lengthy books on Christian morality and justice. But the Christian moral life often requires us to go beyond spontaneous acts of agapic love. Morality then becomes more complex, and when it does, it begins to move from agapic love pure and simple to agapic love that expresses itself in the work of justice.

2. Love into Interpersonal Justice

The great American theologian Reinhold Niebuhr said that Christian love becomes justice when there are three or more people in the room.[8] Expanding on the story of the Good Samaritan, let us imagine that the Samaritan, instead of discovering one robbery victim in the ditch, discovers three. The Samaritan is moved by compassion to go over to the three victims, but as soon as he arrives, he finds himself having to step back from the situation and from his feeling in order to engage in some rational analysis and calculation. He finds himself engaged in what we today call *triage*. Triage is a system of principles and rules by which one judges how one can best treat victims like these, given one's resources. Whenever my family calls our Health Maintenance Organization after hours, we talk first to the triage nurse; using a complex system of principles and rules she decides what the HMO can and should do for us given our ailments and given their resources.

Coming upon the three victims, the Good Samaritan must also practice triage. The principles and rules of triage he uses will be undoubtedly less explicit and formalized that those of the HMO triage nurse; nevertheless, if he is to do *justice* to these three victims he will have to turn his thoughtful attention to *some* principles and rules, however rudimentary they might be.

In practicing triage, the Samaritan does not completely turn from feeling to thought, but he does distance himself enough to allow a rational analysis of the situation. If he lets himself be ruled only by feeling, he might spontaneously attend first to the victim who is screaming and moaning the loudest, but to do so would be unjust. One of the first principles of triage is that one should attend first to the victim who is most seriously injured and then make a judgment about whether one has the resources to help him or her. The Samaritan coolheadedly turns his attention very self-consciously towards this principle and sets about putting it into practice. He first gathers empirical data about the condition of the victims. He discovers that the victim screaming the loudest is a teen-age boy holding his ankle. A second victim is very quiet, is not bleeding, but he has a weak pulse. A third victim is bleeding profusely from the neck. He decides to help her first, and bandages her wounds, and stops the bleeding. On her he decides to concentrate his maximum effort. He has acted justly.

Yet it would be unfair, it would be unjust, if he were to cease thinking about the other two. They, after all, are human beings, with their inherent dignity and worth. He can*not* give them his *maximum* effort in this situation, but he feels bound to give them at least a minimum of attention. But what precisely is the minimum he owes them in this situation? The answer requires another calculation on his part. To the boy holding his ankle, he decides that the injury is not that serious, and he limits himself to wrapping the ankle and uttering words of comfort. And he double-checks the person with the weak pulse to make sure that he still is alive.

At this point the Samaritan is now expressing his love in the form of justice, and specifically, *interpersonal* justice. Interpersonal justice refers to the justice that is practiced by one individual to another in a situation where the person practicing the justice has to distance himself somewhat from his feelings, consult a set of principles and rules, gather data about this situation, and make a rational decision about what should be done. Interpersonal justice requires attention to the questions of what is equal treatment, what is fair treatment, what is the minimum one owes each individual who is present, and what is the maximum one can offer, given one's resources. This kind of analysis tells the Samaritan that it would be wrong, it would violate the principles of interpersonal justice, if he were to spend himself totally in selfless and supererogatory love on only one of the victims that now confront him. He must therefore carefully and rationally distribute his efforts in an equal yet fair manner, giving the most he can give to one without at the same time totally neglecting the others.

Interpersonal justice is not only practiced in the kind of extraordinary situation in which the Samaritan finds himself. It is in fact the stuff of ordinary daily life, in a way that heedless agapic love can never be. Every day we have many encounters with our fellow human beings. Not every encounter is, or should be, an occasion for agapic love in the pure form. Rather, we should treat those individuals we encounter every day with a simple, interpersonal justice, with a basic respect for their worth, dignity, and autonomy.[9] There is a minimum that we owe everyone. Some might require more than the minimum from us. We must weigh matters and decide what we can give. Knowing how this is done takes much training and learning. Some people take to this very well and show an acute ethical intelligence.

Let us return to our story. The Samaritan has bound the wounds of the woman bleeding, attended to the man with the weak pulse, and calmed the boy with the injured ankle. Somehow, after making a whole series of further decisions, all accompanied by considerable rational analysis, he gets them to the nearest town and arranges for their care, though this time a check of his financial resources precludes an offer to pay the innkeeper and the local physician. He has done justice to these people.

But the whole experience has left him angry. For the fourth time this month he has encountered victims of brutal robberies left to die in the ditch. What would have happened to these poor people had he not happened along? The Samaritan thinks on the many others who were passed by and left to suffer and die. This tragic situation is more than he as an individual can manage. He is moved to conclude that one-to-one agapic love and interpersonal justice are not enough. He decides to move into social justice.

3. Love into Social Justice

The Good Samaritan decides to involve the larger community and attempt a more systematic solution to this terrible problem of assault and robbery.[10] He decides thereby to make the move from *interpersonal* justice to the work of *social* justice. Social justice is justice practiced by a group or community towards individuals or other groups or communities. Social justice is a social endeavor, which involves the creation of *social structures*.

Social structures have two elements: the mental and the institutional. The *first* element is concerned with the consciousness, the mind, the attitude, the ethos, of the community. It is obvious to the Samaritan that many people are passing by these victims in the ditch and not doing anything to help. "There is a deeply faulty ethos in these parts," he says to himself. "People around here are indifferent to this kind of human misery."

The Good Samaritan resolves to change the ethos, to raise consciousness, to change the mentality. On his next trip down this road, he stops at each village and gives a little talk to the villagers, alerting them to the suffering of the victims of these robberies and urging them not to pass by the victims. He talks about the basic dignity and equality of all human beings. All human beings, he insists, have a claim on our love and justice, especially those who are suffering. He even includes in his talk a rudimentary introduction to triage. In his efforts to create a new social mentality, the Samaritan enjoys some success. People become more sensitized. More people than before are reaching out with agapic love and interpersonal justice.

In one village this new consciousness becomes so pervasive that helping robbery victims becomes what sociologists call an *institution*, that is, an *established pattern of behavior*, which is the *second* element of a social structure.[11] Helping victims is something that villagers practice without hesitation. The institution in this case is a *custom*, a pattern of behavior that establishes itself quite spontaneously and lacks formal organization.

Nevertheless, this proves to be not enough. There are still many victims and many people are passing them by. The ethos of reaching out to help is indeed deeper and more widespread, but it is far from pervasive. Human beings, after all, are free to defy ethos and custom and are especially prone to do so when they are asked to go outside themselves for someone else's sake. And so the Samaritan decides to move beyond custom and create a more formal institution.

He decides to create an institution in which groups of volunteers will patrol the road in shifts in search of victims.[12] To insure that these volunteers will be skilled in applying triage, he arranges for training sessions. He rents several buildings in the villages in which to hold these sessions. Since those who conduct the sessions will be engaged in virtually full-time work, he decides to pay them. Realizing that he does not have enough money for rent and salaries, he sets out to raise money, trusting that the ethos he created earlier is wide and deep enough to produce people willing to contribute. He organizes a fund drive, to occur on a regular basis. His institution comes thereby to depend on both the willingness of people to volunteer their time to work on the patrols and their willingness to contribute money on a regular basis. And since the contributions of time and money depend on the continued vitality of the ethos, the Samaritan must continue to give talks to raise ethical consciousness; that is, he must continue to be concerned with the element of mentality.

The Samaritan has thus created not only a new mentality, but also new institutions. And many robbery victims are helped.

Yet, many victims continue to die in the ditch, unhelped. The crime rate is up. Also, there are difficulties with the Samaritan's institutional structure. The patrols are staffed largely by unpaid volunteers, who are free to cease volunteering, and quite regularly one or more will suddenly and unpredictably pull out. On nights before holidays, the most dangerous nights, whole patrols have to be canceled for lack of volunteers.

Funding is a continuing problem. The regional economy fluctuates wildly and along with that, financial contributions fluctuate wildly. Sometimes the Samaritan has the funds to do the training, sometimes not. A fickleness and unpredictability pervade the institution making for a fickle and unpredictable service to the victims along the road. One of the principles of justice is universality of coverage: all persons will receive the minimum due them. This institution is failing to provide that coverage, which causes acute pangs of conscience in the Samaritan. The compassion that moved him to that first act of agapic love has now moved him towards the work of justice that aims to reach all those suffering, but he is *not* reaching them all in any consistent way.

For a while the Samaritan considers going to what we now call the free-market approach. In order to guarantee more predictable and reliable staff he could staff the patrols with paid professionals. To pay for them, he could market their services by charging the victims—with some provision for their ability to pay—or by selling their services to villages along the road or to groups of travelers. To raise the initial capital outlay for this service, he could sell shares to the enterprise and then pay the shareholders out of the profits.

But he decides against going into the market. He is not opposed to the market as such, for he is a businessperson and believes firmly that some goods and services are best delivered to people through the market. But he has come to believe that a robbery victim in the ditch has not just a *need* for help, but also a *right* to help. A right means that the victim has an absolute claim on the community for a consistent, predictable, and skilled response to his or her suffering. The free market approach introduces the profit motive and with that the inevitable tendency to provide the best service to those who have the most money to pay for it. But this is the kind of service that every human being has a right to, irrespective of wealth or social position.

So the Samaritan chooses another step, namely, he decides to go to the state, that is, to the institutions of government. This road is in a province under the jurisdiction of Rome. He decides to go to the Roman governor and ask that a new social structure be created. While talking with the governor and his aides, he learns that the problems occurring along this road are occurring on roads throughout the province. The governor is responsive. He petitions Rome for the permission to create a new structure and collect a tax to pay for it. The Roman senate passes a law, the emperor approves it, and the governor's bureaucrats work out detailed policies, that is, principles and rules, to guide the new institution in its service. Paid governmental patrols are put in place along the roads. They deliver medical help more quickly and predictably and thus provide coverage that approaches universal. Because the government owns the means of legalized violence, it equips the patrols with the physical means to pursue, subdue, and arrest the violent robbers who are causing so much human suffering.[13] And since the taxes are set and levied by law, funding is more predictable year-to-year.

The Good Samaritan is quite satisfied with his work. He has moved from agapic love to interpersonal justice, and finally, to social justice. To be sure, he has not ceased practicing agapic love—indeed, just the other night an opportunity again presented itself and he reached out to help a victim—but he has spent most of his time these past several years on the long march through social structures.

Despite his general satisfaction, the Samaritan has frequently found the work of social justice tedious and boring. Giving ethical pep talks, finding buildings to rent, training volunteers, writing up detailed policy suggestions for the governor—more than once during all this he has felt a slackening in his original agapic motivation. Indeed there have been moments when he becomes wistful for the spontaneous purity of that original act of agapic love. He recalls the deep joy and peace he felt after he had paid the innkeeper, knowing that he had done the right thing.

In addition, he is no naïve reformer. He has seen the negative side of this movement from agapic love to social justice. He worries, for example, about the impersonality of the new government structure. He has talked with some members of the patrols and found that quite a few are not motivated by the desire to help their neighbors but by the desire to advance their careers. Some government administrators appear less interested in providing a good service than in protecting their turf and increasing their budgets. He worries that with the movement to a government structure, the community ethos will decline. There is already much grumbling about the new taxes. Taxes, after all, are coercive. They are extracted by law and backed by the organized violence of the state. The other day he heard someone say, "They're confiscating my hard-earned money to pay for these patrols—I never even take those roads. It's not fair!" He fears that giving this work of social justice over to the state will diminish the motivating energy of agapic love to the point where individuals will pass by victims in the ditch with the excuse, "I don't need to stop, a patrol will be by soon." He has even heard rumors that some patrols are abusing their power and using their instruments of violence not to protect the victims but to blackmail them. Social justice, when it is carried out by the structures of government, has its dark side.

But all in all, despite these concerns, the Samaritan remains cautiously proud of his work. He is convinced that this new social structure has reduced the total amount of human suffering. Social justice has accomplished more than his individual acts of agapic love ever could.

As we watch the Samaritan move from agapic love to social justice from our perspective in the twentieth century, we notice something missing from his vision and practice. At no time does the Samaritan engage in an in-depth social, political, and economic analysis of his society. He does not ask himself why there are so many robberies. He does not link the rise in the crime rate with the high concentration of wealth in the hands of a few large absentee landowners. He fails to bring into view the many tenant farmers who live in virtual slavery.[14] Many are so poor that they are drawn to lives of crime. As he journeys to see the governor, he does not wonder if perhaps his work of social justice wouldn't be more effective if this region were not under imperial rule and if Jews and Samaritans were independent peoples with grassroots, egalitarian political structures more immediately responsive to crime and its victims. This kind of analysis might very well have led the Samaritan to a vision of radical and sweeping change in the social, economic, and political structures of his day. But this kind of analysis, and the radical vision that often goes with it, is a relatively recent development in the history of ethical intelligence. Jesus did not undertake this kind of analysis.[15] Nor did the early Church. And the Catholic Church was indifferent, sometimes even hostile, to this kind of analysis until late in the nineteenth century. In our day, however, virtually all Christians engaged in the work of social justice are aware of the need for complex social analysis.

I hope that my revisit of the Good Samaritan story has shown that the distinctions among agapic love, interpersonal justice, and social justice are real, but not hard and fast. Agapic love, Christian love, is not *replaced* by interpersonal and social justice, but continues to accompany both as their motivational fount, energizing both,[16] preventing each from becoming impersonal and bloodless. Justice has been described as the *public* expression of love, a definition that strikes me as particularly apt. The movement from agapic love to social justice is continuous and necessary. Any theology that draws too sharp a separation between love and justice, or which sees them as belonging to utterly different spheres, or which sees them in opposition, is a deeply flawed theology.

Just as there is a natural movement from agapic love to social justice, so too is there a natural move from social justice to agapic love. Even the most intense, one-to-one expression of agapic love does not occur in a social vacuum. Social structures—mentality, ethos, custom, laws, institutions—all pre-shape even the most private actions. The Good Samaritan, after all, is a member of a schismatic Jewish sect whose members followed the Torah, the Jewish law found in the first five books of the Hebrew Bible. The heart of this law is the two-fold commandment to love God and love your neighbor as yourself. This two-fold law was part of the Samaritan ethos and passed on to the Good Samaritan through the institutions of religious learning and instruction. The religious and ethical logic of the two-fold law led him to oppose a mentality that would forbid him to help an injured Jew. And therefore his spontaneous act of agapic love as told in Jesus' story did not arise solely out of his own spontaneity, it was not utterly his own, *sui generis*, but in part was the consequence of a social structure. Indeed the very spontaneity of his action is partly a sign of how thoroughly he was socialized by the redemptive elements of this structure.[17] And we must not forget, the parable of the Good Samaritan was told by Jesus, who was raised a Jew and was taught the same two-fold law of love.

We must, therefore, be wary of drawing overprecise distinctions among Christian love, interpersonal justice, and social justice. The distinctions are real, but within an unfolding unity. In his story of the Good Samaritan, Jesus beautifully captured the first and decisive moment of agapic love. Yet we can well imagine that the logic of love carried the Good Samaritan, as it should carry us, into the work of justice.

But with all this talk of social justice we dare not forget that the direction of agapic love is not only out into the public sphere of social structures.[18] There is the other direction, towards the intimacy of full mutuality, towards friendship, romantic love, and family. What is the final purpose of just social structures if not a world where mutuality can flourish? Mutuality with God and mutuality with others. The full terror of a corrupt social structure is the way its destructive power makes even the intimacy of mutuality impossible. Agapic love achieves public expression in justice, but its fulfillment in mutual self-giving.[19]

Notes

[1] See John Donahue, *The Gospel in Parable: Metaphor, Narrative, and Theology in the Synoptic Gospels* (Philadelphia: Fortress Press, 1988), 126ff.

[2] Joachim Jeremias, *The Parables of Jesus* (New York: Charles Scribner's Sons, 2nd rev. ed., 1972), 198ff.

[3] Donahue, *The Gospel in Parable*, 12f.

[4] Jeremias, *The Parables of Jesus*, 204.

[5] Donahue, *The Gospel in Parable*, 130f., supplies a short history of the relations between Jews and Samaritans to show why they were such enemies.

[6] Jeremias, *The Parables of Jesus*, 202.

[7] Donahue, *The Gospel in Parable*, tells us that the Samaritan's extra help at the inn is more than just a sign of the supererogatory: "As a paradigm for compassionate entry into the world of an injured brother or sister, this final action is indispensable. According to the law at the time, a person with an unpaid debt could be enslaved until the debt was paid (see Matt. 18:23–35). Since the injured man was robbed and stripped—deprived of all resources—he could have been at the mercy of the innkeeper, a profession that had a bad reputation for dishonesty and violence. The parable assures the injured man's freedom and independence" (133).

8   Actually, Niebuhr said it more abstractly than that: "An immediately felt obligation towards obvious need may be prompted by the emotion of pity. But a continued sense of obligation rests upon and expresses itself in rational calculations of the needs of others as compared with our own interests. A relation between the self and one other may be partly ecstatic; and in any case the calculation of relative interests may be reduced to a minimum. But as soon as a third person is introduced into the relation even the most perfect love requires a rational estimate of conflicting needs and interests." Reinhold Niebuhr, *The Nature and Destiny of Man: A Christian Interpretation. Volume II: Human Destiny,* (New York: Charles Scribner's Sons, 1943), 248.

9   Following the rules of common courtesy can fulfill more than a small part of interpersonal justice on a day to day level. It is amazing how much of the advice that Ms. Manners gives in her syndicated newspaper column can be seen as the application of interpersonal justice. She shows an acute sense for the intersection of morality and manners. Though insofar as her rulings on courtesy precipitate a widespread pattern of behavior in society, she is creating a social structure, that is, she is doing the work of social justice.

10   Another re-telling of the Good Samaritan story, which makes much the same move to social justice as I make here, is that of Stephen Mott. See his *Biblical Ethics and Social Change* (New York: Oxford University Press, 1982), 58f. I am not indebted to Mott's re-telling, but the parallel is striking. For the Mott reference I am indebted to Garth L. Hallet, *Christian Neighbor Love: An Assessment of Six Rival Positions* (Washington, D.C.: Georgetown University Press, 1989), 118.

11   On institutionalization, see Peter L. Berger, and Thomas Luckmann, *The Social Construction of Reality: A Treatise on the Sociology of Knowledge* (New York: Doubleday Anchor Books, 1967), 54–61.

12   A volunteer patrol is a good example of what Catholic social teaching calls a "mediating structure" or an "intermediate structure." Such structures carry out the "principle of subsidiarity," which could be summed up this way: before creating larger, governmental structures, first create smaller, local, nongovernmental structures. See Fred Kammer, *Doing Faithjustice: An Introduction to Catholic Social Thought* (New York: Paulist Press, 1991), 184.

13   Here we have an example of the twin functions of government. On the one hand, it has the more positive function of extending medical help to all who need it. On the other hand, it has the more negative function of countering violence with violence, of enforcing order against the forces of anarchy and destruction. There are two traditions in Western political theory that tend to focus on one function at the expense of the other. Martin Luther (and before him Augustine and after him Hobbes) tends to reduce government to the "negative" function, that is, "to bear the secular sword and punish the wicked" (see "Secular Authority: To What Extent it Should be Obeyed," in John Dillenberger, ed., *Martin Luther Selections from his Writings* [New York: Doubleday Anchor Books, first published in 1523, this edition, 1961] 363–402, here 374). Government indeed is willed by God, but by God's "left hand." Its work is God's work, yet an "alien work" (377). If there had been no sin there would be no government. The scriptural source for this tradition can be found in Rom. 13:4 and 1 Pet. 1: 13. Another tradition, going back to Plato and Aristotle, stresses that

government is a good, and natural to human life. Christian socialists and wel-fare state liberals add to this the agapic motivation and welcome government structures in their "positive" function of meeting a broad range of human needs. Reinhold Niebuhr keeps these two traditions in good balance: "All structures of justice do indeed presuppose the sinfulness of man, and are all partly systems of restraint which prevent the conflict of wills and interests from resulting in a consistent anarchy. But they are also all mechanisms by which men fulfill their obligations to their fellow men, beyond the possibilities offered in direct and personal relationships. The Kingdom of God and the demands of perfect love are therefore relevant to every political system and impinge upon every social situation in which the self seeks to come to terms with the claims of other life." See *The Nature and Destiny of Man: A Christian Interpretation. Volume II: Human Destiny*, 192.

[14] One of the effects of the widespread indebtedness among the peasants in Pales-tine was virtual slavery for those who could not pay their debts. Many took to banditry. See Richard A. Horsley, *Sociology and the Jesus Movement* (New York: Crossroad, 1989), 88–90.

[15] I am not denying that people in Jesus' time could not have visions of a new world where life would be radically different. Jesus had that vision, as did the many other "millenarian prophets" of his time. What I don't see is the combi-nation of radical vision and social analysis, as epitomized, for example, in the work of Karl Marx.

[16] In the words of Fred Kammer: "Instead of a tension between love and justice, love as the soul of justice gives the Christian passion for building a more just order." See *Doing Faithjustice: An Introduction to Catholic Social Thought* (New York: Paulist Press, 1991), 181.

[17] An extraordinary example of agapic love practiced spontaneously more because of communal ethos than individual heroic virtue is the story of the French mountain village of Le Chambon, whose 5000 inhabitants sheltered 5000 Jews during World War 11. The documentary, produced by Pierre Sauvage, that tells the story has many interviews with individuals who partic-ipated in this good work. What is remarkable is how self-effacing they are. Indeed, they appear somewhat baffled by the attention. What emerges out of the interviews is that these people performed individual acts of love because that is what one does if one is a member of that community. There appears to have been very little agonizing over the risks. It was the triumph of an ethos and thus of the work of social justice. See also Philip P. Hallie, *Lest Innocent Blood Be Shed: The Story of the Village of Le Chambon and How Goodness Happened There* (New York: Harper and Row, 1979). And yet reading Hallie's book reveals how mysteriously complex all this is. For the ethos of Le Chambon would not have attained its spontaneous strength without the inspired work of two indi-viduals, the pastor and his wife, André and Magda Trocmé. For a very inter-esting philosophical examination of both the village ethos and the moral achievement of the Trocmés, see Lawrence A. Blum, *Moral Perception and Par-ticularity* (New York: Cambridge University Press, 1994), 73–4, 85–9, 91–2, 151–2, 175–80.

[18] Within the public sphere of social justice there are several sub-spheres that cor-respond to different kinds of social justice. These sub-spheres are: 1) basic

human rights and freedoms: freedom of speech, of worship, of movement, and so on; 2) economic justice: the duty of society to ensure that goods and services are fairly and equally distributed and the duty of individuals to contribute to the production of goods and services; 3) political justice: the duty of society to ensure that political power is fairly and equally distributed and the duty of individuals to contribute to political decision-making; 4) criminal justice: the duty of the society to fairly and equally enforce the law and the duty of individuals to obey the law; 5) environmental justice: the duty to protect the inorganic and organic world so that all being will flourish, not just human being; 6) intergenerational justice: duty of the present generation to pass on just social structures to the next generation and not overburden the next generation with debt and environmental degradation; 7) international justice: the duty of nations to live in comity with other nations and to create international social structures to solve social problems that are global in their effects. To all these duties are corresponding rights; indeed, one of the tasks of social justice is to find the proper balance of duties (responsibilities) and rights (entitlements), or to put it another way, the proper mix of what the larger society should distribute to sub-societies and individuals, and what individuals and sub-societies should contribute to the larger society.

[19] The works of two contemporary theorists of agapic love show these two tendencies. Gene Outka in his *Agape: an Ethical Analysis* (New Haven: Yale University Press, 1972), defines agapic love as "universal equal regard." Although he does accept mutuality as a proper fulfillment of agap, his understanding of agap leads his analysis more naturally towards justice. Stephen Post, in his *A Theory of Agape: On the Meaning of Christian Love* (Lewisburg, PA: Bucknell University Press, 1990) shows agapic love as seeking out mutual response in "special relations." My own view is that both tendencies must be kept together in dialectical unity. I like the words of Gilbert Meilander: "We ought not give up the desire for mutual love and try to be stoics. Neither ought we permit our love to be limited to the small circle of those who return it." See *Friendship: A Study in Theological Ethics* (South Bend: University of Notre Dame Press, 1981), 50.

Catherine R. Michaud was born in Salina, Kansas, and grew up in Colorado. She entered the Sisters of St. Joseph of Concordia, Kansas, in 1967 and shortly thereafter completed her B.A. in English at Marymount College of Kansas. She taught English at the secondary level for seven years before being appointed to her religious congregation's retreat center, Manna House of Prayer. She then earned a master's degree at Gonzaga University and joined the theology department of Marymount College, where she served as the department chair. In 1993 she attained a Licentiate in Sacred Theology at Regis College (Toronto) followed by a Ph.D. in systematic theology from the Toronto School of Theology of the University of Toronto. She has taught systematic theology and spirituality at the College of St. Catherine since 1994 and also serves as director of the masters program in theology.

The Catholic Tradition and Social Justice

Sr. Catherine Michaud, CSJ, Ph.D., and Thomas H. West, Ph.D.

The College of St. Catherine is a Catholic, liberal arts college for women that encourages intellectual inquiry in a way that is compatible with the best of the Catholic tradition. Part of the best of this tradition is the teaching on social justice.

This reading is structured as an imaginary dialogue between you, the student of TRW, and the authors, who between them have taught theology for 35 years at the college.

Let's begin!

1. What is the Catholic tradition?

The three great Western monotheistic religions are Judaism, Christianity, and Islam. They are called the "Abrahamic faiths" because they see their origin in God's call of Abraham and the Jewish people to a covenantal relationship: "I will be your God, you will be my people." Out of the Jewish tradition arose the Christian tradition in the first century, and out of both the Jewish and Christian traditions arose the Islamic tradition in the seventh century. The Christian tradition was once unified, but over the centuries it split into three major traditions, Catholic, Orthodox, and Protestant, all of which claim to be the legitimate expression of the original Christian tradition.

The Catholic tradition begins with Jesus of Nazareth, who in the first century was born a Jew, was reared as Jew, and died as Jew. There is no persuasive historical evidence that Jesus intended to replace Judaism with the Catholic Church as we know it. Rather, he felt himself anointed by

God to transform Judaism from within. He was convinced that God was taking a new initiative with the Jewish people, transforming them into a renewed community of love and justice. Jesus and his followers also believed that non-Jews (that is, Gentiles) would be so attracted to this renewed community that they would come to acknowledge the God of Israel as the God of all nations.

Jesus believed that this renewed community, called by Jesus the "Kingdom of God," was coming into existence through his own words and deeds, and would soon come *fully* into existence. But as his mission proceeded, he faced increasing opposition, and he began to anticipate his death as occurring before the full coming of the new rule of God's love and justice. Indeed, he came to see his death on the cross as instrumental in bringing about this new rule of God.

After his death, Jesus' followers experienced him as still in some mysterious way alive, as the "resurrected Christ" who had disabled the power of death and continued to draw people into a loving and just community. They experienced him in their midst when they celebrated the Eucharist and performed works of love. Their experience and their faithful communication of their shared story were the beginning of the Catholic tradition.

This Church at first was hardly more than a collection of individual churches bound together by their memory of the earthly Jesus and their experience of the Spirit of the risen Christ. This memory and experience formed a tradition, literally something "passed on," which at first expressed itself orally and later crystallized itself in written form. Parts of this written tradition formed the nucleus of those writings that later became the New Testament. And thus the "Christian scriptures," the New Testament, joined the "Hebrew scriptures," the Old Testament, to form the Christian Bible, which to this day is a norm against which the tradition measures itself, though not slavishly. Oral tradition thus preceded the written tradition as an authoritative source of Jesus' message. Catholics today believe that this tradition continues in the Church's teaching.

This newly emerging church fanned out over the Mediterranean basin, announcing the call of the risen Christ to form communities of love and justice. This church was thus universalizing itself, spreading itself over that part of the world roughly co-terminous with the Roman Empire. The Latin word for "universal" is "*catholica*," and thus this church came to see itself as the "*ecclesia catholica*," the church catholic or universal.

Anchored in, but not confined by, the Bible, this catholic church passed on its interpretation of the Bible as a living tradition. As a "tradition," this interpretation harked back to the past; as "living," it adapted itself to changing circumstances.

These circumstances were changing rapidly as the church moved out of its originally Jewish culture into Greek and Latin cultures. To some degree, it adopted the culture of the Greco-Roman world. It even came to believe that God's truth and grace could in part be found among the Greeks and Romans: Just as Moses and the prophets were forerunners of Jesus, so too were Socrates and Plato! Despite not having heard God's revelation in Jesus, these "pagans" were not so blind and corrupted that God's truth could not get through, at least in part. Thus the church catholic did not wholly reject Greco-Roman culture, but discriminatingly baptized it, incorporating the best of it into its Christian worldview. This became one of the abiding features of the Catholic tradition: The world outside the Church was not totally estranged from God. Human nature was not completely opposed to the supernatural grace and truth of Christ, but open and susceptible to it. Nor, therefore, could human reason be opposed to faith.

Quite early on, however, the catholic church developed into two distinctive modes, Latin and Greek, Western and Eastern, which produced a tension that led to a separation between the two in 1054 and a divorce in 1453. And thus the catholic church split into the Western Catholic Church and the Eastern Catholic Church (later known as the Orthodox Church), each claiming to be the more authentic continuation of the ancient catholic church.

Both the Greek and Latin churches retained the ancient catholic openness to Greco-Roman culture, especially its great philosophers. In the Latin church this openness reached a climax in the achievement of Thomas Aquinas, who, in the thirteenth century, adopted Aristotle's philosophy (along with a good dose of Platonism filtered through earlier Christian thinkers) into his Christian theology. It is to Thomas that we owe the saying, "Grace does not destroy nature, but builds on it"; that is, the supernatural grace and truth of God that comes through Jesus and the church does not destroy human nature and human culture, but builds on both and transforms both.

The Western Catholic Church (along with the Eastern Orthodox Church) continued its claim to be the legitimate continuation of the ancient catholic church. But then came the second great split in the church, this time within the Western church, known as the Protestant Reformation.

The first great Reformer was Martin Luther, who, in the early years of the sixteenth century, vigorously protested against the corruption he found in the Western Catholic Church. Luther and his fellow Protestants came to believe that these corruptions could already be seen in the earliest centuries of the ancient catholic church, long before the 1600s. As they judged it, very early on, the church had been too friendly with Greco-Roman culture and had departed from the purity of New Testament teaching. The Reformational churches wished a return to the purity of the "primitive church" of Jesus' earliest followers. The authoritative guide to this church was, in Luther's words, "Scripture alone!" rather than "Scripture and Tradition." Scripture (the Bible), therefore, was to be the sole source of Christian truth, not tradition, not reason, not the pronouncements of bishops and popes.

The Reformational churches tended therefore to adopt a more oppositional stance against "pagan culture." Grace does not so much transform human nature and culture as issue a sharp call to a break with both. Human nature apart from grace is so benighted and corrupted that its works require repudiation, not transformation. Thus characteristic Protestant style developed, which is prophetic and either/or—Scripture versus tradition, grace versus freedom, Church versus world, faith versus reason—in contrast to the characteristic Catholic style, which is mediational and both/and—Scripture and tradition, grace and freedom, Church and world, faith and reason. Each style has its own genius, but also its own vulnerability to temptation when not corrected by insistent critique from the other. On the Protestant side, there is the temptation to a sectarian withdrawal from the human world; on the Roman Catholic side, there is the temptation to an uncritical embrace of the human world.

Meanwhile, the Roman Catholic Church continued to declare its unique genius and its claim to most fully represent the ancient catholic church. In making this claim, the Roman Catholic tradition made a special claim on that strain of ancient catholicism which stressed the mediational relationship between grace and nature, church and culture, faith and reason, past tradition and present circumstance, the world that is here and the world that is to come. And we find this mediational style prominently displayed in its teaching on social justice, a teaching that has enjoyed dramatic development since the late 19th century.

2. **A Catholic once told me, "I am a Roman Catholic, but with a small 'c'." What does that mean? Does it have anything to do with this ancient catholic tradition?**

It can mean many things, but usually such a Catholic is saying something like this: "I am Roman Catholic, but I lament the splitting of the ancient catholic church into the Orthodox, Protestant, and [Roman] Catholic churches, and I would to like to see all Christians re-unite on the basis of the ancient catholic tradition. Even though I believe that the Roman

Catholic Church fully expresses the truth of Christ, I believe that the Roman Catholic Church has been weakened by its split from the Orthodox and Protestant churches and has to come part way towards these churches if there is to be re-union. I want the church to once again become truly universal, truly catholic, but I don't think that is possible if we insist that the other churches come back to us solely on our terms."

Other Catholics, however, beg to differ. They designate themselves as Roman Catholics in the large-C sense. They believe that the Roman Catholic Church is the only church that can legitimately claim to embody and continue the ancient catholic tradition. And thus if there is to be re-union, if the church is to be truly universal again, then the Orthodox and Protestant churches must come back to the Roman Catholic Church under the leadership of the Bishop of Rome, the Pope. Many of these Catholics believe that small-c Catholics are losing their hold on the true Catholic faith.

Here at the College of St. Catherine, you will find small-c and large-C Catholics (and blends of both), and you will feel the tensions between them. Despite their differences, however, they share on the deepest level a Catholic mentality that goes back to the ancient catholic tradition. They believe that human nature and human culture apart from Christ are not wholly corrupted by sin and ignorance. They believe that God's grace in Christ reaches out to all human beings and cultures. They believe that Scripture and tradition together guide the Christian community, not Scripture alone, for Scripture comes out of and flows back into the ongoing life of the community and its tradition. They believe that this tradition is living and therefore must adapt to changing circumstances while not losing its essence. And a place where they both see this tradition at its lively best is in the Church's teaching on social justice.

3. What is the relationship between the Sisters of St. Joseph, the founders of this college, and the Catholic tradition?

The Sisters of St. Joseph are a religious order founded in 1650 in LePuy, France. Originally, it was not founded to educate, but to meet the immediate needs of the "dear neighbor," especially homeless and destitute women. But when these needs became educational, they became teachers and college presidents; when these needs became medical, they became nurses and hospital directors. That is, they created social structures and practiced social justice. As a religious order born in the heart of the Roman Catholic Church, the Sisters of St. Joseph carry on the living tradition of the ancient catholic church. They are especially alert to the way this tradition expresses itself in its teaching on social justice.

4. **What does all this mean for the Catholic Church's current teaching on social justice?**

It means that long ago the foundational ideas for this current teaching were in place. We should like now to list some of these ideas more systematically and show their connection to social justice.

  a. **The Catholic tradition does not confine itself to the written form of that tradition that became the Christian Bible.** For Catholics, therefore, the Bible does not provide answers to all the social questions faced by humankind in later times. The Bible, for example, never systematically criticized slavery as a social structure or urged on its abolition. Even Jesus did not reject slavery, and Paul the Apostle accepted its inevitability (while of course urging slave owners to treat their slaves as brothers and sisters in Christ). Circumstances change and the Catholic tradition insists that Christian teaching, while not sacrificing its core teaching, must change, especially when deciding how the imperatives of love and justice apply to the current social situation.

  b. **With respect to the broader "secular" culture, the Catholic tradition at its best counsels a middle ground between withdrawal and surrender.** Just as the Church at one point took the best from Greco-Roman culture, so too it is now open to the best of secular culture. Undeniably, after the Reformation, the Catholic Church retreated from the emerging modern world of science, Enlightenment, and democratic revolution. Indeed, it conducted a defensive war with the modern world, often in an inconsistent and counterproductive way. And so while it rightly opposed the reduction of all truth to scientific truth, it wrongly condemned Galileo. While it rightly opposed excesses of the French Revolution, it wrongly opposed democracy and religious freedom. While it rightly criticized the brutalities of the newly emerging capitalist economy, it idealized a mediaeval economic order (complete with an aristocracy who enjoyed their economic privilege by "divine right") long after such an order had proved its obsolescence and injustice. So yes, the Catholic Church was slow in coming to a nuanced critique and appreciation of the modern world, but it rediscovered the ancient catholic openness to the world, beginning with the social teaching of Pope Leo XIII and breaking through in the extraordinary decree issued by the Second Vatican Council: "The Pastoral Constitution on the Church in the Modern World."

  c. **The Catholic tradition gives a special role to reason in the search for justice.** This respect for reason is one of the great gifts of the ancient catholic tradition which, instead of condemning Aristotle and Plato as benighted pagans, incorporated the best of their rational methods into the theological enterprise. Human reason is wounded by sin, but not wholly corrupted. And thus reason without the help of God's revelation can discover the "natural laws" governing our human nature. It can therefore offer principles and rules that bridge the general gospel imperative to love the neighbor with the concrete needs of the neighbor. How do we, for example, love the neighbor who is dying from AIDs in Africa? There are no sayings from Jesus to tell us precisely how to do this! Faith in Jesus needs therefore to link up with reason to help us know what to do and how best to do it. And thus Catholics believe that in working for social justice they should team up with "all people of good will," theist or atheist, Christian or nonChristian. We all have reason. We all have a sense of what ought to be if human beings are to flourish. We all can analyze the social situation. We all can think together about how to love the neighbor in a world of vast and complex social structures.

d. **The Catholic tradition is grateful for another great gift from the Greeks, and that is the conception of the human being as a "social being."** For the Greeks, social and political association, including government, was natural to human beings. Such association was necessary for human flourishing. For Martin Luther, by contrast, human beings were so entangled in sin that they were always on the verge of running amok. Thus the role of government was basically negative: to punish the wicked and hold back the forces of social anarchy. This deep distrust of government can be found today among some Americans, but not usually among adherents to the Catholic tradition. Government for them has a positive role of creating and supporting social structures (social security, unemployment insurance, protection for union organizing, and so on) that do good things for people, not simply keep people from doing bad things. This is not to say that Catholic teaching automatically favors Big Government. Its opposition throughout the Cold War to the "state socialisms" of the Soviet Union and China shows its profound suspicion of government as Big Brother. Indeed, Catholic social teaching has elaborated the principles of "subsidiarity" (whatever can be done well by a local structure need not be done by a regional or national structure) and vigorously supported "mediating structures" (families, churches, labor unions, businesses, media, nongovernmental organizations—that is "civil society") to guard against handing too much power over to government. And yet, it remains true that the basic disposition of Catholic teaching is pro- rather than anti-government.

e.   **Catholic social teaching, despite its teaching on the good that large social structures can do, is also aware of how unjust these same structures can be. Christians must work against unjust structures.** Large social structures are pervasive and powerful, imposing themselves not only as socially correct, but morally right. It is especially difficult to make Americans aware of these structures, enthralled as they are by the ideology of the "rugged individual" untouched by the broader society. Catholic social teaching is opposed to an individualism oblivious of unjust social structures. It also opposes a Christian individualism that sees the Christian faith as solely a "personal conversion to Jesus Christ" and Christian love primarily as bringing others to that same conversion. While insisting that personal conversion is indispensable to Christian faith, it warns against reducing Christian love to missionary work or one-to-one "works of charity." Christian love thus needs to expand out into the work of social justice, which requires a critique of social structures that do not promote human flourishing. Yes, we need people like Mother Teresa serving the poor with face-to-face love, but we also need social activists like Dorothy Day working to change and perhaps overthrow structures that keep poor people poor.

f.   **With respect to historical progress, the Catholic tradition tends to seek a middle position between optimistic progressivism and pessimistic apocalypticism.** Progressivists believe that the work of social justice will lead to a heaven on earth; the apocalypticists believe that earth will always be infinitely far from heaven. For the apocalypticists, therefore, the work of social justice is ultimately in vain. They are certain that the world can only get worse instead of better. The best thing, then, is to convert to Jesus and wait for him to come, as he surely will, like "a thief in the night" to snatch up the converted into heaven. The Catholic tradition, by contrast, encourages human beings to go about the work of social justice in a spirit of hopeful realism. They should neither puff up their work for justice with the illusion of utopia nor pull down their work with the certainty of disaster. They need to trust that in some mysterious way their work is not in vain and that God and Christ will take what they accomplish for justice in this world and blend it into the content of a renewed heaven and earth. Indeed, the Catholic tradition sees human work for justice as Christ's work continuing on earth by the power of his Holy Spirit.

5. Can you tell me a little more about how Catholic social teaching looks in practice?

Well, we first need to say that Catholic social teaching usually avoids handing out precise policy recommendations. This is especially true of that teaching as it comes from the papal office. Since the pope is speaking to over a billion Catholics around the world, he must, out of respect for local and regional differences, avoid being too precise. For the same reason, even social teaching from national conferences of bishops is usually not very specific.

Perhaps we can best answer your questions by giving you a list of presumptions, oppositions, and supports that currently guide the Catholic practice of social justice.

    a. **There is a presumption in favor of the poor, the powerless, the voiceless, and the oppressed.** This does not mean that the Church teaches that God loves the poor more, but rather that God shows special zeal for those whose basic human needs the current social structures are most obviously failing to meet. We see here the "preferential option for the poor," one of the contributions from "liberation theology" to Catholic social teaching. Catholics are taught to judge a society's justice by how well the bottom 20% are doing, not the top 20%.

    b. **There is a presumption against war and for nonviolence, though this has not led the Church to embrace pacifism.** The Catholic tradition still adheres to the "just war theory," and, properly understood, to the "just rebellion theory," though it must be said that modern warfare is so vicious and destructive that Catholic teaching now pushes very hard against it, approving it only as the very last possible resort.

    c. **There is a presumption in favor of democracy. The Catholic Church teaches that freedom is part of the image of God in human beings and requires democracy for its full exercise.** The exercise of freedom also ensures the continual practice of societal self-criticism, which is needed in a sinful world where groups and societies are prone to arrogantly and self-deceptively claim to be always in the right. Democracy would therefore appear to be the political system best able to do justice to both the divine image of us and the sinful bent within us.

    d. **Catholic social teaching is opposed to all discrimination based on sex, race, class, religion, marital status, ethnicity, disability, language, culture, or nationality.** Some bishops and many lay Catholics, especially in the U.S. and Europe, would want to

include "sexual preference" here, but it is debated among
Catholics, gay and straight, whether the Church's current teaching on homosexuality, which sees it as an "objective disorder"
inclining the person to sinful behavior (the disorder itself is not
seen as sinful), equips the Church to consistently oppose discrimination against gay persons (or persons of any other "disor-
dered" sexual preference). For example, Catholic teaching on the
dignity of all persons would naturally lead most Catholics to
oppose discrimination against gays and lesbians in the workplace; yet, many of these same Catholics would oppose allowing
gays and lesbians to contract a civil marriage. Is the former discrimination, but not the latter? Catholics who say yes and
Catholics who say no will both claim to be relying on the best of
Catholic social teaching. The key point here is this: Any debate
about discrimination presupposes an awareness of the ancient
Catholic teaching about the dignity of the human person: All
human beings are loved by God and called to love God and their
neighbor.

e. **There is a presumption in favor of free market capitalism and
    against top-down "state socialism" of the kind typical of Com-
    munist and authoritarian regimes.** But it must be said here that
    the Church steps very gingerly when it approaches capitalism.
    True, some pro-capitalist Catholics see in the social teaching of
    Pope John Paul II less distrust of capitalism, but he never
    endorses the market economy without careful and extensive
    qualification. Moreover, he refuses to absolutize the rights of pri-
    vate property and capital, insisting in fact on the "priority of
    labor over capital" and on the subjection of the market to the
    common good. Above all, he never makes an idol of the market,
    never claims that it is the highest achievement of economic jus-
    tice and thus "the end of history." Nevertheless, one can see in
    most recent Catholic social teaching a more nuanced apprecia-
    tion for capitalism, especially because of its historical association
    with democracy.

f. **There is a presumption in favor of a friendly separation of
    organized religion and the state apparatus out of respect for
    the fanatical energies that can be unleashed when a govern-
    ment-backed agenda becomes too closely allied with a reli-
    gious group and out of a commitment to protect the religious
    freedom of those who are not members of the majority reli-
    gion.** Admittedly, the Catholic Church has come to this view
    fairly recently. It wasn't long ago that papal social teaching con-
    sidered fascist Spain (which, among other things, enforced state

Catholicism by prohibiting Protestant Christians from having their own church buildings) the paragon of church-state relations. Thanks to the work of a great American theologian, John Courtney Murray, and to the judgment of the majority of bishops at Vatican II, Catholic teaching from the pope on down now favors "friendly separation."

g. **There is a presumption in favor of the government's taking final responsibility for distributive economic justice.** State involvement in distributive economic justice helps ensure universality and impartiality when meeting basic human needs with the appropriate goods and services. Nevertheless, governmental structures must be set up so as not to stifle "mediating structures" (families, labor unions, non-governmental organizations, businesses, advocacy groups, etc.) or local initiative (the principle of subsidiarity).

h. **Catholic social teaching strongly supports the protection of human life from conception to death.** This is the famous "seamless garment," or "consistent life ethic" for which the Catholic Church has been both praised and pilloried. This ethic includes the teaching against birth control by artificial means though the Church is not opposed to birth control by "natural means" (nor is it opposed to population control); the teaching against abortion; and the teaching against active euthanasia, though the Church is also opposed to prolonging human life by "extraordinary means." This same ethic is pushing Pope John Paul II and many bishops to the point where they are a hair's-breadth away from advocating the total abolition of capital punishment. Not all Catholics line up behind the Church on all these teachings.

i. **There is a presumption in favor of feminism.** Of course, the pope and most bishops would not call themselves "feminists." Yet, the official Church teaching is that men and women are in every fundamental way equal. True, many church leaders, including the current pope, are inclined to a "difference feminism" that sees men and women as different biologically and psychologically and thus sees the two sexes as carrying out "complementary," rather than exactly the same, roles in the home, society, and church. Many Catholic feminists would protest our claim that official Catholic social teaching is in favor of feminism. They contend that the way this teaching construes the differences between males and females and the way it carries out its difference feminism in practice (e.g., the prohibition of women priests) contradict the Church's contention that men and women are fundamentally equal.

j. **There is a presumption in favor of the have-nots in the less developed countries.** This takes the form of urging the developed countries to use their great wealth to help speed up development in the less developed countries. In effect, this is a global application of the Catholic teaching on the "preferential option for the poor." It also leads Catholic social teaching to be skeptical of unqualified enthusiasm for the global economy.

6. **Under letter "g" above, you mention distributive economic justice. I have been under the impression that economic justice was social justice. Are they different according to Catholic social teaching?**

The emerging consensus among Catholic thinkers is that social justice is the genus and economic justice is a species within that genus. Or to put it another way, social justice is the wide sphere within which are located eight sub-spheres of social justice, among which is economic justice.

Here is a list of these eight sub-spheres:

a. **Basic Human Rights and Freedoms.** Basic rights and freedoms without which there can be no justice in the other sub-spheres of justice.

b. **Political Justice.** Rights and duties with respect to how political power is exercised and distributed.

c. **Economic Justice.** Rights and duties with respect to the production and distribution of goods and services.

d. **Criminal Justice.** Rights and duties with respect to how laws enacted by political decision are obeyed and enforced.

e. **Environmental Justice.** Duties to the inorganic and organic world: water, land, plants, and animals.

f. **Intergenerational Justice.** Duty of the present generation to pass on to the next generation social structures that are just and to hand over a planet that can sustain human life in a humane manner.

g. **Multicultural Justice.** Rights and duties of the society with respect to minority groups within the society.

h. **International Justice.** Rights and duties of one nation (or group of nations) vis-à-vis another nation (or group of nations).

Later in your education here at the college, you will take the second core course, The Global Search for Justice. In this course you will study one or more of these eight sub-spheres of justice in the context of a culture (or cultures) that differs from the majority culture of the United States. May you find this course a launching pad for a lifetime of working for social justice!

Recommended Readings

Bokenkotter, Thomas A. *A Concise History of the Catholic Church.* 2nd ed. New York: Doubleday, 2004. A lively and interesting history of the Catholic Church. Covers both ideas and institutions. An earlier paperback edition may be available. A page-turner!

————. *Church and Revolution.* New York: Doubleday, 1998. The author traces the history of Catholic social teaching since the French Revolution. Covers both liberal and conservative strains.

Catechism of the Catholic Church. New York: Doubleday, 1995. If you want to know what is official Catholic teaching on almost any theological or ethical matter, this is your best source.

Curran, Charles A., Margaret A. Farley, and Richard A. McCormick, eds. *Feminist Ethics and Catholic Moral Theology: Readings in Moral Theology No. 9.* New York: Paulist Press, 1996. An excellent anthology of articles, covering a wide range of views.

Curran, Charles E. *Catholic Social Teaching 1891–Present: A Historical, Theological, and Ethical Analysis.* Washington, DC: Georgetown Univ. Press, 2002. A progressive Catholic theologian, Curran offers here a very thorough and fair-minded analysis of Catholic social teaching since 1891.

DeBerri, Edward P., Peter J. Henriot, and Michael J. Schulteis. *Catholic Social Teaching: Our Best Kept Secret.* Maryknoll, NY: Orbis, 4th ed., 2003). A magnificent compendium of Catholic social teaching that provides detailed outlines of the most important documents of modern Catholic social teaching.

Dwyer, Judith A., ed. *The New Dictionary of Catholic Social Thought.* Collegeville, Minn: Liturgical Press, 1994. For any topic on social justice this is probably the best reference book to go to first.

Ellacuria, Ignacio, and Jon Sobrino, eds. *Mysterium Liberationis: Fundamental Concepts of Liberation Theology.* Maryknoll, NY: Orbis Books, 1993. This anthology offers the best entrance into liberation theology.

Maritain, Jacques. *Integral Humanism.* South Bend: Univ. of Notre Dame Press, 1976. A re-issue of the 1938 classic. Maritain did more than any other Catholic thinker to reconcile official Catholic social teaching with democracy.

Massaro, Thomas, S. J. *Living Justice: Catholic Social Teaching in Action.* Franklin, Wisconsin: Sheed and Ward, 2000. If we could recommend only one book to CSC students this would be it. Thorough, but not long-winded, this reasonably priced paperback is an excellent introduction.

Mechmann, Edward T. *God, Society and the Human Person*. New York: Alba House, 2000. Also an excellent book for someone looking for a paperback introduction. Distinguished by its many quotes from key documents.

Novak, Michael. *Freedom with Justice: Catholic Social Thought and Liberal Institutions*. San Francisco: Harper and Row, 1984. Along with George Weigel and Richard Newhaus, Novak ranks as one of the most prominent spokespersons for a neoconservative interpretation of Catholic social teaching. Like all his works, this one is very well written.

O'Brien, David J., and Thomas A. Shannon, eds. *Catholic Social Thought: The Documentary Heritage*. Maryknoll, NY: Orbis Books, 1992. There is no official canon of Catholic Church documents on social teaching, but if there were, the documents in this book would be included. Ten are by popes, three are by the college of bishops (including two of the most important decrees of the Second Vatican Council), and two are by the American bishops.

Eyes Open on a World *was written as part of the 150th anniversary of the arrival of the Sisters of St. Joseph in St. Paul. In it, the sisters reflect on the many changes of the past fifty years and the effects of these changes on their community. As stated in the preface by Sr. Karen Kennelly, CSJ, "In showing the Sisters of St. Joseph as pioneering feminists, this book brings out the meaning of religious life for a new generation alert to feminist concerns."*

Eyes Open on a World: Responding to Societal Needs

A Collaboration by the Sisters of St. Joseph of Carondelet St. Paul Province

The story of Sister Rita Steinhagen reflects the evolution of many sisters from institutionally based ministries to direct social services and then to social justice issues and political action. As Sister Rita explains, "One thing led to another." After illness demanded she leave her work as a medical technologist, Sister Rita opened a Free Store on the West Bank in Minneapolis, a place where people could "shop" for what they needed. She became acquainted with many people, including runaway youth who spent their days and nights on the streets. One day a youth asked her, "Why don't you get us a place to stay?" So Sister Rita founded the Bridge, a shelter for runaway youth, not far from the Free Store.

"I was learning about the oppressive and unjust systems—what it is like to be poor with a constant struggle just to survive," recalls Sister Rita. Because many of the people she met spoke Spanish, "I decided it was time to learn that language. So I went to a small language school in El Paso, Texas, and worked at a nearby shelter for refugees. It was there that I first learned about the School of the Americas." After hearing the refugees' stories, Sister Rita went to Central America as a Witness for Peace and lived in the war zones in northern Nicaragua.

When she returned home, Sister Rita worked for seven years at the Center for Victims of Torture. Haunted by her experience of seeing the results of torture and by her knowledge of U.S. complicity in training Latin American soldiers in methods of torture, she went to Fort Benning, Georgia, to participate in demonstrations opposing the School of the Americas. Because she "crossed the line a second time," a judge sentenced her to six months in federal prison, where "I got a crash course in our prison system and the unfairness of it all." Now, besides continuing to work to close the School of the Americas, she is involved with changing prison policies that are especially harsh on women with children.

Like Sister Rita, many sisters have become active in social justice movements. With the growing understanding in the 1960s that our religious vow of obedience meant much more than listening to the directives of our superiors and included being open to the Spirit by listening to the people and events of our times, we felt called to confront injustices wherever we saw them.

Like our first sisters in France we continue to give direct service to those in need and work for systemic change. Sister Florence Steichen uses the phrase "walking on the two feet of justice," a metaphor developed in the 1970s to describe this dual task. Our stories from the past fifty years show how leadership has emerged whenever sisters have seen needs and responded to them.

Sisters, of course, have been responding to needs all along. Sister Lillian Meyer went to political caucuses in the early 1950s, subscribed to the *Congressional Record*, and vigorously contributed her knowledge and opinions in Saturday classes on current affairs she took at the College of St. Catherine. In the 1940s and 1950s Sister Julienne Foley taught Mexican children and adults. Downtown St. Paul merchants and cab drivers recognized her resolute gait as she fearlessly approached them for food and clothing for "her people" or asked for free rides. Throughout the years sisters visited students and families in their homes and provided clothing and other necessities. They also visited those who were poor and elderly at the Ramsey County "poor farm," in hospitals, and in prisons, as our earliest members had done.

Some of our sisters worked at the Catholic Infant Home, a residence program for pregnant girls. The sisters provided child care and personal and spiritual enrichment classes for the girls, while other organizations provided health care services. As attitudes toward single pregnant women changed, so did the program. This ministry, now called Seton Center, is no longer a residence and offers a variety of services for single parents and married couples.

As social issues and reform movements surfaced in the 1960s, our community experienced transition from total separation to deep involvement in world affairs and ambivalence over our sisters being involved in public issues. By the end of the decade, however, we had a clear affirmation from our congregational leaders and from one another that social activism is part of our call. We welcomed the pastoral letter *Justice in the World*, issued by the U.S. bishops in 1971. One statement reinforced our conviction that working for justice is not an optional pursuit but is integral to the gospel: "Action on behalf of justice and participation in the transformation of the world appear to us as a constitutive dimension of the preaching of the gospel, or, in other words, of the church's mission for the redemption of the human race and its liberation from every oppressive situation." We celebrated this liberating statement as a landmark.

Sisters participated in political caucuses and demonstrations, including vigils for slain civil rights workers and protests against the Vietnam War and the Gulf War. Some also protested Honeywell's production of cluster bombs. Sisters Char Madigan and Rita Foster were among the early organizers of nonviolent protests there. In the early 1990s when Honeywell moved its weapons making to Alliant Technical Systems in Hopkins, the protesters moved there, too. Several sisters took part in antiwar demonstrations protesting the U.S. bombing of Iraq, the sanctions on Iraq, and intervention in Yugoslavia.

Societal conditions and movements provided impetus for political action. Some sisters became active in the Civil Rights movement, which in the beginning was primarily concerned with voting rights of African Americans. The notion of civil rights soon expanded to include the right to be born, to be housed adequately, and to be employed. Civil rights further evolved to encompass Native Americans and other ethnic minorities, sexual minorities, and women.

The *Roe v. Wade* Supreme Court decision in 1973 legalizing abortion in every state brought our deep convictions about the sacredness of life to the forefront. As a community we support all efforts to reverence and enhance the life of each person from beginning to end. Some of us are active in the prolife movement. Others focus their energy on abolishing the death penalty. After Sister Helen Prejean, a Sister of St. Joseph from the Medaille congregation and a well-known author and advocate for abolishing the death penalty, spoke at a gathering of the Federation of Sisters of St. Joseph in St. Louis in 2000, the 1,550 sisters present released a public statement on their stand against capital punishment. Also in the summer of 2000 Sister Mary Mark Mahoney, retired for many years, and Sister Carol Neuburger testified at a court appeal in Oklahoma and tried, unsuccessfully, to commute the death sentence of a prisoner with whom Sister Mary Mark had been corresponding for three years. She continues her special ministry by corresponding with other prison "pen pals."

As we moved from convents and from institutions into neighborhoods, many of us became more involved in public issues. When some of us moved from the College of St. Catherine into neighborhood housing in 1968, the college's student publication, *The Catherine Wheel* (May 10, 1968, p. 8) described the experience as not a departure from traditional religious living but rather as an opportunity to open up new possibilities of religious life in the spirit of renewal.

Moving into different living situations brought us into new ministries and political involvement. In the mid-1970s, Sisters Jean Campbell and Jackie Slater moved into the Cedar-Riverside housing project in Minneapolis, a multiracial, multi-economic, integrated community. Sister Jackie's work there led her to run for the city council. She reported: "A few of the older and more traditional Catholics were upset about my candidacy for office. They were concerned that a nun would have a hard time in the nasty world of politics, or they were clinging to the notion that sisters should be either teachers or nurses. But there were also many who were very much in favor of it and they gave me their support and votes" (*Minneapolis Star Tribune*, December 24, 1977). Jackie won the election and became an influential as well as controversial council member. After her sudden death in 1984, the city of Minneapolis honored her by naming a renovated block of housing near downtown Minneapolis Slater Square.

Sister Jackie was not the first sister from the St. Paul Province to seek public office. Running on a prolife platform, Sister Elizabeth Regnier narrowly missed being elected to the North Dakota state legislature in 1972. Two years earlier in Jamestown, North Dakota, Sister Rose Alma Woychik lost the election to a ward precinct post by two votes.

While some sisters sought to influence public policy through elected office, Sister Mary Madonna Ashton received a state appointment from Minnesota Governor Rudy Perpich. During her tenure as Commissioner of Health from 1983 to 1991, Minnesota led the nation in addressing major health concerns by implementing tobacco control programs and HIV/AIDS prevention measures.

A number of us received our political initiation when Senator Eugene McCarthy from Minnesota sought the Democratic nomination for president in 1968. At the precinct caucus so many sisters showed up that we overwhelmed the proceedings. Some of us remember how upset the politician who chaired the meeting was when he saw all of us. Suspicious of the sisters' unaccustomed activism, he told us in no uncertain terms that he expected us to continue to come to the subsequent caucuses, and we did.

Some of us believed that protesting was part of our mission. In addition to her political involvement, Sister Rose Alma Woychik protested at missile bases in Jamestown, North Dakota, beginning in the mid-1960s. In a 1975 letter to Sister Frances Babb, she expressed the pivotal shift from suspicion of the world and withdrawal from it to wholehearted engagement with the world, which came to characterize the thinking of many sisters in the remaining decades of the twentieth century. She wrote: "I am not willing to admit that being interested in politics necessarily means that I am less interested in the love of God and my neighbor, or the spread of the gospel."

While some sisters protested against the Vietnam War and others demonstrated against legalized abortion, still others lobbied for fair housing, jobs, health care, education, and welfare legislation. Seeing government cuts in human services and increases in military spending, we insisted that enormous expenditures for weapons to protect the national security were creating havoc in our cities. As Sister Rita Steinhagen keeps saying, "One thing led to another." We did social analysis, asking who benefits and who suffers. We learned from our sisters in Peru that multinational success and security for developed countries meant tragic insecurity to the majority in developing countries.

When Sister Char Madigan began working in a downtown parish in the 1970s, she realized she was saying good night to people at 5:00 P.M. knowing they had no home to go to. Sisters Rita Steinhagen, Laura Geyer, and Char Madigan began offering shelter in their upper flat convent. That eventually led to the opening of St. Joseph's House, Ascension Place, and Incarnation House, all in Minneapolis, which were transitional housing shelters designed to empower women to live healthy, independent lives. In November 2000, Incarnation House began a new phase of service to women and children as it held an open house to celebrate its partnership with Wayside, a Minneapolis-based program designed to help women achieve their full potential and become productive members of the community.

Experience in these newly established shelters and runaway centers led Sister Marguerite Corcoran and three of the McDonald sisters, Rita, Brigid, and Jane, to question what was going on in the broader world community. A fourth McDonald sister, Kate, who along with others taught English to refugees and immigrants, had the same question. Her sister, Sister Brigid, while working at Incarnation House, connected us with Women Against Military Madness (WAMM) to pressure legislative bodies to direct government funds to welfare rights instead of to military spending. A growing interest in liberation theology, which focuses on the struggles of those who are poor and encourages religious people to champion nonviolent resistance, motivated many sisters to support WAMM's work.

Sisters have joined in solidarity with our Native American sisters and brothers seeking to preserve their cultural beliefs. At the invitation of Ojibwe elder woman Bea Swanson, Sister Jane McDonald helps staff an intergenerational and interracial prayer lodge at All Nations Church in Minneapolis. That experience led her to stand in solidarity with Native American struggles against land pollution—for example, the pollution of Prairie Island Indian land with the storing of nuclear waste. In the late 1990s Sisters Jane McDonald, Jan Dalsin, and Mary O'Brien and others joined the Native American protest against a highway reroute that sacrificed sacred sites, including trees and spring-fed waters, for the sake of a highway expansion. Other sisters helped Native Americans adjust to urban life by providing basic necessities and connecting them with social service agencies.

For twenty years our sisters have worked with the Resource Center of the Americas and other Sanctuary movements, both for indigenous peoples in other lands and with refugees fleeing those lands. While serving as director of a sanctuary house in Waco, Texas, Sister Marie Richard King worked to provide temporary safe haven for undocumented persons from Mexico. Sisters have been arrested, and some imprisoned, for such "illegal" activities as supporting the César Chavez United Farm Workers grape boycott in 1968, standing with Salvadoran refugees who sought sanctuary in the Cathedral of St. Paul, and demonstrating against the manufacture of nuclear weapons. After more than twenty years of involvement in human rights issues, Sister Betty McKenzie connected sisters to the St. Paul Ecumenical Alliance of Churches (SPEAC), an ecumenical effort to work locally for housing, fair wages, and environmental issues.

The plight of persons who are homeless continues to be of deep concern to us. In one instance, both serendipity and providence played a part in the opening of an overnight shelter. Sister Dolore Rochon, an administrator at St. Joseph's Hospital in downtown St. Paul, was having coffee with Sister Rita Steinhagen one blizzardy December day in 1981. Sister Rita, then working at the nearby Dorothy Day Center, expressed concern that so many homeless people were sleeping in downtown doorways and in caves near the river. Sister Dolore, aware there was an empty floor in Mary Hall, the nurses' residence at the hospital, persuaded hospital and province leaders to convert this space into overnight housing for homeless persons. A week later, on New Year's Eve, with a wind chill of seventy degrees below zero, the doors of Mary Hall opened. Sisters volunteered to spend nights with the guests until Catholic Charities assumed responsibility for the residence.

Another dream became reality when Sister Rose Tillemans established Peace House, a space where people gather during the day for sharing and prayer. To her, Peace House is "one answer to the seldom looked-at question of what do the poor and disadvantaged do after they have some food, clothing, and shelter." She set up a storefront in 1985 on Franklin Avenue in Minneapolis, and since then people have come each day for coffee, food, and meditation. Together, they form community in a safe atmosphere built on acceptance, a sense of belonging, friendship, dignity, and mutuality of service.

Our commitment to supporting people who experience poverty, abuse, torture, mental illness, or discrimination remains strong. In Minneapolis, sisters are involved in INSTEP, a child care program that helps low-income parents pursue work and/or educational opportunities to become more self-sufficient. When the Derham Convent building in St. Paul became available in the 1990s, the province opened Sarah's Oasis, a temporary home for women, including refugees, some of whom come from the Center for the Victims of Torture in Minneapolis. At Sarah's women live in a safe environment that fosters relationships, reflection, and self-empowerment.

As a psychologist, Sister Karen Hilgers worked with many adult women who had survived abuse. She dreamed of a peaceful residence—not a hospital—where women in crisis could spend a few days with a supportive staff to regain their equilibrium. In collaboration with a small group of other psychologists Sister Karen developed this new approach to treatment. In 1996, Cornelia Place opened its doors in Minneapolis, providing the care and support the women needed. Although the model Sister Karen and her colleagues created proved to be a successful crisis management model, the residential portion of the program closed because of lack of funding. Cornelia Place now operates as a mental health clinic specializing in the treatment of women with posttraumatic stress disorder.

Through our experiences in pastoral and social ministries, we realized that unjust economic systems are significant factors leading to the oppression of people. This insight led Sister Mary Ellen Foster to complete a master's degree at the New School for Social Research in New York City, a school that critiques economic systems with an eye towards social transformation. Following her studies, Sister Mary Ellen began to teach classes in economics stressing the impact of economic systems on the world and urging her students to engage in activities that lead to systemic change.

Clearly, our concerns for social justice extend beyond the U.S. boundaries. Recognizing needs around the globe, sisters have responded in various ways. While Sister Florence Steichen served as registrar at Bethlehem University in the occupied West Bank, the Israeli military governor closed the university for three years because of the *Intifada*, the struggle of Palestinian young people to gain independence. Sister Florence played a major role in arranging for off-campus classes to help Palestinian students continue their education. She and other sisters who taught at Bethlehem University returned home with a commitment to further Palestinian rights by speaking, writing, contacting legislators, and seeking funds for Bethlehem University from our Partners in Justice fund. Continuing her advocacy for peace in the Middle East, Sister Florence works with Minnesota Middle East Peace Now and the Middle East Committee of Women Against Military Madness.

Representing our province at the United Nations Fourth World Conference on Women in Beijing in 1995, Sister Susan Oeffling learned firsthand about the status and plight of women throughout the world. While she was in Beijing, at the invitation of Minnesota Public Radio, Sister Susan called in regularly to report on the conference and answer listeners' questions. Upon returning home, she gave numerous talks on her Beijing experience to parish, school, corporate, and religious groups and published an article entitled "Keep on Keeping On" in *Sisters Today*. She joined the nonviolence working group of the Justice Commission, which then changed its name to Beyond Beijing: Women and Violence to focus on implementation of the Beijing platform.

As we struggled to "walk on the two feet of justice" in these last fifty years, we realized that we needed education and support in our efforts. As coordinator of the Social Justice Secretariat from 1979 to 1982, Sister Kathy Roehl kept us informed about justice issues and actions we could take to address the issues. We then established the Social Justice Task Force in 1982, which evolved into the Justice Commission in 1984. Sister Carol Neuburger, the first chair of the commission, brought energy and initiative to the work of justice. With her guidance, the province developed a process for sisters in the province to take a "corporate stand," that is, to make a public statement in the name of the Sisters of St. Joseph of the St. Paul Province. The process ensured that a corporate stand would represent the will of a majority of sisters, not a small group within the province. We took our first corporate stand in 1986 as a strong symbolic action for peace: "To declare as nuclear-free zones properties owned by the Sisters of St. Joseph in the St. Paul Province."

The province hired Joänne Tromiczak-Neid, a former Sister of St. Joseph, in 1992 as the full-time justice coordinator to help us address issues of social justice discussed at the congregational chapter and written in our Acts of Chapter. In addition to networking with local and national justice groups, Joanne was instrumental in starting Women Religious for Justice, a collaborative effort of area religious communities. Among the founders of www.Sistersonline.org, a collaborative venture begun in 1996 with other communities of women religious in Minnesota, Joänne sees the website as facilitating outreach "to women and children who suffer from the multiple manifestations of injustice" (*Together*, November 1999, p. 13). As part of a global movement of women who care deeply about what is happening with the world, the earth, and its people, Sistersonline's 1999–2000 focus included debt relief and women in prison.

The role of women in the church is the concern of many of us. Sister Frances Babb, throughout her long life, was an ardent feminist. At the age of six in 1912, she handed out women's suffrage pamphlets with her mother. From the age of sixteen, she was certain that she had a vocation to the ordained priesthood, and throughout her life she was a persuasive spokeswoman for the ordination of women. In 1975 she spoke eloquently and painfully, with her commanding voice and strong Maine accent, of her desire to be a priest when she presented a petition to the official board for the Permanent Diaconate asking that the St. Paul and Minneapolis Archdiocese permit women to enter the Permanent Diaconate Training program. No action was taken on her petition.

Our first public efforts on behalf of gay, lesbian, bisexual, and transgendered (GLBT) persons were undertaken by Sister Sarah O'Neill, who dedicated much of her time and energy to seeking reconciliation and support between the Catholic Church and Catholic gays and lesbians. She worked tirelessly to assist with the founding of the Catholic Pastoral Committee on Sexual Minorities (CPCSM). In the years since Sister Sarah's death, some sisters have participated in demonstrations against repression of GLBT persons and sought to help families/friends both understand the church's position on GLBT persons and respect the individual's conscience. In June of 1999, twenty-two sisters and consociates marched in the Twin Cities Gay Pride Parade. They carried a large banner stating, "Sisters of St. Joseph of Carondelet, St. Paul, MN, Justice Commission, Standing for Human Rights and Justice." It was the first time we had walked in the parade so publicly.

As we look to the future, we recognize that the need to "walk on the two feet of justice" at times exceeds our ability to be involved personally and directly. In recent years we have found additional ways to support our quest for justice. After we sold St. John's Hospital in Fargo, North Dakota, we established the Giving Board in 1987, which allowed sisters to request grants for persons with immediate needs such as child care and living expenses. The sale of St. Mary's Hospital in Minneapolis presented us with a unique opportunity and challenged us to use the money generated to fulfill our mission. We developed a focus statement to guide our vision: "We, the community of the Sisters of St. Joseph [of the St. Paul Province], in keeping with our commitment to the gospel, choose, in dialogue with one another to use our spiritual, material, and personal resources in collaborative efforts to support those in need."

An Allocations Task Force recommended that the funding of ministries be spread across a range of categories representing a continuum of risk, from sponsored institutions and affiliated ministries to new, ongoing, or collaborative projects and individual radical responses to the gospel. As a result of the work of the task force, we established the Partners in Justice fund, which supports ministries that respond uniquely to unmet needs of the economically oppressed and to ministries that further our historical commitment to women and children.

Another vehicle for funding our ministries, the Partners in Ministry fund of our Ministries Foundation, "seeks to make a difference in the lives of those in need by generating and allocating funds to support present and future ministries of the Sisters of St. Joseph of Carondelet" (Ministries Foundation mission statement, 1995). Foundation board members, both sisters and laypeople, dedicate their time and efforts to ensuring that our mission and ministries continue into the future.

As we look back on the last fifty years we see how we have divided the city and sought to be attentive to the needs of our neighbors. Although, at times, tensions existed among us and we do not always agree on how to address the needs, we have grown in respect for one another as we realized that there are many ways to do the works of justice. Our Congregation of the Sisters of St. Joseph of Carondelet "encourages each sister [and consociate] to witness in areas of concern according to the dictates of an informed conscience and supports the rights of members to take a public stand on matters of justice" (Complementary Document 1984, p. 12). As needs continue to manifest themselves, we are confident that, like our foremothers, our sisters, consociates, and partners in ministry will divide the city and stand with the dear neighbor.

Acknowledgments

Acknowledgments

pp. 149–150: "The Low Road" from *The Moon Is Always Female* by Marge Piercy. Copyright © 1980 by Marge Piercy. Used by permission of Alfred A. Knopf, a division of Random House, Inc.

pp. 169–174: First appeared in *The Wind's Twelve Quarters* by Ursula K. Le Guin. Copyright © 1973, 2001 by Ursula K. Le Guin; Reprinted by permission of the author and the author's agents, the Virginia Kidd Agency, Inc.

pp. 183–196: As appeared in *One Hundred Years of Catholic Social Thought: Celebration and Challenge* edited by John Coleman, S J. Copyright © 1991 by Bishop Raymond Lucker.

pp. 197–205: From *Teaching to Transgress: Education as the Practice of Freedom* by bell hooks. Copyright © 1994 by Routledge, NY. Reprinted by permission of the publisher via the Copyright Clearance Center.

pp. 206–228: From *Staying Alive: Women, Ecology and Development* by Vandana Shiva. Copyright © 1988. Published by Zed Books.

pp. 229–242: As appeared in *Signs,* Summer, 1989. Copyright © 1989 by Charles Payne. Reprinted by permission of University of Chicago Press.

pp. 245–256: From "Working Paper #189 of the Wellesley College Center for Research on Women" by Peggy McIntosh. Copyright © 1988 by Peggy McIntosh. Reprinted by permission of the author.

pp. 257–262: From *The Gandhi Sutras* by Mohandas K. Gandhi. Copyright © 1949 by Devin-Adair Publishers, Inc., Old Greenwich, CT, 06870. Reprinted by permission.

pp. 263–277: Reprinted by arrangement with The Heirs to the Estate of Martin Luther King, Jr., c/o Writers House, Inc. as agent for the proprietor. Copyright © 1963 by Martin Luther King, Jr., copyright renewed 1991 by Coretta Scott King.

pp. 278–282: From *Do You Know Me Now? An Anthology of Minnesota Multicultural Writings* edited by Elisabeth Rosenberg. Copyright © 1997 by Elisabeth Rosenberg.

pp. 283–286: From *The Cancer Journals* by Audre Lorde. Copyright © 1980 by Aunt Lute Books. Reprinted by permission of the publisher.

pp. 287–288: From the *New Revised Standard Version of the Bible.* Copyright © 1989 by the Division of Christian Education of the National Council of the Churches of Christ in the USA. Used by permission. All rights reserved.

pp. 317–326: From *Eyes Open on a World: The Challenges of Change* by the Sisters of St. Joseph of Carondelet. Copyright © 2001 by North Star Press of Saint Cloud, Inc.